The Making of America's Soviet Policy

A COUNCIL ON FOREIGN RELATIONS BOOK

COUNCIL ON FOREIGN RELATIONS BOOKS

THE MAKING OF AMERICA'S SOVIET POLICY

Edited by Joseph S. Nye, Jr.

Yale University Press   New Haven and London

Published with the assistance of
the A. Whitney Griswold Publication Fund.

Set in Baskerville Roman.
Printed in the United States of America by
Edwards Brothers, Inc., Ann Arbor, Michigan.

Library of Congress Cataloging in Publication Data
Main entry under title:

The Making of America's Soviet policy.

   "Council on Foreign Relations books."
   Includes index.
   1. United States — Foreign relations — Soviet Union.
2. Soviet Union — Foreign relations — United States.
I. Nye, Joseph S.
JX1428.S65M34 1984   327.73047   83 – 51295
ISBN 0 – 300 – 03140 – 8
       0 – 300 – 03416 – 4 (pbk.)

*The paper in this book meets the guidelines for permanence
and durability of the Committee on Production Guidelines
for Book Longevity of the Council on Library Resources.*

10   9   8   7   6   5   4   3   2

Contents

Preface

For four decades, the Soviet Union has been the central problem for American foreign policy. It is the one country that could destroy us. At times, we have treated the Soviet relationship as virtually the only problem of foreign policy; at others, we have tried to banish the Soviets to the peripheries of our concern. Managing the relationship has not been easy.

An obvious reason for this is the Soviet Union itself. The marriage of the Russian empire and a universalistic ideology has produced a state that looks to some people like a defensive status quo power and to others like an expansionist revolutionary power. The fact that defensive motives can be combined with aggressive policies further confuses our perceptions, and a repressive and secretive political system frustrates efforts to fathom Soviet intentions. It is small wonder that Americans often have divided views about the nature of the Soviet state, and the issue will not be settled here.*

A less frequently studied reason why the relationship has been diffi-cult to manage has to do with the American foreign policy process. This process is notoriously untidy and seems to be particularly so in our deal-ings with the Soviet Union. This book does not try to deal with the nature of the Soviet challenge or both sides of the history of the relationship. Rather, it focuses on our own institutions and capabilities for dealing with the problem. Assuming that the Soviet Union will remain both an enigma and an inescapable fact, is there anything we can do to manage the rela-tionship better than we have done in the past? In an earlier era, we could evade some of the difficulties inherent in our political institutions by following George Washington's warning against foreign entanglements. But this solution no longer suffices in a world where nuclear missiles can reach within our borders in a matter of minutes.

The chapters that follow will approach the problem of understanding and improving the management of American policy toward the Soviet

*See Walter Laqueur, "What We Know about the Soviet Union," *Commentary* 75, no. 2 (February 1983):13; also John Van Oudenaren, *U.S. Leadership Perceptions of the Soviet Problem since 1945* (Santa Monica, Calif.: The Rand Corporation, 1982).

Union from three different perspectives: by major domestic actors, by subject matter, and chronologically.

The first part looks at the postwar period from the perspective of the major actors in the U.S. policy process. William Schneider describes the changing structure of public opinion; I. M. Destler examines the Congress; and Robert Bowie surveys the presidency and the executive branch.

The second part focuses on the major issues in the relationship and how they have been managed over time. Richard Betts looks at nuclear issues; Alexander George, at crisis management and prevention; Marshall Goldman and Raymond Vernon, at trade and economics; and Strobe Talbott, at social issues.

The third part takes a chronological approach. It examines the three major periods and turning points in the postwar period. Ernest May analyzes the domestic roots of our policy during the cold war; Stanley Hoffmann studies the rise and fall of the foreign policy of détente; and Samuel Huntington looks at the political origins and prospects of the current period of renewed hostility. All of these chapters focus on the American side of the U.S.–Soviet relationship; the final chapter in part 3, by Dimitri Simes, presents in summary fashion, and to the extent that is known, what was happening in Soviet policy during this period. This is the one chapter that looks at the other side of the coin and allows the reader to compare Soviet policy with American images of it.

In the fourth part of the book I summarize the policy recommendations made throughout and draw my own conclusions.

Over a century ago, Alexis de Tocqueville expressed grave doubts about the institutional capabilities of the American democracy in the field of foreign policy. In the words of the constitutional scholar Edwin Corwin, the American Constitution established an "invitation to struggle" for the control of foreign policy. In 1979, Daniel Yankelovich wrote: "In its statements to the American public, the U.S. leadership blows hot and cold. The tone is rarely balanced, ambiguities are played down, subtlety is sacrificed to overstatement."*

No book can hope to solve such a forbidding problem, but it can aspire to contribute toward intelligent and informed debate on ways of improving our performance, when the stakes are so high.

J.S.N.

---

*"Farewell to 'President Knows Best,'" *Foreign Affairs,* special issue, *America and the World, 1978* 57, no. 3 (1979): 687–88.

Acknowledgments

Each of the essays in this volume, including the conclusion, is, of course, the responsibility of the author, but the book has also been a collective enterprise. Robert Legvold persuaded me to undertake this study in 1980; the Council on Foreign Relations and two Harvard University centers—the Center for International Affairs and the Center for Science and International Affairs—cosponsored a study group in Cambridge early in 1981. Participants included Graham Allison, Abram Bergson, Robert Bowie, John Burns, Albert Carnesale, Abram Chayes, Antonia Chayes, Richard Cooper, Steven David, Paul Doty, Roger Fisher, Leslie Gelb, Guido Goldman, Marshall Goldman, William Griffith, Samuel Huntington, William Hyland, Jack Keliher, Anthony Lewis, Michael Mandelbaum, Arto Mansala, Ernest May, Michael Nacht, William Odom, Robert Paarlberg, Robert Putnam, Marshall Shulman, Steven Sternheim, Wolfgang Rudolph, and Adam Ulam.

A smaller group met at the Council on Foreign Relations in New York in April 1981 to comment on my suggested framework for the book. Participants included Richard Betts, Robert Bowie, I. M. Destler, Alton Frye, Alexander George, Stanley Hoffmann, Samuel Huntington, Ernest May, William Schneider, Marshall Shulman, Helmut Sonnenfeldt, Strobe Talbott, and Richard Ullman. Authors were then selected for the individual chapters. They prepared extended outlines and spent two full days discussing and criticizing each other's outlines before proceeding to write first drafts. When drafts were in hand, we met again for two days, this time with a small group of outside critics, who included McGeorge Bundy, William Hyland, Richard Pipes, and Malcolm Toon.

Each author received comments from his fellow contributors, as well as a detailed criticism from the editor, to guide the rewriting. Because of this group process, the authors and editor are mutually indebted in a manner that is most efficiently described here rather than in a multitude of acknowledgments throughout the book.

In addition, I am indebted to a number of people for their help. Robert Legvold not only conceived the idea for the book and relentlessly pursued me until I agreed to edit it, but he was ever the helpful colleague and critic throughout the process. Andrea Zwiebel at the Council was tireless in her administrative and editorial labors, as was Valerie Grasso at Harvard. Bob Beschel provided research assistance for the charts in chapter 13. I received helpful comments on the Introduction and Conclusion not only from my fellow authors but also from McGeorge Bundy, Mark Garrison, Roger Hamburg, Robert Keohane, James Leonard, Richard Neustadt, Richard Pipes, Richard Solomon, Helmut Sonnenfeldt, William Taubman, Scott Sagan, and Adam Ulam.

1

The Domestic Roots of American Policy

JOSEPH S. NYE, JR.

Americans tend to view international politics from a liberal historical perspective in which peaceful and harmonious relations are the "normal" condition. But U.S.–Soviet relations have not fit this norm. There are several deep-seated reasons to believe that tension is likely to be a continuing feature in those relations. First, as Tocqueville already saw in the nineteenth century, the enormous size and resources of the Russian and American nations foreshadowed a future bipolar rivalry. Then, in 1917, the Bolshevik revolution added a layer of deep ideological incompatibility. When the Second World War destroyed the multination balance of power that had existed before 1939, it left a bipolar structure of world power centered on the U.S.–Soviet rivalry. The accumulation of vast nuclear arsenals overshadowing those of all other nations has consolidated that special relationship, and the probability of tension is now built into its international structure.

Nonetheless, at different times there have been different degrees of tension and hostility. In fact, there have been six major phases in U.S. policy toward the Soviet Union. Our first policies toward the Soviet Union included intervention and ostracism. In the 1930s we turned to recognition and trade; and in the 1940s, of course, came the wartime alliance. Since the war, there have been three major phases: cold war from the late 1940s to the early 1960s; relative détente in the late 1960s and early 1970s; and renewed tension since the mid-1970s. In no period, however, has the relationship been warm or easy.[1]

Although there have been significant changes in Soviet foreign policy and in the Soviet polity—today's Russia is certainly not the same as Stalin's—Soviet objectives have probably changed less than American perceptions of them. Both Russian history and communist ideology have lent Soviet foreign policy consistency. While there are differences of views among experts regarding the defensive versus offensive intentions of

1. See, for example, Peter G. Filene, *Americans and the Soviet Experiment, 1917–1933* (Princeton: Princeton University Press, 1967), or Charles Bohlen, *Witness to History: 1929–1969* (New York: Norton, 1969).

Soviet expansion, its planned or opportunistic nature, and the degree of risk that Soviet leaders would bear to achieve these goals in the face of constraints, most tend to agree with the position outlined by Dimitri Simes later in this book that there has been consistency in Soviet objectives, albeit considerable variety in their tactics.

At the same time, American attitudes, responding in part to Soviet moves and in part to the political competition inherent in our democratic politics, have tended to alternate between overemphasis and under-emphasis on the threatening nature of Soviet objectives. The result has been an inconsistency in policy and possibly missed opportunities. During the cold war, our exaggeration of Soviet capabilities prevented us from negotiating at a time when our position was strong. For example, Adam Ulam argues that "long-range solutions can be reached in this sinful world only through short-range and partial accommodations. The trag-edy of 1949–50 was that no such negotiations took place."[2] The same argument is sometimes made about the period after Stalin's death in the mid-1950s. Subsequently, the ideological interpretation of policy and domestic political constraints prevented American policy from exploiting the diplomatic opportunities in the Sino–Soviet split for more than a decade after it occurred in the late 1950s. Conversely, the enthusiasm for détente in the 1960s and early 1970s led American officials to underesti-mate the Soviet military buildup, to delay an appropriate response, and to encourage false domestic expectations of future restraint in Soviet inter-national behavior.[3] Certainly, changing Soviet tactics have helped trigger American policy changes, but the exaggeration in American attitudes may develop as much from domestic political pressures and reactions toward previous swings of the policy pendulum as from the actual changes in Soviet behavior.

In the early part of the 1970s, American power was limited by intro-spective moral and social concerns in the aftermath of Vietnam and Watergate. The United States spent less in real terms on defense, foreign aid, embassies, and foreign broadcasting in 1980 than it did in 1960. Moreover, there was no political consensus on how to bring the nonmili-tary aspects of American power (such as our nearly 2:1 advantage in GNP, our grain reserves, our advanced technology) to bear upon U.S.–Soviet relations. Different groups resisted or insisted on their preferred link-ages. In these circumstances of shifting power, domestic disagreement,

2. Adam Ulam, *The Rivals* (New York: Viking, 1971), pp. 19, 156, 102; but for a contrary view, see William Taubman, *Stalin's American Policy* (New York: Norton, 1973).

3. See, for example, William G. Hyland, *Soviet–American Relations: A New Cold War?* (Santa Monica, Calif.: The Rand Corporation, 1981), p. 55. See also Albert Wohlstetter, "Is There a Strategic Arms Race?" *Foreign Policy*, no. 15 (Summer 1974), and "Rivals, But No Race," *Foreign Policy*, no. 16 (Fall 1974).

and ambiguous rules, it was not surprising that Soviet tactics proved adventuresome.

By the end of the decade, American attitudes had changed again, well before the 1980 election and even before the Soviet invasion of Afghanistan. As American policies switched from détente to renewed hostility, one could not help but wonder how such changes occur, whether a policy with fewer oscillations would be more effective in managing the relationship, and whether the United States is institutionally and politically capable of following a consistent and coherent policy toward the Soviet Union.

THE FOREIGN-POLICYMAKING PROCESS

Is the Soviet relationship uniquely difficult for the American policy process to handle? To some extent, the Soviet case is merely a particular instance of a more general problem, whose roots are deep in American political culture and institutions. The American Constitution is based on an eighteenth-century liberal view that power is best controlled, not by centralizing and civilizing it, but by fragmentation and countervailing checks and balances. In the area of foreign policy, the Constitution establishes the open "invitation to struggle" for control by the executive and legislative branches alluded to by Edwin Corwin.[4] This struggle is complicated by the federal and relatively geographically dispersed nature of the political elite; the weakness and poor discipline of the national political parties; the strength and legitimacy of economic, ideological, and ethnic pressure groups; the depth and frequency of political turnover in the executive branch after elections; and the almost constitutionally entrenched role of the press as a virtual fourth branch of government. All these features are familiar to Americans, but they are strange to most other governments. One cannot help but smile when imagining the difficulty a Soviet official would have trying to explain the American system to his masters in the Politburo.

Not only are the institutions rare and complex, but they are embedded in a distinctive political culture that places strong stress on American uniqueness, moralism, isolation, and quick solutions to problems. Dexter Perkins once asked, "What is unique about American foreign policy?" His answer was, "moralism and publicity."[5] Moreover, a number of students

4. Edwin S. Corwin, *The President: Office and Powers* (New York: New York University Press, 1940), p. 200. See also Arthur Schlesinger, Jr., *The Imperial Presidency* (Boston: Houghton Mifflin, 1973), and Thomas Franck and Edward Weisband, *Foreign Policy by Congress* (New York: Oxford University Press, 1979).

5. Dexter Perkins, "What Is Distinctly American about the Foreign Policy of the United States?" in Glyndon Van Dusen and Richard Wade, eds., *Foreign Policy and the American Spirit* (Ithaca, N.Y.: Cornell University Press, 1957). Also Frank Tannenbaum, *The American Tradition in Foreign Policy* (Norman, Okla.: University of Oklahoma Press, 1955).

have observed cyclical tendencies in American foreign policy. There have been oscillations between inward- and outward-oriented attitudes; between realist and moralistic approaches; and between executive and legislative domination of the process.[6]

There has been a variety of explanations of these swings. The cultural explanation stresses the optimism and moralism of liberal culture, which successively encounters and withdraws from the harsh outside reality of the world balance of power. Foreign policy reflects "the impulse to make overseas affairs a vehicle for expressing unresolved internal tensions."[7] The geopolitical explanation stresses the degrees of freedom that a Western hemisphere location (plus the British navy) allowed us, except on rare occasions when intrusion or encirclement looked possible and stimulated our response.[8] The institutional explanation turns to the pluralism and separation of powers designed to prevent tyranny that is enshrined in our eighteenth-century constitution. In Stephen Krasner's terms, the result is a foreign policy of a strong society but a weak state.[9] The electoral politics explanation stresses the alternation between political parties with different geographical and class bases. At a more general level, each of these considerations may contribute to lags in response to outside events—in cybernetic theory: the slower the feedback mechanisms, the wider the oscillations in observed behavior.

MAKING POLICY TOWARD THE USSR

Although these characteristics of American foreign policy are general, there is reason to believe that the Soviet relationship is more difficult to manage than others. For one thing, the secretive nature of Soviet society makes it something of a "black box" to us. It is difficult to bring evidence to bear on differences of opinion over Soviet intentions or the nature of their internal processes. Obviously this situation can result in misperceptions, but it is hard to prove what is or is not a misperception, because secrecy renders "evidence" fragmentary and subject to contradictory interpretations. There is none of the relative transparency that characterizes relations with most countries. This indeterminacy exacerbates the struggle for definition and control of policy in the United States. American foreign-policymaking is sometimes colloquially called "zoo-like." To extend the metaphor, it is particularly hard for a "zoo" to figure out and agree upon what is going on inside a "black box."

6. Dexter Perkins, *The American Approach to Foreign Policy* (New York: Atheneum, 1961), chap. 7. See also Stanley Hoffmann, *Gulliver's Troubles* (New York: McGraw-Hill, 1968), chap. 6.

7. Robert Dallek, *The American Style of Foreign Policy* (New York: Knopf, 1983), p. xiii.

8. Nicholas Spykman, *America's Strategy in World Politics* (New York: Harcourt, 1942), p. 449.

9. Stephen Krasner, *Defending the National Interest* (Princeton: Princeton University Press, 1978), chap. 3.

Cultural differences also exacerbate the problem of managing the Soviet relationship. As a liberal society, the United States has an ahistorical sense of innocence about international politics that periodically recoils from its encounters with Hobbesian reality. Encounters with the Soviet Union are the epitome of this process. Ahistorical liberal moralism meets Russian history married to amoral communism. While the Soviet leaders view capitalist America in relatively unchanging terms, the pragmatic lawyers and bureaucrats who guide American foreign policy are more responsive to Soviet tactical behavior. False hopes are raised and dashed because of American naiveté about the supposed change in the Soviet Union. A Soviet variant of this hypothesis argues that the capitalist system of the United States produces an elite that cannot accept the Soviet Union because the latter's success is a repudiation of capitalism, and communism is seen as both immoral and implicitly threatening. From time to time, goes this Soviet view, the elite produces realistic leaders who accept Soviet equality and the changing correlation of forces; but they are periodically overcome by other parts of the elite who see communism as immoral and refuse to accept Soviet equality.[10]

In any case, the rise of Soviet power may be resented because it has become identified with the end of the utopian idea of isolation in American political culture. In the past, threats severe enough to overcome America's geographic buffers were relatively rare, and popular attitudes of isolation toward Europe could flourish for long periods. Such attitudes linger in the postwar period, but Soviet nuclear weapons and progress in military technology have brought more frequent threats and alarms from outside: the Soviet A-bomb in 1949; the bomber-gap scare in the 1950s; the missile-gap scare and Sputnik in the late 1950s; ICBM vulnerability in the 1970s. As geographical buffers are eroded and shocks become more frequent, periods of oscillation shorten. The post-Vietnam period of inward-turning attitudes, for example, lasted less than a decade. But latent isolationism still exists (or "noninternationalism," as William Schneider calls it below) and may contribute to the sense of resentment against the principal country identified with its frustration. Indeed, Richard Barnet argues that "as the Second World War ended, the symbol of national insecurity became Russia and world communism. The insecurity had less to do with the reality of Russian power—much of the Soviet Union was still in ashes—than with the bureaucratic revolution in the United States and the staggering social and political upheavals that accompanied World War II."[11]

Whatever the merits of these general arguments, there *is* evidence that

10. Based on discussions with members of the Institute of the United States and Canada of the Soviet Academy of Sciences, January 1982.

11. Richard J. Barnet, *The Giants: Russia and America* (New York: Simon and Schuster, 1977), p. 56.

the management of the Soviet relationship is different from the rest of foreign policy. For one thing, the change in public attitudes toward China—another relatively opaque society—went through one shift in the postwar period rather than the ups and downs that have characterized our policy toward the Soviet Union.[12] Second, over a longer period, the oscillations in our Soviet policy have not corresponded very closely with the broader oscillations in U.S. foreign policy. The period 1920–40 is generally regarded as one of inward orientation in attitudes and legislative dominance of the foreign policy process, yet there were two separate policies toward the Soviet Union. Similarly, the period 1941–69 is generally characterized as one of outward-oriented attitudes and executive domination of the foreign policy process, but it encompassed three different policies.

The simplest explanation for these changes in American policy toward the Soviet Union should be shifts in Soviet behavior. Certainly, there is some relationship between the two, but at best the fit is so imperfect that further explanation is necessary. As Ernest May shows in chapter 9, the 1947 turning point in U.S. policy was a delayed response to postwar Soviet actions, but domestic politics caused policy to take an exaggerated form by 1950. Conversely, the turning point in Soviet policy following the death of Stalin elicited little change in American policy. The turning point of 1963 was more clearly a response to Soviet action in the Cuban missile crisis and its aftermath, and the 1979–80 changes were also somewhat delayed responses to underestimation of Soviet military and political behavior in the 1960s and 1970s. Moreover, as John Gaddis has argued, the alternation between narrowly and broadly defined strategies of containment in 1953, 1961, and 1969 had more to do with domestic electoral politics than with Soviet behavior.[13] In short, American policy is affected by Soviet behavior, but so imperfectly that other causes must also be involved.

Several of the institutional factors noted above contribute to oscillations in U.S. policy toward the Soviet Union. The constitutional fragmentation and geographical dispersion of power in the United States are critical features. Because of the far broader and more dispersed political elite here than in the Soviet Union (or most European countries), it takes longer to develop and change a consensus on policy. The lags accentuate oscillation. In order to try to shorten the lags in formulating consensus in our democracy, the political leadership must exaggerate the degree of external threat. An example is Dean Acheson's admission that the purpose of National Security Council document 68 was to "so bludgeon the

12. Richard H. Solomon, ed., *The China Factor* (New York: Prentice-Hall, 1981), pp. 12–13.

13. John L. Gaddis, *Strategies of Containment* (New York: Oxford University Press, 1982).

mass mind of 'top government' that not only could the President make a decision but the decision could be carried out."[14]

A particular instance of this institutional fragmentation is the division of foreign policy powers between the executive and legislative branches. Not only does this contribute to incoherence per se, but the executive tends to simplify and exaggerate to overcome the inertia of a diverse and loosely structured body of 535 individuals with weak party loyalty. An example is President Truman's justification of flamboyant rhetoric with the view that the Senate would not approve his 1947 policy change "without the emphasis on the Communist danger."[15]

A third institutional factor that contributes to oscillations is the practice of political appointments deep in the executive branch. Not only does this weaken the ability of the career civil service to pursue a constant policy, but many members of this "government of outsiders" are lawyers and others with a problem-solving orientation, or visionary academics who will hold office for only a few years.

Electoral politics also contribute to the problem. Given the fact that political power must be defended at the polls every four years, it is hardly surprising that electoral politics contribute to changes in U.S. policy toward the Soviet Union. One variant of this hypothesis is a simple "outs vs. ins" proposition. Given the centrality of the Soviet Union to American security, mishandling of that relationship is a handy stick for an outsider to seize and try to beat the incumbent with, particularly if the latter appears not to hold a strong enough position against the Soviet Union. The years 1952, 1960, 1976, and 1980 followed this pattern. Then, at least at the beginning of the next administration, there is generally an effort to differentiate the new policy from that of the defeated predecessor before reverting to a central tendency.

A second variant of the electoral hypothesis draws distinctions between Republicans and Democrats. Gaddis argues that, until the Reagan administration, the fiscal orthodoxy of Republican presidents (Eisenhower, Nixon, Ford) made them more cautious in their assessment of the economic costs of containment, and they followed a narrowly defined selective strategy. Liberal Democratic presidents were more optimistic about economic constraints and followed a broader approach to containment. Thus the particular strategy of containment altered with partisan success at the polls rather than in response to changes in Soviet behavior.

Alan Wolfe suggests a similar explanation but adds that Republican presidents are better protected on their right flank politically and have

14. Dean Acheson, *Present at the Creation: My Years at the State Department* (New York: Norton, 1969), p. 374.

15. Charles Bohlen, *Witness to History, 1929–1969* (New York: Norton, 1973), p. 261.

more leeway to reach accommodation with the Soviets.[16] He argues that "bipartisanship insured that debates over national security policy would always be skewed sharply to the right" and that the Soviet threat was more exaggerated by Democrats, who were egged on by Republicans. However, one must be cautious about this partisan explanation. Not only does the Reagan administration not fit this pattern but, as William Schneider shows in chapter 2 (and as I discuss further in the Conclusion), a complex process of party realignment occurred over the past two decades that is not adequately captured by the simple partisan thesis.

A variety of techniques can be imagined to improve the coherence, consistency, and efficacy of U.S. policy toward the Soviet Union. At the cultural level, better education about the Soviet Union and the incorporation of more expertise in the policy process might help. At the institutional level, some have suggested constitutional amendments to lengthen and strengthen the presidency, though this is a slow process and a debatably effective solution. More modest suggestions include new legislative committees and special compacts to govern executive–legislative interactions. In the executive branch, different organizational procedures could be attempted for handling issues like trade and intelligence. But it is also possible that the nature of our democratic system does not permit us to overcome easily the effect of "iron triangles" of bureaucrats, congressional committees, and interest groups (for instance, in agriculture) or the unpredictable and unavoidable oscillations arising from electoral campaigns. If this is true, then those aspects of our process that are unchangeable must set limits on the types of strategies we can choose. We may have to settle for simpler approaches that are more robust and durable in terms of the realities of American life.

16. Alan Wolfe, *The Rise and Fall of the Soviet Threat: Domestic Sources of the Cold War Consensus* (Washington, D.C.: Institute for Policy Studies, 1979), p. 38.

PART I

The Actors

If we think of the United States foreign policy process in terms of a sports metaphor, the first section of this book looks at the players; the second section looks at particular plays; the third section looks at how past games have been played; and the conclusions focus on how to play better in the future. This section on the key players starts with public opinion—the basic place to start in a democracy—and then, moving up the pyramid, focuses on the Congress and the presidency.

Public opinion in the United States has often been characterized as "isolationist" or, in William Schneider's term, "noninternationalist." Indeed, only a minority of the public pays close attention to foreign affairs. Traditionally in the past, at least the attentive and better-educated minority of the public tended to follow presidential initiatives in foreign policy. Not so any longer, says Schneider. Elite consensus and "followership" eroded under the pressures of party realignment and the events surrounding the Vietnam War. Elite opinion became more divided than mass opinion. The situation was further complicated by the adversarial role of the media, the rise of more ideological special interest groups, and some of the unintended effects of television news. The result, writes Schneider, is a complex public opinion. The elite has lost its consensus, while the general public wants both peace and strength in America's relations with the Soviet Union. Why have these twin objectives proven so difficult to reconcile in practice, and why is public opinion so often driven toward one or the other pole in response to changing events, fears, and concerns? These are the key questions that Schneider explores.

If public opinion provides the most basic but also the most amorphous players in the democratic game, the Congress is intermediate between public opinion and the presidency. The ambiguities in public opinion are often reinforced rather than reconciled by the congressional process. While the Congress shares control over foreign policy with the executive branch, it is organized in a manner that tends to emphasize particular interests and, in the case of U.S.–Soviet relations, the conflictual more than the cooperative dimensions. Ironically, as I. M. Destler points out, the reforms of congressional procedures in the 1970s tended to exacerbate rather than diminish the focus on particular interests, and the weakening of the leadership made executive-legislative consultation more difficult. Why this situation exists and what steps might be taken to improve congressional procedures are the central concerns of his chapter.

At the apex of the pyramid of actors is the presidency. The president is the key actor in the system who must set a course both to reflect and guide public and congressional opinion and also be responsive to other leaders in the alliance of democracies that has played such an important role in the postwar balance of power between the United States and the Soviet Union. Without a clear strategy and an effective process, it is virtually impossible to coordinate the tasks of managing the bureaucracy, working with the Congress, informing the public, and leading the alliance. In principle, the president should be like a captain introducing coherence into the team. Robert Bowie explores how and why this has not always occurred when different presidents have performed very differently in fulfilling the leader's tasks.

2
Public Opinion

WILLIAM SCHNEIDER

THE DECLINE OF "FOLLOWERSHIP"

In an analysis entitled *War, Presidents, and Public Opinion* published ten years ago, political scientist John E. Mueller found that there exists, particularly in the area of foreign affairs, an important group of citizens—they can be called "followers"—who are inclined to rally to the support of the president no matter what he does.[1] Is this the great mass of uneducated, unthinking Americans who, having few ideas of their own about foreign policy, simply follow the cues of whoever happens to be in power? Not at all. According to Mueller, "It is the well-educated segment of the population that most nearly typifies the follower mentality."[2] These people were found to be attentive to foreign affairs, internationalist-minded, and receptive to the often complex justifications for U.S. involvement in the rest of the world. They literally "followed" foreign policy, and, until very recently, to follow meant to support.

Thus, throughout the period of the Korean War and until the last few years of the Vietnam War, college-educated Americans were the ones least likely to express the opinion that involvement in those conflicts was a mistake.[3] Poorly educated Americans, who knew or cared little about foreign policy, saw no point to our becoming involved in other countries' business. They were suspicious of alliances, diplomacy, treaties, and trade and were relatively unsupportive of such activities. And they were totally unsupportive of lengthy, costly, inconclusive foreign wars that had no obvious justification in terms of U.S. national security. Furthermore, the mass public was generally uninterested and uninvolved in the foreign policy process except at presidential election time, when it passed judgment on the performance of its leaders.

The period when this model prevailed, roughly from 1948 to 1968, was also a period of bipartisan consensus in U.S. foreign policy. Prior to

1. Mueller, *War, Presidents, and Public Opinion* (New York: John Wiley & Sons, 1973), p. 69.
2. Ibid., p. 122.
3. Ibid., pp. 124–25.

1948, the noninternationalist public tended to hold sway over foreign policy, at least during peacetime, because of the influence of a substantial segment of ideological isolationists among American political leaders. Isolationism had a long history in American politics and was associated with both the Left (Progressivism) and the Right (conservatism). After World War II, however, instead of rejecting an activist role in world affairs and "returning to normalcy," as was the case after World War I, American leaders drew together around a new internationalist consensus. "The dominant views from the late 1940s through the early 1960s," one historian of public opinion writes, "had such powerful influence even on its critics that it may be called the Cold War consensus."[4]

The cold war consensus was facilitated by the reversal of alliances on the part of the United States during the 1940s. Left-wing isolationism virtually disappeared after the 1930s, as Franklin D. Roosevelt, the hero of the Left, led the United States in a crusade against international fascism. Right-wing isolationism had a mild resurgence in 1945–56, but its most prominent leaders, such as Senator Arthur Vandenberg, had already become convinced as a result of Pearl Harbor of the necessity of an active U.S. role in the world.[5] The watershed came with the pronouncement of the Truman Doctrine in 1947, in which the United States shifted from support for the international Left (the antifascist alliance) to leadership of the international Right (the anticommunist alliance). As Samuel Lubell has argued, conservative isolationism in the 1930s and 1940s was strongly motivated by the conviction that the United States should stay out of world politics because it was on the wrong side. The cold war reformulated America's world role and made it possible for former isolationists to become internationalists.[6] When Gallup took a poll shortly after the Truman Doctrine speech in March 1947, Republicans and Democrats were equally supportive of $250 million in aid to Greece (56 percent of each partisan group approved). The major factor in degree of support was level of education: 65 percent of the college-educated, 57 percent of the high-school group, and 48 percent of the grade-school-educated favored the proposal.[7]

The Truman Doctrine also precipitated a sharp increase in public hostility toward the Soviet Union. As Ernest May points out in this volume, during the last years of World War II, roughly half of the U.S.

4. Ralph B. Levering, *The Public and American Foreign Policy, 1918–1978* (New York: William Morrow, 1978), p. 104.

5. Ole R. Holsti and James N. Rosenau, "Vietnam, Consensus, and the Belief Systems of American Leaders," *World Politics* 32, no. 1 (October 1979): 1.

6. Samuel Lubell, *The Future of American Politics* (Garden City, N.Y.: Doubleday Anchor Books, 1956), pp. 150–67.

7. Levering, *The Public,* p. 99.

public told the Gallup poll in repeated questionings that they thought Russia could be trusted to cooperate when the war was over. In January 1947, 43 percent continued to hold the view that Russia would cooperate with us in world affairs. By June 1949, however, the figure had fallen to 20 percent. The proportion of the public who described Russia as "an aggressive nation that would start a war to get something she wants" rather than "a peace-loving nation, willing to fight only if she has to defend herself" went from 38 percent in September 1945 to 66 percent in October 1947. The view that "Russia is trying to build herself up to be the ruling power of the world" rose from 58 percent in July 1946 to 76 percent in October 1947.[8]

The "followership" model entailed a leadership stratum that was largely agreed on the goals and methods of U.S. foreign policy, an attentive public that "followed" their leadership, and a noninternationalist but essentially inert mass public. The foreign policy values that prevailed during this period were those that will be described below as conservative internationalism: a continuity of goals—essentially containment of Soviet aggression—and an oscillation between cooperative and confrontational strategies. Foreign policy "followers" tended to support both kinds of strategies. Ralph Levering, for instance, found that "during the 1950s the college-educated consistently gave the most support to proposals to ease East–West tensions," such as commercial ties with Russia and increased contacts with China.[9] On the other hand, the well-educated were also the most supportive of military intervention when that was defined by the president as an official foreign policy objective.[10]

The argument of this chapter is that the "followership" model, which sustained a bipartisan foreign policy consensus for eighteen years, began to break down after 1964. This breakdown had two causes: ideological polarization over foreign policy within the attentive public, and the rise of anti-Establishment feeling in the mass public during the late 1960s and 1970s.

Anti-Establishment themes became prominent at both the mass and elite levels in American politics after 1964. At the elite level, anti-Establishment sentiment was heavily colored by ideology. Counterelites emerged on both the right and the left to challenge the supremacy of the old foreign policy Establishment and the traditionally moderate party leaders. The result has been a division between conservative and liberal internationalists and a fracturing of the postwar elite consensus.

The polarization of elites has, to a considerable extent, been institu-

8. Rita James Simon, *Public Opinion in America, 1936–1970* (Chicago: Rand McNally, 1974), pp. 151–53.

9. Levering, *The Public*, p. 113.

10. See Mueller, *War*, pp. 122–36.

tionalized within the party system. American political parties have been deeply ideologized as a result of the protest movements of the sixties, which challenged and, to a large extent, either displaced or converted the Establishments of the two major parties. This institutional divergence militates against the reemergence of a politically effective elite consensus in foreign policy, as in other areas.

The predominantly noninternationalist mass public continues to support a two-track policy of peace and strength. However, important changes have also occurred at the mass level. In the first place, the mass public has become less inert and more activated, partly as a result of television, which brings news about foreign affairs to the attention of a large, mostly inadvertent audience. In addition, the period since 1964 has witnessed a widespread decline of confidence not only in political leaders but also in the leaders of every major institution of American life. Public opinion has, in sum, become less passive and more distrustful. At the mass level, anti-Establishment feeling is not so much ideological as repudiative, a rejection of those in power as corrupt, incompetent, and ineffective. This mood has been sustained by the mass media, whose influence is less ideological than anti-Establishment. What has replaced "followership" is an unstable model of competing coalitions in which the noninternationalist mass public swings left or right unpredictably, in response to its current fears and concerns. Instead of a stable, two-track foreign policy, there is a situation of erratic alternation from one track to the other.

The consequences of a polarized and vacillating foreign policy environment are just beginning to be felt. They include a change in the role of elections from their traditional function of reaffirming the national consensus; an ideologization of executive–legislative relations and interest-group activities; and political obstacles that make it difficult for an administration to pursue a centrist foreign policy—assuming that it wants to. Foreign policy has become more political. The effect has been to challenge and demoralize the traditional foreign policy Establishment and to raise the risk of substantial policy discontinuities between—and sometimes within—administrations.

Liberal and Conservative Internationalism

In 1976, Ole R. Holsti and James N. Rosenau surveyed 2,282 American leaders, including a random sample of persons listed in *Who's Who in America* and quota samples of military personnel, Foreign Service officers, labor leaders, politicians, clergy, foreign affairs experts outside government, media leaders, and prominent women. Their purpose was to assess the impact of the Vietnam experience on the beliefs and attitudes of American leaders. What they found was evidence of a deep and profound division that was consistently related to the respondents' recalled policy positions on the Vietnam War. "The broad consensus among American leaders that marked the period following World War II has been shattered."[11] The absence of consensus was demonstrated by the failure of the leaders, when grouped by policy preference on the Vietnam War, to agree on the meaning or lessons of that experience or the future conduct of U.S. foreign policy. Holsti and Rosenau concluded that "the divergent sets of beliefs about foreign policy are sufficiently coherent to be properly described as competing belief systems."[12]

Jerrold E. Schneider conducted extensive personal interviews with 108 members of the House of Representatives in 1970, probing their views on a variety of foreign policy issues: Vietnam, military aid to Greece and Brazil, defense spending, foreign economic aid, the Rhodesian trade embargo, and relations with Cuba. He examined the intercorrelations among the congressmen's positions on these issues and related their interview responses to their voting behavior on a set of foreign policy roll-calls in 1971–72 (for the 97 representatives still in office). His conclusion: "We can infer from a set of strong relationships . . . that there were definite, seemingly distinct, foreign policy ideologies in the Congress in the summer of 1970. One ideology is basically liberal, and one basically conservative."[13]

Schneider's findings for the 1970s contrasted sharply with the results of earlier studies showing much lower constraint within the foreign policy domain and across foreign and domestic policy. He concluded that ideological consistency had increased since the 1950s and that foreign policy had been the area of significant polarization.[14]

In 1979, Michael Mandelbaum and William Schneider carried out a detailed analysis of data from a 1974 survey of American foreign policy attitudes sponsored by the Chicago Council on Foreign Relations. Their analysis revealed that certain themes consistently divided internationalists, those generally better-educated Americans who are attentive to foreign policy and supportive of an active U.S. role in world affairs. These polarizing themes included any reference to the military, such as military aid, troop commitments abroad, and defense spending; the notion of U.S. hegemony or world leadership; the CIA, the military, and business as agents of or forces influencing U.S. foreign policy; sympathy for Third World liberation movements; support for dictatorial regimes in countries otherwise friendly to the United States; and anticommunism as a foreign

11. Holsti and Rosenau, "Vietnam," p. 5.
12. Ibid., p. 6.
13. Jerrold E. Schneider, *Ideological Coalitions in Congress* (Westport, Conn.: Greenwood Press, 1979), p. 63. See pp. 59–67 for statistical results.
14. Ibid., pp. 146–47.

policy priority. It was possible to differentiate conservative and liberal internationalists according to their views on these issues.[15]

During the Nixon and Ford administrations, two foreign policy issues became matters for intense disagreement—détente and antimilitarism. The first, of course, was the product of Nixon and Kissinger's dramatic decision to normalize relations with the People's Republic of China and to reach agreements with the Soviet Union to stabilize the international status quo. Antimilitarism was the Left's interpretation of the "lesson of Vietnam"—to wit, that military power was no longer the most critical resource in "the new world order" and that the United States should think less in terms of national security and more in terms of global economic interdependence. The worldwide energy crisis was taken as further justification for this position.

Conservative internationalists were found to picture the world primarily in East–West terms: democracy versus totalitarianism, capitalism versus communism, freedom versus repression. They were supportive of military power and gave high priority to national security as a foreign policy goal. They also showed a strong commitment to traditional anticommunist containment and were suspicious of détente as a kind of cartel agreement whereby the two superpowers agreed to limit competition in order to stabilize the market and protect their interests.

Liberal internationalists emphasized economic and humanitarian problems over security issues and rejected a hegemonic role for the United States. They wanted leaders to think in global terms—of the scarcity of natural resources, environmental and oceanic pollution, and international economic inequality. They tended to regard the common problems facing all of humanity as more urgent than the ideological differences between East and West. Liberal internationalists approved of détente as a necessary first step toward a new world order based on global interdependence. The impact of Vietnam could be seen in this group's deep suspicion of military intervention and military power as instruments of foreign policy.

Détente and antimilitarism were the issues that split the internationalist public and destroyed the cold war consensus. Both liberal and conservative internationalists perceived foreign policy in moralistic terms, and both attacked Henry Kissinger for the lack of moral commitment in his diplomacy. Conservative internationalists are anti-détente and promilitary. They align ideologically with the international Right, which is to say that their primary moral commitment is to the free world in its confronta-

15. Michael Mandelbaum and William Schneider, "The New Internationalisms: Public Opinion and Foreign Policy," chap. 2 in Kenneth Oye, Donald Rothchild, and Robert Lieber, eds., *Eagle Entangled: U.S. Foreign Policy in a Complex World* (New York: Longman, 1979), pp. 40–63.

tion with communism. Liberal internationalists are pro-détente and anti-military. They align ideologically with "the forces of change" in world affairs—not communism, but the "Third World Left," including national liberation movements, oppressed minorities such as Palestinians and blacks in southern Africa, and, indeed, the Third World as a whole in its claim for economic justice against the industrialized "North."

The basic assumption of Kissinger's balance-of-power approach was, of course, the dominance of the national interest over all other moral commitments. His policies were, in fact, pro-détente and promilitary, and therefore ideologically confusing. For a while, conservatives were willing to go along with détente because Nixon and Kissinger were pursuing a "tough" military policy in Vietnam. Liberals expressed grudging approval of Nixon and Kissinger's overtures to China and Russia but were never unreservedly enthusiastic about the policy. Conservatives remained suspicious, while liberals felt that détente was no more than a precondition for a globalist foreign policy. As I. M. Destler notes in this volume, good U.S.–Soviet relations were not the principal foreign policy objective of any major constituency in Congress.

Eventually, both sides turned against the secretary of state, once the issues on which they differed with him became more salient than those with which they agreed. The Left attacked his preoccupation with military strength and big-power diplomacy, while the Right passed a "Morality in Foreign Policy" amendment to the 1976 Republican party platform criticizing their own administration's policy of détente. Both sides seized upon the human rights theme as the perfect reproach to the cynicism and casuistry of Kissinger-style diplomacy, although the Left and the Right had different notions of which specific forces in the world were the chief perpetrators of human rights violations. It was enough for Jimmy Carter to claim in 1976 that American foreign policy had paid too little attention to human rights and leave it at that.

Détente and human rights were both themes that appealed strongly to all internationalists and were typical of the kinds of issues that, in an earlier era, would have been promoted and sustained by the foreign policy Establishment as elements of the bipartisan consensus. In the polarized environment of the 1970s, however, détente and human rights became sources of division, and their proponents were subject to political and ideological criticism.

Noninternationalists

Noninternationalists, who comprised almost half of the American public in the 1974 study, do not share this moralism. They are suspicious of international involvements of any kind. They tend to be poorer and less well-educated than internationalists and to know and care little about foreign affairs, which they see as remote from their daily concerns. This large, inattentive public is neither consistently liberal nor consistently conservative in its foreign policy beliefs. Nor is it ideologically isolationist in the sense that many Americans were between World Wars I and II. The inattentive public is simply not internationalist-minded. It is predisposed against U.S. involvement in other countries' affairs unless a clear and compelling issue of national interest or national security is at stake. If we are directly threatened or if our interest *is* involved in any important way, this group wants swift, decisive action, not long-term involvement.

The foreign policy attitudes of the noninternationalist public are not ideological. Instead, this group swings left and right unpredictably, in response to its current fears and concerns. The issue of détente, for example, has split liberal and conservative internationalists. But détente also comprises a powerful nonideological theme—namely, *peace*. The Nixon-Kissinger détente policy was extraordinarily popular with the public during the 1970s because it was interpreted, not as a liberal policy, but as a way to promote peace. Peace, which liberal internationalists tend to regard as an ideological position and noninternationalists as a consensual theme, draws these two constituencies together.

Similarly, liberal and conservative internationalists differ profoundly over military policy. But *strength* is a nonideological sentiment that appeals strongly to noninternationalists. The desire for military strength draws conservative internationalists and noninternationalists into a "conservative" coalition. Peace and strength are the two issues of surpassing concern to noninternationalists, and as the relative salience of these issues changes, so does the coalition pattern and the dominant ideological complexion of foreign policy opinion.

One additional factor contributes even greater instability to this inherently unstable coalition pattern. That is the impact of the media, particularly television. The primacy of television has expanded the audience for news, especially foreign policy news. As print-media reporters are painfully aware, the public now relies on television as its primary source of news and information. In polls conducted since the late 1950s by the Roper Organization for the Television Information Office, television surpassed newspapers as "the source of most news" in 1963. Today, 74 percent of Americans say they rely on television for information about foreign affairs, compared to 54 percent who rely on newspapers.

The dominance of television has had a substantial impact on public opinion. Watching television is a different kind of activity from reading newspapers or magazines. When people read newspapers or magazines, they edit the material by selecting only those articles that interest them. If they are not interested in foreign affairs—and most Americans are not— they simply pass over the foreign affairs articles.

Television news, on the other hand, edits the information for the viewer. Few people turn off the television or walk away when they are confronted with news stories that do not particularly intrigue them. Television thus exposes its audience to a much wider range of information than the viewing public would normally select for itself.

Television also creates opinions where formerly there were none. Before the advent of television, much of the public was insulated from a great deal of political information because they edited it out of their lives. That was particularly true of foreign policy. The public probably would never have heard of El Salvador, much less cared about it. Today the sheer volume of exposure to new information relayed by television assures a more involved public. Television has created a vast, *inadvertent* audience for news about foreign policy.

Another dimension can be associated with the prominence of television. The television news audience is qualitatively different from the print-media audience. The person who regularly follows foreign affairs tends to have strong predispositions on the issues. The person who is exposed to foreign policy news (or any other kind of news) irregularly or only occasionally tends to have weakly held opinions about these issues simply because he is not interested in them.

Social scientists have shown that when people with strongly held opinions are exposed to new information, they use that information to bolster their opinions. New information does not, as a rule, change their minds. On the other hand, when people with weak opinions are exposed to new information, the impact of that information is very strong. They form new opinions, and if the information they receive is negative or critical, their opinions will develop in that direction.

The mass audience, which is not interested in foreign affairs, is noninternationalist in outlook and automatically suspicious of American involvement with the rest of the world. It is exposed inadvertently, through television, to more foreign policy information than ever before. This group is not converted by any editorial policy on the part of television, but it is made aware of what is going on in the world and, in particular, of how deeply the United States is involved in world events. That information is brought home to these people in a very dramatic way on their television sets night after night, and it offends their noninternationalist sensibilities. They simply don't see the point of it.

As a result, the public has become less patient with foreign policy initiatives. The attentive elites compete for allies in the noninternationalist public, each on its own grounds. The net impact is a good deal more cynicism and distrust among a public that finds its leaders deeply divided and increasingly critical of each other. There is no evidence that television changes the nature of the public's concerns in the area of foreign policy. Those concerns remain what they always have been: peace and strength.

Television simply intensifies these concerns and creates more negative and unstable public moods.

Public opinion between 1964 and 1974 was totally preoccupied with the issue of peace. The result was to pull noninternationalists to the left. After 1968, for instance, the noninternationalist public turned against the Vietnam War as a wasteful, pointless, and tragic U.S. involvement. The antiwar coalition was a potent alliance between liberal internationalists and noninternationalists. The latter, however, never accepted the more extreme contention of the antiwar activists that U.S. purposes in Vietnam were evil or corrupt.

The noninternationalist public allies with the Left on questions of intervention because they see no point to American involvement in most of the world. They are profoundly anti-foreign aid, anti-troop involvement, anti-anything that smacks of foreign entanglement. To call this viewpoint "isolationist," however, is a bit too strong. Isolationism implies a principled opposition to U.S. participation in world affairs. Noninternationalists are not so much opposed as they are nonsupportive.[16] Being less well-educated—that is the strongest demographic correlate of noninternationalism—this group has a limited understanding of the relevance of events that are complex and remote from their daily lives. They feel that most of what the United States does for the rest of the world is senseless, wasteful, and unappreciated. And sometimes they are right.

In cases like Vietnam and El Salvador, noninternationalists find a natural alliance with the Left. But that alliance is not automatic or constant. The noninternationalist public is also oriented toward a strong military posture. After 1975, the mass public began to feel insecure about Soviet military strength and adventurism, and public opinion began to drift to the right. Noninternationalists were pulled into an alliance with conservative internationalists out of a shared concern over the nation's military security. Virtually every month from 1974 to 1981 saw greater public support for increasing the size of the defense budget. Noninternationalists voted heavily for Reagan, in part because of his promises of a defense buildup and a tougher line with the Soviet Union. This constituency likes strength and toughness in foreign affairs because they prevent us from becoming involved in the business of other countries. They see the United States as protected so long as we are the toughest kid on the block. The basic impulse is defensive; the public wants to see the United States beef up its military power in order to protect itself from a growing Soviet threat, not in order to assume an interventionist role in world affairs. Thus, noninternationalists support the conservative elite on many issues having to do with defense and toughness. But they support the liberal elite when it becomes a question of involvement.

16. See the discussion in Mueller, *War*, pp. 124–26.

The Conservative Trend

An analysis of trends in foreign policy opinion from 1974 to 1978, when the Chicago Council on Foreign Relations repeated many of the same survey questions, shows shifts in the direction of greater conservatism and less internationalism. Thus, public support for "defending our allies' security," "containing communism," and "protecting weaker nations from foreign aggression" increased over this four-year period, while endorsement of such liberal internationalist goals as "combatting world hunger" and "helping to improve the standard of living in less developed countries" tended to decline. Approval of foreign economic aid fell by 5.5 percentage points; approval of foreign military aid rose by 7 percentage points. Support for NATO rose by 10 points. The view that the United States should increase its level of defense spending rose by fully 17 points. On the other hand, the attitude that the United States should take an active part in world affairs—an almost pure measure of internationalism—actually fell by 6 percentage points between 1974 and 1978.[17]

The conservative trend surely had something to do with the election to the presidency in 1980 of the best-known conservative internationalist in American public life. It can be argued, however, that the foreign policy "mandate" in 1980 was ambiguous at best. Virtually every poll showed that Ronald Reagan had a clear advantage over Jimmy Carter on domestic issues, particularly the economy, while Carter was consistently rated better for handling foreign relations—a reversal of the usual party advantages. For instance, in a Gallup poll taken in September 1980, Carter led Reagan by 25 points as the best candidate for keeping the United States out of war. On the other hand, Reagan had an equally strong lead as the best candidate for strengthening the national defense. Carter was preferred for dealing with the Middle East situation; but Reagan was preferred for increasing respect for the United States overseas. Generally, peace issues benefited Carter, while Reagan had the advantage on issues related to strength and national defense. Balancing all these issues together, Carter maintained a slight margin as the candidate who would "best handle foreign policy."[18] Indeed, Carter used the foreign policy issue, particularly the widespread fear that Reagan might get America into a war, as the principal theme of his campaign. The mass public, still heavily noninternationalist, was with Reagan on the issue of strength but

17. William Schneider, "Conservatism, Not Interventionism: Trends in Foreign Policy Opinion, 1974–82," chap. 2 in Kenneth Oye, Robert Lieber, and Donald Rothchild, eds., *Eagle Defiant: United States Foreign Policy in the 1980s* (Boston: Little, Brown, 1983), pp. 44–47.

18. Ibid., pp. 37–38. Also, William Schneider, "The November 4 Vote for President: What Did it Mean?" chap. 7 in Austin Ranney, ed., *The American Elections of 1980* (Washington, D.C.: American Enterprise Institute for Public Policy Research, 1981), pp. 231–34.

fearful of him when it came to peace. It is fair to conclude that Reagan won the 1980 election in spite of his foreign policy positions, not because of them.

These ambiguities became apparent during the first eighteen months of Reagan's presidency. In the area of defense spending, for instance, the president had enormous public support for the increases he proposed—and got—during his first year in office. By the end of 1981, however, the public appeared to be basically satisfied with the president's military buildup and was reluctant to endorse further increases in military spending. According to the NBC News/Associated Press poll, the proportion of Americans favoring an increase in defense spending fell by almost half, from 65 percent in January to 34 percent in November 1981. In the spring of 1980, the National Opinion Research Center found 56 percent of the public in favor of higher defense spending and 11 percent for cutting the defense budget. In the spring of 1982, the two proportions were almost equal, 29 percent for more defense spending and 30 percent for less, with a plurality, 36 percent, expressing the view that we were spending "about the right amount" on defense.

In the area of interventionism, the president ran into serious problems with public opinion during the sequence of foreign policy crises between December 1981 and July 1982—namely, Poland, El Salvador, the Falkland Islands, and Lebanon. Though the public had strong sympathies in each of these conflicts, polls showed decisive margins opposed to U.S. military intervention. The El Salvador issue brought these sentiments into sharpest relief. In a March 1982 ABC News/*Washington Post* survey, 64 percent of respondents agreed that a pro-Communist government in El Salvador would endanger the security interests of the United States, whereas 27 percent disagreed; but 79 percent disapproved of sending U.S. troops to fight in that country, compared to 18 percent who were in favor. The public disapproved of the way the administration was handling the situation in El Salvador, 45 to 40 percent. They were evenly split (42 to 42 percent) over whether the Reagan administration was in fact telling the truth when it claimed it had no intention of sending American soldiers to fight in El Salvador. And by 51 to 42 percent, Americans said they would support young men who refused to go to El Salvador if the United States were drafting soldiers and sending them to fight there.

None of these attitudes had changed significantly a year later, after President Reagan delivered a nationally televised address before a joint session of Congress on the subject of Central America on April 27, 1983. The view that a pro-Communist government in El Salvador would endanger U.S. security went up slightly, according to a poll taken in May 1983 by ABC News and *The Washington Post* (69 to 22 percent agreed). Opposition to sending U.S. troops to fight in El Salvador remained strong, however (80 to 14 percent). The public was almost as strongly opposed to President Reagan's request for increased military aid to the government of El Salvador (70 to 19 percent). When asked which side the United States should support in El Salvador, only 15 percent said the government, 3 percent said the rebels, and fully 69 percent replied that the United States should "stay out of the situation." The ABC/*Post* survey also asked people which they saw as the greater danger to the United States: "The spread of communism in Central America because the U.S. doesn't do enough to stop it" or "the U.S. becoming too entangled in internal Central American problems as a result of trying to stop the spread of communism." A majority, 55 percent, saw U.S. entanglement as the greater danger, compared to 34 percent who were more concerned about the spread of communism.

Finally, the movement in support of a nuclear freeze was an essentially spontaneous public initiative in reaction to fears that the military buildup and the president's tough foreign policy rhetoric were increasing the risk of war. Public pressure was strong enough to get nuclear freeze initiatives onto one-quarter of the ballots cast nationwide in the 1982 congressional elections. A March 1982 *Los Angeles Times* poll found 57 to 37 percent of the public in favor of a nuclear freeze. In the same poll, however, respondents supported a tougher rather than a more conciliatory stand toward the Soviet Union by 53 to 27 percent.

In November 1982, the Chicago Council on Foreign Relations carried out its third quadrennial survey of public opinion and foreign policy. As noted, the interval between the 1974 and the 1978 Chicago Council surveys had shown a marked conservative trend. The 1982 results, however, were generally similar to those obtained in 1978—conservative, but not especially internationalist. Thus, the view that the United States should stay out of world affairs continued to rise, from 24 percent in 1974, to 29 percent in 1978, to 35 percent—over one-third—in 1982.[19]

The data did show two shifts of opinion between 1978 and 1982, and these were seemingly contradictory. One has already been noted—namely, the declining demand for higher military spending. In 1978, those who wanted to expand the defense budget had outnumbered those who wanted to cut the defense budget by two to one. Data from 1980 and 1981 reveal the margin growing to as high as six to one. By the end of 1982, however, as in the spring, the proportions favoring higher and lower defense spending were about equal.

At the same time, the 1982 results reveal a continuing increase in hostility toward the Soviet Union. One question in the Chicago Council

19. John E. Rielly, ed., *American Public Opinion and U.S. Foreign Policy 1983* (Chicago: The Chicago Council on Foreign Relations, 1983).

survey asked respondents to rate various countries on a "feeling ther-
mometer" running from zero degrees (very cold or unfavorable) to 100
degrees (very warm or favorable). The average rating for the Soviet
Union dropped from 34 degrees in 1978 to 25 degrees in 1982. The
public's favorability toward Cuba, a close Soviet ally, also declined, from
32 to 25 degrees. However, the public's feelings toward Poland became
more positive (50 to 53 degrees). The inference that the trend was specifically anti-Soviet rather than generally anticommunist is confirmed by the
shift in attitudes toward the People's Republic of China; China's image
improved between 1978 and 1982, from 44 to 48 degrees. Elsewhere, the
1982 results revealed an 8-point increase since 1978 in the percentage of
the public willing to use U.S. troops "if Japan were invaded by the Soviet
Union" and a 10-point increase in willingness to use U.S. forces "if Soviet
troops invaded Western Europe." Public support for restricting U.S.–
Soviet trade and for limiting the sales of advanced computers to the
Soviet Union also rose significantly between 1978 and 1982.

Thus, one finds continuing hostility toward the Soviet Union but less
demand for increasing the defense budget. Much of the explanation, of
course, lies with President Reagan's economic program. The president
had already increased defense spending quite substantially in 1981 and
1982, while cutting spending on domestic social programs. Faced with an
enormous federal deficit, the public tended to prefer that Congress look
first at the military budget rather than at the domestic budget in deciding
where to make further reductions.

Paradoxically, then, an atmosphere of strong anti-Soviet feeling gave
rise to public fear and insecurity and, consequently, to a demand for arms
control. At the end of 1982, 58 percent of the public said they favored "a
mutual, verifiable freeze on nuclear weapons . . . right now, if the Soviets
would agree." Only 21 percent endorsed President Reagan's position that
such a freeze should be agreed to "only after the U.S. builds up its nuclear
weapons more," while 12 percent opposed a freeze altogether. In the
1982 midterm elections, the nuclear freeze resolutions were passed by
voters in 8 out of 9 states and 28 out of 30 localities. The freeze movement
certainly did not imply any great feeling of trust in the Soviet Union. The
prevailing view, expressed by 49 percent of the public at the end of 1982,
was that the United States should stop building nuclear weapons only if
the Soviet Union agreed to do so. Twenty-six percent felt that the United
States should continue to build nuclear weapons regardless of what the
Soviets do, while only 19 percent were of the opinion that we should stop
building nuclear weapons even if the Soviets do not.

The public appeared to approve of Reagan's initial defense buildup
and his tough anti-Soviet line. But the cost of those policies was a greater
risk of war. People demanded some assurances that the president was

equally strong in his commitment to peace and arms control. In the end, on the nuclear freeze, as on defense spending and El Salvador, the administration essentially got its way. But it first had to adapt its policies to public and congressional pressures and, in each case, face a major political test.

Anti-Establishment Politics

Probably the most pervasive theme in American political life since 1964 has been antagonism toward established interests. Anti-Establishment hostility has affected politics at both the mass and elite levels, although in very different ways. At the elite level, it has assumed a mostly ideological mode of expression, namely, the emergence of counterelites on both the left and the right in opposition to the traditionally moderate leadership stratum in American politics. The latter was closely identified with the bipartisan foreign policy consensus of the cold war period. The left and right oppositionists made foreign policy the principal theme of their attack on the Establishment; more specifically, the new liberals and the new conservatives opposed the lack of moral consistency inherent in a two-track foreign policy. How could we pursue cooperation with an essentially evil adversary? How could we seek confrontation at the expense of the interests of "innocent" third parties—and at the risk of world survival? These confrontations between old and new Establishments involving foreign policy as a central issue occurred mostly within the Democratic and Republican parties.

The 1960s witnessed the emergence of protest movements on the left and right that challenged the Establishments of the two major parties. In 1964, Barry Goldwater mobilized conservative activists to attend Republican caucuses and wrest party control from the liberal Eastern Establishment which, they claimed, had not been vigorous enough in opposing communism. The left protest movement sprang up with the antiwar candidacy of Eugene McCarthy in 1968. McCarthy's followers challenged the Democratic party Establishment in the primaries and on the streets of Chicago. In 1972, liberal activists mobilized their strength in the primaries and caucuses in order to defeat the party Establishment that had "stolen" the nomination from them four years earlier. Thus, both conservatives and liberals waged war against their respective party Establishments. Foreign policy was the principal rallying theme for both movements. And, despite many setbacks and defeats, both protest movements have become major, if not dominant, forces in their respective parties.

The political alignment that has been emerging since the mid-1960s is two-dimensional in nature. The system of class politics associated with the New Deal remains strong and, in fact, was revitalized by the predominance of economic issues since 1973 and by the policies of the Reagan administration. Overlying that dimension are the newer ideological cleavages associated with the social, cultural, and foreign policy conflicts of the past two decades. Ronald Reagan retains the old economic conservatism of the traditional Republican party but adds to it the vigorous social and foreign policy conservatism of the New Right (which first brought him to prominence in California in the 1960s as a law-and-order candidate). Edward Kennedy represents a similar melding of old and new liberal traditions on the left. The current realignment has been in the direction of ideological consistency, with the Republican party becoming socially as well as economically conservative and the Democrats moving toward a more liberal philosophy on social and foreign policy issues to match the party's historic economic liberalism.

A realignment in the direction of ideologically consistent parties, however, may create sociological inconsistencies with the electorate. As much survey research has shown, lower-status voters tend to be liberal on economic issues and conservative on social issues, while higher-status voters tend to be just the reverse. Thus, the typical voter is probably ideologically inconsistent and therefore feels cross-pressured by the realignment trends in the party system. Many working-class voters seek economic protection from the Democratic party but do not trust its social and foreign policy liberalism. Middle-class suburbanites favor Ronald Reagan's fiscal conservatism but are disturbed by the Moral Majoritarian, antienvironmental, and interventionist signals on foreign policy that sometimes emanate from the Republican party. In many ways, the New Deal party system, with its ideologically inconsistent parties, may have fit the electorate better. The problem with the realigned party system, in short, is that it leaves many voters without a comfortable home.

The situation is far different from that in 1964, when Goldwater activists saw themselves as an outside force attempting to overthrow the party Establishment, or in 1968, when Eugene McCarthy's followers fought the Democratic party Establishment on the streets of Chicago. To a considerable extent, New Right Republicans and New Politics Democrats *are* the Establishments of the two parties. Liberal Republicans and conservative (mostly southern) Democrats have seen their influence decline sharply. Moderates in both parties continue to have significant influence, largely because of their credentials and their ability to offer practical policy alternatives, most notably in the area of foreign policy. Moderate influence in both parties is really based on professionalism. The problem is, in an age of anti-Establishment politics, professionalism is not always an undisputed advantage. Republican conservatives and Democratic liberals are able to argue, with some reason, that "moderate" solutions have been tried under presidents like Johnson, Nixon, Ford, and Carter, and they have, by and large, failed. Moderates in both parties operate under suspicion of illegitimacy and are constantly forced to justify themselves in ideological terms.

Anti-Establishment feeling has also increased at the level of mass public opinion since 1964. In their analysis of "the changing American voter," Nie, Verba, and Petrocik found evidence of two major trends in public opinion after 1964. The first was a sharp rise in ideological consistency in the American electorate beginning that year. This was followed by increasing political distrust, growing alienation from political parties, higher levels of political independence, and greater instability in voting behavior.[20] The mid-1960s also saw antibusiness and antilabor sentiment rising more or less in tandem with disaffection from government. Indeed, confidence in the leaders of every major institution in American society, including education, religion, the military, and the press, suffered serious deterioration after 1964.[21]

The interesting point found by Nie, Verba, and Petrocik is that the two trends were largely unrelated:

The rise in the proportion of Independents is found on the left, on the right, and in the center. The same is true for the proportion who express negative views about the parties. The proportion expressing such views goes up across the political spectrum. . . . In short, though the increase of political distrust and the weakening of party ties comes on the heels of the increase in the coherence of political attitudes, there is no clear evidence that distrust and the abandonment of parties takes place among those who have developed those coherent attitudes.[22]

The evidence suggests that the loss of public confidence in the Establishment—the leaders of government and other major institutions—was not fundamentally an ideological or partisan phenomenon. It affected the electorate across the board.

What caused it? Research by Seymour Lipset and William Schneider found little relationship between confidence in institutions and people's sense of personal well-being. Yet there were strong relationships between confidence in institutions and the condition of the economy. It appears that the troubled economy of the 1970s primarily affected people's conception of how things were going in the country and only secondarily their sense of personal satisfaction and optimism.

Moreover, the period of sharpest deterioration of public confidence was between 1964 and 1974, which was also a period of relative economic

20. Norman H. Nie, Sidney Verba, and John R. Petrocik, *The Changing American Voter* (Cambridge, Mass.: Harvard University Press, 1976), pp. 281–84.

21. For a review of these trends, see Seymour Martin Lipset and William Schneider, *The Confidence Gap: Business, Labor, and Government in the Public Mind* (New York: The Free Press, 1983), chaps. 1 and 2.

22. Nie, Verba, and Petrocik, *American Voter*, p. 286.

prosperity. Confidence in institutions seems to be mostly a response to events, a reaction to the way things are going in the country. The downturn in the economy after 1973 should be treated as one of a long sequence of events interpreted by the public as "bad news." The sheer quantity of "bad news" increased rapidly beginning in the mid-1960s. In the late 1960s, most of the "bad news" was noneconomic in nature—a disastrous foreign war, racial strife, and social conflict. That was also true in the early 1970s, when the Watergate scandal cut short the country's efforts to return to normal. Finally, beginning with the oil embargo of late 1973, "bad news" about the economy began to monopolize the country's attention—albeit with a regular smattering of social unrest, foreign policy failures, and political scandal.

The role of the press in bringing this "bad news" to the attention of the public has been much commented upon. It would be simplistic to argue that the mass media are uniquely responsible for destroying public confidence. That would be blaming the messenger for the message. Nevertheless, several observations can be made regarding the subtle ways in which the media have influenced the public mood.

The first is that negative news makes good press. Consequently, the media have a tendency to emphasize conflict, criticism, and controversy in their news presentations. Michael Robinson has argued a theory of "videomalaise," that television news in particular has an inherent bias toward reporting negative and critical information: "The highly credible television news organizations have been compelled to bombard the American television audience with interpretive, sensational, aggressive, and anti-institutional news items"—in other words, bad news.[23] It is undeniably true that the quantity of bad news has been great in recent years, and the media have a duty to report it. But the press, and perhaps television in particular, displays a proclivity for reporting bad news, especially scandals and controversies that make good video. In a political debate or in a conflict between two countries, producers rarely show the two sides agreeing with one another. There may be a kind of Gresham's law operating in the mass media—the bad news drives out the good.

Second, researchers have found strong connections between political cynicism and exposure to negative information in the media. Using an experimental research design, Robinson found that a controversial CBS News television documentary critical of the military—"The Selling of the Pentagon"—lowered viewers' sense of political confidence. He also used survey data to demonstrate that reliance on television as a primary source

23. Michael J. Robinson, "Public Affairs Television and the Growth of Political Malaise: The Case of 'The Selling of the Pentagon,'" *American Political Science Review* 70, no. 2 (June 1976): 426.

of news increased social distrust and political cynicism.[24] A subsequent study by Miller, Goldenberg, and Erbring investigated the relationship between political trust and the actual content of news stories. They found that the "representation of news in a manner that conveys a high degree of political conflict or criticism leads to a sense of distrust and inefficacy among newspaper readers."[25]

Third, research by Lichter, Lichter, and Rothman has shown the national media elite to be "one of the most liberal, anti-Establishment groups in American society."[26] Of course, they interviewed the top journalists at the major national networks and news organizations, as well as students at the most prestigious journalism school in the country (Columbia). While the ideology of this elite may not be characteristic of the journalistic profession as a whole, one suspects that an anti-Establishment orientation is widely shared by media professionals. It is, after all, the business of the press to keep an eye on those in positions of authority. There is some evidence, for instance, that the public perceives the press as being in an adversary relationship with government. Long-term trends in confidence in institutions reveal something of a seesaw relationship between trust in the president and trust in the press—when one goes up, the other tends to go down.[27]

Of course, confidence in the press has declined over the long run, along with confidence in government. That is because the press is identified as part of the Establishment. In 1981 *The Washington Post* asked a national sample of Americans whether they thought the news media were too critical of the government in Washington or not critical enough. While 25 percent thought the media were too critical, 40 percent said they were not critical enough. By 53 to 35 percent, those interviewed agreed that "the major news media often cover up stories that ought to be reported." Thus, it is not the case that the public particularly trusts the press. In 23 different ratings of institutions taken between 1966 and 1980, the press came out, on the average, in seventh place—behind medicine, religion, education, the military, business, and the Supreme Court. But Congress and the executive branch of the federal government came

24. Ibid., p. 425.

25. Arthur H. Miller, Edie N. Goldenberg, and Lutz Erbring, "Type-Set Politics: Impact of Newspapers on Public Confidence," *American Political Science Review* 73, no. 1 (March 1979): 77.

26. Linda Lichter, S. Robert Lichter, and Stanley Rothman, "The Once and Future Journalists," *Washington Journalism Review* 4, no. 10 (December 1982): 26; and S. Robert Lichter and Stanley Rothman, "Media and Business Elites," *Public Opinion* 4, no. 5 (October/November 1981): 42–46, 59–60.

27. Lipset and Schneider, *The Confidence Gap*, p. 55.

out lower than the press. The point is that the public trusts government even less than it trusts the press. When the *Post* asked people who they thought was usually more truthful, "high government officials in Washington" or the major news media, the answer was decisively in favor of the media, 57 to 17 percent.

The experiences of the Vietnam War and Watergate in the late 1960s and early 1970s were not so much ideological as anti-Establishment victories for the press. The press challenges those in positions of power, including liberals like George McGovern and Edward M. Kennedy when their turn comes. The public approves of this relationship. It accepts the press as an anti-Establishment institution and criticizes it for not being even more so. It may not be too much to argue that, today, the major "check and balance" against presidential power is not Congress or state governments or the opposition party. It is the countervailing power of the national media.

PUBLIC OPINION AND FOREIGN POLICY

Foreign policy is, of course, a surpassingly Establishment enterprise. Almost twenty years of anti-Establishment politics have certainly had consequences for foreign-policymaking. It is important to point out, however, that these consequences are more procedural than substantive. At the level of the mass public, there is no evidence to indicate that the basis for a bipartisan, two-track foreign policy consensus has eroded. While activist opinion has become much more bimodal, the foreign policy attitudes of the mass public remain unimodal. The public continues to hold the core values of peace and strength as strongly as ever, if not more so. Thus the anomalous results of the Chicago Council's 1982 survey, which showed strong hostility to the Soviet Union accompanied by diminishing support for President Reagan's massive defense buildup and increasing support for arms control. What has eroded at both the mass and elite levels is confidence in the president and in the nation's foreign policy leaders and the sense that our foreign policy expresses a set of widely shared values. It is the *process* of building and maintaining a foreign policy consensus that has changed.

The question is sometimes asked whether, and how, public opinion constrains foreign policy. Does public opinion compel foreign-policy-makers to take certain actions or not take others? Putting the question this way reverses the actual direction of causality. Public opinion is reactive, not prescriptive; the operative relationship is one of support, not constraint. Policymakers do not look to the public for specific policy direction. But they must mobilize public support for the policies they want to pursue, or at least preempt opposition to them. Ernest May argues in this volume that the necessity of building political support explains the "great shift of the postwar decade or two" to cold war interventionism: "All else was secondary." The reason is that a policy without political support can be frustrated so easily in our system—through the interference of Congress; as a result of interest-group pressure on the executive and legislative branches; and by means of the threat of voter rejection at the polls, a prospect that is never more than a few years away.

Throughout the first two postwar decades, the problem was one of mobilizing support for an internationalist policy from an essentially noninternationalist public. May writes of a divergence between leadership opinion and perceived public and congressional opinion. During the immediate postwar years, leaders were more hawkish in private than in public, being fearful that the public was not yet prepared for a major new internationalist commitment. In the 1950s and early 1960s this relationship reversed, as officials whose private views were often moderate and flexible found it necessary to "oversimplify the antagonism with the Soviet Union and to exaggerate the nature and immediacy of the peril it entailed." The point was to keep the public, and therefore Congress, from questioning or challenging the internationalist thrust of cold war policy— foreign economic and military aid, U.S. bases and troops in the rest of the world, treaties and alliances, all of which are inherently suspect to a noninternationalist public. Support for such policies is not natural; it must be mobilized and maintained against the constant threat of unraveling. Certainly the hardest kind of support to sustain is for a prolonged intervention by U.S. troops, which may be considered the outer limit of public tolerance for internationalism.

The difference between the mass public and the attentive public is still one of internationalism. What has helped to bridge the gap is the steadily rising educational level of the mass public; the one clear relationship that can be documented in any foreign policy survey is that between education and internationalism. But other forces have worked to offset the effect of education, that is, to increase mass–elite differences over foreign policy. One is the effect of events. Two experiences in particular—the Vietnam War and the economic downturn of the 1970s—have had the effect of souring the public's taste for international involvement and turning the focus of the public's concerns inward. The result, as the three Chicago Council surveys reveal, is declining internationalism despite rising educational levels. Second, the effect of the mass media, and television in particular, has been to expand the inadvertent audience for news about foreign policy and to activate the previously inert noninternationalist public. The viewing public is more aware of America's foreign policy commitments— and failures—than the reading public ever was. Finally, the cushion of public trust has been replaced by a high level of public cynicism and suspicion toward all elites. The public is much less willing to give presidents the benefit of the doubt. Thus, despite Ronald Reagan's striking successes with Congress in 1981, his popularity with the public faded more quickly than was the case with any other newly elected president since scientific polling began in the 1930s.[28] The public is more willing to listen to, and ally with, critics of the administration's foreign policy.

And critics are precisely what the polarization of political activists has produced—in greater numbers, with higher intensity, and with more influence in the major political parties than was the case before 1964. The traditional divergence between elite and mass over internationalism is now accompanied by a new divergence within the elite between liberal and conservative internationalists. Virtually any foreign policy espoused by an administration is likely to be suspect to those who feel that they do not share the same basic foreign policy values. Stanley Hoffmann makes the point in this volume that the détente policy of Richard Nixon and Henry Kissinger met exactly this fate. Hardliners used every advance made by the Soviet Union and every U.S. setback in the world as arguments to discredit détente. Liberals were suspicious of détente because they were suspicious of Nixon and Kissinger's bipolar and power-oriented view of world politics; they saw détente as a cartel arrangement between the two great superpowers that ignored or endangered the interests of the Third World.

The impact of ideology is more visible so far in the process than in the substance of foreign-policymaking. For one thing, there has been a change in the role of elections. Presidential elections, like that of 1960, used to confirm the national consensus on foreign policy. The parties and candidates would agree on what needed to be done and then contend bitterly over who could do it better. To some extent, that is still true, as both parties in 1980 condemned the decline in U.S. military security (although they blamed the policies of different administrations), and both promised a significant defense buildup. Since 1960, however, every incumbent president has been challenged for renomination within his own party. These challenges exposed deep ideological cleavages, particularly on foreign policy, in 1968 and 1976, when they were very nearly successful. The centrifugal forces that pull the two parties apart in the primaries are now a major feature of presidential elections and create strong coun-

28. In the November 1982 Gallup poll, Ronald Reagan's approval rating was 43 percent. Compare this with the following ratings for previous elected presidents two years after they took office: 68 percent for Dwight D. Eisenhower at the end of 1954: 76 percent for John F. Kennedy at the end of 1962: 52 percent for Richard Nixon at the end of 1970: and 51 percent for Jimmy Carter at the end of 1978. See *The Gallup Opinion Index,* Report no. 182 (October–November 1980), pp. 3–39, for detailed historical data on presidential approval ratings.

tervailing influences against the inherent centrism of general election campaigns.

Interest groups must also operate in a more ideological context. Ethnic constituencies, business interests, and farmers used to participate in foreign-policymaking as nonideological "interests" pressuring for their private advantage or special concern. All now find themselves embroiled in politics of values and ideology. Business groups and farmers are challenged by conservatives, who argue that they are enriching themselves and selling out America's larger interests by supporting détente and pressuring for increased foreign trade. Supporters of Israel have either been thrown on the defensive by criticism from the Left or have taken the moral offensive themselves, by enlarging their views into a new foreign policy ethos whereby American and Israeli interests are joined in an aggressive new conservatism. One of the most successful foreign policy "interest groups" in recent years, the Committee on the Present Danger, had no apparent self-interest except to expose U.S. military vulnerability and advocate a stronger anti-Soviet line. Cause groups like the antiwar movement and the Nuclear Weapons Freeze Campaign, like many other single-issue groups, advanced their goals almost entirely in the public domain, through protest, media campaigns, and electoral politics. In the new style of pressure-group politics, values are more at stake than interests.

Similarly, the resurgence of Congress as a force in foreign-policymaking had its origins as much in ideology as in institutional rivalries, as the Democrats after 1974, emboldened by Watergate, sought to check "the imperial presidency" and limit the president's power to commit U.S. forces overseas. Ideological politics has, as noted, placed moderates in both parties under suspicion and tended to demoralize the traditional foreign policy Establishment, who find themselves besieged from both sides (and most of whom, like Zbigniew Brzezinski and Alexander Haig, do not have the brilliance or the flair for public relations that enabled Henry Kissinger to fight back). In short, we are in a situation where there is more politics in foreign policy than has been the case for the last thirty years. Foreign-policymakers must demonstrate not only that their policies work but that they are morally and ideologically consistent and express the values of major constituencies in American political life.

One approach that presidents have used with considerable success might be described as confounding the opposition—that is, doing exactly the opposite of what is expected on ideological grounds. (Nixon did this in the case of détente.) The president appeals not so much to the opposition as to the mass public in terms of its core value of either peace or strength. Nixon and Kissinger, who were "tough" on military policy and realistic about world affairs, could call for rapprochement with the Communists with less risk of being attacked for softness or idealism. Senator William S. Cohen recently depicted this paradox as follows:

The shift in public opinion . . . suggests that conservative Republican Presidents (moderates or liberals need not apply) may be able to open doors to China and secure support for arms control treaties yet be unable to sustain a significant or even stable growth in military spending. By contrast, liberal or moderate Democratic Presidents may be able to secure support for strategic and conventional modernization (few questioned the need for the MX, Stealth aircraft, Trident submarine, or a Rapid Deployment Force under Jimmy Carter) but will be less able to obtain ratification of arms control treaties.[29]

The problem is, it took the Soviet invasion of Afghanistan to convince Carter to adopt a tough line toward the Soviet Union. And so far at least, Reagan has taken no bold steps toward arms control despite the pressure of the nuclear freeze movement and the opportunity provided by the change of leadership following Leonid Brezhnev's death.

At the very minimum, the confounding strategy requires a president to be reasonably pragmatic, if not opportunistic. Presidents usually meet this requirement—even ideological ones like Ronald Reagan—or else they could hardly get as far as they do in politics. But the confounding strategy also requires that a president be fairly secure in his political base, unthreatened by the opposition, and confident of his ability to sustain the confidence of the mass public. Watergate contributed to the undoing of détente since it undercut all three of these political requirements. It can be argued, however, that the long-term changes in American politics described in this chapter have weakened the political preconditions that enable any president to exercise independent foreign policy leadership.

In the end, however, the public judges a foreign policy as it judges any other policy—by its results. In the American system, public opinion is never very constraining, even in an area quite close to home, like domestic economic policy. The public never approved of most of the detailed provisions of Ronald Reagan's economic program—particularly the deep cuts in domestic social spending—but public opinion remained remarkably supportive of the program for almost two years: it was bad medicine, but it just might have been necessary to get the country out of the economic crisis. The public turned against the program only when a major recession set in and it became clear that the president's program was not working—in fact, was making the condition of the country considerably worse.

Similarly, the public elected Richard Nixon in 1968 to end the war in Vietnam. Polls taken that year showed that the public was not sure

29. William S. Cohen, "Presidential Paradoxes," *The New York Times,* December 19, 1982, sec. E, p. 17.

whether Nixon was a dove or a hawk; but that did not matter: he was a Republican, and it was the Democrats who had gotten us into the war. In fact, Nixon turned out to be both a dove and a hawk, withdrawing American troops and intensifying the bombing at the same time. What mattered to the electorate was whether the policy worked—whether, by 1972, "peace was at hand." Ronald Reagan's foreign policy mandate in 1980 was to restore America's military security. The president chose to do so by means of a massive military buildup. Given the damage to the economy and the risks to foreign policy that such a strategy entails, it is not clear that the American public feels substantially more secure as a result of it. In any event, presidents and legislators will need to find ways to build upon a noninternational public opinion that seems committed to the dual (and not always easily reconcilable) objectives of peace and strength.

3

Congress

I. M. DESTLER

Senator Henry Bellmon was concerned. The Foreign Relations Committee was considering the SALT II treaty, but the Congress as a whole was confused and deeply divided about the broad range of issues to which the treaty was clearly related. So in September 1979 he introduced a resolution to create a new Senate select committee, which would conduct "a thorough examination and evaluation of U.S. foreign policy and defense and security needs . . . *particularly with respect to the Soviet Union.*"[1]

Bellmon was a respected conservative from Oklahoma, a Senate "elder statesman" planning to retire in 1981. How did his proposal fare? Foreign Relations Committee Chairman Frank Church agreed that a broad review was needed but feared encroachment on his panel's prerogatives (even though the inability of Foreign Relations or any other committee to speak for the Senate on these matters had been one of Bellmon's avowed reasons for proposing a select committee combining their perspectives). So Foreign Relations decided it should conduct such a study itself, with senior members of armed services, appropriations, and budget committees invited to participate. After some closed hearings focusing especially on the Persian Gulf, the Committee invited Secretary of State Cyrus Vance to present "a comprehensive statement of U.S. foreign policy on a global scale."

Vance did so on March 27, 1980, with Senator Jacob Javits, in his opening remarks, heralding the onset of a "revolution in American foreign policy and in American military policy." "Thanks to Senator Bellmon of Oklahoma," Javits continued, "we are going to decide first on the foreign policy of our country, hopefully, and then we are going to decide what military means are needed to realize this foreign policy."[2] The secretary then proceeded with his broad statement.

I am grateful to Timothy Reif and Jonathan Sack for the research assistance they provided as Carnegie interns.

1. *Congressional Record,* September 17, 1979, p. S12793 (emphasis added).
2. "U.S. Foreign Policy Objectives," hearing before the Senate Committee on Foreign Relations, 96th Cong., 2d sess., March 27, 1980 (Washington, D.C.: U.S. Government Printing Office, 1980), p. 3.

37

But members' minds were largely elsewhere. A few did raise broad, if idiosyncratic, questions. But Senator S. I. Hayakawa wanted to know why thousands of Iranians were still being admitted to the United States, Senator Edward Zorinsky tried to get Vance to admit that we really had "at least two Secretaries of State," and future Chairman Charles Percy gave priority to getting Vance to deny a report that he planned to resign. Chairman Church trumped everybody by using the occasion to unveil a proposal that stole the headlines—that the committee issue a "White Paper" on U.S. historical involvement in Iran. And the review which Bellmon called for was never completed.

Bellmon's idea reflected a premise that many liberals as well as conservatives would endorse—that the Soviet connection in all its manifestations is the most important and difficult issue American foreign policy has to address, and that the United States needs, above all, to establish a comprehensive approach and pursue it steadfastly. So the fate of his proposal is instructive. Put forward at a time of widespread public recognition of the need for such an approach, and of widespread belief that the Carter administration was not providing it, Bellmon's experience illustrated how difficult it was for the Congress itself to meet this need.

In fact, a case can be made that the primary congressional impact on U.S.–Soviet relations since 1972 has been the opposite: to disrupt such purposive policies as the executive branch was pursuing. For instance:

1. In 1974, the Jackson-Vanik and Stevenson Amendments led to Soviet renunciation of Henry Kissinger's bilateral trade agreement because they linked U.S. adherence to a new, congressionally imposed issue—Jewish emigration.

2. The Clark Amendment, enacted in early 1976, blocked the Ford administration's efforts to counter, "covertly," Soviet-supported forces in Angola.

3. Congressional pressure weakened, and contributed to lifting of, suspensions of grain sales to Russia in 1975 and 1980–81.

4. The Senate failed in 1979–80 to ratify the SALT II treaty, and the most serious and sophisticated agreement we have ever reached with the Soviet Union became the casualty of conservative concerns over defense policy, "linkage," and positioning for the 1980 elections.

5. Then, by 1982, Congress was pressing the Reagan administration from the liberal direction, urging modification of its hard-line approach and that greater priority be given to arms control.

How much is this the product of things peculiar to the Congress? How much does it reflect the broader American politics of Soviet relations? And what, if anything, might be done about it?

HOW CONGRESS ADDRESSES U.S.–SOVIET RELATIONS

In our system of government, the congressional role in making Soviet policy is every bit as legitimate as that of the president and the executive branch. Both find their legal base in the United States Constitution, that "invitation to struggle for the privilege of directing American foreign policy."[3] Still, if we look at how Congress actually deals with U.S.–Soviet relations, almost everything that might encourage policy stability and comprehensiveness seems absent. There is no regular "Soviet bill," no ongoing statutory program. Hence there is no committee or subcommittee that gives primary attention to the Soviet connection. Individual members may try to shine a spotlight on U.S.–Soviet relations in general, but Congress as a whole addresses them mainly in two ways: (1) most frequently, in the context of ongoing, programmatic international activities like defense, intelligence, foreign assistance, arms sales, information; and (2) occasionally, when a specific negotiated agreement is up for approval.

These two types of congressional involvement coincide nicely with the two sides of the relationship. Ongoing programs serve mainly its predominant side—*competition*. Agreements seek to broaden the limited dimension of *cooperation*.

Ongoing Programs

In deciding the shape and magnitude of programs for defense, intelligence, aid, and so on, Congress is, among other things, determining what resources will be available to the U.S. government in its competition with the Soviet Union. At the same time, that competition is employed as a rationale for programs which have other goals also, and has been ever since Joseph Stalin's denunciation made it easier for the 80th Congress to approve the Marshall Plan. Debate on particular programs, and items therein, often focuses on the nature of the Soviet threat and the appropriate American response. But the bills are processed separately, through several different committees in each chamber. Budget and appropriations processes notwithstanding, no one on Capitol Hill has the power to link these with one another in a systematic way.

Specific U.S.–Soviet Agreements

Negotiated arrangements for U.S.–Soviet cooperation engage Congress far less frequently, but more intensively. Beginning with the limited test-

3. Edwin S. Corwin, *The President: Office and Powers* (New York: New York University Press, 1940), p. 200.

ban treaty of 1963 and the consular convention completed in 1964, such agreements multiplied in the early seventies. Congress addressed two SALT I agreements in 1972 and a general trade agreement in 1973–74. And SALT II dominated the Senate in the second half of 1979, despite its failure to reach the floor. Major agreements do bring a certain broad attention to Soviet relations, as their review gives Congress heightened policy leverage. But since 1972 this leverage has been employed in idiosyncratic ways, as agreements become targets for campaigns to change U.S. (or Soviet) policies beyond their formal scope.

The Impact of Congressional Reforms

For much of the postwar period, the lack of a central congressional process for Soviet matters was offset by the existence of reasonably strong leaders who could, within limits, control congressional procedures and at least predict major policy outcomes. This held true particularly for foreign policy, where there was broad interbranch consensus on goals and major means, and where one legacy of World War II had been deference to the president on matters of action, if not rhetoric.

Things changed dramatically in the early seventies, when democratizing congressional reforms coincided with the Vietnam-triggered reaction to postwar U.S. policy. The reforms had their roots in electoral politics. Senators and congressmen were becoming better educated, more issue- and media-conscious, more self-selected in the sense of initiating and organizing their own campaigns. As policy entrepreneurs, they were expanding their substantive staffs. They were less willing than their predecessors to wait their turn for leadership. Liberals were particularly impatient, since they linked the seniority system with dominance of Congress by the "conservative coalition" of southern Democrats and Republicans.

In the Senate, power spread gradually beginning in the late fifties, the process marked by the aging of grandees like Richard Russell and the leadership succession from Lyndon Johnson to Mike Mansfield. In the House, committee chairmen clung to effective power longer despite the growing challenge from liberals loosely joined in the Democratic Study Group. But this meant only that the explosion was more dramatic and far-reaching when it came. Most dramatic was the removal of three committee chairmen by the Democratic Caucus after the 1974 elections. Most enduring was the institutionalization of subcommittees, each with its separate chairman, staff, and legislative jurisdiction. Important also were the opening up of committee markups and the democratization of floor procedures, making the legislative process more visible and accessible to junior members and outside interests.

Because internal reform came at the same time as unhappiness about

Vietnam and a determination to apply its "lessons," the new congressional decentralization had particular impact on foreign policy. From the Nixon administration onward, Congress has been more important, creative, fractious, and unpredictable in its policy impact. To explore this congressional impact more fully, we turn now to an examination of the three main periods of postwar U.S.–Soviet relations.

CHANGING CONGRESSIONAL POLITICS OVER TIME

The Cold War (1947–63)

The White House scene on February 27, 1947, immortalized by Dean Acheson in *Present at the Creation*, is worth recounting once again. The participants were leaders of the Truman administration and the Republican-led 80th Congress; the subject was the new plan for aid to Greece and Turkey, whose governments Great Britain was no longer able to support. Secretary of State George Marshall gave a cryptic explanation, stressing humanitarianism and British–American relations. As this pitch fell flat, Under Secretary Dean Acheson asked "in desperation" to speak. "In the past eighteen months," he said,

Soviet pressure on the Straits, on Iran, and on northern Greece had brought the Balkans to the point where a highly possible *Soviet* breakthrough might open three continents to *Soviet* penetration. Like apples in a barrel infected by one rotten one, the corruption of Greece would infect Iran and all to the east. It would also carry infection to Africa through Asia Minor and Egypt, and to Europe through Italy and France, already threatened by the strongest domestic *Communist* parties in Western Europe. . . . These were the stakes that British withdrawal from the eastern Mediterranean offered to an *eager and ruthless opponent.*

A long silence followed. Then Arthur Vandenberg said solemnly, "Mr. President, if you will say that to the Congress and the country, I will support you and I believe that most of its members will do the same."[4]

Throughout the years of the cold war, this dynamic was replayed. It was hard to sell Congress on costly, multipurpose international engagements. It was much easier to sell responses to the Soviet/Communist threat. Thus this threat—its substantial reality, its exaggerated appearance—became the political engine for American internationalism. Marshall would declare that his European recovery proposal was "not directed against any country or doctrine," fully aware that he was taking a domestic gamble—if the Russians said yes, Congress might say no. But perhaps to his relief, Stalin did not put the proposition to the test. In denouncing the Marshall Plan and pulling Eastern Europe out, he proved an unwitting lobbyist on Capitol Hill.

4. Dean Acheson, *Present at the Creation: My Years at the State Department* (New York: Norton, 1969), p. 219 (emphasis added).

With the "loss" of China, the war in Korea, and the rise of Senator Joseph R. McCarthy and his Communist-hunting allies, the public debate became, at times, stringently Manichean. Broad defense commitments won overwhelming endorsement—NATO, SEATO, and bilateral treaties with Japan, Korea, and Taiwan. U.S. military assistance reached billions annually—in the dollar of the fifties.

What is more remarkable, viewed with 1982 hindsight, is the degree to which liberal and humanitarian programs were also dressed in anticommunist clothing. The best-selling novel *The Ugly American*, whose argument for grass-roots American engagement in Asia helped to prepare the political ground for the Peace Corps, argued its case in particularly strident cold war terms. Even such diverse causes as aid to education and highway construction and stimulation of the U.S. economy were sold, in important part, as means of pursuing the world struggle more effectively.

For most of the cold war period, congressional action was dominated by the competitive instruments. On defense, the predominant pressure—after Korea—was to spend more, to press for weapons like the B-70 bomber, and to deploy a thousand Minutemen, a decision made after the "missile gap" had disappeared. On foreign aid, Congress regularly cut administration requests by an average of about 20 percent. It also tended to favor military programs and military allies. Nonetheless, it generally appropriated at least $3 billion annually.

In the day-to-day battles for program authorities and funds, it was in the interest of program advocates to maximize all aspects of the Soviet threat: military strength; scientific prowess; revolutionary goals; ideological appeal; control over the international communist movement; political influence and adroitness in the Third World. Thus, ironically, the congressional process most tended to exaggerate Soviet power in the very period when, objectively, we had the least to fear: the danger of upheaval in Western Europe had largely passed, and Russian military "parity" was far away.

Congress supported and reinforced administration efforts to constrain East–West trade: the Export Control Act of 1949 for American products; the Battle Act of 1951 to discourage allies from selling strategic goods. But Congress was most permissive regarding the most serious competitive instrument—the use of military force against Soviet allies. Truman's quick decision on Korea won overwhelming support, though the Senate did insist on passing a resolution supporting the dispatch of four divisions to Europe the following year. Eisenhower seized upon this device as a means of broadening his base and protecting his political flanks. The Formosa Resolution, authorizing use of U.S. forces to counter the Chinese Communist threat, was adopted in 1955, four days after the president transmitted it, with only three dissenting votes in each house.

Congressional doubts did play a role in Eisenhower's 1954 decision not to send major U.S. forces to Indochina, doubts that reinforced the president's already strong reservations.[5] And Eisenhower encountered greater difficulty in 1957 with his request for open-ended authority to send American forces to combat "international communism" in the Middle East. Still, Eisenhower's dispatch of marines to Lebanon in 1958 was little contested. And four years later, Kennedy could cite the recently passed Cuba resolution, pledging the use of force to resist communism in the Western Hemisphere, as an endorsement of his constitutional authority to impose the Cuba blockade.

Thus, as James Sundquist has noted, "a wealth of precedent had been established, through a dozen years of successive crises, that in the worldwide confrontation with communism it was for the president to set the policy, the Congress to support."[6] And as John F. Kennedy discovered when critics found his performance unequal to his hawkish campaign rhetoric, the pressure that did come from Congress came mainly from the hard-line side. Only Kennedy's success in the Cuban missile confrontation gave him partial relief from this pressure and the political opening to move cautiously toward limited cooperation in 1963.

But there was, in the later cold war period, some congressional pressure in the cooperative direction. Eisenhower's repeated initiatives toward U.S.–Soviet cooperation did much to legitimize it as a goal; his failure to achieve much in concrete terms left an opening for critics. Senator Hubert Humphrey was an early arms control exponent, and he was joined by figures like Joseph Clark in the Senate and Chester Bowles in the House. Such voices were fewer in number and weaker in impact than the Henry Jacksons who declared that the United States was "losing the cold war." Nonetheless, in 1961, with Kennedy administration encouragement, Congress passed the Arms Control and Disarmament Act which created the Arms Control and Disarmament Agency (ACDA), established arms control as a statutory foreign policy goal, and safeguarded congressional prerogatives by requiring that "no action shall be taken . . . that will obligate the United States to disarm or . . . limit . . . armaments . . . except pursuant to the treaty-making power of the President under the Constitution or unless authorized by further affirmative legislation by the Congress."[7]

In 1963, conservative and military resistance limited Kennedy's flexibility on the key issue of on-site inspections and thus made a comprehen-

5. Richard Immerman, "The Anatomy of the Decision Not to Fight," paper delivered at APSA Convention, Denver, Colo., September 1982.

6. James L. Sundquist, *The Decline and Resurgence of Congress* (Washington, D.C.: The Brookings Institution, 1981), p. 118.

7. Arms Control and Disarmament Act of 1961, section 33.

sive test-ban treaty unreachable. But he did conclude a limited U.S.–United Kingdom–USSR treaty banning atmospheric nuclear tests. The actual negotiation had been preceded by some astute administration efforts to create a balanced if not favorable record in Armed Services Committee hearings on the subject, and to persuade skeptical conservative Democrat Thomas Dodd to join Humphrey and thirty-two other senators in introducing a "sense of the Senate" resolution supporting a limited test ban. Still, it took the better part of two months before the treaty was ratified on September 24 by a vote of 80 to 19, with pragmatic conservatives like minority leader Everett Dirksen casting key votes in favor. This demonstrated that there was a political market for arms restraint, but also that conservatives who took cues from the military establishment held an effective veto over specific treaty terms. Indeed, Kennedy and McNamara gave strong assurances that underground nuclear testing would be vigorously pursued.

Kennedy's American University speech, which preceded the treaty, had called for reexamining Americans' attitudes toward the cold war. And in other administration programs like the Alliance for Progress he had sought, at least intermittently, to downplay cold war rationales. His administration had mistakenly dramatized Khrushchev's speech about "wars of national liberation," and had made "counterinsurgency" a Washington obsession. But it had also emphasized more benign policy instruments—development assistance, the Peace Corps. Still, the political pattern remained that of the late forties and the fifties. Liberal internationalists were significant but junior partners in alliance with security-minded conservatives. Together they formed a coalition to provide needed political support for broad-scope American engagement in the world.[8]

Johnson-Nixon-Ford: Détente's Slow Rise and Fast Fall (1964–76)

Over the decade after Kennedy's assassination, congressional sentiment moved toward tolerance, sometimes even encouragement, of U.S.–Soviet cooperation. By the late sixties, however, Vietnam was beginning to undercut support for competitive U.S. policy instruments, extending even to the defense budget.

In the Johnson administration the picture was decidedly mixed. Congress initially endorsed, then increasingly challenged, the Vietnam policy, with the attack coming from right as well as left. With the escalation in Vietnam and the shift from the adventurous Khrushchev to the methodi-

---

8. Thomas L. Hughes labels this a "workable dissensus." See "The Crackup," *Foreign Policy*, no. 40 (Fall 1980), p. 52.

cal Brezhnev, direct U.S.–Soviet issues declined in congressional visibility, with the temporary exception of the 1968 intervention in Czechoslovakia. A treaty limiting military uses of outer space was ratified unanimously in 1967, and U.S.–Soviet cooperation on nonproliferation received broad support. But congressional resistance doomed the 1966 Johnson administration proposal to authorize the president to grant limited most-favored-nation (MFN) status to Eastern bloc countries.

Congress was flashing an amber light on other issues as well. Kennedy had initiated U.S. sales of wheat to Russia that were modest by contemporary standards, and encountered sharp union resistance. The resistance continued under Johnson, and a requirement that half the grain sold be shipped in American bottoms priced American grain out of the Soviet market. This left the American farmer and the U.S. merchant marine with "50 percent of nothing," as farm-belt legislators increasingly noted. But grain interests were not yet fully mobilized on this issue.

There was also persistent conservative pressure on defense. Urged by senators like Richard Russell, Henry Jackson, and Strom Thurmond, Johnson ordered Secretary of Defense Robert McNamara to announce deployment of an ABM system. On the other side, Democrats who agonized over Vietnam offered a receptive market for arms control initiatives; by raising the issue at Glassboro in 1967 and moving to open talks in 1968, Johnson could placate this group as well as reach for historic accomplishment. Nonetheless, Hill initiative on this issue was limited.

The political cross-currents of this period were well illustrated by the fate of the U.S.–Soviet consular convention signed in June 1964. Its substance was innocuous: it simply established a legal framework for the operation of such new consulates in either country as the president might (under existing authority) agree to allow. But as the first *bilateral* U.S.–Soviet treaty it had broad symbolic significance. Reported favorably by Senate Foreign Relations in early 1965, the consular convention was delayed for two years, as conservative groups—notably the Liberty Lobby—mobilized against it. Senator Karl Mundt insisted that it would make Soviet espionage easier. (The name of J. Edgar Hoover was invoked in support of the latter worry, and was neutralized by a carefully worded exchange of letters with Dean Rusk in which the FBI chief refrained from endorsing the treaty but said it would not keep him from countering Soviet spies.) Senator Dodd worried that it would feed the "dangerous delusion that the cold war is ending." Finally, when President Johnson gave it priority and influential Republicans like Everett Dirksen and Thruston Morton came to its support, the convention was ratified with three votes to spare.

Conditions changed sharply in 1969. Liberal Democrats, now overwhelmingly critical about Vietnam and liberated from pressure to support their party's president, were also drawing broader foreign policy conclusions: that we weren't fighting China in Southeast Asia; that Russia was a bitter rival of China, which was a historical rival of Vietnam; that the notion of a worldwide, integrated, Moscow-directed communist "threat" didn't hold up. Simultaneously, advocates of arms control—very much the "in" subject in the foreign policy community—were encouraged by the progress under Johnson but alarmed by the emergence of a new and threatening generation of offensive and defensive weapons, and worried about whether Richard Nixon and Henry Kissinger would give arms control sufficient priority.

Thus Congress suddenly became a source of liberal initiative. Nixon's ABM—a scaling-down of the program Johnson had adopted under congressional pressure—survived an unprecedented congressional challenge in 1969, with one anti-ABM amendment to the defense procurement bill failing on a tie (50-50) vote. Senator Edward Brooke got forty senators to cosponsor a resolution calling for a joint U.S.–Soviet moratorium on MIRV testing. There were also moves to ease cold war barriers to trade. Senators Edmund Muskie and Walter Mondale were able to amend the Export Control Act so as to reduce the range of commodities it restricted. Their arguments combined pragmatism with cautious optimism. Restricting trade wasn't hurting communist economies but U.S. firms, which lost the business to West European competitors. On the positive side, there was, in Mondale's words, the hope that "Western trade can have a profound effect on the nature of life in Russia and in Eastern Europe," fueling demand for consumer goods, strengthening technocrats who would seek a freer internal economy, and so on.[9]

Among the liberals it was a time of ferment, of shifting positions. A number, for example, were becoming hostile to foreign assistance, because so much money was being allocated to Vietnam, and because a few followed Senator J. William Fulbright in seeing the aid program as a prime cause of U.S. entanglement there. And the "guns vs. butter" issue was emerging, as Vietnam costs limited funding of Great Society social legislation. Until 1965, liberals had favored increased spending for cold war *and* domestic purposes. Now they were seeing a trade-off and favoring the domestic side.

In combination, these developments gave the Nixon administration unusual political running room in 1971 when it shifted suddenly from resisting "détente" initiatives to leading the parade. The Left seemed to be already on board. The Right was on the defensive—defending presi-

9. "Export Expansion and Regulation," hearings before the Subcommittee on International Finance of the Committee on Banking and Currency, United States Senate, 91st Cong., 1st sess., April 23, 24, 28, 29, and 30, and May 1 and 28, 1969. (Washington, D.C.: U.S. Government Printing Office, 1969).

dential flexibility in Southeast Asia, seeking to limit and control cuts in defense spending.

So great was the Nixon-Kissinger political advantage that they could submit a SALT I offensive arms arrangement which allowed the Soviet Union significantly more missile launchers than the United States—one over which both the ACDA director and the Joint Chiefs of Staff had had important eleventh-hour reservations—and yet win Senate approval by 88 to 2. This margin did not come free; it required acceptance of Senator Jackson's amendment calling on the president to "seek a future treaty" that "would not limit the United States to levels of intercontinental strategic forces inferior to the limits provided for the Soviet Union." But this reflected Jackson's current weakness: he was targeting future negotiations because SALT I was beyond his power to reshape. And it, like the "purge" of senior Arms Control and Disarmament Agency personnel which he triggered, was accomplished in collaboration with conservatives within the administration.[10]

Yet the political foundation for détente proved remarkably fragile. Within one year, Jackson would mobilize overwhelming support for his amendment to make the grant of MFN trade status, which the Nixon administration had promised Moscow, conditional upon removal of Soviet barriers to Jewish emigration.[11] Within two years, Congress was taking a range of steps restraining use of political-military instruments to compete with Russia—arms sales, covert operations, deployment of troops in combat. And in the last year of the Ford administration, conservatives blocked Kissinger's effort to complete the SALT II treaty that he and Ford wanted.

Why did what seemed so promising fade so quickly? Certainly Watergate was one cause: Nixon's political authority had collapsed at least a year before he was forced from office in August 1974. Another was the fact that the huge Soviet wheat sales of 1972 were followed by virulent food-price inflation in 1973, giving popularity to labels like "the great grain robbery" and casting Russians as enemies of American prosperity. In fact, of course, what Soviet officials did in 1972 was play by the capitalist rules of the grain trade, with official U.S. encouragement! Still, the inflation brought strong political pressure on the Ford administration to limit such sales in 1974 and 1975, and then bitter counterpressure from farmers when it did so.[12]

10. See Duncan L. Clarke, *Politics of Arms Control* (New York: Free Press, 1979), especially pp. 50–54.

11. See Paula Stern, *Water's Edge* (Westport, Conn.: Greenwood Press, 1979).

12. See I.M. Destler, *Making Foreign Economic Policy* (Washington, D.C.: The Brookings Institution, 1980), chaps. 3 and 7.

But there were also several interrelated, broader causes of the rapid disintegration of détente's congressional base.

One cause, certainly, was the peculiarly isolated way in which Nixon and Kissinger had achieved their Soviet breakthroughs. This featured a lot of *articulation* of what they were seeking to achieve with the Soviet Union, but little *engagement* of domestic allies who, had they shared credit for achievements in 1971 and 1972, would have developed both obligations and stakes in defending them thereafter. Instead, Nixon and Kissinger went it alone. Liberals were resisted in 1969 and 1970 and preempted thereafter. Conservatives were supposed to go along because of Nixon's proven toughness. This gave the two geostrategists sole credit but also sole burden, as opportunities for domestic alliance-building were missed. If, for example, moderates like Ways and Means Chairman Wilbur Mills or the respected Republican Barber Conable had been brought into the trade negotiations with Moscow, they might have done more to counter the Jackson amendment.

A broader phenomenon was the fact that no important congressional group placed high priority on good U.S.–Soviet relations. As Kissinger later noted, "Liberals took the relaxation of tensions for granted while conservatives assailed it."[13]

Jackson, a key Nixon ally in the Vietnam and defense struggles of the first term, began his attack in the waning months of 1972, disrupting the nascent negotiating relationship. But liberals did not spring to its defense either, for they stressed, not the short-term government-to-government dialogue that Kissinger thought crucial, but the longer-term trends which seemed clearly favorable. In their eyes, the Soviet Union was proving to be an ordinary great power, with strong stakes in the status quo. "Communism" was a many-splintered thing, and its spread was not always to Russian advantage. And liberals saw the nuclear balance as stable, perhaps even weighted in America's favor. These views meant not an *attachment* to U.S.–Soviet relations but a *detachment* from them, a sense that we could abandon our cold war obsession with Moscow. So liberals were not at all inclined to resist when Jackson pressed his amendment. Both its morality and its politics appealed to them. They too supported human rights. They too had Jewish (and labor) constituents. U.S. diplomatic credibility or economic ties with Moscow were not of comparable importance. So when Charles Vanik, Jackson's House collaborator, proposed on the floor to add credit to MFN sanctions, Northern Democrats voted 130 to 16 in favor. And Senator Adlai Stevenson III was the sponsor of a credit-limiting amendment to the Export-Import Bank legislation which reinforced Jackson's efforts.

13. Henry Kissinger, *Years of Upheaval* (Boston: Little, Brown, 1982), p. 984.

Liberals combined a relaxed feeling about bilateral dealings with a lack of anxiety about Soviet involvements in the Third World. To them the "lessons" of China and Vietnam were that postwar U.S. foreign-policymakers had grossly exaggerated the "threat" of expanded Soviet power through "wars of national liberation." So they focused on exposing cold war and Nixon-Kissinger excesses, from assassination plots against Patrice Lumumba or Fidel Castro to efforts to destabilize the Allende regime in Chile. Conservatives, of course, saw these things differently: geostrategists felt we must engage in a complex game of countering Soviet influence; ideologues, who saw the enemy as "Communism," were driven to counter radicals everywhere. So any arena where the Soviet Union was engaged—like Angola—also became an arena in America's domestic struggle. In the short run, liberals won on Angola, with Congress prohibiting covert U.S. operations there. Later, it was to be conservatives who exploited Angola most effectively as an example of Soviet aggressive expansionism which belied any commitment to world peace and stability. Since Americans were sharply divided about what mattered in the Third World, we could only fight among ourselves about what standard should be applied in judging Soviet conduct. And since no one was *defending* Soviet behavior—a ridiculous burden for a politician to assume—the debate tended to strengthen the view that the Russians were not fit partners to do business with.

All of these issues were being fought out in a Congress where reforms were reaching their peak. Leaders were losing leverage by the day. The Jackson-Vanik amendment hit the House in 1973, a year of waning power for Wilbur Mills, who had long dominated tax and trade policy. Congressional foreign policy action was constrained more generally in 1973 and early 1974 by a desire to support America's prime remaining foreign policy asset, Henry Kissinger, at a time of constitutional crisis. For a time, a close Kissinger-Fulbright relationship blossomed in support of this goal. But with the Ford succession and the sweeping Democratic gains in the fall election, the dam broke. In the month of December 1974 alone, as Congress gave final approval to a modified Jackson amendment still strong enough to bring Soviet rejection of the trade agreement, action was also being completed on a foreign aid authorization bill that embargoed arms sales to Turkey, established a legislative veto on large arms sales in general, required that CIA covert operations be discussed with six relevant congressional committees, and allocated 70 percent of U.S. food aid to countries of greatest need (thereby limiting its "political" uses).

The result of all this, as everywhere noted, was that by 1976 Congress had taken away from Ford and Kissinger both the carrots and the sticks with which they hoped to enforce the détente policy. The political rout became complete when Reagan challenged Ford for the Republican presidential nomination, arguing that détente had been "a one-way street," with the United States winning nothing more important than "the right to sell Pepsi-Cola in Siberia," and attacking the Vladivostok agreement which sought to establish the basis for a SALT II treaty. Reagan found Republican primary crowds particularly responsive to his hard-line foreign policy views, and Ford backpedaled progressively. He put SALT II on hold rather than confront Jackson (and Reagan), even though its formula of equal ceilings could be defended as responsive to Jackson's 1972 amendment. He even swallowed a "Morality in Foreign Policy" plank in the Republican party platform, which was, as Ford later characterized it, "nothing less than a slick denunciation of Administration foreign policy."[14]

Thus, when Jimmy Carter came to the White House in January 1977, he faced a Congress divided rather sharply about key U.S.–Soviet issues. On arms control, Senators like Hubert Humphrey, Alan Cranston, Jacob Javits, and John Culver championed the liberal-to-moderate view, contesting with conservative Democrats like Jackson and increasingly aggressive Republicans like ranking Armed Services Committee member John Tower. These divisions mirrored the post-Vietnam polarization of "internationalist" opinion described in the preceding chapter by William Schneider in this volume.

The ultimate direction Congress would move in was unclear. It was clear, however, that there had never been much Hill "euphoria" about détente, and that the Kissinger approach was now discredited on both left and right. It was clear also that the Congress had reclaimed its foreign policy powers and would persist in seeking to exercise them. Yet support for foreign policy-related *programs* was at a low ebb.

Renewed Hostility: Years of Dissensus (1977–83)

In the 1976 campaign, Carter responded to polarization of public opinion by attacking Ford from both left and right. Once in office, he disappointed conservatives by appointing liberals or moderates to most key foreign and defense posts, seeking to deliver (at least initially) on promises to reduce defense spending and overseas troops, and canceling weapons systems (notably the B-1 bomber) on cost-benefit grounds. Thereafter he was, in the main, on the defensive. Hill-based conservatives pointed to Soviet arms buildup and adventurism—Angola, Ethiopia, Yemen, and ultimately Afghanistan—and castigated Carter for weakness and vacillation in response.

There was difficulty from the start on arms control. The nomination

14. Gerald R. Ford, *A Time to Heal* (New York: Harper & Row, 1979), p. 398.

as arms-control negotiator of Paul Warnke, a strong, articulate defense critic, gave hawks an opportunity to show their strength. When forty senators voted no, this signaled the difficulty any SALT II treaty would face in winning two-thirds support. When Carter, responding in part to hard-line pressure, sent Vance to Moscow in March 1977 with the famous "deep cut" proposal which bore Jackson's influence, the Russians rebuffed it. When the administration then shifted back to a formula closer to what Ford had negotiated at Vladivostok, critics resumed their attack, with the added argument that Carter was now abandoning a principled position in his search for agreement.

For two years, Jackson led an assault on the evolving SALT II treaty. And Senate Republicans were mounting a more partisan challenge: in May 1978 they issued a unanimous declaration which denounced the administration's softness on national security, including the "frightening pattern of giving up key U.S. weapons systems for nothing in return." Pro-SALT senators countered by organizing informal meetings to weigh the issues, develop counters to hard-line attacks, and prepare for the coming SALT ratification debate.[15]

In June 1979, Carter and Brezhnev met in Vienna to put their initials to the SALT II treaty and its accompanying protocols. Experts generally found this treaty much more tightly written, and more favorable to the United States, than the SALT I offensive arms agreement that had sailed through the Senate seven years before. But it nonetheless faced withering assault. To some degree this focused on its specific terms, though the most obvious imbalance—the fact that the United States, unlike the Soviet Union, was forbidden "heavy missiles"—was mitigated by the fact that we had no prospect of deploying them. More important, however, was the irresistible opportunity which SALT II afforded for congressional "linkage." Senators across the political spectrum, but particularly in the center-right, used the two-thirds ratification requirement to press for policy changes on related issues. Senator Sam Nunn had little problem with the treaty itself, but he had long been concerned about weaknesses in U.S. conventional forces. So he explicitly linked his vote to the administration's overall defense budget plans and called for a 5 percent real annual increase in defense spending. The Senate, which had been cutting defense budgets for most of the decade, now reversed itself and voted 55 to 42 in September 1979 in support of Nunn's objective. On the liberal side, senators like Mark Hatfield and George McGovern denounced the Vienna pact for not restraining arms enough.

---

15. For more detail, see I. M. Destler, "Trade Consensus; SALT Stalemate: Congress and Foreign Policy in the Seventies," in Thomas Mann and Norman Ornstein, eds., *The New Congress* (Washington, D.C.: American Enterprise Institute, 1981), pp. 329–59.

All of these burdens and qualifications meant that SALT II would be ratified, if at all, in substantially encumbered form. When the Senate Foreign Relations Committee finally recommended it on November 9, by the narrow margin of 9 to 6, it attached twenty specific conditions: thirteen stating unilateral U.S. declarations; five understandings which the president would be required to communicate to the Soviet Union; two reservations requiring explicit Soviet assent. And while each of these was so worded that it might have won reluctant Russian acquiescence, it seemed certain that more stringent amendments or reservations would be imposed on the floor. The Armed Services Committee, with its Republicans unanimously in opposition, rallied 10 to 7 behind a counterreport, drafted by Jackson aide Richard Perle, calling the treaty totally unacceptable without "major changes."

But what finally buried SALT II was the perennial question of Soviet geopolitical behavior. The administration seemed to be making progress selling the treaty until the end of August, when Senator Frank Church, embattled in his Idaho reelection campaign, leaked an intelligence finding of a 2,600-man Soviet "brigade" in Cuba and demanded its withdrawal. This created a foolish, month-long furor, with Carter declaring it "unacceptable" before he was forced, in effect, to accept it. The November seizure of American hostages in Teheran further poisoned the atmosphere by intensifying Americans' sense of impotence. Finally, the Soviet move into Afghanistan dealt the coup de grace. By mutual agreement, Carter asked Senate Majority Leader Robert Byrd—who had become a strong SALT supporter—to remove the treaty from the Senate calendar until further notice.

Even without Afghanistan the treaty was probably doomed. The most optimistic scenario for its proponents was that Byrd would take it to the floor with far less than 67 votes lined up in advance, winning some votes by forcing senators to face the prospect of taking responsibility for explicit rejection, and winning others through reservations and amendments that would certainly require renegotiation with the Soviet Union. The Russians would have been unlikely to accept Senate changes as written, and unlikely to talk seriously until they saw the results of the 1980 election. Then, with a Reagan victory, its status would not have been greatly different from what it in fact was on January 20, 1981, and remains to this day—an arrangement which the administration has denounced as "fatally flawed" but is nonetheless living within.

The politics of grain sales was an exception to the hardening trend. And the reason was clear: the tight market which had stirred consumer complaints about earlier Soviet sales had disappeared. Throughout the Carter administration, grain prices remained well below their 1974–75 peaks; under Ronald Reagan, they would decline still further, as part of the worst farm-belt economic conditions since the Great Depression. General public hawkishness in the wake of Afghanistan meant that Congress still mounted only token resistance to the embargo of January 1980, and Carter himself got a temporary political boost from his willingness to take such a tough, politically risky stand. But candidate Reagan promised to lift it and President Reagan did so in April 1981. Agricultural interests then nailed down this victory through an amendment to the Export Administration Act: any "selective" embargo (i.e., on agricultural exports only) after Reagan's first term could be maintained only if Congress gave its explicit approval.

The 1980 elections brought surprise Republican control to the Senate for the first time since 1954, in the same landslide that swept Ronald Reagan into the White House. Yet while the 96th Congress had pushed Carter to the right, the 97th began to pull Reagan toward the center, and the 98th continued this trend. The new administration's ambitious defense-spending plans won overwhelming congressional endorsement in 1981 but were under broad bipartisan assault by 1983, as the federal budget deficit ballooned alarmingly. Hard-line Reagan rhetoric helped to fuel the grass-roots "nuclear freeze" movement, which surged onto the political scene in 1982 and won qualified House endorsement a year later. Perhaps most significant for future U.S.–Soviet relations, moderate Senate conservatives like Nunn and William Cohen were insisting that the president adjust his extraordinarily demanding arms control positions in order to make a new agreement at least plausible. And while the ultimate impact of their campaign was unclear as of mid-1983, they were able to win some verbal concessions as the price for their support of the controversial MX missile. Congress was also resisting administration efforts to restrict East–West trade. Hawks were strengthened in early September, however, when Soviet air defense forces shot down an off-course, unarmed Korean airliner, and Moscow offered neither a credible explanation, nor an apology, nor compensation for the 269 people aboard who lost their lives.

As in the cold war period, the Soviet threat was once again a major force in American politics. And as in that period, advocates of military approaches to combat that threat were preeminent. But advocates of development and humanitarian programs were now much less likely to be riding the anticommunist bandwagon than in that earlier, more harmonious time. Nor did they stand to gain much support if they did. Whereas the fifties and sixties had seen a coalition of conservative and liberal internationalists, subordinating their sharply different priorities to their common goal of American world engagement, the late seventies and early eighties saw the two domestic sides deep in quasi-ideological combat with one another. Occasionally they might join in fragile union, as when House of Representatives security conservatives like Jack Kemp joined with development liberals like Matthew McHugh and Stephen Solarz in winning House enactment of aid appropriations in 1981. But the unity was short-lived.

THE POLITICAL VULNERABILITY OF U.S.–SOVIET RELATIONS

It is hard to avoid rather bleak conclusions. Congressional provision of resources for U.S.–Soviet *competition* (weapons and aid, for example) is limited and shaky, constrained by budgetary tightness and disagreement about which programs are appropriate. Currently, defense programs have by far the greatest support, but they are feeling the fiscal squeeze and the nuclear freeze. Agreements providing for limited *cooperation* have proved to be vulnerable political targets because legislators use them as vehicles to pry new policy concessions from the Soviet government or from our own.

In the cold war period, three things combined to make Congress a tolerable policy partner: deference to the president on the big things; centralization of power; and, if not consensus, a functioning internationalist coalition. By the 1970s all had disappeared. This meant not that Congress seized power consistently but, rather, an unpredictable, sporadic engagement in issues, a surging in and out.

Congress was not always a negative influence. Sometimes a demanding legislator, backed by his colleagues, could actually win important Soviet concessions. Henry Jackson accomplished this on Jewish emigration in 1973, though the gains were lost after he upped the ante in 1974. At other times, when a presidential transition was bringing abrupt changes in executive branch people and policies, Congress even offered an element of continuity. In 1981, Europeans could be reassured when the Senate Foreign Relations chairman stressed the need for continued arms control negotiations, and could even align themselves with forces in American politics seeking to push Reagan policies toward the center.

But congressional pressure for continuity is limited by the relatively weak influence of interest groups with stakes in steady policies. Farmers and the grain trade have become such a group, but they have sought to insulate their transactions from swings in the relationship rather than take on the more daunting task of moderating these swings. Business groups have usually been marginal players, though they did work to get Reagan to lift his sanctions against the Soviet natural-gas pipeline to Western Europe. The U.S. military has not consistently embraced arms control as a means to a more manageable defense environment. Polish-Americans and other ethnic groups of East European origin were strong supporters of hard-line policies in the cold war period, but less so after détente opened new opportunities for human contact. Jewish groups played a key role on the emigration issue, but they used Jackson less than he used them, and they were chastened when the outcome was a precipitous decline in the number of Jews leaving the Soviet Union.

So Congress continues to be a volatile force on Soviet issues, usually pressing presidents toward a tougher line. This reflects the balance in the broader policy community: it was the Committee on the Present Danger that became a formidable influence in the seventies, not the Committee on East–West Accord. And this is related in turn to the enormous difficulty that Americans, hawks and doves alike, seem to have with the idea of an adversary relationship within which limited cooperation is both possible and urgently needed. We believe, not without reason, in the moral superiority of our system to that of the Russians and in our defensive, peaceful, status quo motivation. It is hard for us to believe that our rival could reasonably, from its perspective, feel threatened by us or challenged by our global reach and moved to emulate it. But if we cannot conceive of this, then we are likely to see Soviet weaponry and world engagement as not just contrary to our interests (as indeed they generally are), but morally wrong *because* they conflict with our interests. It then becomes reasonable to demand that the Soviets follow U.S. rules of restraint to prove that they are choosing, to paraphrase a recent president, cooperation over confrontation.

Soviet repression at home compounds the problem. Americans cannot but identify with its victims, and in periods of détente it is hard to resist the idea of using improved relations as a lever to ease their plight. Indeed, most Americans feel a deep ambivalence about U.S. policies aimed at building shared, mutual interests with the Soviet regime if these policies seem to ignore—or, worse yet, facilitate—its despicable treatment of the Soviet people.

For all of these reasons, we have trouble accepting the legitimacy of the Soviet Union both as an enduring domestic order and as a world power which quite naturally competes with us and will seek—if, as we hope, it does not obtain—parity of political influence.

So U.S.–Soviet agreements are vulnerable to two very sweeping and unproductive sorts of linkage. The first is to *Soviet* behavior. The Russians "shouldn't" be limiting emigration or involving themselves in a particular country if they want peace; it is costly for us to counter them directly (Angola) or to manipulate concrete incentives (grain availability); hence the political attraction of demanding that they withdraw (Church and the Soviet "brigade") as a condition of continuing to do business with us.

A second sort of linkage is aimed at Washington, as a Kissinger trade agreement or a Carter SALT II treaty become targets for campaigns to change U.S. policy on matters beyond their formal scope. Jackson used the former to toughen U.S. policy toward Russia generally; George Meany was among those who assisted, in part because he wanted to sink the trade liberalization bill to which the Jackson-Vanik Amendment was attached. SALT II presented the perfect opportunity for the rising Senate defense coalition to win military spending increases. And in both cases, the goals of the "linkers" were accomplished even as the U.S.–Soviet accords were being undermined.

What can be done? The goal is congressional participation in building and supporting more stable and balanced U.S. policies toward the Soviet Union. One thing Congress clearly will not do is generate and sustain a comprehensive policy package by itself—Senator Bellmon learned that. Congress needs to be led. And reforms notwithstanding, there remains considerable congressional readiness to defer to the president and his people, at least most of the time, if they are seen as competent, effective, trusted; if their national political standing is good; and if they are pursuing a policy approach that makes sense and reflects broad American values.

The harder question is what sort of policy might meet these criteria. Polls show consistent majorities for military parity, a tough and wary stance toward Russia, and arms control negotiations. Support seems a good bit shakier for certain competitive instruments: foreign aid, major arms sales, or actual use of military force in Third World areas. And as Schneider points out, our domestic divisions make a coalition backing centrist policies hard to develop and maintain. Still, public support for the main elements of a policy of constrained or managed competition seems adequate if means can be found to formulate, articulate, and implement one.

An impressive, self-confident U.S. military posture is a prerequisite in building support both for competitive engagement with the Soviet Union and for arms negotiations. Pragmatic conservative senators were vital to ratification of the limited test ban and the consular treaty. Their notable absence from the ranks of SALT II supporters proved fatal. And they take their cues from the military. Achieving such a solid defense posture, *and* a belief in it at home and abroad, is no easy matter. There will always be disagreement about how much constitutes enough, and campaigns for arms buildup will inevitably dramatize U.S. weaknesses and Soviet strengths. Still, an administration giving priority to defense stands a good chance of meeting this political imperative.

To the degree that our leaders are perceived as effective in defending American interests *against* the Russians, they will gain credibility in negotiating and presenting to Congress agreements *with* them. Kennedy's Cuban missile crisis of 1962 paved the political path to the limited test ban of 1963. The fact that Nixon was fighting the hawks' fight in Vietnam gave him running room on SALT I. Conversely, the perception that American interests were *not* protected on wheat sales in 1972 reinforced the notion that his trade agreement was a favor we were doing the Russians, making it more vulnerable to congressional assault. Similarly, Carter's perceived unreadiness to counter specific Soviet challenges undercut the reception of the treaty he signed in Vienna.

But tough language can underscore impotence—what if the "unacceptable" brigade does not depart? Moreover, in a world of global Soviet power and reach and 150 sovereign states, visible Russian gains *somewhere* are almost inevitable. They are likely to be used politically against whoever is president, whatever their durability or intrinsic importance. Recall the Kennedy campaign of 1960: not just Cuba but "Ghana and Guinea falling into the Soviet orbit." Few Americans will welcome these gains, but we will not always, at reasonable cost, be able to prevent them. But if Americans believe that our president should be able to prevent them, and believe also that the Russians, if they truly want peace, ought not to be engaging aggressively in the global influence game at all, then such gains will do double damage to SALT-like agreements. They will undermine presidential credibility. They will render the Soviets unfit partners for any negotiated accord.

How can these effects be muted? One way is to engage loudly and visibly in countering Soviet Third World influence; Central America presently comes to mind. But this will not always be productive in particular country situations, and when it is not, it will surely deepen divisions at home. A second approach is preventive diplomacy to reduce Soviet opportunities—Zimbabwe and Namibia are apt cases—but not all doors can be closed in this way. A third method is to try to negotiate "rules of the game" for Third World engagement—a long-shot undertaking at best and one which, if successful, would doubtless be followed by charges that the Soviets were breaking the rules.

A fourth, more ambitious approach would be to try to change the predominant way Americans think about U.S.–Soviet relations. This would build on an argument Senator Gary Hart has used: that the reason we need SALT is that we distrust and fear the Russians and need all the handles on them that we can get. It would begin with the picture of the Russians as powerful, ambitious, unattractive, opportunistic rivals whose presence on the world scene, however disadvantageous and threatening to us, is beyond our power to alter in any fundamental way. But we have the strength and capacity both to compete with them and to live with them. Kennedy's "twilight struggle" metaphor is grimmer than our prospects justify, but its spirit is the proper one. Defense, arms control, aid, and diplomacy then become not competing policies but components of an overall policy.

Such a formulation ought to be able to command support across a pretty broad range of our political spectrum. But in practice it would be advanced or retarded by how our leaders characterize, and respond to, specific international events, and whether they can bring our political dialogue within this framework. And it would need to be implemented by our divided government, by our system—in Richard Neustadt's apt characterization—of "separated institutions *sharing* powers."[16] What sort of changes in congressional structure and process might make sensible Soviet policies easier to conduct?

CHANGES IN CONGRESS?

Congressional influence is rooted, of course, in the United States Constitution. On balance, that document gives the president the advantage: he has particular powers to negotiate treaties, to command the armed forces, to appoint and receive ambassadors. This, combined with the widely recognized need, in Alexander Hamilton's words, for "decision, activity, secrecy, and dispatch,"[17] makes it possible for the executive branch to keep the initiative—most of the time. But it is equally legitimate under our system for the Congress to employ *its* powers—over appropriations, general legislation, ratification of treaties, confirmation of appointments—to control or constrain United States foreign policy.

When Congress does so, this can destroy an administration's Soviet policies, as Kissinger learned from Henry Jackson and Carter found when he submitted SALT II. The United States is left with no policy and—worse yet—a foreign perception that we may be constitutionally incapable of one. So reform prescriptions often begin there. Lloyd Cutler, Carter's counsel for SALT II, has argued that the United States lacks a capacity "to form a government" which can carry out coherent policy and suggests a number of possible constitutional changes aimed at bringing president and Congress closer together by linking their electoral fates.[18] Carter's deputy secretary of state, Warren Christopher, advances a proposal that is modest only by comparison: for a "compact" between the branches which "would affirm the President's basic authority to articulate and manage our foreign policy," with the executive in turn sharing information, offering consultation, and abiding by the (hopefully broad) policy constraints that the Congress does impose.[19] Senator John Tower

16. Richard E. Neustadt, *Presidential Power* (New York: John Wiley and Sons, 1980), p. 26.

17. *The Federalist,* no. 70 (Modern Library edition), p. 454.

18. Lloyd N. Cutler, "To Form a Government," *Foreign Affairs* 59, no. 1 (Fall 1980): 139–43.

19. Warren Christopher, "Ceasefire between the Branches: A Compact in Affairs," *Foreign Affairs* 60, no. 5 (Summer 1982): 999.

would tilt power even more toward the president, "proposing a return to the situation that prevailed in the 1950s and 1960s." "Chess," he would remind us, "is not a team sport."[20]

Of the three, Christopher's prescription offers the most practical approach for the 1980s. But he deals only briefly with the crucial question of how either branch might get its act together, both to negotiate such a compact and to enforce it. For neither goal is the recent record very encouraging. Looking at the Congress, the focus of this chapter, one central issue is whether there can be developed legislative subgroups which can speak for their parent bodies on major issues of U.S.–Soviet relations, groups that can work with the executive in developing substantive and procedural consensus and winning broader Senate and House support.

All of this brings us full circle, back to Henry Bellmon. The standard congressional way of providing subject-matter leadership is through committees. Bellmon wanted a select committee to conduct a broad analysis and perform a task of political integration, putting together a balanced approach to U.S.–Soviet issues which most of his colleagues could then endorse, making it easier to sustain a consensus and harder for the subject to be exploited for partisan advantage.

But successful select committees are rare. The effective congressional enterprises are those that are attached to streams of legislative business— the standing committees. They do not, of course, always prevail. On both the SALT II and trade agreements, the responsible congressional committees proved utterly unable to keep control of the central political action. Senate Foreign Relations was in a constant struggle with Armed Services over SALT II. House Ways and Means and Senate Finance found the politics of Jackson-Vanik beyond their reach in 1974.

Recent trade experience on non-Soviet issues, however, offers an example of more constructive executive–congressional collaboration. In the Trade Act of 1974, Congress set policy goals for the multilateral "Tokyo Round" negotiations; Finance and Ways and Means representatives monitored the talks in Geneva. The final accords were implemented through the Trade Agreements Act of 1979, formally submitted by the president, and considered under procedures (established by the Trade Act) which barred amendments and assured a timely up-or-down vote. To ensure that this vote would be favorable, the executive branch worked intimately with the two committees in shaping the bill. And the House and Senate endorsed their work overwhelmingly.[21]

20. John G. Tower, "Congress versus the President," *Foreign Affairs* 60, no. 2 (Winter 1981/82): 234, 243.

21. I. M. Destler, "Trade Consensus; SALT Stalemate . . ." provides a fuller description and comparative analysis.

Such a system might well be employed for SALT—which Reagan has renamed START—if means could be found to bring it into being. It would require, as its base, a committee with broad political-military jurisdiction, including authority over arms control agreements, one that was representative of, and could run political interference for, the Senate as a whole.

SALT II suffered from the lack of such a committee and from the Foreign Relations–Armed Services strife that arose in its stead. After 1980 this jurisdictional conflict intensified as the aggressive John Tower replaced the courtly John Stennis as Armed Services chairman. This conflict strengthens the case for Senate reorganization but simultaneously makes the normally slim prospects for such reform even slimmer. It will hardly help future arms control agreements if the Senate's repository of military expertise has a vested interest in attacking them.

There are at least four reform possibilities, any one of which might make U.S.–Soviet arms agreements more manageable politically:

1. A merger of key Armed Services and Foreign Relations jurisdictions, creating a *Committee on National Security;*
2. A *Joint Subcommittee on Arms Control* to which both committees supplied members;
3. A *Select Committee on Arms Control,* also with SALT jurisdiction, but drawing members from Intelligence, Appropriations, and perhaps Budget as well;
4. *Giving SALT jurisdiction to Armed Services,* on the same political effectiveness argument that justifies Finance and Ways and Means authority over trade.

With a strong, credible committee to collaborate, fence, and bargain with the executive, it might be possible to legislate procedural changes of the Trade Act variety. An administration might seek, at the start of a negotiation, a bill through which Congress would set arms-control goals and establish rules for expeditious action on any agreement that resulted. These rules might limit or prohibit amendments and promise action within, say, ninety days. This would tend to force advance consultation with the committee(s) and influential members of Congress.

Finally, we could consider making changes in the content and form of what Congress acts upon. Leslie H. Gelb has proposed smaller agreements, more frequently submitted.[22] These might be less likely to become major political targets, and congressional rejection of any single one would be less disruptive of U.S. policy and Soviet relations. But the lesser damage from rejection might in fact increase the chances of rejection (or

22. Leslie H. Gelb, "A Glass Half Full," *Foreign Policy,* no. 36 (Fall 1979): 22–32.

of encumbering amendments if procedure did not prohibit them). Another frequent suggestion is to lower the threshold—make agreements, not treaties. This course would probably have been suicidal for Carter on SALT II in 1979, but it makes political sense from a longer-range perspective. A majority approval requirement in both houses offers Congress ample opportunity for influence but allows greater flexibility in negotiations because it removes the veto of the one-third-plus-one minority that can prevent treaty ratification.

One should not exaggerate either the likelihood of such changes or their impact, taken alone. They cannot substitute for effective congressional or administration leadership. On the contrary, they are conceivable only if developed and pressed by adroit leaders in both branches, as, once again, the Trade Act procedures were. And they would only work if an administration moved to capture the policy center, responding to "peace" and "strength" constituencies alike, in an attempt to pursue balanced Soviet policies of the sort crudely outlined in the preceding pages of this chapter, and to reinforce Capitol Hill leaders and institutions that were similarly inclined.

4

The President and the Executive Branch

ROBERT R. BOWIE

The president has the central role in conducting relations with the USSR. But he performs it, well or badly, with the executive branch, the Congress, and interdependent allies.[1]

In analyzing how it has been done since World War II, key questions are: What is the nature of the president's tasks? How do strategy and the policy process relate to their performance? What factors affect the capacity of the president to marshall domestic support and to concert with allies? And finally, what are the implications from this range of experience?

THE TASKS

The tasks of the president in managing relations with the Soviet Union have flowed from the nature of U.S. objectives: to prevent nuclear war; to contain Soviet expansion; and gradually to develop better relations, as feasible.

These objectives impose three requirements for an effective policy: (1) the dedication of large military, economic, and political resources; (2) collaboration with other nations, especially the advanced industrial states of Western Europe and Asia; and (3) consistent pursuit over an extended period. In meeting these requisites, the role of the president is basic.

At home, only he can mobilize the support of Congress and of the public for the policy itself and for the means needed to pursue it. Congress has or shares control over essential policy instruments: funding for defense and foreign military and economic assistance; trade and other legislation; approval of treaties; and declaring war. And it can also exercise influence by resolutions, hearings, and investigations. Yet Congress cannot manage foreign policy; it can only facilitate, influence, or frustrate the president's handling of it.

---

1. Although sharing many powers with the Congress under the Constitution, the president was expected from the start to enjoy primacy in the conduct of foreign affairs. See *The Federalist,* Essay no. 70 (Washington, D.C.: National Home Library Foundation, 1937). See generally, E. S. Corwin, *The President* (New York: New York University Press, 1957), chaps. 5 and 6.

In the alliance, joint policies do not come easily. Despite shared interests, the allies differ in situation, concerns, and priorities, which change over time. The leadership in concerting policies for defense, negotiation, and other issues, must come largely from the United States through the president and executive branch.

Finally, his leadership is essential in assuring the effective functioning of the executive branch, on which he depends for information, analysis and advice, and for implementing his decisions and policies.

Thus the president's job in foreign policy has two aspects: to make wise and informed decisions and to lead in carrying them out. How can he do it? Obviously, the personal capacities of the president are critical. But just as important are adequate procedures for making and conducting policy. Those procedures must be shaped, it is often said, by the president's own habits and predilections. But besides satisfying him, the policy process must also fulfill certain objective requirements inherent in the nature of the containment policy.

1. The purpose of the process is to mobilize and orchestrate many kinds of decisions and actions by the United States, its allies, and other nations to create the conditions and environment needed to maintain deterrence and influence Soviet conduct. To be effective, such actions and decisions must be consistent at any time and over an extended period.

2. Within the executive branch, the president can consider and decide only a miniscule part of all the issues that will arise from day to day in relations with allies and adversaries. Most will have to be handled at various levels of the executive branch from cabinet officers on down and in embassies abroad. If these many actions are to reinforce each other, they must be guided by an understanding of the purposes and priorities of the president.

3. For a coherent course, the president needs the steady support of Congress (and the public) on specific actions which most members will not be able to assess in detail. Their support for a particular measure is likely to depend heavily on the conviction that the general policy of the president and his administration is reasonably clear and sensible and is being pursued competently and with consistency.

4. For concerted action among allies, leaders of other democratic states will often need to use political capital to subordinate competing interests in order to align the action of their governments with an alliance course. They will be willing or able to do so only within the context of a reliable and predictable U.S. policy.

Thus an effective containment policy toward the USSR requires consistency and coherence to achieve its objective of influencing Soviet behavior and to maintain the public support and allied cooperation necessary to ensure the means. Hence a president needs a well-articulated strategy and a policy process adequate to assure consistency in the policies adopted. He needs to understand his dual task of deciding and leading and the relation of a strategy and the policy process to both functions.

A strategy is obviously not a detailed blueprint of future policies; clearly, that is not feasible in an unsettled world where crises and unforeseen events are inevitable. What is required is a framework relating U.S. interests, the Soviet threat, and the means for countering it. By clarifying objectives, priorities, and means, it will help guide or shape specific policies.

Some presidents have explicitly developed such a strategy. Others have proceeded more by ad hoc decisions and procedures. In either case, of course, interests, threat, and means are not givens—each president consciously or otherwise forms his own concept of each, based on his preconceptions, his knowledge and judgment, the inputs of his advisers, and the impact of events at home and abroad.

How far these elements are combined into a coherent and feasible strategy depends on the quality of the information, analysis, and judgment brought to bear. How far it enlists domestic support and allied cooperation also depends on the president's capacity to lead. The policy process affects both.

PRESIDENTIAL CAPACITY

"Today no one can come to the Presidency of the United States really qualified for it."[2] Certainly, of the eight presidents since World War II, most have not been well equipped by knowledge or experience for the broad task of managing relations with the USSR.

Four (Truman, Kennedy, Johnson, and Ford) had prior public service primarily in Congress, and two (Carter and Reagan) as governors. Congressmen make speeches about the Soviet threat, attend committee hearings, and vote on relevant appropriations or legislation, but their job seldom calls for deeper analysis or understanding of Soviet policies and actions or for a strategy to cope with them. Nor does it provide any executive experience in making complex decisions and living with their consequences or in directing large organizations or leading an alliance. On the contrary, a congressman is used to working with a small personal staff and dealing with specific issues separately as they arise. He need have no larger strategy in adopting positions on specific issues and can change them without undue concern. And service as a governor involves even less exposure to Soviet or alliance issues, while the executive experience has little relevance to the conduct of foreign policy. As vice presi-

2. Dean Acheson, *Present at the Creation: My Years at the State Department* (New York: Norton, 1969), p. 730.

dent, neither Truman nor Johnson had been actively involved in foreign policy.

Eisenhower was an exception. He had had extensive experience in policymaking in Washington and abroad. As Supreme Commander in World War II and in NATO in 1951–52, he had worked intimately with civilian and military leaders of many European countries. He had already had some direct dealings with the Soviets during World War II and the German occupation, including talks with Stalin and negotiations with top military leaders.

While not comparable to that of Eisenhower, Nixon too had had a wider experience than most. He had been exposed both to the policy process in foreign affairs and to Soviet issues during his eight years as vice president. He had attended National Security Council (NSC) meetings, traveled, and met Soviet and other leaders, but he had not had direct executive responsibility for making or carrying out policies.

Frequently, presidents only compound their own shortcomings by their staffing of their administration. In practice they replace the whole upper layer of officials concerned with foreign affairs and defense, from Cabinet officers and the NSC assistant and staff down through the assistant secretaries, and even lower in some cases. Many of these appointees have limited backgrounds in foreign affairs and little or no experience in policymaking or the workings of the federal government. In general, secretaries of state have been an exception.

This extensive turnover of the top officials is disruptive of continuity. The new officials have to get to know each other, the Congress, and allied leaders, and have to learn how to utilize the expertise of the bureaucracy, which they often distrust. Yet they tend to be confident of themselves and believe the external world more malleable than it is. Thus policymaking, especially in the early, formative stage, tends to suffer from the lack of institutional memory and the orderly input of professional experts. It takes some months or longer for events to shake the confidence, confound the campaign rhetoric, and force a greater awareness of the limits on the capacity to reshape policies and direction.

In short, at the time when the president most needs to define his strategy and set up his policy process, he is least qualified and equipped to do so. One president glimpsed an aspect of this dilemma when he said that he had to choose appointees at once but would only know their capabilities to perform a year later.

By the time the president and his cabinet have settled in, they have become too immersed in the current demands to allow much chance for educating them about the broader background of problems or issues. They do not have the time or the patience to learn enough about Vietnam or Iran or some other situation really to be able to assess the significance of the "current intelligence" for which they are so avid.

In the last two decades, these difficulties have been heightened by the succession of one-term presidents. In the case of Truman, Johnson, and Ford, however, the carryover of appointees mitigated the effect somewhat.

CHANGES IN STRATEGY

While the United States has pursued containment of the Soviet Union since 1947, the strategies for doing so have shifted over time as administrations have sought to define and balance their conceptions of U.S. interests, the Soviet threat, and suitable means.[3] The main sources of variation have been differing appraisals of the Soviet Union and divergences as to the means which could or should be used in countering it.[4] Concepts of U.S. interests have been global in scope but were modified, at least de facto, in the 1970s by the constraints on the means for pursuing some of them.

Strategy toward the USSR has been articulated most explicitly and systematically by three presidents—Truman, Eisenhower, and Nixon. Broadly, the other five tended toward a more ad hoc or partial approach. Some resisted efforts to define a strategy as tying their hands or foreclosing options (i.e., Kennedy); or apparently did not naturally think in such terms (Carter, Johnson); or mistook rhetorical stance for strategy (Reagan). Ford, with Kissinger as secretary of state, appeared simply to carry on the strategy inherited from Nixon until he abandoned the term *détente* in the reelection campaign as a result of Reagan's criticism. Two of these five (Kennedy and Carter) substantially modified their approach to the USSR in reaction to crises, Kennedy after the Cuban missile crisis and Carter after the invasion of Afghanistan.

The two most significant changes in U.S. policy since World War II— those made by Truman and by Nixon—reflected major revisions in the appraisal of Soviet purposes or priorities. Eisenhower's shifts in that respect were more subtle, but seminal, and were more explicit in military strategy.

Truman's strategy evolved under the impact of events and his advisers. From 1945 to 1950 he gradually moved from the policy inherited

3. For a comparative appraisal of the successive approaches to containment, see John L. Gaddis, *Strategies of Containment* (New York: Oxford University Press, 1982).

4. William G. Hyland, *The Soviet Union in the American Perspective: Perceptions and Realities,* Adelphi Paper no. 174 (London: International Institute for Strategic Studies, 1982), p. 52.

from Roosevelt to the all-out containment of NSC 68. The premise of the Roosevelt policy had been that Stalin, though difficult and suspicious, was pragmatic, and could be persuaded to join in maintaining a stable peace after the war by assuaging his deep-seated insecurity. By the time of Roosevelt's death, disputes over Poland were raising doubts for him and especially for his advisers—W. Averell Harriman, Admiral William D. Leahy, James V. Forrestal, and others. "The air the new President [Truman] breathed was permeated with advice to be firm, to keep his commitments and demand that the Soviets keep theirs."[5] Initially, through Secretary of State James F. Byrnes, he tried to follow Roosevelt's policy, but in a more demanding style. During 1946, he read the report on conditions in Eastern Europe by Mark Ethridge, a U.S. newspaper publisher who had been sent by Byrnes on a special assessment mission; George Kennan's "Long Telegram" from Moscow, which ascribed Soviet hostility to deep-seated, systemic causes; and the report by Clark Clifford, which reflected a wide official consensus on the gravity of the Soviet challenge, stressing the military threat more than Kennan had.[6] This analysis was reinforced by the Greek–Turkish turmoil, the foreign ministers' stalemate, the Communist takeover in Czechoslovakia, and the Berlin Blockade.

Until mid-1950, however, Truman seemed to see the danger mainly as Soviet subversion and pressure rather than military, and to rely heavily on the U.S. monopoly of the atom bomb. He kept the defense budget at about $14 billion against the advice of Forrestal, the Joint Chiefs of Staff (JCS), and other key advisers because of his deep conviction that higher defense spending would jeopardize the economy and civilian needs. Finally, the Soviet atomic test and Mao's victory in China led him to request a review which produced NSC 68 early in 1950. The image of the Soviet Union embodied in NSC 68 was of an implacably hostile, expansionist, military threat that had to be countered by greatly expanded Western military strength, nuclear and conventional. That view was confirmed by Korea. The defense budget was tripled.[7]

Eisenhower's changes in strategy were much less radical than Truman's and dealt mainly with means. In contrast to Truman, however, he formulated his view of the USSR and his strategy by a unique, organized, in-depth review early in his tenure. In the Solarium exercise in mid-1953, three teams of experts developed alternative strategies over five or six

5. Robert J. Donovan, *Conflict and Crisis: The Presidency of Harry S Truman* (New York: Norton, 1977), p. 37.

6. The Clifford memorandum (*American Relations with the Soviet Union*, September 24, 1946) is reprinted as an appendix to Arthur Krock, *Memoirs* (New York: Funk and Wagnalls, 1968), pp. 419–82.

7. Donovan, *Conflict and Crisis*, chaps. 5 and 15.

weeks, which they presented to the president and NSC for discussion and initial policy choices. Despite campaign rhetoric, Eisenhower quickly re-affirmed containment and jettisoned "roll-back" in Eastern Europe as an operational objective. He did, however, revise military strategy substantially, broaden Third World policy, and eventually seek negotiations.

Eisenhower's defense policy was greatly influenced by domestic factors and a sense of limits. Like Truman, he was a firm fiscal conservative, committed to a balanced budget and resistant to excessive military spending, which he thought would damage economic growth and could not be sustained over the long haul. In his view, NSC 68 would be too costly. Actually, his annual defense spending ($40.2 to $46.6 billion) was three times that of Truman before Korea but below what NSC 68 implied, and it favored air and naval power over ground forces. After the Korean War, Eisenhower was opposed to U.S. intervention with ground forces in a limited war.

Eisenhower's "New Look" military strategy downplayed reliance on conventional ground forces. Instead, the United States (1) would respond to any future aggression "at times and places of its own choosing"; and (2) would treat nuclear weapons, including tactical ones, as a part of the arsenal to be employed where militarily and politically useful. This did *not* mean that the response to local attacks would be massive nuclear retaliation on Moscow or Beijing. It did imply exploiting enemy weak points rather than necessarily responding at the point of attack. It also meant stressing U.S. mobile power, air and sea, rather than ground forces.

Eisenhower was confident that this strategy would deter "nibbling" as well as major attacks and apparently believed that tactical nuclear weapons, if used, could be limited. In 1954, however, he refused to intervene in Indochina with air or ground forces. In the Quemoy-Matsu crises in 1954 and 1958, the threat worked, but it was clearly risky. By 1958, Secretary Dulles urged the JCS to begin planning for more conventional means for resisting local aggression. And toward the end of his tenure, Eisenhower began to consider this issue.[8]

To resist Communist advances in the Third World, Eisenhower also was prepared to use covert means, as in Guatemala and Iran. And seeing nationalism in the developing nations as a barrier to Soviet control, he sought to bolster them through military and economic assistance, and by security guarantees like the SEATO treaty and the Middle East resolution of 1957. Despite Dulles's ill-advised criticism of neutralism, Eisenhower assisted India and understood, and indeed favored, its nonalignment.

Finally, Eisenhower gave negotiation with the USSR a different role.

8. Douglas Kinnard, *President Eisenhower and Strategy Management* (Lexington: University of Kentucky, 1977); Gerard Smith, *Doubletalk: The Story of SALT I* (Garden City, N.Y.: Doubleday, 1980), p. 10; conversations with the author, 1960.

The doctrine of NSC 68, like Kennan's 1946 concept of an implacably hostile Soviet Union, left little basis for negotiation until the "Kremlin design" for expansion had been frustrated by extended containment. Eisenhower was less rigid. After Stalin died, he wanted to probe for possible openings, initially by his speech of April 1953. Once Malenkov and then Khrushchev recognized the suicidal nature of nuclear war in 1955, Eisenhower sought repeatedly to find a basis for agreeing to reduce the arms burden, or at least the danger of nuclear war, at the 1955 summit, in various expert and other negotiations, and during the Khrushchev visit of 1959 and the abortive summit meeting of 1960.

While these initiatives had little practical result, they did legitimize negotiations to control nuclear arms or risks while maintaining the deterrent and adversarial rivalry. Subtly, they modified the image of the Soviet Union as compared to that of NSC 68. The Soviet Union's interest in avoiding nuclear war might possibly induce it to join in measures for that purpose, without abandoning expansive rivalry.

As said above, Nixon's pursuit of détente represented the most marked shift in strategy after that of Truman. It rested on a very different concept of how to influence Soviet external conduct. A revision in the appraisal of the Soviet Union had already begun in the last months of Kennedy's administration and continued through Johnson's. The outcome of the Cuban missile crisis fostered some complacency about U.S. predominance and Soviet acquiescence in it. The Soviets came to be seen as a limited adversary with a shared concern for stability. Two factors were thought to favor accommodation: (1) the Soviet Union's need for Western trade, credits, and technology to maintain its economic progress; and (2) a common interest in achieving military balance, based on mutual assured destruction, and in stabilizing the arms buildup. Indeed, McNamara apparently believed the Soviets would not attempt to surpass the United States militarily. This more hopeful attitude was nurtured by agreements on the "hot line," grain sales, the Limited Test Ban, Johnson's "bridge-building," and by trade and exchanges with Eastern Europe, the Non-Proliferation Treaty, and plans for strategic arms talks. The momentum was not slowed by Vietnam or, for long, by the invasion of Czechoslovakia in 1968, although the scheduled arms talks were suspended.

The notion that antagonism and conflicting interests could be compromised and bridged was ingrained in Johnson's mentality by his whole career. The belief that similar methods would also work with the Soviet Union was congenial and natural. Politically, successes in efforts to ameliorate tension with the USSR were a welcome counterweight to Vietnam. And the policy was rationalized and put into a larger perspective by Walt

Rostow, later National Security adviser, as well as Brzezinski, who was for a time on the Policy Planning Council in State, and by academic experts.[9]

But only with Nixon was the concept of the Soviet Union as a traditional great power fully adopted and acted upon. As such, it could be induced to join in building a stable structure of peace, if recognized as an equal and given a stake in the international order by means of arms control, trade, credits, and cooperative ventures of various sorts. But it was still necessary to balance its military power. In doing so, however, the new element was China, which sought to enhance its security by links with the United States. The Nixon Doctrine reaffirmed treaty commitments and the nuclear shield but limited other U.S. support for security to military assistance and excluded U.S. ground forces. The new U.S.–Soviet relationship was to be governed by principles agreed to at the 1972 and 1973 summits, which purported to commit each side to avoiding confrontation or taking unilateral advantage. Yet from the start the Soviets stated that the basis of relations was peaceful coexistence, which they had defined since the 1950s as cooperation to avoid nuclear war without giving up the struggle to expand Soviet influence through all other means, including wars of national liberation. Ford, relying wholly on Kissinger, seemed to have no strategy other than continuing Nixon's course. In real terms, defense spending in 1975 had dropped to one-half that in 1965, before the Vietnam buildup (see chap. 13, chart 1).

Kennedy and Carter had only a shallow understanding of the USSR on taking office. Both were predisposed to focus on specific issues rather than on strategic frameworks. Both shifted their approaches to the Soviet Union during their terms. Having criticized Eisenhower's policy as complacent, passive, and starving defense, Kennedy initially reverted to the sweeping concepts and prescriptions of NSC 68 and proclaimed a U.S. global role almost unlimited in its extent and commitment. Khrushchev's speech of January 1961, asserting active Soviet support for wars of national liberation, underscored for Kennedy the danger to the Third World; and the crises in Berlin, Southeast Asia, and over the Cuban missiles confirmed the seriousness of the Soviet threat.

The actual changes were mainly in means and were more modest than the soaring rhetoric. Kennedy and McNamara espoused "flexible response" with some buildup in ground forces, as well as expanding ICBM, Polaris, and tactical nuclear programs already under way (defense spend-

9. Walt W. Rostow, "The Third Round," *Foreign Affairs* 42, no. 1 (October 1963): 1–10; George F. Kennan, *On Dealing with the Communist World* (New York: Harper, 1964); Zbigniew Brzezinski, *Alternative to Partition* (New York: McGraw-Hill, 1965); Marshall D. Shulman, *Beyond the Cold War* (New Haven: Yale University Press, 1966).

ing rose about 15 percent from 1961 to 1964). To counter Third World vulnerability, Kennedy increased economic assistance and developed special counterinsurgency forces to resist guerrilla and other subversive forces. The change in approach which took place after the Cuban missile crisis and marked the beginnings of détente has already been discussed.

Much more radically than Kennedy, Carter also modified his assessment of the Soviet Union and his approach during his term as a result of Soviet actions. So far as can be judged, his original perception of the Soviet Union seemed to be similar to that of Secretary of State Vance. The USSR was difficult, assertive, and secretive, but the adversarial rivalry might be modified or limited by agreements and better understanding. Initially he hoped to downgrade the priority for U.S.–Soviet relations in favor of other concerns. His focus was much more on specific issues than on a strategic framework. He continued efforts for SALT II within the Vladivostok framework, after the Soviet rebuff of major cuts; and he did not respond at this stage to the steady Soviet military buildup or its actions in the Third World. Yet he attacked Soviet denial of human rights while also broadening efforts for arms control.

By 1978–79, however, elite and public opinion became more concerned about (1) the steady buildup of Soviet military power absolutely and relatively; (2) growing Soviet influence in Angola, Ethiopia, and Yemen; and (3) the increasing vulnerability of the Middle East, especially after the fall of the shah of Iran.

In reacting to these concerns, the divergences in advice and appraisal by his National Security adviser and his secretary of state led to Carter's vacillation. This was not resolved until the Soviet attack on Afghanistan radically changed Carter's perception of the USSR. It prompted the various efforts at sanctions; contributed (along with the SALT debate) to a larger defense budget and to the Carter Doctrine for the Middle East and the Rapid Deployment Force; and led to the withdrawal of the SALT treaty.

Reagan's deep distrust of the Soviet Union is not matched by any conception of a coordinated policy integrating interests, threat, and means. The rhetoric is strident; the greatly expanded defense program lacks a convincing strategy; and East–West issues have been raised to highest priority. The Siberian pipeline was opposed, while grain sales are promoted. The result has been confusion at home and abroad. The impact of reality, domestic criticism, and pressures from allies have pushed the president toward more balanced positions, especially on arms control. But they have not overcome much of the confusion or produced a coherent strategy.

POSTWAR POLICY PROCESSES

Even a well-conceived strategy achieves its purposes only if supported by an effective system for the making of policies and decisions on specific issues and actions. An adequate policy process must fulfill demanding requirements.

1. It must provide the president and his top advisers, including the secretaries of State, Defense, and Treasury, with the data and analysis for decisions. Even if they were more widely experienced in foreign affairs than they often are, their personal knowledge could cover only a tiny portion of the vast range of countries, regions, and issues involved in policymaking, including the Soviet Union itself, allied nations, and developing societies. Yet effective actions must start from valid premises, data, and judgments. Hence expert advice is essential for understanding the situation, projecting future trends and reactions, and assessing the probable effects of alternative courses.

2. The policy process must also assure the balancing and integrating of diplomatic, military, economic, and other interests and means.

3. In dealing with any issue, there is bound to be a wide range of uncertainty, even among experts, as to existing and future conditions, intentions and reactions of others, and the effects and risks of alternative courses. Hence, in making judgments and choices, it is essential for the president to understand the extent and nature of such uncertainties in the situation and the relative merits and risks of alternative courses. Debate and advocacy before the president by his chief advisers offer the best means for examining competing perspectives, analyses, and judgments on the issues and choices. Written analyses of options will seldom be as effective: they are unlikely to reveal as clearly divergences in defining the problem or assessing various courses and means.

4. The time a president can devote to foreign policy decisions is relatively limited and will partly be preempted by crises. If he is to keep control, he needs to focus on decisions which are strategic or seminal—that is, those which set or modify a general course of action. That will allow him to delegate much of the execution of policy to his secretary of state and other officials with greater confidence that their decisions and actions will conform to his perspective; and, by the same token, they will be able to act with more assurance and to take initiatives by knowing the parameters. Thus the process should result in a record of decision which can also be made known to lower-level officials for their information and guidance.

5. Finally, to ensure allied support and cooperation, the process must

provide a way for them to feed their views into the policymaking in some recognized manner before policy becomes fixed.

In short, the policymaking process should assist the president both in reaching informed decisions and in leading the executive branch, the Congress, and the alliance.[10]

Since the creation of the National Security Council in 1947, presidents have utilized two quite different models for policymaking.

Truman and Eisenhower built theirs on two pillars: they relied on the secretary of state as their principal adviser and executor for foreign policy and utilized the NSC and a supporting structure as a policy forum. Kennedy, Johnson, and Nixon downplayed the NSC in favor of less formal methods of decision; and they gradually expanded the role of the National Security Assistant as adviser and executor at the expense of the secretary of state, until the latter was virtually eclipsed when Kissinger was National Security Assistant under Nixon. In Nixon's last year and under Ford, however, Kissinger enjoyed primacy as secretary of state, even keeping both posts for a while. The system under Carter began on the Johnson pattern but veered steadily toward a dominant NSC adviser. In theory, Reagan adopted a Department-of-State-centered model, but in practice Judge Clark as NSC assistant steadily expanded his authority.

Both Truman and Eisenhower depended heavily on a strong secretary of state (Marshall, Acheson, and Dulles) and his department in making and carrying out foreign policy. The primacy of the secretary of state did not mean allowing him a free hand or abdication by either Truman or Eisenhower. Both had high regard for their secretaries, but they expected to be kept fully advised of the conduct of policy by the secretary and to make all significant decisions themselves. When in Washington, Acheson saw the president nearly every day and often spoke with him on the telephone. When abroad, he sent detailed reports, with a copy and a condensed summary for the president, asking for guidance if needed; and several times a week or more, a personal assessment. "As a result of this systematic flow of information, the President was kept as familiar with what was going on as though he were present himself."[11]

The practice of Dulles and Eisenhower was much the same. Contrary

10. For analyses of various aspects of presidential policymaking, see Alexander L. George, *Presidential Decisionmaking in Foreign Policy* (Boulder, Colo.: Westview Press, 1980); I. M. Destler, "National Security Advice to U.S. Presidents," *World Politics* 24, no. 2 (January 1977): 143–76; Andrew J. Goodpaster, "Four Presidents and the Conduct of National Security Affairs," *Journal of International Relations* 2, no. 1 (1977): 26–37; William P. Bundy, "The National Security Process," *International Security* 7, no. 3 (Winter 1982–83): 94–109.

11. Dean Acheson, "The President and the Secretary of State," in *The Secretary of State* (Englewood Cliffs, N.J.: Prentice-Hall, 1960), pp. 27–50.

to the myth, Eisenhower was in full control of foreign policy. Dulles took no significant action and made no decision, speech, or statement of substance without discussing it with Eisenhower beforehand and getting his approval, usually by going to the White House or by telephone. When out of Washington, he reported as fully as Acheson had.[12]

In practice, the NSC under Truman and Eisenhower brought together the secretaries of state, defense, and treasury, the Director of the CIA, chairman of the JCS, and others to advise the president on major decisions. An executive secretary (under Truman) or Special Assistant for National Security (under Eisenhower) was charged with overseeing the preparation of policy analyses and proposals by a group of senior officials (at the level of assistant secretary) from the key departments. They were able to draw on the expertise of their departments and agencies in preparing these papers, which served as a basis for discussion in the council. Under Eisenhower each policy paper was accompanied by a CIA estimate bringing together the relevant intelligence from that agency, state and defense. The NSC special assistant had a small staff to make sure that issues were fully presented, but neither he nor his staff provided policy advice.

The experts in the departments also had an opportunity to discuss the paper with their Secretary, in a regular briefing held before the NSC meeting. Thus the president had the benefit of the experts' paper and the comments or debate by the NSC members, who in turn had heard from their experts. The council system was especially valuable for discussing basic policies or approaches to issues, regions, or countries. From 1950 to 1960, the NSC produced a Basic National Security Policy document each year, updating strategy toward the Soviet Union. The council also provided an effective forum for considering reports prepared by Special Task Forces (like NSC 68) or by outside groups (like the Killian Report).

Under Eisenhower, an Operations Coordination Board, made up of under secretaries, was charged with overseeing the carrying out of the policy decisions by the responsible departments and agencies. Since it acted by unanimity, it had no ready means to resolve disputes, but the more intimate meetings confined to the members and the executive secretary were useful in coordinating the execution of policy.

This formal process was not suited to day-to-day tactical decisions, such as those relating to ongoing negotiations or detailed handling of crises or implementing policy. Such decisions were handled directly by the president with the secretary of state, and with others present as re-

12. Fred I. Greenstein, *The Hidden-Hand Presidency: Eisenhower as Leader* (New York: Basic Books, 1982), pp. 87–91.

quired. Under President Eisenhower, a staff assistant (Paul Carroll, followed by Andrew Goodpaster) took care of this part of his activities. He kept the president abreast of intelligence reports, brought to his attention other materials, and arranged for discussions with outside experts.

This system had considerable merit. It often raised issues for discussion before they became crises; it provided systematic channels for expert advice; it exposed the president to face-to-face discussion with his chief advisers, who had had a chance to fully inform themselves on the issues; it assured participation in the making of policy by those charged with executing it; it did integrate the various elements of policy; and it produced a record of the decision made available to subordinate officials. Furthermore, since the relevant assistant secretary of state took part (in preparation or briefing or both), foreign ministries of allies had a clear channel for inserting their views while the policy was still fluid, and defense ministries had a similar channel through Defense Department participants. The NSC system was especially valuable in the period where the administration was charting its course, and later on for reviewing and revising its direction. In the course of two terms, however, it risks becoming less useful or routine, as it apparently tended to do in the last Eisenhower years.

Both presidents considered the NSC system well suited to sound decisions and presidential control of foreign policy. While Truman did not usually attend until 1950, Eisenhower almost always did so. In a 1950 directive, Truman specifically stated how he expected the NSC to function to give him "the benefit of the collective views" of the relevant officials. He requested frequent meetings, small enough to encourage free discussion and preceded by carefully coordinated staff work by "the best qualified individuals." Each agency was to nominate a member for this senior NSC staff group for appointment by the president. This system fit Truman's "passion for orderly procedure" and his desire for adversary debate and adequate staff preparation.[13]

Eisenhower felt even more strongly about the vital importance of these procedures to good policymaking. Members of the Planning Board were specifically appointed by him and were directed not merely to represent their department but to adopt a broader approach. Their joint papers, which organized, analyzed, and criticized all available data, provided the basis for full discussion of conflicting views (which he insisted should not be concealed). He stressed the value of the active debate to the president in reaching informed decisions. The NSC discussion and the president's written decision ensured a common understanding of the

13. *Foreign Relations of the United States, 1950,* vol. 1 (Washington, D.C.: U.S. Government Printing Office, 1951); Acheson, *Present at the Creation,* p. 733.

issues and the president's thinking by the key cabinet officials and their subordinates.[14]

Besides these benefits, Eisenhower valued the NSC discussion of longer-term policies as a means of preparing the ground for emergency decisions that might be taken more informally. "To my mind," he wrote, "the secret of a sound, satisfactory decision made on an emergency basis has always been that the responsible official has been 'living with the problem' before it becomes acute. Failure to use, on a continuing basis, the National Security Council, entails losing the capacity to make emergency decisions based on depth of understanding and perspective—that is, on a clear comprehension of the issues involved, the risks, the advantages to be gained, and the effects of this particular action."[15]

The NSC also helped to gain political support. "One of the important reasons for using an advisory body of the stature of the National Security Council is that the public, knowing the quality of the advice, will be apt to develop a strong feeling of confidence in the adequacy of the nation's security."[16]

In making military policy, the practices of Eisenhower and Truman differed radically, though both imposed ceilings on the military budget in the interest of the economy (though Eisenhower's was three times that of Truman before Korea). Truman left the secretary of defense (Forrestal and then Louis Johnson) to allocate resources among the services, apparently without concerning himself with strategy or weapons decisions. Eisenhower exercised a much more active and personal control. He dealt directly with the Joint Chiefs of Staff in insisting on the "New Look" strategy and with the secretary of defense and Joint Chiefs in keeping spending within the budget allocation. He also was actively involved in the decisions regarding missiles and other major weapons systems.[17]

The alternative model of policymaking was less structured or formal, relying much less on the NSC system and more on the NSC assistant for policy advice, but with variations within the general pattern.[18] Kennedy disbanded the NSC underpinnings and used the council very little. Instead he favored small, informal meetings, finding the NSC rigid and

14. Robert Cutler, *No Time for Rest* (Boston: Little, Brown, 1966); Goodpaster, "Four Presidents," p. 26; Dwight D. Eisenhower, "The Central Role of the President in the Conduct of Security Affairs," in Amos A. Jordan, Jr., ed., *Issues in National Security in the 1970s* (New York: Praeger, 1967), pp. 212–16; Bundy, "National Security Process," pp. 95–99.

15. Eisenhower, "Central Role," p. 214.

16. Ibid., p. 217.

17. See Kinnard, *President Eisenhower*.

18. For a review of the role and functions of the National Security assistant from Truman to Nixon, see David K. Hall, "The 'Custodian-Manager' of the Policymaking Process," appendix D (chap. 12) of *Report of The Commission on the Organization of the Government for the Conduct of Foreign Policy* (Washington, D.C.: U.S. Government Printing Office, 1975).

cumbersome. While the secretary of state was still supposed to be chief adviser, the special assistant became more active in the policy process, although still seeking to ensure that issues were fully presented. In effect, the special assistant combined the roles of the NSC assistant and the staff assistant and the functions of the Operations Coordination Board, with a small but substantive staff. The staff, especially the academics, who were much interested in intelligence estimates, were a conduit for feeding them into the policy process.

The heavy stress on a "pragmatic" approach and keeping options open entailed resistance to developing a strategic framework. President Kennedy decided not to issue a Basic National Security Policy prepared by Walt Rostow and the State Department's Policy Planning Staff, lest it constrict flexibility. The first formal coordinated interagency study of Soviet policy and its implications was not prepared until August 1962, prompted by new intelligence estimates on Soviet nuclear capability; apparently it was not discussed with the president, who was merely advised that it required no change in the U.S. policy.[19]

In theory, Kennedy may have favored a State-centered system, but Dean Rusk did not display the initiative which that would have required (as McNamara did in Defense). In reality, Kennedy undoubtedly wanted to conduct policymaking himself in a manner that inevitably elevated the NSC assistant and his staff to more than "holders of the ring." Kennedy's style in the presidency reflected that of a senator's office: comfortable with a small, agile, personal staff, and critical and distrustful of a large bureaucracy like the State Department. But in the area of defense, Kennedy largely delegated to McNamara the handling of strategy, forces, and budgets. After the Bay of Pigs, however, he brought General Maxwell Taylor into the White House as an adviser, until he became chairman of the JCS.

This system did not necessarily assure thorough staffing or adequate preparation for decisions or full debate of issues, as the Bay of Pigs showed. Apparently sensing this, Kennedy created the special Executive Committee (ExCom) of the NSC to advise him in the Cuban missile crisis. In reflecting later on the Cuban episode, Robert Kennedy said that it showed the vital need that the president be exposed to the recommendations and opinions of more than one individual or department, and for vigorous debate, in order to assure him the expert knowledge and judgment of the various agencies concerned with foreign affairs.[20] The costs of ad hoc decision-making without adequate preparation and staffing are

19. See Raymond L. Garthoff, *Intelligence Assessment and Policy-Making: A New Window on American Foreign and Defense Policy in the Kennedy Administration* (Washington, D.C.: The Brookings Institution, 1983).

20. Robert F. Kennedy, *Thirteen Days* (New York: Norton, 1969), pp. 111–12.

evident in the Kennedy meeting in Nassau with the British after his cancellation of the Skybolt missile program.[21] The decision to provide the Polaris system to the United Kingdom undercut the administration's opposition to national nuclear forces and its proposal for a multilateral force, and contributed to de Gaulle's veto of British entry into the European Community. Afterward, Kennedy said, "We didn't know the meaning of the words we were using."[22]

Kennedy's approach to policymaking was largely carried on by Johnson, though he tried briefly to revive the NSC and was closer to Rusk than Kennedy had been. Even so, McGeorge Bundy, and Rostow much more so, moved more into the role of adviser. With Vietnam, the "Tuesday luncheons" with the top advisers became the principal forum for decisions, as Johnson became more and more preoccupied with the details of military operations. The supporting staff work was rather haphazard, the discussions "rambling, lacking a formal agenda or clear conclusions, infinitely wearing to the participants, and confusing to those at the second level who then had to take supporting actions."[23]

Nixon's campaign promise to restore an effective NSC was formally carried out at the start, but the council's role soon atrophied and the system was perverted to serve the secretive policymaking virtually limited to Nixon and Kissinger. As National Security assistant, Kissinger used the various NSC committees he headed to obtain studies and analyses and an array of options from the experts in the departments, while excluding their chiefs, including the secretary of state, from any significant role in the decision-making. (This, of course, was reversed when Kissinger became secretary of state under Nixon and Ford.) Kissinger also used his substantial staff for advice and expertise.

The secretary and officials of the State Department were kept in the dark about many of the decisions and initiatives. Kissinger moved from adviser to executor on many matters. He utilized a "back channel" for negotiations on some matters like SALT, keeping the official delegation in ignorance of their course. This practice was feasible where so much attention was focused on direct negotiations with the leaders of the Soviet Union and China. But the costs were very high in relations with allies and in congressional and public support. When officials in Washington were not able to explain or defend the policies or actions, and ambassadors in the field were equally uninformed, it inevitably created suspicion and

21. See *Public Papers of the Presidents of the United States: John F. Kennedy, January 1–December 31, 1962* (Washington, D.C.: U.S. Government Printing Office, 1963), pp. 908–09.

22. Smith, *Doubletalk*, p. 486; see George W. Ball, *The Past Has Another Pattern* (New York: Norton, 1982), chap. 18.

23. Bundy, "National Security Process," p. 10.

resentment both at home and abroad. Ford largely delegated foreign policy to Kissinger as secretary of state.

Carter went both ways. His National Security adviser was given cabinet status and tended toward an active role like Kissinger's, but the secretary of state was more like Rusk under Kennedy than Rogers under Nixon. Much of the policy discussion took place in two committees of the NSC, made up of cabinet members, which met without the president, and often without adequate preparation of papers or proposals. The results were summarized by the Special Assistant in a memo, not seen by the secretary of state, which was transmitted to the president for approval or decision. Thus he did not have the benefit of hearing the discussion by his advisers unless an NSC meeting was held, which was relatively infrequently. Carter also had a "Friday breakfast" each week for unstructured discussion and decisions on foreign policy. Initially limited to the vice president, Vance, and Brzezinski, it was gradually expanded to include Harold Brown, Hamilton Jordan, and others. Without an advance agenda, decisions were often casually made and not formally recorded until 1980.

In some cases, subcommittees or special groups devoted elaborate efforts to developing analysis and recommendations, as in the case of PRM 10, but they did not succeed in imposing coherence on much of the policymaking. In relations with the USSR, where the National Security adviser and secretary of state often held different views, the tug-of-war resulted in vacillation until the Afghan war tipped the balance. The active role of the National Security adviser in meeting with ambassadors, as public spokesman, and in executing policy directly, as in Iran, resulted in competing channels and confusion.[24]

Before the election, Reagan promised to restore coherence to foreign-policymaking and to make the secretary of state his "principal spokesman and adviser" and the NSC assistant a staff coordinator. Alexander Haig and Richard Allen were appointed on that basis. Soon, however, Haig was feuding with Allen and other White House advisers, and clashed publicly with the secretary of defense, who construed his mandate broadly. When William Clark moved from deputy secretary of state to replace Allen, with expanded authority to coordinate, the respite was short, as Clark began to take a more active hard line on Soviet issues. Haig lost the support of the president as he became more assertive and more erratic. In resigning, he decried the lack of "consistency, clarity, and steadiness of purpose" of Reagan's foreign policy.

24. For differing perspectives on the Carter policy process, see Jimmy Carter, *Keeping Faith* (New York: Bantam Books, 1982), especially pp. 35–62; Cyrus Vance, *Hard Choices* (New York: Simon and Schuster, 1983), especially pp. 34–44; and Zbigniew Brzezinski, *Power and Principle* (New York: Farrar, Strauss, Giroux, 1983), especially pp. 17–78.

His successor, George Shultz, more low-key but seemingly holding more authority, has sought to make the process of decision-making more orderly. Yet after a year, on many aspects of foreign policy—such as arms control or Central America—he is still struggling with the Defense Department and the White House for control. Undoubtedly the temperament and work habits of the president, his lack of experience in the conduct of foreign policy, and his reliance on trusted advisers who themselves are inexperienced compound the confusion about authority and policy.

The review of the policy process under Kennedy and his successors suggests several comments.

A National Security assistant has a serious role conflict if he is also a key adviser on substance. Under Truman and Eisenhower, his sole responsibility was to make certain that the process worked and that issues were fully staffed and presented for decision. With the backing of the president, he had great authority to compel the departments to fulfill those requirements and to air and debate disagreements. If the assistant is also an adviser, the temptation to push his preferred solution, and the suspicion that he may use his access to do so, can be extremely corrosive and disruptive.

When the National Security assistant also deals directly with ambassadors and the media, the result is almost certain to be confusion and the impression of conflicting voices.

While an informal policy process is less cumbersome and quicker, those advantages are often bought at the cost of adequate staffing and full discussion, which can lead to unwise or casual decisions. The Tuesday luncheons of Johnson and the Friday breakfasts of Carter display those weaknesses clearly. The formal NSC-type process is best suited to more basic decisions which justify the time and effort, leaving tactical decisions to more informal methods. But the latter also benefit from the more thorough analysis and participation which has taken place through formal machinery.

When the president is making the decision, he should normally have the benefit of discussion among his advisers in his presence. Summaries of separate discussions are no substitute for this, and easily lend themselves to distortion and manipulation.

A State Department–centered system also has great advantages in execution and in relations with allies and the Congress.

Bureaucratic Expertise

The professionals in State, Defense, and the CIA, as well as the economic agencies, are the main source for the specialized knowledge and analysis needed for making policy. Even a large NSC staff can only be a supplement, and indeed is usually recruited largely from the career officials of the departments. How well or badly their talents are used depends largely on the policy process.

The career staffs inevitably have their special strengths and weaknesses in relation to policymaking:

- In general, the distrust of some presidents like Nixon or the disdain of Kennedy is not justified. As a group, senior career officials are competent, dedicated, and loyal; they do not willfully go their own way or seek to sabotage the policies of a president. Their principal interest is in having an opportunity to take an active part in the policymaking.
- The charge that the State Department is by nature routine, stodgy, and resistant to innovation is often made by the White House, especially when the NSC assistant and staff are active policy advisers. Those tendencies are most marked when the State Department is not in the center of policymaking and lacks strong leadership at the top. An effective and respected secretary who is the main adviser and clarity about objectives evoke energy and initiatives in proposals and execution by the Department.
- Regional bureaus of State or the Services in Defense do tend to be parochial in outlook and priorities. Yet that tendency can even be an asset if the policy process encourages multiple advocacy and debate which assure diverse inputs and clarifies points of difference. The Secretary or others who decide should be able to weigh the differing perspectives and integrate them. Since policy toward the USSR is inevitably many-sided, forceful analysis from different points of view is essential.
- The Departments tend to be weak on strategic analysis. The Joint Chiefs of Staff are not well organized or staffed to develop military strategy, as has been stressed by General David Jones, recently retired as chairman of the Joint Chiefs of Staff. And the Policy Planning staff of the State Department, which was to focus on questioning the premises of policy and analyzing the relation of specific measures to longer-term objectives, has at times become too topical or operational. Its impact also depends on whether the Secretary tends to approach issues in strategic terms.
- Intelligence estimates in many fields, such as Soviet military capabilities, international economics, the Soviet economy, and so on, are on average excellent. In the past, projections of future Soviet military capability have sometimes been influenced by current policy premises (as in the McNamara period).

- A major problem in State and CIA is the shortage of in-depth expertise on many foreign countries. Sound policies often require insight and understanding regarding the basic political and social forces, the culture and values of allies, developing nations, and adversaries in order to analyze events or future trends and the impact of proposed actions. That kind of knowledge and "feel" about a country or region comes only from specialized study, living there, and mastery of the language. The normal career pattern in State or CIA does not encourage or reward such specialization, with few exceptions. And budgets do not favor standby expertise. Reporting from the field is also biased toward current intelligence rather than more basic data and analysis.
- Too often, top policymakers do not make effective use of intelligence estimates (as distinct from current intelligence). If used, they could help to overcome some of the lack of background and understanding which frequently skews decisions and actions regarding unfamiliar areas or issues. They are more likely to influence policy if the Director of Central Intelligence is closely involved in the policy process, and if it allows for adequate preparation and staffing.
- The ambassador, if qualified and respected, can be a very valuable asset, even in the jet age. Too often the asset is wasted. In an allied country, his authority (held since Truman) to oversee the activities of all elements of his mission can assure more coordinated policies in Washington as well as in the country. And the ambassador to the USSR can be a special source of information and advice if his regular use as the channel to the Soviet regime gives him access to the Soviet leaders. But his usefulness is greatly curtailed by the practice in recent years of dealing mainly through the Soviet ambassador in Washington, which has been fostered by the active role of the National Security assistant and the reliance on "back channels."

MARSHALLING DOMESTIC SUPPORT

Every president recognizes that he requires the support of Congress and ultimately of the concerned voters in order to have the requisite instruments and authority to conduct an effective policy toward the USSR. How far does such support depend on his methods and policies and how far on other factors?

Until about 1968, as I. M. Destler explains in this volume, Congress provided bipartisan support for the president's handling of foreign policy (except perhaps for Truman's last year). Thus Eisenhower enjoyed strong congressional support, even during six years of Democratic control, as did Johnson through most of his term, despite Vietnam. And the attentive public tended to follow the same pattern.

What were the conditions which underlay the predominance of the president over these two decades?

First was the shared consensus on the gravity of the Soviet threat and on the strategy of containment for resisting it. Forged largely by events from 1945 to 1950, it reflected the conviction that failure to resist Hitler earlier had led to World War II. The partisan cleavages from the Korean War were soon mended. And the consensus was reinforced by the later crises over Hungary, Berlin, Cuba, and Czechoslovakia, which united liberal Democrats with internationalist Republicans.

So strong was the anti-Soviet sentiment in Congress that it may have contributed to distortions by the Executive. On Greek-Turkish aid, it was Senator Arthur H. Vandenberg who urged Truman to describe the threat in sweeping terms in order to assure passage. In general, foreign aid requests were customarily presented in cold war dress. Kennedy, who had sought to stress the positive aims of development aid, eventually had to adopt this course to get appropriations approved.

Second, the Congress had substantial confidence in the competence and leadership of the president and his Cabinet. While Truman initially had few credentials, he inherited a group of key advisers of both parties from the Roosevelt era, and grew in stature by his handling of the early phase of the cold war. Moreover, he was from Congress and knew its members. In the close 1948 election, foreign policy was not the issue. Loss of confidence rapidly erodes the president's influence, however, as happened to Truman in his last year, after the perceived mishandling of Korea.

As a national hero, Eisenhower enjoyed much more respect and influence with Congress (and the public) than was reflected in the media. By ending the Korean War he revived the bipartisan consensus, and his initiatives toward the USSR responded to public hopes for better relations and peace. Under both Kennedy and Johnson, Congress continued to look to the president for leadership. Only at the end of the Johnson administration did confidence begin to decline significantly, once more as a result of a protracted limited war.

Third, these presidents all actively consulted with Congress on proposed measures. Under Truman, some of the major steps, like the Greek-Turkish aid, the Marshall Plan, and the Atlantic Treaty, were developed with participation of key members of Congress, such as Vandenberg. In some instances, Republicans linked to the international wing of the party were appointed for specific tasks, as was John Foster Dulles to negotiate the Japanese Peace Treaty. (Yet Truman did not consult on his decision to intervene in Korea or to send four divisions to NATO).

To bolster his hand, Eisenhower obtained congressional resolutions approving his use of U.S. forces as he might find necessary in defending Formosa in 1955 and in the Middle East in 1957. Under Kennedy, Congress adopted similar resolutions regarding Cuba and Berlin. In 1964, Johnson obtained the Tonkin Gulf resolution with almost no debate; and the next year he sent the marines into the Dominican Republic on his own, without congressional objection. Such resolutions were devices for committing Congress to the policy in advance.

Consultation was greatly facilitated by the structure of Congress. In the Senate and House, both parties had established and respected leaders with substantial influence over the proceedings of each House and with members. Knowing what each House could be led to support, they could speak within wide limits for their respective chambers. Thus the president could genuinely consult the Congress by meeting with a dozen or so of the leaders, and could candidly discuss his proposals and revise them as necessary on the basis of their advice. And throughout these two decades, secretaries of state and their deputies spent large amounts of time and energy testifying to and briefing congressional committees. On major issues the members of Congress were generally prepared to defer to the president and be guided by the judgment of their leaders.

In essence, in defining its role in this period, the Congress recognized its own limitations. Too decentralized to be able to plan a coherent strategy, it looked to the president to do so and to submit his proposals for review or revision. Lacking the capacity to act quickly, Congress delegated to the president the authority needed to protect the interests of the country. And in this period, despite campaign rhetoric, Congress largely treated foreign affairs as bipartisan. Conversely, the president respected the authority and prerogatives of the Congress.

After 1968, conditions changed. Congress began to assert more independence and more control over military and foreign policy. As casualties rose and opposition to Vietnam grew in the media and public opinion and on campuses, Congress adopted a resolution against making foreign commitments without the consent of Congress (1969), and ultimately the War Powers Act of 1973, overriding Nixon's veto. Thereafter, it foreclosed any renewal of the Vietnam involvement, adopted the Jackson-Vanik Amendment (1974), blocked military aid to Turkey over Cyprus, barred covert intervention in Angola (1976), cut aid to various countries for violations of human rights or other reasons, and made a variety of actions, including arms sales, subject to the legislative veto.

From 1968 on, the conditions favoring collaboration of the president with Congress were lacking.

First, Vietnam eroded the shared consensus on foreign policy that had prevailed in the preceding period. Congress and the attentive public divided over the premises and conduct of intervention. Nixon's effort to create a new grand design for U.S.–Soviet détente was flawed in concept and based on misjudgments about the Soviet Union and its priorities and U.S. capacity for leverage. While initially popular, it polarized opinion rather than unifying it, as Soviet actions undercut its assumptions and premises. Carter did no better in forging a strategy or a renewed consensus. The incipient one on defense and Soviet policy that was starting to emerge in 1980–81 was disrupted by the more extreme positions taken by Reagan.

Second, the presidency no longer commanded confidence in its handling of foreign policy. Distrust of the Executive by Congress began with suspicions of having been misled on the Dominican Republic and Tonkin Gulf resolution. It reached its high point under Nixon as a result of deception regarding the Vietnam War, secrecy in general, and Watergate. Ford overcame the legacy of personal distrust but failed to create confidence in his competence or command of the problems. Carter appeared to vacillate between Vance and Brzezinski in his assessment of Soviet purposes and to lack the capacity to integrate his various policies toward the USSR. And until the Afghan invasion, he seemed out of step with growing public concern about Soviet actions. The result was public confusion rather than consensus. Inevitably, in 1980 Reagan campaigned on policy toward the Soviet Union and the adequacy of defense. But in its first two years the Reagan administration has failed to convince Congress or the public of its competence in making and conducting a coherent foreign policy.

Finally, Congress was more fragmented and less disciplined than ever before, as Destler discusses. The changes in its structure and the personal basis for election undercut hierarchy and many of the bases for leadership. Efforts to consult Congress as in the earlier period were bound to falter on the ambiguity as to whom to consult. Who could speak for either House with any confidence when the members were so deeply divided on the various issues related to U.S.–Soviet relations and defense and arms control?

Moreover, Nixon's and Kissinger's highly personal and secretive methods hardly lent themselves to close collaboration with the Congress. The Carter administration sought to mend relations by offering timely information and consultation, but it offended Congress by actions like the abrupt decision on withdrawing forces from Korea and the unilateral recognition of China and termination of the Taiwan defense treaty.

In both periods the attitudes in Congress largely mirrored those of the attentive public. While foreign and defense policy were issues in the electoral campaigns in 1952, 1956, 1960, and 1964, the debates did not undermine the essential bipartisan consensus. The issues were not about the essentials of containment but about mistakes in managing it, or means for pursuing it, and they tended to be buried or to disappear after the elections. Eisenhower settled the Korean War and quickly abandoned the talk of "roll-back" in Eastern Europe; Kennedy dropped the alleged missile gap and adopted "flexible response."

After 1968, however, the issues were more basic, raising questions about the scope of U.S. interests, the character of the Soviet threat, and the strategy and means for coping with it. The splits in opinion and policy were more polarized and persisted after the election was over to an extent which had not been true earlier. The fact that the Vietnam War continued until 1973 was a major factor; and that was soon followed by the disillusion created by the unraveling of the Nixon détente.

COOPERATION WITH ALLIES

A strategy of containing the Soviet Union by frustrating its efforts to expand inherently depends on joint action by the major threatened states. They must organize relations among themselves, agree on military strategy and forces, regulate economic and other relations with the USSR, and work out joint positions for negotiations with it.[25]

The process of concerting policy and action on such a wide range could not be easy in a coalition of democracies. To achieve a common policy on such issues, each allied leader has to be satisfied with the policy and able to convince his government and public to subordinate competing interests or concerns which often are supported by strong domestic political groups. The leader must be willing to use political capital for this purpose.

The alliance has gone through several phases. From 1947 to 1955, the task was to work out the structure of the alliance, its political and military organization, and its initial strategy and forces. But the hardest issue was to find an agreed way of including the Federal Republic of Germany as a member so soon after World War II. In the middle period the Europeans were sorting out relations among themselves: in the European Community, especially on the issue of British entry; in French–German relations under de Gaulle; and in France's relations to Europe and NATO under him. That process complicated alliance efforts to cope with the strategic issues related to the Soviet atomic arsenal and control of nuclear weapons. In the phase of détente, the allies adopted the Harmel dual formula of deterrence and dialogue, and embarked on *Ostpolitik* and the Nixon détente, with more emphasis on direct negotiations and relations with the USSR. But expansion of negotiations and of trade and other relations

25. See "Managing Alliances," appendix K, pt. 4 of *Report of the Commission on the Organization of the Government for the Conduct of Foreign Policy* (1975).

tends to increase risks of cleavage and friction among the allies, as a result of differing interests and priorities. Since the mid-1970s, such divergences have intensified on East–West, security, and economic issues.

Changing conditions have influenced the process of coordination. In the early years, when fear of the Soviet threat gave security top priority, and when the United States was most predominant, that facilitated cooperation. Yet even then it could be slow and arduous. Finding a basis for including the Federal Republic in the alliance that was compatible with its domestic politics and also acceptable to France and other allies required five years of patient and persistent effort.

While this was an extreme example, extended negotiations have often been required to achieve joint policies on other issues, like handling the Berlin or other crises, strategy for NATO, or preparing for conferences with the Soviet Union. Special task groups have had to be set up for some critical topics, such as the Harmel study of the Soviet Union, détente, and defense in 1967–68.

As the allies recovered strength and self-assurance and the imminent fear of the USSR receded, the pressure to subordinate parochial interests or to follow the U.S. lead declined. Thus, in the 1960s de Gaulle, confident of the stability of the deterrent, felt free to pursue an independent policy within Europe and toward the USSR, despite its disruptive impact on the alliance. By the later 1960s, the Federal Republic had regained sufficient self-confidence to embark on its *Ostpolitik*. And for a younger generation, without memory of the war or the early postwar period, secure peace in Europe has come to seem the normal condition, not calling for sacrifices in the interest of the alliance.

In the last decade, the greater Soviet capacity and readiness to extend its power and influence outside Europe has produced divergences in the U.S. and European concepts of détente and relations with the USSR. For the Europeans, especially the Germans, détente has succeeded in ameliorating human contacts, stabilizing conditions in Berlin, and expanding trade in Europe—benefits they do not wish to jeopardize because of Soviet activities outside Europe or even in Eastern Europe. For the United States, détente as a constraint on Soviet global expansion has been a disappointing failure. These differences have impeded efforts for joint reactions to Poland, Afghanistan, and elsewhere.

Achieving the concerted action that is indispensable for the alliance requires constant consultation, compromise, and adjustment, and some readiness to live with differences. The United States has had and will still have a primary role to play in this process. It can be played only by the executive branch, with the support of Congress. Relative success or failure depends greatly on the respect the president commands and on his methods of making policy and conducting relations with the allies.

A critical factor is the degree of allied confidence in the competence and effectiveness of the president and his key advisers. Does the administration have a sense of direction, sensible objectives and priorities? For the reasons discussed, it is important for allied leaders that U.S. policy be predictable and reliable so that they can plan their own course with assurance. They need to feel that the administration is following a coherent strategy that they understand and accept, and that provides a common starting point for specific policy decisions consistent with it. That coherence lessens concern over unilateral action or surprise.

Unfortunately, such confidence has been declining in the last fifteen years or so, when the allies' own self-assurance has been growing. The causes have been various and somewhat cumulative. Vietnam eroded confidence in the Johnson administration: many of the allies considered the war a mistake and out of proportion to U.S. interests. Nixon was discredited by the handling of Vietnam, Watergate, and his secretive methods of policymaking, and was resented for his unilateral actions and general disregard for the allies. Carter appeared to vacillate and be confused about his larger strategy or priorities, and to have limited command of foreign affairs. Reagan seems ideological and rigid, as well as lacking both experience and an overall coherent framework. The early attitude of the president and his associates on nuclear weapons and arms control was deeply unsettling for the allies.

To some extent, the shortcomings of the individual presidents have coincided with more general allied concerns about the U.S. capacity to manage its affairs effectively. Especially troubling have been the weaknesses in the functioning of the economy and of some major industries, as well as in the political system, with Congress undercutting the president.

Also, the readiness of the allies to follow U.S. leadership has been greatly influenced by how far they have felt the United States has understood and taken account of their views and interests in devising policies. When policymaking is wholly centralized, as under Nixon, the allies are certain to feel excluded. But even when the departments have a more active role, the nature of the U.S. policy process makes allied coordination difficult. Proposed policy takes shape as it is worked out in and among the departments and with congressional leaders, and tends to become frozen or hard to adapt thereafter to reflect allied views.

The problem can be managed by a policy process based on the secretary of state and the State Department. Then the allies have a variety of channels for registering their views and exerting influence while policy is still fluid. Of course, under any system allied leaders can occasionally alert the president and his key associates directly as to issues which especially concern them. But when the secretary of state is recognized as the chief adviser on foreign affairs, he and his associates can serve as a conduit for assuring allies of being heard on any issue concerning them. When assistant secretaries and their deputies and country officers are actively involved in the policymaking, an allied government can readily feed its viewpoint into the system during the formative stage when adjustments and compromises are being made. Under these conditions, their own embassy and that of the U.S., as well as the NATO Council and other joint bodies, can all be used to contribute to the dialogue.

The allies tend to be most frustrated and resistant when they feel cut out of the process. If they do not understand the framework within which the policy is being developed or are deprived of means for an effective input, alliance cohesion is naturally strained and common policy is far harder to achieve. Dissatisfaction with their ability to influence U.S. policy and actions and their loss of respect for the president and for the operation of the U.S. polity have combined to undercut confidence in U.S. leadership and the readiness of the allies to follow it. Since no substitute is apparent, the consequence has often been disarray and tension among the allies.

CONCLUSIONS

Over thirty-six years, eight presidents have conducted a policy of containment toward the Soviet Union. They have pursued various strategies—some explicit, some implicit, and some erratic. The actual policies have often been inconsistent and inconstant, and their course has oscillated over the period. What can one conclude from this experience?

It can be said, of course, that the policy has largely served its basic purpose. Nuclear war has been avoided. While the Soviet Union has extended its reach and its influence in some areas, it has not taken over any region vital to the United States, despite the steady growth of its military power. How far Soviet purposes have moderated is debatable, however, though the USSR of today is not that of Stalin.

That these results have been achieved in spite of the shortcomings and vacillations in Western policy may reflect a tolerance for deficient performance allowed by favorable circumstances. In future, conditions are likely to be more demanding than in the past. With military parity and proxies, the Soviet Union has greater means to exploit vulnerable situations. The relative strength and prestige of the United States have substantially declined. The cohesion among the allied nations is weaker. And the Third World, on which the West is more dependent, has many areas of potential instability and conflict.

The necessity for a coherent policy is as great or greater: (1) to influence Soviet behavior and avoid miscalculations which could be disastrous; and (2) to maintain Western cohesion and cooperation despite the divisive tendencies. That will require a viable strategy integrating interests, threats, and means, and a policy process suitable to avoid past oscillation and inconsistency. The record since 1947 can teach us lessons on both counts.

Strategy

The most costly mistakes in postwar strategy were the Vietnam War and the Nixon détente. Both, however, exemplified persistent shortcomings in U.S. policy.

Relating Interests and Means. Vietnam was an extreme case of the failure to clarify the nature of our interests and to keep interests and means in balance. This has been a repeated source of vacillation in U.S. policy, especially in coping with Soviet penetration into the Third World. Thus, Truman's low ceiling on defense from 1947–50, by prompting the exclusion of Korea from the U.S. defense perimeter, may well have contributed to the decision to attack. Conversely, NSC 68, which was a "bludgeon" to crack that ceiling, overstated the scale and imminence of the Soviet threat, was open-ended as to U.S. interests, and did not specify the resources required. Popular disenchantment with Korea was a warning as to limits on intervention. In reaction, Eisenhower's New Look was designed to avoid ground involvement in Asia as well as to control defense spending; but he did not explicitly narrow the global scope of U.S. interests in opposing aggression. Yet in 1954 he accepted the "loss" of North Vietnam without intervening. Kennedy's sweeping assertion of U.S. interests and the intention to defend them was hardly matched by his defense program.

In Vietnam, whatever Kennedy might have done, his definition of U.S. interests and objectives was applied by Johnson in pressing the intervention. The turmoil over Vietnam established that the U.S. polity could not sustain extended hostilities of that kind and scale. That fact was recognized by Nixon's Guam doctrine but not in the last stage of Vietnam. The reactions to Angola, Ethiopia, the Persian Gulf, and Central America show that the United States now seeks to distinguish in practice between what are seen as vital interests and more peripheral concerns. But the controversies over these issues also show that consensus has not been achieved on the extent of U.S. interests in such areas and the resources it is prepared to devote to them. The absence of consensus impedes limited action because of doubts and suspicions about the possible expansion of involvement.

The Image of the Soviet Union. The appraisal of the Soviet Union and of how to influence it as reflected in U.S. policy has tended to oscillate over time between two conceptions.[26] The image of the implacable enemy with a systemic drive to expand was embodied in Kennan's analysis of 1946 and in NSC 68. It underlay the concept of containing that expansion by deterrence and external resistance until the Soviet system mellowed or collapsed. Apart from crises, almost no basis was seen for influence by diplomacy or negotiation. Gradually, however, the focus on direct dealing developed, leading by stages to a different concept. When Khrushchev and his successors recognized the suicidal nature of nuclear war, it appeared that the West and the USSR would share an interest in avoiding it. From Eisenhower on, that hope led to the pursuit of arms control and related measures to reduce the danger of nuclear war. Yet the USSR did not necessarily perceive such agreements in the same terms as the West. It might wish to reduce risks of nuclear war, but it did not share the Western aim of stability based on parity and restraint. In the minds of many Western political leaders and their electorates, however, both sides were engaged in a *common* effort for *shared* goals. One major consequence was to nurture the Western tendency to "mirror-image" the USSR—to view it as difficult and pushy, but essentially a traditional great power, basically pragmatic and opportunistic. Thus negotiation seemed the best means (as in the Western political culture) to resolve "misunderstandings" and to compromise differences.

The Nixon détente policy seemed to be founded on such a conception. The United States and the USSR were committed to a joint goal of building a "stable structure of peace" based on restraint. The policy presupposed a U.S. ability to manipulate the Soviets directly by benefits and penalties. Conversely, the Soviets appeared to think that the United States, recognizing the shift in the correlation of forces, had accepted coexistence as they define it. The U.S. hopes for restraint were proved illusory by Soviet actions in Angola, Ethiopia, and finally Afghanistan, and by the inexorable Soviet military buildup during the 1970s, while real U.S. defense spending dropped to half the level before Vietnam. The Europeans, especially the Germans, continued to derive benefits from a selective détente. The result has been confusion and division.

The Need for a Balanced Strategy. The combined effect of the Vietnam quagmire of Johnson, Nixon's deceptions in extricating the U.S. from it, and the overselling of détente was disastrous. It undermined public and congressional trust and support, provoked constraints on the president by Congress, and severely strained allied confidence and unity. And the disillusion with the fruits of détente contributed to overcompensation regarding the USSR.

26. Hyland, *The Soviet Union in American Perspective* (see n. 4).

In 1981 conditions seemed favorable for reviving a centrist consensus on policy toward the USSR. The divisions over Vietnam were fading, the Afghan invasion and awareness of the Soviet military buildup had brushed away many false hopes, and public opinion seemed ready to support a firm but moderate policy, including larger spending for necessary defense. Unfortunately, that opportunity was missed by the Reagan administration. The uncritical defense budgets, the attitude toward nuclear weapons and arms control, the intemperate rhetoric, and undue stress on East–West trade were divisive both at home and in the alliance.

Thus one of the most difficult tasks ahead (as in the past) will be to develop a strategy which balances interests, threat, and means on a basis which can enlist the requisite support at home and among allies for a reasonably stable policy. It will have to start from a realistic view of the Soviet Union, recognizing the continuing clash of purposes and the limited Western leverage for directly influencing Soviet behavior. The corollary is that Western policy must continue to maintain direct and indirect constraints based on strength, vitality, and unity in the noncommunist world. Yet it must also pursue negotiation and dialogue without illusions both for substantive agreements and for subsidiary benefits: for effective arms control; to keep open channels of communication and reduce risks of miscalculation; to hold out to Soviet leaders the option of better relations, if and when they are interested; and to reassure Western publics. Finally, it will be essential to clarify the range of Western interests and objectives, their relative priority, and the resources that will be devoted to pursuing them. Incoming presidents might be well advised to emulate Eisenhower's "Operation Solarium" as a means for developing an integrated strategy on the basis of competing analyses.

Policy Process

The experience since World War II has shown both the necessity and difficulty of having a policymaking process that will enable the president to: (a) make sound and consistent decisions which reinforce each other over time; (b) provide leadership in utilizing the executive branch, in enlisting the support of Congress, and in maintaining alliance cooperation. The eight presidents have tried a wide gamut of structures and procedures for making and executing their policy. Neither the informal methods of Kennedy, the unstaffed "Tuesday luncheons" (Johnson), the concentrated and secretive system of Nixon, nor the Carter or Reagan operations seem to have met the requirements both for sound decisions and for coordinated action.

The postwar experience seems to me to show that these requisites can best be achieved:

1. By a decision-making process which utilizes both: (*a*) the NSC system, organized and managed substantially as under Truman and Eisenhower, which draws on the expertise of the department staffs and involves them in the policy process, and which regularly exposes the president to debate on important issues by adequately prepared top officials; (*b*) more informal methods for day-to-day, tactical, specific, or negotiating decisions.
2. By making the secretary of state the principal adviser and executor of foreign policy, subject to the discipline of the NSC process and with full participation of other interested top officials.
3. By making the NSC assistant primarily a facilitator of the policy process (not a policy adviser), with the authority from the president to assure effective staff work by the responsible departments and agencies and presentation of options and diverse views both in the NSC and in the day-to-day, informal decision-making.

Such a system can best provide the basis for sound and informed decisions, coherence and consistency, and for the leadership essential to maintaining domestic support and allied cooperation. The view that the State Department cannot provide the necessary initiative is belied by the first decade after 1947, which was remarkably creative by any standard. But to perform well the Department must have strong and respected leadership and clear guidelines. It will also need to continue to develop more expertise in the many fields now involved in the international arena.

The Congress could also assist in achieving more orderly and consistent policymaking by modifying many of the specific restrictions or controls adopted in the 1970s.[27] Those measures reflected genuine concern about the policies and actions of the president, but they are a poor way to manage foreign policy. Congress can best play its legitimate role in foreign policy by the normal exercise of its extensive constitutional powers and by insisting that the president develop and justify an adequate strategy and consistent policies. In doing so, the president should, of course, involve the Congress through full consultation with its leaders and other influential members. A more constructive relationship is not likely to come about by constitutional reform, or even by formal pact.[28] It will only result from the reassessment by Congress of its proper function and by restoration of confidence in the competence and judgment of the president.

27. See Senator John G. Tower, "Congress versus the President," *Foreign Affairs,* vol. 60, no. 2 (Winter 1981–82).
28. See Lloyd N. Cutler, "To Form a Government," *Foreign Affairs*, vol. 59, no. 1 (Fall 1980); Warren Christopher, "Ceasefire between the Branches," ibid., vol. 60, no. 5 (Summer 1982).

PART II
The Issues

A second way to look at the problems of shaping American policy toward the Soviet Union is to examine how we have handled the key issues involved in the relationship: strategic defense, political crises, economic transactions, and social concerns. Or, to return to our sports metaphor, how have different parts of the game been played?

Managing the defense and nuclear issues is most important, because domestic and allied confidence in our deterrent is basic to all the rest of the policy toward the Soviet Union and because of the disastrous consequences of failure. Richard Betts points out the dangers in our tendency to exaggerate as a means of generating political support for defense programs and explores a number of steps that could counter this tendency and provide more long-term policy consistency in this area. Alexander George looks at the record of managing and preventing crises, including the difficulty of maintaining domestic support for a graded degree of interest in Third World conflicts. He suggests a combination of presidential education of the public about the problems of limited ends and means and an active effort to engage the Soviet Union in quiet discussion of classic diplomatic techniques for avoiding crisis escalation.

Examining our experience in handling the economic issues in our relationship with the Soviet Union, Marshall Goldman and Raymond Vernon describe a record of inconsistency and ineffectiveness. But what can be done? They admit the value of controlling a narrowly defined set of technologies where we are sure of the direct military significance, but they caution that we have too poor a grasp of our own or allied political processes to succeed in an ambitious effort at economic denial or to engage in a policy of detailed and finely tuned economic leverage. Finally, Strobe Talbott surveys the record in the social and humanitarian area. If we are to escape the current conflict, then we have an interest in trying to change Soviet society. Moreover, by our very nature we Americans cannot avoid a concern for human rights. But our policies in this area have often been counterproductive when given too high a prominence—generally as a result of domestic political pressures inside the United States. Though less frequently analyzed than the political or economic issues, the social problems explored in Talbott's chapter are among the most difficult-to-manage plays in the policy game.

95

5

Nuclear Weapons

RICHARD K. BETTS

This is the greatest thing in history.
> —President Harry S Truman on receiving word of the bombing of
> Hiroshima, August 6, 1945

The atomic bomb does not adhere to the class principle.
> —Official Soviet Communist party statement, 1963

Two revolutions coincided in 1945. The political revolution of bipolarity determined the first priority of U.S. foreign policy—containment of Soviet power—which, despite fluctuations, has endured ever since. The technological revolution of nuclear fission dominated strategy for supporting containment in the central zone of interest—Western Europe. Intervening military and political factors have made nuclear strategy far less consistent than foreign policy. At a general level of analysis, though, the most striking thing about nuclear weapons is the clarity and stability they have imposed on the superpower relationship. Without the awesome spectre of nuclear devastation, it is less certain that peace would have survived confrontations over Berlin, Cuba, or the Middle East. The nuclear problem did not freeze strategic maneuver but constrained it.

POLICY, STRATEGY, AND POLITICS

Only in specific policy is inconsistency or incoherence notable. The problem has been the difficulty of fixing the constraints that the nuclear spectre can impose on superpower competition as other constraints or opportunities wax, wane, or evolve at unsynchronized rates and in conflicting directions.

Strategic Dilemmas: Ambivalence and Avoidance

The persistent tension in Western strategy is the lack of agreement about how much mileage can be gotten from nuclear weapons. There is consensus on their *primary* function: deterrence of Soviet nuclear attack. Were that the only requirement, the superpower relationship might have stabilized long ago. The roots of inconsistency and inconstancy of Western strategy lie in the second imputed function—"active" or "extended" deterrence of Soviet *conventional* attack, by threatening U.S. *nuclear* first use. If nuclear war would be apocalyptic, and both contenders' rationality and willingness to take risks are symmetrical, the first function contradicts the second. To deter nuclear attack the United States relies on retaliatory capabilities that make Soviet first use suicidal and therefore unthinkable. By that logic, comparable Soviet retaliatory capabilities make U.S. first use unthinkable. To escape this bind several solutions have appealed to different constituencies.

First is to accept the logic that the role of nuclear forces is to immobilize each other, abandon the contradiction of extended deterrence, and replace it with very confident (and more expensive) conventional deterrence. This preference has been strongest among U.S. elites but has never achieved alliance-wide consensus. Second is to negate the contradiction and overcome the mutuality of nuclear deterrence by developing effective first-strike or damage-limitation capabilities. This was the air force preference but has not been feasible since the early 1960s, if it ever was. Third is to refute the contradiction by denying the symmetry of risk and rationality, relying on the credibility of the West's willingness to court suicide through first resort to nuclear fires and the incredibility of Soviet willingness to risk testing the bluff. This has been preferred by European elites but considered insufficient by most U.S. administrations. Fourth is to mute the contradiction by developing options for limited first use to control escalation. This has been pursued episodically since 1961 but has instilled little confidence even among its proponents. Fifth is to ignore the contradiction, wish it away, or deny the need to deter conventional attack. These have been responses of mass opinion on both sides of the Atlantic in rare periods when the public was mobilized on nuclear issues.

All of these avenues of escape have been partial or temporary elements in the evolution of strategy. Their influence has varied according to perceived Soviet capabilities and intent. In this respect nuclear strategy is Eurocentric. In no other region has there been such long-standing concern that stakes are so high or conventional capabilities so weak that nuclear force would be unleashed in a crisis. But military balances, perceived threats, and strategic concepts have coincided less often than they have been out of phase.

For most of the postwar era European military equilibrium was conceived in the West to rest on countervailing superiorities: Soviet conventional advantage countered by U.S. nuclear advantage.[1] The equilibrium

---

1. See Richard K. Betts, "Elusive Equivalence: The Political and Military Meaning of the Nuclear Balance," in Samuel P. Huntington, ed., *The Strategic Imperative: New Policies for American Security* (Cambridge: Ballinger, 1982), pp. 102–05, 109–11.

was most stable in the mid-1950s and mid-1960s. At most other times military trends were seen to be moving gradually in Soviet favor. Since 1960 there has been scant variation in Soviet investment in military power—a steady increase commensurate with a growing economy. Over the same period the proportional U.S. effort has varied by nearly 100 percent (between almost 10 and barely 5 percent of GNP). After World War II, U.S. military spending fluctuated, never rising for more than three years in a row until 1983. The magnitude of buildups in the early 1950s and 1960s sapped the sense of threat, allowing competing concerns (fiscal restraint or domestic programs) to gain support. But given lags between spending and deployment, budget fluctuations sometimes left incongruities between threat and response. U.S. nuclear force levels spurted in the early 1950s and early 1960s (when Soviet capabilities for striking the United States were modest) and were improved more leisurely from the mid-1960s through the 1970s as Soviet capabilities were expanding. Existing U.S. capabilities have rarely been closely calibrated to existing Soviet capabilities in a manner prescribed by strategic doctrine.

Political Asymmetries: Soviet Tortoise, American Hare

At most times since 1945, U.S. commitments have exceeded the military capabilities to back them up simultaneously with high confidence of success. In the netherworld of the pure strategist, such a gap should be closed by trimming commitments or increasing capabilities. But international politics is more like poker than chess, and acceptable risk is the intervening variable between commitments and capabilities. With the exception of formal statements in the Joint Chiefs of Staff planning process about levels of risk—formulations that have never had discernible impact on policy—risk is never specified, agreed upon, or admitted at the policy level. Rather, it emerges tacitly, vaguely, and by default from the interplay of views about threats and competing claims on resources. Threats are always far more ambiguous than the economic price of countering the worst possible interpretation of them.

In the West interacting trends in domestic politics, economic development, and threat perception produced undulation in defense spending. In the 1950s fiscal conservatism yielded the "New Look," which substituted "cheap" nuclear firepower for conventional forces; in the 1960s Keynesianism yielded both more guns and butter; in the 1970s the evolution of welfare states on both sides of the Atlantic, stagflation, the Vietnam trauma, and détente reduced inclination to match Soviet military power. The discrepancy between commitments and capabilities was often rationalized by exaggerating the Soviet threat in terms of conventional capability (making the option of matching it appear hopeless) and minimizing it in terms of intent (allowing more acceptable risk). The gap in the conventional balance has been managed by varying combinations of: substitution of U.S. nuclear superiority; half-measures to narrow the gap; and hope that arms control could achieve more stable equilibrium and reduced danger of war. The inconstancy of policy was compounded by the diffusion of sovereignty and transience of authority. Far more than in the Warsaw Pact, the preferences of the dominant NATO power were often not shared throughout the alliance, and those preferences changed too fast to sustain coherent strategy.[2] As the military balance shifted to the East, strategic dilemmas were papered over with calculated ambiguity, tinkering with force structure and doctrine, and evasion.[3] Ironically, alliance unity on nuclear issues has usually been least when U.S. efforts to improve the equilibrium were most energetic, because such efforts highlight the strategic dilemma and, by making the issue of acceptable risk explicit, raise doubts about U.S. commitment.

The Soviet approach has been to tolerate less risk. The Khrushchev period was an exception that ultimately reinforced the tendency. Initially opposing Malenkov's acceptance of finite deterrence, Khrushchev later moved toward emulating Eisenhower's New Look, briefly planning to reduce conventional forces by one-third.[4] In contrast to Eisenhower, he put this approach to work to change rather than preserve the European status quo, brandishing the Soviet nuclear deterrent as a shield for a squeeze on Berlin. NATO did not prove to be as intimidated by Moscow's nuclear threat as it expected the Soviets to be by that of the United States,

2. "But whenever consensus seemed to emerge in Western Europe after painful processes of adaptation and reappraisal, the conditions that had determined American unilateralism in the first place ceased to exist. Thus when the alliance finally agreed . . . to accept a major West German conventional contribution the United States pushed through the decision to nuclearize NATO forces, thus changing dramatically the rationale for the German defense contribution. When West European governments . . . came around to supporting this new NATO posture, a new administration in Washington again turned things upside down by forcefully favoring stronger conventional defense. But when the alliance . . . agreed on a flexible response doctrine (MC 14/3), congressional pressure was mounting to reduce American forces in Western Europe. . . . when governments gave up their resistance to the deployment of IRBMs on their territory, Washington had already changed its deployment policies. . . . Again, as at least some West European governments became committed to the American MLF . . . that project became the victim of President Johnson's rising interest in offsetting the impact of the Vietnam War with the conclusion of a nonproliferation agreement with the Soviet Union." Uwe Nerlich, "Continuity and Change: The Political Context of Western Europe's Defense," in Johan J. Holst and Uwe Nerlich, eds., *Beyond Nuclear Deterrence* (New York: Crane, Russak, 1977), p. 14.

3. Richard Hart Sinnreich, "NATO's Doctrinal Dilemma," *Orbis* 19, no. 2 (Summer 1975): 472–75.

4. Arnold L. Horelick and Myron Rush, *Strategic Power and Soviet Foreign Policy* (Chicago: University of Chicago Press, 1966), pp. 19–30; Thomas W. Wolfe, *Soviet Power and Europe, 1945–1970* (Baltimore: Johns Hopkins University Press, 1970), pp. 144–46.

and Khrushchev was ousted for his adventurist "harebrained schemes." If subsequent Soviet perceptions can be gauged at all from public indications, three appear notable: (1) Soviets do not differentiate deterrence from "compellence" as clearly as American theorists do, claim to have been coerced by U.S. nuclear superiority, and view flexible response as an offensive strategy;[5] (2) the objective "correlation of forces"—not risky bluffs—is the logical basis for strategy; (3) U.S. attempts to rationalize nuclear doctrine for first use reflect a lack of reconciliation to nuclear parity and exhibit a potential for adventurism. In short, American adaptive doctrinal measures undertaken both to preserve NATO's capacity for deterrence and to maintain political unity of the alliance, and thus to stabilize the superpower relationship in the face of growing Soviet capabilities, could be just the movements that Moscow considers *de*stabilizing.

U.S. administrations have addressed nuclear problems with unilateral military solutions which became subverted by political conditions and negotiated solutions which became subverted by military conditions. The problem of controlling disparate trends is compounded by the need to pacify numerous audiences within the West while conveying credible and consistent signals to the East.

ACTORS AND PROCESSES

The political arena of nuclear policy involves more participants than domestic policy (external allies and adversaries play a role), but the central actors and mechanisms are more limited. The confusing interrelationships between deterrence concepts, weapons programs, technical assessments of Soviet capabilities, and diplomatic objectives leave specialists in the analytical community and bureaucracy with the greatest leverage on how programs and issues are defined and integrated. Congress and the media focus on particular high-profile issues, allies and Russians function as kibitzers or anticipated constraints, and the public's passivity is only occasionally punctuated by high concern, which is rarely translated into compelling political action. Refined theories that make sense to many in the small expert elite (such as limited nuclear war or civil defense) may founder in public, but because actors outside the Executive tend to fasten on specific elements extracted from the strategic calculus, their influence may be deflected or confined as the administration calls other considerations into play. The Executive, however, does not have a free hand. As the recent "freeze" movement suggests, amorphous frustrations can accumulate and, when ignited by careless official rhetoric that sounds insensitive

5. Henry Trofimenko, *Changing Attitudes toward Deterrence*, ACIS Working Paper no. 25 (Los Angeles: UCLA Center for International and Strategic Affairs, July 1980), pp. 1, 5.

to nuclear horror, can hamper the most ambitious elements of administration strategy.

Professionals

More than other aspects of public policy, nuclear issues have been influenced by theoreticians. Because deterrence has never failed, concepts have never achieved the status of applied science, so none of the contending theories of what deterrence requires has ever been disproved. In debate about strategy, programs, and arms control, scholasticism interacts with competing visceral notions of risk. Untested abstractions and arcane disputes about capabilities dominate decisions within the bureaucracy and negotiations with Moscow; generalized moods about Soviet intentions and global trends dominate public, congressional, and allied support.

Numerous theoretical sects that have framed elite debate can be grouped in two categories. One is oriented to *relative* military power and focuses on operational doctrines meant to buttress deterrence by demonstrating that credible options exist (especially "counterforce" attacks to reduce enemy striking power) were deterrence to fail. The other is oriented to *absolute* capabilities for "assured destruction" of civil society ("countervalue"), and asserts that inexorable mutual nuclear deterrence issues from them. Academic analysts and scientists were instrumental in defining the terms of reference for variations on these theories and have dominated political debate about them.

Theoretical inclinations are refracted within the permanent government. The air force favors maximal counterforce capability, but—mindful of the problem of "friction" in combat, the difficulty of coordinating complex operations, and Hindenburg's principle that in war only the simple succeeds—the service has not been very responsive to theoreticians (or presidents) when they asked for varied and finely tuned flexible options.[6] Though the idea has not been publicly discussable since the days of Curtis LeMay, Strategic Air Command (SAC) planners strapped to a polygraph would say that full-scale preemption is the only hope in event of war. There are, however, military counterweights to the air force. The navy (whose submarine missile force is oriented to the countervalue mission) and army (opposed to diverting expenditures from conventional forces) have been less enthusiastic for counterforce. Before parity was imminent, the military were least amenable to arms control, but in SALT I military representatives were sometimes more supportive than Defense Department civilians.[7] In Reagan's first year, the Joint Chiefs of Staff

---

6. Henry Kissinger, *White House Years* (Boston: Little, Brown, 1979), pp. 216–17.

7. Gerard Smith, *Doubletalk: The Story of SALT I* (Garden City, N.Y.: Doubleday, 1980), pp. 28, 42, 114.

were on the left of the administration in concern about limiting Soviet programs through treaty constraints.

Military views are dominated by program aims, and abstract doctrine often becomes a malleable justification for concrete weaponry. Viewing the nuclear problem in terms of mutual assured destruction and insulating arms control from other aspects of the superpower relationship are more prevalent among State Department careerists. Nixon and Kissinger from the beginning of the Strategic Arms Limitation Talks (SALT) were exasperated with State's attempts to undercut "linkage"[8] (the aim to make arms concessions dependent on political concessions), and State was usually the most resistant to increased emphasis on counterforce. For professional diplomats, successful negotiation is the counterpart of the military's priority on weapons programs. In both cases there is a premium on not belaboring theoretical ambiguities in strategic doctrine. Efforts focus on concrete inputs over which bargains can be struck more than on hypothetical outputs that would constitute an elegant strategy. Expertise unencumbered by policy responsibilities is concentrated in the CIA. (Other intelligence units—the Defense Intelligence Agency, the service intelligence staffs, and the State Department's Bureau of Intelligence and Research—are entangled with the interests of their parent departments.) Yet this freedom limits CIA's contribution, since it can address Soviet capabilities and intent but not U.S. responses.

Normal bureaucratic fragmentation in principle is resolved at the National Security Council (NSC) level, but it ramifies politically because Congress deals more with separate agencies, programs, and treaties than with an organic strategy that crosscuts defense programs. The result in governmental debate is disaggregation of strategy—avoidance of the vexing link between conventional and nuclear deterrence, and a focus on the nuclear balance alone. Those whose real worry is maintaining extended deterrence without nuclear superiority sublimate their arguments in exaggerations of Soviet nuclear advantages. Those whose real concern is saving money or bolstering détente have to deny such advantages. This fosters gamesmanship in estimating Soviet capabilities. In early years gamesmanship focused on data about Soviet deployments; in more recent years, given greater consensus about basic data, disputes revolve around the relative *significance* of different aspects of capability and specific scenarios of hypothetical attacks.

Until the 1960s poor intelligence collection capabilities made estimates of the Soviets' forces difficult, but the principal concern was simple: how many delivery systems could they deploy? Wrangles over the false "bomber gap" and "missile gap" hobbled estimates even after the reconnaissance revolution provided much more reliable data—analysts were

8. Kissinger, *White House Years,* pp. 134–38.

reluctant to overestimate mistakenly again. The significance of subsequent underestimates of Soviet missile deployments has been exaggerated, because by the middle of the 1960s the U.S. administration—which had determined to freeze our own intercontinental ballistic missile (ICBM) numbers—had no intention of preserving the old ratio of forces. Yet McNamara softened the doctrinal shift to emphasis on assured destruction by continuing to proclaim that U.S. nuclear superiority would be preserved. To counter hawks' focus on megatonnage, he relied on comparisons of the number of delivery vehicles. The Soviet buildup in launchers then led him to focus on the favorable ratio in warheads.

Emerging parity and richer intelligence increased politicization of the analytical debate by broadening it. By the mid-1970s some administration leaders' image of CIA analysts as liberal optimists prompted more purposeful politicization with the appointment of the conservative "Team B" to provide an alternate interpretation of Soviet objectives and capabilities. Politicization of estimates of Soviet intent is inevitable, because such judgments are inseparable from fundamental assumptions and evidence is too ambiguous to prove anything without being filtered through ideological prisms. Ironically, however, the exponential growth of evidence on Soviet forces did not ease disputes about capability. Judgments came to focus obsessively on complex calculations and scenarios. Before parity, professional disputes were politically cushioned by the diffuse notion that the United States was still ahead. Acceptance of parity lent greater urgency to anticipating nuances of Soviet advantage. Parity raised the salience of analytical precision, which aggravated professional dissension. Normative anxieties increasingly were played out in manipulations of data: "Beyond a certain point, analysis becomes an end in itself—a substitute for internally agreed-upon goals."[9]

Politicians

When professional threat assessments are clear and consensual, the Executive responds and eventually fixes the problem. This was the case with the 1955 Rand Corporation basing study, which eventually prompted measures to reduce SAC's vulnerability. When judgments are contested, specific calculations provide ammunition for politicians, who use it selectively, and technicalities or scenarios can become surrogates for overall concepts in debate about strategy. In the 1970s theoretical calculations about heavy Soviet missiles eventually yielded a consensus on the near-total vulnerability of U.S. ICBMs. The "window of vulnerability" in turn

9. John Newhouse, *Cold Dawn: The Story of SALT* (New York: Holt, Rinehart and Winston, 1973), p. 8.

became shorthand for the inadequacy of U.S. forces. Considerations that would raise practical questions about the real degree of vulnerability were ignored, and doves' attempts to dampen alarm rested on the sufficiency of assured destruction capabilities. Hawks discredited that view by the end of the decade by emphasizing scenarios of a Soviet counterforce attack and countervalue reserve that could leave U.S. leaders "self-deterred" from retaliation.

Underlying the fixation on ICBM vulnerability was the old problem of extended deterrence,[10] but outside of smoky seminar rooms this was rarely acknowledged. Those most alarmed in Congress promoted the issue in great part out of general anxiety over falling behind the Russians militarily. Greater effort could no longer respectably be promoted by the norm of nuclear superiority; rather, it had to be justified for denial of *Soviet* superiority. Given rough parity, this required resort to abstruse calculations, but these were politically more a pretext than a motive.

More than among professionals or the bureaucracy, threat assessment at the political level involves vague perceptions of trends in Soviet power. Congressional response is seldom calibrated to careful professional analyses of the military balance. In 1961 McNamara did not believe analysis demonstrated a need for as many ICBMs as he planned to request but believed he could not ask Congress for fewer than 950 without getting "murdered."[11] Congressional support is not calibrated to the balance because sophisticated analyses are impenetrable to most politicians and there is always a contending analysis available that appears equally reasonable to the untutored. Disillusionment about Vietnam spilled over into distrust of hawkish assessments of nuclear requirements, and détente made nuclear parity easy to accept. When the Vietnam hangover and détente dissipated, the mood shifted; but the new consensus on ends (more military power) was not matched by clarity about means (programs and doctrine).

The Public

When the chips are down, presidents have seldom been outflanked to the left by Congress. Close to exceptions were the one-vote margin for the anti-ballistic missile (ABM) in 1969 and the dalliance over MX under Reagan. Few major programs or doctrinal concepts have been killed by legislators. The Scoop Jacksons have been more potent constraints than

10. The Soviets would not plausibly strike first unless war in Europe was imminent *and* they believed the U.S. would indeed use strategic forces before accepting defeat. If the U.S. were to use strategic forces, ICBMs would be the most appropriate weapons.

11. Quoted in Desmond Ball, *Politics and Force Levels* (Berkeley: University of California Press, 1980), pp. 86–87.

the Les Aspins. There are similarities at the broader level of public opinion, but the differences are greater. The mass public has usually been strong in support for general military effort. There is no appreciable constituency for "weakness." For example, the hawkish Committee on the Present Danger was a more potent lobby than the dovish Federation of American Scientists when the public debate revolved around the general issue of the balance of military power. On specific strategic doctrine, however, the picture is different. The public has scant grasp of deterrence theory and, if anything, assumes the simple apocalyptic notion of mutual assured destruction. Most of the time—particularly from the mid-1960s to the early 1980s—public attention to the danger of nuclear war has been slight.[12] But when the *implications* of official doctrine are made starkly evident, the only visible reaction of the public occurs toward the left. This happens so ambiguously and infrequently, however, that there is scant evidence that mass opinion influences policy. Official strategy has public opinion to thank mainly for muteness or inability to express opposition in terms stronger than dismay.

In the early 1960s the controlled-response doctrine led to more emphasis on civil defense, but promotion of private shelter construction met underwhelming success. The Limited Test Ban Treaty proved more of a solution to public concern about fallout than did the civil defense program, which soon lapsed. This was less because of public resistance, however, than because McNamara saw it as prohibitively expensive for the protection it would provide, given the ease with which the prospective Soviet offensive buildup would negate defensive measures. When the ABM program was initially planned, the only audible public reaction was protest in some communities where sites were to be constructed. But Nixon gave up ABM in SALT because of technical doubts about its efficacy and for Soviet reciprocity, not because sit-ins would prevent deployment. The antinuclear movement of the early 1980s was energized in part by unease over Reagan's belligerent rhetoric, but also because his loose talk about limited nuclear war simply thrust into wider consciousness the reality of what official doctrine has been for over two decades. The same phenomenon—alarm over programs that simply reflect old doctrinal logic—had occurred on a smaller scale in the 1978 flap over the neutron bomb. Extended deterrence and first use have never been endorsed by referendum.[13] This may be why staunch assurances to NATO

12. Barry Sussman and Robert G. Kaiser, "Survey Finds 3-to-1 Backing for A-Freeze," *Washington Post,* April 29, 1982, sec. A, p. 17; Rob Paarlberg, "Forgetting about the Unthinkable," *Foreign Policy,* no. 10 (Spring 1973), pp. 133–34, 136–37.

13. In the poll showing overwhelming support for a freeze, 52 percent of respondents agreed that it would "make it much easier for the Soviet Union to invade other countries, including those in Europe, without worrying about U.S. retaliation." Sussman and Kaiser, "Survey Finds 3-to-1 Backing for A-Freeze," sec. A, p. 17.

governments about coupling of strategic forces to European defense are not replicated in statements for U.S. domestic consumption.

The nuclear freeze movement represents the broadest manifestation of nuclear dread since Hiroshima. Anxieties were high in the late 1950s and early 1960s, but the cold war consensus was more solid and anti-nuclear activism was confined to specialists or the political fringe. Though dramatically visible (voters in eight out of nine states approved freeze resolutions in the 1982 elections), the movement's significance is tempered by several qualifications.[14] The movement does not reflect a *qualitative* change in mass sentiment but higher consciousness of old fears; it represents visceral frustration—as Congressman Charles Schumer said, "Forget the numbers, forget the throw-weights, forget the abstract concepts"—not a coherent program for deterrent stability; and the mood exists hand-in-hand with continued support for deterrence, distrust of Moscow, and preserving military equality. What is not clear is that this sentiment extends beyond defense of the United States to protecting allies. There is no indication that opposition to reliance on nuclear weapons coincides closely with support for greater spending on conventional forces. Congress responded to freeze proponents, but with so many hedges and loopholes that continuation of new programs could actually be accommodated within resolutions that nominally mandate a freeze. The version the House passed in May 1983 endorsed a freeze if it were mutual, verifiable (including on-site inspection), negotiated in terms compatible with alliance commitments, "consistent with the maintenance of essential equivalence," included air defenses, and excluded submarines as delivery systems.[15] These conditions left enough interpretive latitude for the Executive to avoid a genuine freeze without violating the letter of the resolution. The contradictions, diffuseness, or ambivalence of public mood allowed even a highly hawkish administration to escape decisive constraint.

Allies

The U.S. nuclear dilemma lies in Western Europe, where governments have refused to maximize conventional defense; had they been willing to invest as much of their GNPs in the military as the United States, the need for extended deterrence would have receded. European elites have responded to the dilemma by wishing it away, embracing contradictions

14. The following is based on: Everett Carl Ladd, "The Freeze Framework," *Public Opinion* 5, no. 4 (August/September 1982): 20; "Reagan Arms Control Stance Was Focus of Freeze Debate," *Congressional Quarterly* 40, no.33 (August 14, 1982): 1971, 1973; "Americans Assess the Nuclear Option," *Public Opinion* 5, no. 4 (August/September 1982): 36, 38, 39.

15. "Excerpts from Resolution on Freeze," *The New York Times,* May 6, 1983, sec. B, p. 6.

between declaratory policy and operational strategy, and relying on Soviet prudence.

In 1967 NATO governments finally accepted the flexible response concept with its emphasis on avoiding quick escalation only because of the event that actually made conventional defense less feasible—withdrawal of France from the alliance military structure. In the 1970s European leaders were even more insistent than Americans that nuclear parity be codified through arms control, when their preference for reliance on extended deterrence should have made parity less acceptable to them than to Washington. Three conditions account for this divergence: comparatively less European sensitivity to demands of operational military logic (there has been no European corps of civilian strategic analysts comparable in influence to those in the United States); comparatively greater sensitivity to ways in which diplomatic accommodations could reduce risk of war and with it the salience of military deficiencies (European leaders are generally more professional in the realm of diplomacy, better schooled in international relations, and less mechanistic or moralistic than leaders of some U.S. administrations); and the absence of a realistic alternative (given the limits of domestic tolerance for more ambitious military policies, the price of baldly admitting the nuclear dilemma would be admission of Soviet hegemony). When NATO *did* undertake a response to the shift in the military balance by deciding in 1979 to deploy new long-range theater nuclear forces, the response provoked the most widespread antinuclear movement in postwar history. For European populations as much as the American, the logic of extended deterrence is acceptable only when it is out of mind.

Adversaries

The Soviet Union has driven U.S. nuclear policy. China never figured as a significant influence; its role in adjusting U.S. policy has been as an afterthought (Chinese nuclear capabilities remained so modest that they were a minor included case in U.S. targeting requirements); an excuse (McNamara sought to stanch pressure for a massive ABM program oriented to the Soviets, so he resorted to the "thin" system against China when President Johnson made clear that *some* ABM deployment was politically irresistible); or an opportunity (Nixon used triangular diplomacy to induce Soviet cooperation in SALT). The Soviet actions most visible in determining U.S. nuclear policy were the three Berlin crises, which underlined the need for extended deterrence, and the nuclear buildup over the past two decades. The most dramatic event, the Cuban missile crisis, determined U.S. policy less than it reflected it. Relative U.S. power, especially counterforce capability, was at its apex in 1962. But soon after going to the brink (ostensibly to preserve the imbalance of vulnerability), policy became resigned to growing vulnerability.

Among the U.S. elite another recent influence has been "evidence" about Soviet strategic *doctrine,* used to support preferred policies for the United States. The evidence, however, is mixed. U.S. analysts tend to focus on the elements that coincide with their own ideological orientations and explain away those that do not. Hawks focus on military writings from the 1960s and early 1970s that emphasize victory as the purpose of nuclear strategy; doves find contrary affirmations of mutual assured destruction (MAD) in the same sources. Confronted by more equivocation in recent military writings, or MADish statements by Soviet leaders, hawks dismiss them as temporary recognition of what the Soviets hope is a transient reality, or as disinformation. Confronted by emphasis on counterforce capability, doves deny military control of Soviet policy or dismiss the worrisome doctrine as wishfulness that will always remain frustrated by the U.S. deterrent. Ambiguity of evidence makes it grist for all contenders in U.S. policymaking.[16]

The extent to which Soviet approaches to the nuclear problem differ from American ones has been the crux of recent debate. One variation in Soviet behavior has significant consequences. In the United States, loud assertions of weakness in deterrent capability have been prominent. This is inevitable because democracy requires public awareness of danger to allocate more resources to defense programs, even though such assertions undercut deterrence if the Soviets consider them sincere. In contrast, given no comparable requirement to mobilize support outside the oligarchy, official Soviet declarations often exaggerated their *strength* rather than their vulnerability. This tendency, however, proved even more counterproductive for Moscow, because it fed the inverse U.S. propensity, supporting hawks' arguments in Washington. In 1955, the Soviets deceived U.S. observers of an air parade by having Bison bombers fly

16. For hawkish interpretations, see Richard Pipes, "Why the Soviet Union Thinks It Could Fight and Win a Nuclear War," *Commentary,* vol. 64, no. 1 (July 1977); Fritz W. Ermarth, "Contrasts in American and Soviet Strategic Thought," *International Security,* vol.3, no. 2 (Fall 1978); Donald G. Brennan, "Commentary," *International Security,* vol. 3, no. 3 (Winter 1978/1979); John J. Dziak, *Soviet Perceptions of Military Power: The Interaction of Theory and Practice* (New York: Crane, Russak, 1981), p. 3. For dovish views, see Raymond L. Garthoff, "Mutual Deterrence, Parity and Strategic Arms Limitation in Soviet Policy," in Derek Leebaert, ed., *Soviet Military Thinking* (London: Allen & Unwin, 1981); Robert L. Arnett, "Soviet Attitudes towards Nuclear War: Do They Really Think They Can Win?" *Journal of Strategic Studies,* vol. 2, no. 2 (September 1979). For compromise interpretations that synthesize the contrasting evidence, see Dimitri K. Simes, "Deterrence and Coercion in Soviet Policy," *International Security,* vol. 5, no. 3 (Winter 1980/1981); Dennis Ross, "Rethinking Soviet Strategic Policy: Inputs and Implications," *Journal of Strategic Studies,* vol. 1, no. 1 (May 1978).

over, out of sight, and back again, creating the illusion that they had far more Bisons than they did. This supported revision of U.S. intelligence estimates that provoked the "bomber gap" scare in Congress.[17] When evidence of the overestimate accumulated, it actually reinforced an even more counterproductive Soviet deception—the "missile gap"—since analysts assumed that Moscow was skimping a major bomber program to pour resources into ICBMs. Khrushchev reinforced this reaction with post-Sputnik bluffs, exacerbating American alarm by boasting that Soviet missile power negated U.S. nuclear capabilities.

Soviet assertions of strength continued even during SALT, when such arguments logically supported U.S. demands for a better bargain. During the 1974 Moscow summit a Soviet officer "told his US counterpart that the US was underestimating Soviet missile accuracies."[18] By the 1980s, however, Soviet spokesmen got smarter. U.S. critics' charges of emerging inferiority had become so strident that the SALT II treaty was shelved, and plans for new NATO missile deployments had become vulnerable to dovish opposition in Western Europe. The time was ripe to recognize the benefits of modesty, and Moscow responded with an uncharacteristically sophisticated propaganda campaign (including analyses designed to show how favorable the military balance is to the West),[19] statements affirming the mutuality of assured destruction and denying that Soviet doctrine included a war-fighting nuclear strategy, and a no-first-use pledge.

Lobbying with Western elites became more effective as analysts from research institutes gained wider access. Such contact is desirable, though broader U.S. access to Soviet military elites—especially the General Staff—would be more helpful; civilians influence nuclear policy less in Moscow than in Washington. This was evident in SALT I, when Soviet civilian delegates were not permitted to ask their own government how many missiles the USSR had and relied on U.S. data.[20] If there is genuine Soviet pluralism on strategy as in the West, it has yet to be incorporated in the institutional balance of power; the USSR has no agencies comparable in automony, size, or status to the Arms Control and Disarmament Agency or Office of the Secretary of Defense.

17. When Soviet Defense Minister Zhukov tried to repair the damage by telling U.S. Air Force Chief of Staff Twining that the U.S. estimate was too high, "American officials dismissed this remark as a well-coached leak." John Prados, *The Soviet Estimate: U.S. Intelligence Analysis and Russian Military Strength* (New York: Dial Press, 1982), pp. 42–45.

18. Lawrence Freedman, *U.S. Intelligence and the Soviet Strategic Threat* (Boulder, Colo.: Westview Press, 1977), p. 173.

19. *The Threat to Europe* (Moscow: Progress Publishers, 1981); *Whence the Threat to Peace* (Moscow: Military Publishing House, 1982).

20. Smith, *Doubletalk*, p. 335.

A charitable view is that Soviets see fewer differences in actual doctrine or the distribution of internal influence than U.S. hawks do. Soviet analysts often identify the U.S. first-*use* policy with a war-winning first-*strike* doctrine. This is not necessarily disingenuous: the dilemma underlying extended deterrence makes first use without effective damage limitation extraordinarily risky. Since even many U.S. doves cynically rejected their own government's rationales in Schlesinger's retargeting program or Carter's Presidential Directive 59 as covers for serious counterforce efforts, Soviet suspicions should be expected. And they may see SAC's doctrinal preferences as more relevant than the public rhetoric of transient political leaders. Soviet analysts also offer a variant of American concerns about extended deterrence in Europe—that flexible response and pursuit of even marginal nuclear superiority were meant to liberate U.S. conventional forces for intervention on the periphery (such as in the Dominican Republic and Southeast Asia).[21] If declared doctrine in the West seems incoherent or reckless to Soviet observers (not surprisingly, since it seems so to many U.S. analysts as well), it may be interpreted as disinformation to complicate Soviet planning or as evidence of American unrealism, unpredictability, and irrationality. Neither view is conducive to communication, though the latter one might bolster deterrence.

On balance, however, more access to the West has given Soviet analysts a more realistic view of the genuine fears about Soviet power and the dynamics of political debate in Washington and Europe. This cuts two ways. The optimistic interpretation is that it enhances the influence of "doves" in the Soviet policy process and will make Moscow more reasonable. The pessimistic interpretation is that greater understanding has simply strengthened Moscow's hand for intervening in the development of Western policy, making better use of sharp instruments and less of the blunt ones. Now more confident of their own deterrent power, and aware of leverage that opposition movements could have in the West, the Soviets can afford to poor-mouth their military might in hopes of crippling transatlantic consensus-building.

UNILATERAL SOLUTIONS

The major shift in the strategic equation was the gradual and grudging U.S. acceptance of the loss of nuclear superiority. Cumulative Soviet

---

21. Henry A. Trofimenko, "Counterforce: Illusion of a Panacea," *International Security* 5, no. 4 (Spring 1981): 35–36; William D. Jackson, "Soviet Images of the U.S. as a Nuclear Adversary, 1969–1979," *World Politics* 33, no. 4 (July 1981): 615–16. Moscow's attitude toward limited options is "that one does not hit a king unless one is determined to kill him." Benjamin S. Lambeth, *Selective Nuclear Options in American and Soviet Strategic Policy*, R-2034-DDRE (Santa Monica, Calif.: The Rand Corporation, December 1976), p. 42.

effort made maintenance of the old U.S. margin exponentially more expensive, and bearing the cost would not have eliminated the dilemma of extended deterrence (it became contentious as early as the late 1950s, well before parity) as long as Moscow could retain a capacity to inflict unacceptable damage. Administrations have tried to resolve the dilemma (by conventional buildup), temper it (by keeping nuclear superiority), or adapt to it (through détente), but none of the attempts succeeded for more than a few years.

Building Up Force Levels

The simplest way to deal with military challenges is to overwhelm them by increasing capabilities in gross form—numbers of nuclear delivery systems and conventional force manpower. This occurred in the early 1950s and early 1960s. In both cases the solution proved ephemeral, as fiscal pressures, Soviet military development, and diversion to other foreign policy issues prevented the solution from being sustained. After the Korean War broke out, defense expenditures climbed precipitously, the U.S. atomic stockpile grew, and NATO undertook a buildup for serious conventional defense. At the February 1952 Lisbon meeting, the alliance settled on a goal of ninety divisions to be met by 1954—the most ambitious of postwar benchmarks for conventional deterrence. The impracticality of fulfilling it crippled subsequent commitment to conventional deterrence. By the time the date for the ninety divisions arrived, the Eisenhower administration had shifted to the massive retaliation strategy as the economical solution for the "long haul." Vast nuclear superiority was the underpinning, and conventional imbalance was uncontested. The long haul proved short. By 1955, Soviet capability to strike the continental United States was recognized and the mutuality of nuclear deterrence began to emerge. In the latter part of the 1950s alarm over the prospect of Soviet superiority in new ballistic missiles aggravated debate. Yet Eisenhower continued to reduce conventional forces and adopted a policy of nuclear sufficiency: while not matching the Soviets in all categories of delivery systems, the diverse U.S. force structure would continue to exceed the USSR's in destructive capacity. Nuclear superiority, though reduced, would continue to compensate for conventional inferiority. Critics challenged the credibility of massive retaliation without massive superiority.

Kennedy's answer was to build up across the board. Flexible response was backed not only by greater conventional forces but by dramatic nuclear expansion. One thousand Minuteman ICBMs were programmed, even after it became evident that the "missile gap" was actually reversed. Procurement of bombers and submarine-launched ballistic missiles

(SLBMs) also expanded. For a brief period U.S. superiority was so over-whelming that it approached a disarming first-strike capability, but by the mid-1960s Soviet missiles had become so numerous and hardened that Moscow's deterrent was secured. Eisenhower's fiscal philosophy did not inhibit the Johnson administration from maintaining the balance of ca-pabilities that Kennedy had achieved, but three other pressures did: di-version of funds from military investment to operations in Southeast Asia; expansion of budgets for domestic programs; and the conviction that no level of spending could prevent the Soviets from keeping their capability to inflict unacceptable damage on the United States. Through the 1970s the option of building conventional force levels up to parity in Europe was foreclosed by economic and political constraints, while the option of building up intercontinental nuclear force levels was foreclosed by SALT (though qualitative improvements proceeded). Reagan launched a buildup as ambitious as Kennedy's, but not likely to resolve strategic dilemmas even as briefly as in the 1960s. The conventional buildup is concentrated in the navy, which cannot prevent the Soviet army from overrunning Europe. The planned nuclear buildup involves modernization, not force levels, and is obstructed by vulnerabilities aris-ing from past attempts to substitute technical innovations for expanded force levels.

Technological Fixes and Frustrations

U.S. delivery system force levels stabilized with the buildup of the early 1960s. Thereafter improvements came mainly from qualitative moderni-zation. Some innovations have been unambiguously beneficial—most no-tably, ballistic missile submarines. The most significant innovation since establishment of the triad has been multiple independently targetable reentry vehicles (MIRVs). This case in contrast exemplifies the problem of integrating technology with politics, strategy, and diplomacy. Condi-tions made exploitation of the technological option sensible at the point that it become possible, investments in the option mortgaged adaptability of policy to the sunk costs, and by the time the option matured, changed conditions made it counterproductive. A cure evolved into a curse.

In the 1960s bombers were considered vulnerable while ICBMs were not, so U.S. force structure shifted in the latter direction. When MIRVs were conceived later in the decade, they offered a solution for coping with the Soviet buildup while keeping U.S. force levels stable (since the same number of missiles could carry more warheads). By the early 1980s *Soviet* exploitation of MIRVs had turned the tables and rendered the U.S. ICBM force vulnerable (because a small number of Soviet missiles could then target the entire U.S. force). One of the rationales for MIRV had also been to negate a prospective Soviet ABM system. The 1972 treaty obviated this requirement. But even before Reagan's 1983 "Star Wars" speech, inability to solve the problem of ICBM vulnerability without some active defense had raised pressures to revise the ABM treaty, thus throwing into doubt the only achievement of SALT still legally in force.

Considering how destabilizing MIRVs became, the decision to develop them is striking because there was so little opposition. In the early research and development (R & D) phase the only doubts were in the air force, while civilian analysts embraced the innovation as a way to limit spending.[22] "MIRV was put to the service of restraint and became a strong bureaucratic instrument for discouraging other new systems and higher numbers of systems."[23] Lack of dispute within the Executive, in turn, gave Congress no incentive to focus on MIRV. As the system neared deployment in 1969, Senator Brooke's suggestion for a moratorium was swamped by his colleagues' clamor against ABM. The possibility of a MIRV ban was considered in SALT, but not pursued seriously by either side.[24] (In part, this was because of doubts that the number of warheads on a missile could be verified. This concern was later resolved by the standard that the maximum number of MIRVs *tested* on any missile would be the assumed loading for all such missiles. But by the time that standard was accepted, MIRVs were already rampant.)

The result (MIRV without ABM) would have made strategic sense only if the Russians lacked MIRVs to threaten U.S. ICBMs, or the United States rested deterrence solely on assured destruction capability (which could be retained without ICBMs). Neither is the case. But exploiting superior technology had always been an American value, and when MIRV was developed, the spectre of ICBM vulnerability seemed distant. The contradiction between the original appeal of MIRV and its eventual destabilizing effect might have been averted if another technological fix—a survivable undefended basing mode for the MX—had become available. The alternate solution (defense against MIRVs by ABM) is inhibited by a vicious circle. Paying the political and financial prices of abandoning the treaty and investing in a massive new system require confidence that it would be effective; confidence comes from ample testing; and ABM testing is constrained by the treaty. Thus we cannot be sure the treaty is worth giving up without first violating it.

22. Ted Greenwood, *Making the MIRV: A Study of Defense Decision Making* (Cambridge, Mass.: Ballinger, 1975), pp. 37–43, 50.

23. Newhouse, *Cold Dawn,* p. 76. McNamara used MIRV as an argument not only for holding offensive force size level, but also for not wasting money on ABM. Thomas W. Wolfe, *The SALT Experience* (Cambridge, Mass.: Ballinger, 1979), pp. 6–7.

24. Graham T. Allison et al., "The Management of Defense and Arms Control Issues," vol. 4 of Commission on the Organization of the Government for the Conduct of Foreign Policy, *Appendices* (Washington, D.C.: U.S. Government Printing Office, June 1975), p. 341; Greenwood, *Making the MIRV,* pp. 14–15; Smith, *Doubletalk,* pp. 154–78.

Operational Doctrine

Before concern with Soviet deterrent power gelled, rationales behind U.S. targeting plans were not controversial. In the 1940s the low number of bombs in the U.S. stockpile precluded wasting many of them against anything but economic targets. In the 1950s targeting plans were simple (because they rested on one all-out strike against *both* civil and military targets in the Warsaw Pact countries and China) and not widely debated (because they were the preserve of the air force and navy). Since 1960, however, intricacies of operational doctrine have been integral to strategic debate.

To back up flexible response, the Kennedy administration implemented theories spawned in the Rand Corporation for discrimination between countervalue and counterforce strikes. A "no cities" counterforce option was the core of the revision. But as the number and survivability of Soviet missiles grew, McNamara shifted to emphasis on assured destruction as the standard for adequacy of U.S. forces. Yet ever since, U.S. leaders have sought to maintain options for selective use of nuclear forces, against military as well as civilian targets, in an attempt to straddle the dilemma of extended deterrence. Doctrinal evolution has confused U.S. debate and unsettled alliance relations as much as it has bolstered deterrence. The evolution confused U.S. politicians because, like suspicious Soviet observers, they found it hard to distinguish between limited counterforce options and pursuit of a first-strike capability. McNamara's rhetorical emphasis on the stark principle of assured destruction, and the abstruseness of rationales for limited options, led nonspecialists to see doctrinal choice in dichotomous terms. Among specialists, doves criticized any counterforce as destabilizing and hawks criticized limited options as anemic. Moreover, for years the distinctions between different types or degrees of counterforce were never explained clearly.[25] The air force aspired to full first-strike capability and had to be beaten down by McNamara, who worried about how the Soviets would read U.S. ambitions. When Schlesinger tried to improve limited options in the mid-1970s, the public debate over what were really modest adjustments generated far more heat than light. Allied governments were uneasy because pursuit of limited options underlined the tentativeness of U.S. commitment to escalation in conventional war: better for deterrence

25. In 1969, when Air Force Chief of Staff Ryan justified MIRV for its capability against hard targets, Senator Brooke complained to President Nixon, who affirmed that the administration did not have a "hard-target-kill" program. When Ryan repeated his rationale, Secretary of Defense Laird reaffirmed that there was no first-strike policy but that Ryan was referring to second-strike counterforce—at that time a bizarre notion to nonspecialists. Ronald L. Tammen, *MIRV and the Arms Race* (New York: Praeger, 1973), pp. 117–18.

that the dilemma be denied than publicized. Soviets were disturbed for the opposite reason—that the doctrine reflected U.S. unwillingness to accept the equality enforced by change in the correlation of forces.[26]

Another problem is the inverse relationship between urgency of doctrinal adaptation and availability of appropriate forces. The need for adjustment becomes more insistent as relative Soviet power grows, but that growth threatens the U.S. forces appropriate for doctrinal change. Pursuit of limited options dragged in the 1960s, when U.S. forces remained largely invulnerable and erosion of superiority was gradual. Attention to flexibility became most pressing when vulnerability appeared to increase dramatically. As a result, the Carter "countervailing strategy" was proclaimed but was a goal more than a reality. The most applicable weapons—fast, accurate ICBMs with more secure command communications than other elements of the triad—were precisely those whose vulnerability had provoked the fascination with using doctrine to compensate for deficiencies in force structure. The disjunction of adjustments in doctrine and structure by the 1980s was reflected in the irony that the NATO theater nuclear modernization program was "a set of weapons without a corresponding strategy," while "the countervailing strategy [for intercontinental forces] is one without a corresponding set of weapons."[27]

Unilateral initiatives are necessary for maintaining equilibrium and in earlier years were sufficient. Competing in gross quantities of weaponry proved economically and diplomatically difficult. Technical sophistications proved to be brief solutions, as they bred their own obsolescence, undercut themselves with unforeseen consequences, provoked controversy about strategic purpose, or reached fruition after the conditions motivating them at the time of conception had changed. Increased difficulty of funding or inventing means to neutralize the progress of Soviet power lent increasing weight to cooperative alternatives to unregulated competition.

NEGOTIATED SOLUTIONS

During the U.S. nuclear monopoly, arms control proposals were visionary (the Baruch Plan for an international authority). During the period of U.S. superiority, proposals were hardly more practical (Eisenhower's "Open Skies," Johnson's "freeze" initiative) because Moscow would not accept inequality. During rough parity in the 1970s, arms control was most feasible and successful. But by the 1980s, with images of U.S. in-

26. Jackson, "Soviet Images of the U.S. as Nuclear Adversary," pp. 624–26, 631–32, 637.

27. Christopher Makins, "TNF Modernization and 'Countervailing Strategy,'" *Survival* 23, no. 4 (July/August 1981): 157.

feriority ascendant, U.S. proposals were again impractical, since they sought reductions that would require Moscow to sacrifice more than Washington and were backed by leverage of dubious credibility—the threat of a Western nuclear buildup that would redress the balance. The window of opportunity shrank as the window of vulnerability opened. The fortunes of negotiated accommodation have been hostage to unsynchronized evolutions of the military balance, the pace of negotiation, and domestic constraints.

Prerequisites and Obstacles

Three developments that facilitated arms control in the early 1970s bedeviled it by the end of the decade. First was confidence in intelligence surveillance, which relaxed U.S. demands for on-site inspection. When satellite reconnaissance was complemented by high missile accuracy, however, verification became synonymous with improved counterforce targeting, and monitoring capability became as much a destabilizing problem as a stabilizing solution. Second was consensus on parity and détente, which provided the incentive for bargaining. But when rough parity with a tilt in favor of the United States turned into rough parity with an apparent tilt in favor of the USSR,[28] the roughness became politically as destabilizing as it had been facilitating. The Soviet view is that change in the global correlation of forces had forced Washington to realistic acceptance of parity and a détente (apparently in Moscow's eyes) akin to condominium. The predominant American impression had been that détente was compatible with containment. Continued change in the correlation of forces therefore eroded détente and buttressed U.S. hawks' arguments about the perils of parity. Third was a simple and manageable currency of negotiation: the number of strategic launchers. After agreement against ABMs, the agreement on offensive limitations was eased by temporary U.S. confidence in qualitative advantages that offset Soviet advantages in missile payload. Warnings from hawks like Senator Jackson that the Soviets would close the qualitative gap and exploit their edge in numbers and size of ICBMs could be contained by hopes that negotiation would avert the problem or that availability of a new missile by the late 1970s could close a throw-weight gap. Neither happened. Dealing with the thornier qualitative disparities underlying an equal level of launchers drew out

28. In 1970 the U.S. had an advantage in all principal static indices that dominate public debate (delivery vehicles, warheads, throw-weight, equivalent megatonnage) except for megatonnage; in 1980 the Soviet Union led in all but warheads. Detailed analyses can make the situation look better or worse, depending on which variables and scenarios are included. For an assessment that indicates U.S. advantage, see Raymond Garthoff, *Perspectives on the Strategic Balance* (Washington, D.C.: Brookings Institution, 1983) pp. 26–31.

SALT II (which took twice as long to negotiate as SALT I), and inability to field the MX left critics armed with calculations demonstrating U.S. counterforce inferiority.

Shifting technologies helped codify parity and technical stability early in the 1970s, but undermined both by the 1980s. Shifting fortunes of the overall global relationship allowed magnanimity in SALT I but revived linkage by the time SALT II was complete—when Washington had less leverage to enforce linkage. Agreement based on simple measures of the balance forced subsequent wrangling over complexities, which in turn pushed consensus on terms of accommodation farther away.

Avenues of Approach

Arms control has three axiomatic goals. First is to save money by slowing or reducing competitive deployments. The ABM treaty may have done this, but it is unclear whether either side would have spent more on offensive arms without SALT than with it. (Indeed, SALT treaties were sold by assuring critics that modernization would proceed, to compensate for weaknesses embraced in the agreements.) Second is to limit the destructiveness of war if deterrence fails. The ABM treaty, combined with failure to achieve radical reductions in offensive forces, negated this objective. (Indeed, preservation of assured destruction capabilities was the cornerstone of SALT). Third is to reinforce strategic stability. This is the most difficult result to gauge, largely because negotiations were conducted in terms of concrete technical inputs (weaponry) without consensus over desired conceptual outputs (the structure of security or stability). Doing otherwise is complicated by three asymmetries.

First is strategic geography. Washington could not accept Moscow's concept of "equal security" (based on vulnerability of the superpowers' homelands, not of the aggregate alliances) because the formulation would imply U.S. decoupling from NATO. The Russians grudgingly gave up insisting that SALT I include U.S. forward-based systems (FBS) in Europe (which could hit Soviet territory) but not Soviet theater systems (which could not hit the continental U.S.). But in SALT II Moscow fastened on the protocol limiting Western cruise missiles in Europe. When this provoked anxiety in NATO, and the Carter administration neutered the protocol with firm plans for such deployments after its expiration, Moscow saw this as circumvention of treaty limits.

Second is organizational sociology. U.S. strategic forces grew out of the air force and an R&D tradition emphasizing exploitation of technological sophistication. Soviet strategic forces grew out of army artillery and a need to compensate for technological lags with missiles of large payload. As a result, the force structure which U.S. negotiators had to bargain with was heavy on bombers and light on land-based missiles, while the Soviet structure was the reverse.

Third is deterrent philosophy. Soviet negotiators were less concerned with deterrence in terms of U.S. theories of technical stability, saw the danger of war as related to political tension more than force configuration, and viewed stability in terms of the aggregate size of forces. Thus they focused on *new* U.S. systems as destabilizing, refusing to differentiate between them according to which enhance survivability without increasing first-strike capability.[29] U.S. canons of stability impute innocence to bombers and SLBMs (too slow or inaccurate for preemptive counterforce), which together constitute most of the U.S. force—and evil to ICBMs (the bulk of the Soviet force). These canons did not evolve until *after* the triad was established. (Indeed, a quarter-century ago bombers were considered better for counterforce and a first strike than were ICBMs).[30] Thus Soviet conceptual resistance may be reinforced by suspicion that the U.S. formulation is a rationalization for investments in which Washington happens to have high sunk costs, and a ploy to force expensive changes in Soviet force structure. As U.S. proposals justified in terms of stability became more demanding (asking for asymmetrical reductions in 1977 and 1982), the Soviets countered emphasis on equal results in output with emphasis on equal concessions on inputs. The U.S. stability standard is intellectually correct but not diplomatically compelling.

Scope, Pace, and Mode of Bargaining

The principal arms control agreement before parity (the Limited Test Ban Treaty) succeeded because it was simple and symmetrical. Success of SALT I followed from wider but still simple terms of reference, ascendancy of moderates in the strategic debate, and a residue of U.S. technical advantage. As these conditions changed, the urgency and speed of negotiations became disjoined. Anxieties about adversary advantages led to demands for more inclusiveness. In 1974 Moscow accepted exclusion of forward-based systems from negotiation in exchange for U.S. dropping of demands for reductions in heavy ICBMs,[31] but the Vladivostok accord was derailed by disputes about whether Soviet Backfire bombers or U.S.

---

29. Robert Legvold, "Strategic 'Doctrine' and SALT: Soviet and American Views," *Survival* 21, no. 1 (January/February 1979): 12–13; Jack L. Snyder, *The Soviet Strategic Culture: Implications for Limited Nuclear Operations*, R-2154-AF (Santa Monica, Calif.: The Rand Corporation, September 1977), p. 18; Smith, *Doubletalk*, p. 86.

30. Lawrence Freedman, *The Evolution of Nuclear Strategy* (New York: St. Martin's Press, 1981), pp. 168–69.

31. Strobe Talbott, *Endgame: The Inside Story of SALT II* (New York: Harper & Row, 1979), p. 33.

air-launched cruise missiles would count as strategic delivery systems. SALT II dragged on for almost five more years. By then the failure to reduce heavy Soviet ICBMs opened the window of vulnerability, which helped kill the treaty. The United States solved some anxieties by planning theater missile deployments, but this reopened the FBS issue for the Soviets. The result by the time of the Reagan administration was expansion of negotiations—intermediate-range nuclear force (INF) talks parallel to strategic arms reduction talks (START)—but the two sides' positions were such that dramatic rather than marginal compromises would be required for agreement. Simplicity and momentum had given way to overload and immobilism.

Closure of SALT I was also facilitated by fast-and-loose diplomacy. Clandestine "back-channel" contacts between Kissinger and Soviet leaders developed behind the scenes of the formal talks. This mode of operation was criticized by the professional negotiators as being reckless, disruptive, and the cause of careless concessions. Questionable as the back-channel method may have been, the one thing that may be said for it is that it prodded movement. Cutting a Gordian knot leaves messy and perhaps dangerous loose ends; unraveling it is safer but may be overtaken by events. The subsequent process was more careful and orderly but interminable. By the time SALT II was concluded, Soviet activism in the Third World and extraneous events like discovery of a Soviet brigade in Cuba had eroded the consensus behind the enterprise and rendered *any* feasible agreement suspect.

The contribution of secrecy to the earlier phase contrasted with the increasingly public nature of negotiation. In March 1977 Carter announced the initial U.S. offer *and* the fallback position before talks commenced. The Reagan administration announced U.S. proposals for both START and INF in advance. In both cases the motive was to secure domestic support. (The Russians, probably aiming at Western Europe, also revealed their proposals.) The ultimate effect, however, is the reverse. Open posturing anoints an ambitious aim and makes inevitable compromise appear a retreat. By making positions harder to modify, publicity contradicts the essence of negotiation.

Another problem that has complicated and extended negotiations is the instability of U.S. politics and leadership. Soviet leadership may be calcified but more consistent. For almost a decade and a half after the first stirrings of SALT there was one General Secretary in charge in the USSR while *five* American presidents passed through office. The Soviet orientation remained the same: to establish mutual constraints that would not drastically alter force levels already programmed. As negotiations became longer and more controversial, however, U.S. approaches became erratic. The last two presidents (who both came into office with extremely

ambitious aims and no experience in foreign policy) radicalized the negotiations by shelving previous accords and tabling new proposals for significant reductions. Carter's initiative outraged the Soviets, momentum was
lost, and the delay proved fatal to SALT II. Moscow reacted more cautiously to Reagan's even more radical proposals, but breakthrough still
depended on the possibility of an unprecedented degree of retreat by one
side or the other.

Political-Military Incongruities

Arms control can secure a satisfactory military balance at least feasible
cost by constraining the opponent's forces, and it can symbolize the potential for peace. Logically the former aim should take precedence, because
military terms are the only palpable regulations embodied in a treaty,
superpower amity is subjective and fluid, and importance of the military
balance varies inversely with the prospects for peace. In the United States,
however, practice diverges from logic. Since SALT began, domestic support for treaties has been highest when the balance was most favorable
and lowest when it was becoming most dangerous. Psychologically understandable and politically inevitable, this trend was strategically counterproductive because there was no alternative to fix the deteriorating
balance: during the term of the abortive SALT II treaty, none of the new
weapons that the United States could realistically deploy to improve the
balance were foreclosed by the treaty, while it limited the most worrisome
Soviet option (putting more than ten warheads on heavy ICBMs) and
required Moscow to dismantle 10 percent of its launchers. Yet those most
worried about the balance and Soviet intent were those most opposed to
the treaty. Senate hearings produced the bizarre spectacle of Henry Kissinger and the Joint Chiefs of Staff saying they would be reluctant to
endorse the treaty unless future U.S. nuclear programs were assured. In
terms of strategic logic, if new programs were not guaranteed, treaty
restraints on the Soviet side of the equation would be even *more* necessary.

The logic for accepting the treaty was recognized more than it was
admitted (Reagan rejected SALT II but accepted informal mutual obser-
vance of its limits), because hawks recognized that in the political arena
the symbolic aura of arms control agreements predominates, so ratification fuels opposition to military programs. The intuitive popular feeling
is that arms control means less need for more or better arms. Prompt
modernization is harder to sell because the threat is harder to sell. After
SALT I several major programs were canceled (B-1) or delayed (MX,
Trident). SALT did not cause the braking (it was in part a response to
constraints on arms competition already imposed by the public mood
poisoned by Vietnam), but it was seen by hawks as reinforcing the lull in

concern with growing Soviet power. But to secure support for a buildup, the threat has to be painted in lurid colors; which in turn discredits the peace-and-coexistence rationale for a treaty. In the end, cold calculations about effects on the military balance seem to dominate the priorities of neither hawks nor doves. In the early 1970s, with opposition doves ascendant, pressure for lower military spending and hopes for détente took precedence over refined assessments of trends in the balance. By the late 1970s, hysteria had replaced complacency as the opposition center of gravity, but ascendant hawks subordinated near-term military concerns (the balance as affected by the treaty) to securing support for longer-term programs. At the beginning of the 1960s, a massive U.S. nuclear buildup was undertaken when it was least urgent in terms of the nuclear balance; and at the beginning of the 1980s, treaty restraints were rejected when they were most needed to maintain balance. Both decisions were arguably wise, given the relationship between military and political trends, but only because those trends were disjoined in practice rather than integrated as they should be in principle.

BETWEEN COHERENCE AND CHAOS

Stepping back from a litany of inconsistencies, the big picture does not look so bad. Peace in Europe has endured, more because of nuclear weapons than despite them. The only superpower that may yet have been cowed by nuclear threats in crises was not the United States but our adversary.[32] The shift of the relative military balance in favor of Moscow may be less significant than the absolute increases in U.S. striking power available for deterrence. SALT agreements, though not legally in force, are still being observed. Proliferation has occurred much more slowly than most expected, and to the enemies of the USSR rather than those of NATO. (And on the issue of preventing proliferation U.S. and Soviet interests coincide, and the superpowers have cooperated efficiently to that end, fostering the Nonproliferation Treaty and restricting supplies of sensitive equipment to third countries.) Operational doctrines designed to straddle the dilemma of extended deterrence have no demonstrable public support when their content is thrust into view, but public opinion has usually been permissive. Nuclear forces are comparatively cheap, claiming only 10 to 20 percent of defense budgets. When program paralysis occurs (as with the MX), it is due more to problems of physics than to policymaking. Evading contradictions is part of the normal business of politics and has been done no less adeptly on nuclear matters than in any other area of policy. Indeed, evasion has been more functional

32. Betts, "Elusive Equivalence," pp. 113–16.

than not, since forced clarity would do more to wreck alliance cohesion and public support than to improve deterrence. At these levels of generality, continuity and stability appear quite remarkable.

Old Tensions on a New Threshold?

Most continuities eventually end. Might we now be on the brink of major departures? The current Soviet succession period coincides with economic constriction. The U.S. Executive, however, appears insensitive to the extent to which Soviet administrative superiority (political capacity to milk the civilian economy for military power) can compensate for Western economic superiority. Conditions for negotiated accommodation may be simultaneously opportune militarily and economically for both sides but politically most difficult to grasp. Tensions between Washington and NATO capitals have ballooned; disputes over military policy are compounded by differences over the fundamental fabric of relations with Moscow. In contrast to past peaks of discord, the issue is less whether Washington is dependable for defense than whether it is too dangerously dependable. And Soviet diplomacy has never before been as skillful in playing to NATO disarray. The U.S. antinuclear movement is broader and more energetic than ever before (now even including Catholic bishops). Congressional opposition to some major nuclear modernization programs has intensified.

Benign continuities may be preserved by muddling through, but those trying to manage the muddle need clearer recognition of how evolving conditions, constituencies, and concepts interact. The conditions underlying dissension are the shifting military balance, incomplete Western reconciliation to the loss of nuclear superiority, and tenuousness of détente. None of the three basic views of these issues can sustain a consensus. Conservatives (Nixon and Kissinger) who viewed parity as undesirable but inevitable, because domestic politics would not sustain an arms race, aimed to get the best negotiated deal possible but were squeezed by groups on left and right. Liberals (Vance and Warnke) who considered parity inevitable and desirable as a stabilizing condition came to power just as the domestic mood turned in the opposite direction. Hawks (Reaganites) who considered parity neither desirable nor inevitable capitalized on this shift, but undertook domestic economic policies and belligerent diplomatic initiatives bound to frustrate attempts to reverse it.

The obstacles to policy coherence are largely inherent in: the strategic dilemma; objective differences between U.S., allied, and Soviet interests; the difficulty of sustaining support for resolving the dilemma through unilateral military solutions; and the difficulty of sustaining technological fixes to the military balance when the political climate does support more effort. Real solutions can only, if ever, come from basic and not readily manageable shifts in political mood, macroeconomic performance, and technological opportunity. Realistic policy management should aim to chip away at the obstacles while obfuscating the inherent contradictions.

Managing Strategic Ambivalence

Improvements in process are often misidentified with structural change in bureaucracies. The problems in both the U.S. government and NATO, however, are more constitutional than organizational. Most reorganizations change little and create as many problems as they solve. A few measures—structural, procedural, or simply hortatory—could help at the margins:

Threat estimates. The primary need is more objective net assessment. With temporary and controversial exceptions, National Intelligence Estimates—theoretically the most important intelligence products—have been enjoined from evaluating Soviet capabilities in relative terms—that is, in comparison with U.S. capabilities. Net assessment has been dominated by military agencies which have a conflict of interest (justifying defense programs). The CIA should not have sole responsibility for net assessment but should be the senior partner in the interagency process, and the umpire should be from the NSC staff, not the Pentagon. Given uncertainties in nuclear exchange calculations, rigorous net assessment must present a range of alternatives from best to worst. If either extreme is leaked, the full range should be revealed lest the leak bias political debate. Sanitized versions of the assessments should be emphasized in negotiations. If the Soviets challenge the data, the United States should demand reciprocal revelation of Soviet calculations and methodology. This may not work but is necessary if U.S. concepts of technical stability are to mold the contours of a treaty.

Coordinating military planning and arms control. Doves and hawks must confront two political facts: that treaties are not salable unless they appear to preserve military equality, and that unilateral efforts sufficient to substitute for treaty restraints on Soviet forces are not long sustainable. Because doves' preferences cost less money, there is no economic discipline that can be invoked to constrain them, but there is for the hawks. For more coherent policy, professional debate has to be forced away from the false polarities of reliance on arms control or military investment, reversing the political dynamics that encourage partisans to exaggerate arguments. One way to do this is to abandon the strategic fiction (prominent under Kennedy and Reagan) that defense investment will be determined by adding up needed capabilities according to the standard of how much is enough, and accept the political reality (admitted by Eisenhower and

Nixon) that allocations will be made within a budget limited arbitrarily by vague notions of how little is enough. This could nudge internal debate from the danger of specific treaty constraints on U.S. power toward the danger of lack of constraints on Soviet power. In public, leaders should stress that a secure military balance must take precedence over economization, but in private they should stress the consequences of underestimating Moscow's commitment to the same principle.

Bite the bullet or avoid gratuitous frankness. A democratic approach to nuclear policy entails risk to long-standing U.S. commitments. The strategic dilemmas are insoluble and at best malleable. Oversell of the Soviet nuclear threat necessary to mobilize public support for defense spending in the short term soon becomes counterproductive. To refute the adequacy of simple assured destruction capabilities, such arguments ultimately draw attention to the dilemma of extended deterrence. European allies then become alarmed that Washington has doubts about the commitment, or mass publics become alarmed that the commitment is all too real. The result is either confusion or backpedaling in U.S. policy, either of which complicates signals to Moscow. The virtuous alternative is to educate U.S. and European publics by explaining much more clearly why there are only three logical alternatives: strong conventional defense (requiring more domestic sacrifice); continued reliance on the threat of nuclear first use (raising the risk of apocalypse if Soviet tanks roll into Germany); or forswearing credible deterrence (which might lead to U.S. disengagement and Soviet hegemony in Europe). The danger would be that more information would not make publics less selfish or frightened, but make them see the third alternative as less unpalatable than the first two; the more hopeful gamble would be that once they understood the dilemma, stable support for one or both of the first two options would result. Minimizing public discord and diplomatic discoordination, however, requires more stability in political consensus, leadership, and economic growth than has obtained for years. Longer presidential tenure, partisan identification of Congress with the Executive, more hierarchical organization of legislative activity, allies more submissive to Washington's will, and a less exacting tradeoff between guns and butter would help, but this amounts to nostalgia for the good old days. If public education is not the solution, administrations should avoid maladroit statements about the rationales for limited nuclear options.

Semantic finesse. If a dilemma must be managed rather than resolved, the trick is to have a policy that is all things to all men. This requires military suboptimization, doctrinal compromise, and reassurance of opposed constituencies—a tall order to be filled without an un-American amount of dissimulation. Declarations can help bridge the gaps by orchestrating emphasis. To pursue a stable nuclear balance without alarming

Western doves or Soviet negotiators, the rationale for equal counterforce capabilities should be larded with emphasis on the impossibility of disarming either side's countervalue reserve forces. The Carter administration integrated these concerns intellectually in the "countervailing strategy" but faltered in the public presentation of it and accepted a SALT II treaty that did not guarantee the desired U.S. options. Reagan integrated the rationale with his arms control proposals and mastered the presentation to the Western public (though his loose talk about nuclear war vitiated the public-relations gains from the "zero solution" initiative), but at the price of unnegotiable proposals. To preserve alliance cohesion while minimizing Soviet propaganda gains, Washington should mount a counteroffensive based on a *conditional* no-first-use pledge—a semantic nuance obvious to specialists but not to mass opinion. The president should emphasize that we *do* have a no-first-use doctrine, noting only parenthetically the exception of a Soviet invasion of allied territory and failure of conventional defense. This might then be used to induce more commitment to conventional defense, exploiting antinuclear movements' reaction to the high profile of extended deterrent doctrine in order to reduce elite opposition to military initiatives to soften the strategic dilemma.

The net effect of nuclear weapons on the U.S.–Soviet relationship has been both stabilizing and unsettling. They have reduced the danger of war through miscalculation because the apocalyptic consequences make risk-taking less thinkable. But because the consequences are so awesome, maintaining stability is so vital, and technology does not stand still, neither side can long remain satisfied with the quality of its deterrent. Keeping the nuclear spectre at bay turns out to mean continuing competition in exploiting technology and seeking advantage from negotiation. Shifting political fortunes intrude further to complicate the military relationship. Many critics yearn for a static equilibrium, some neat combination of force structures and diplomatic arrangements to anchor stability across the board. But the complexity of the relationship and the endurance of conflicts of interest mean that dynamic equilibrium is the only feasible hope.

Domestic politics in the United States and Europe have affected nuclear policy in three conflicting ways. First, because most of the time we do not really believe the danger of armed conflict with the USSR is very high, it is easy to allow economic constraints to supersede defense investments (stronger conventional forces) that would reduce reliance on nuclear weapons. Second, when the possibility of war does come to seem less remote, the consequences of nuclear reliance provoke confusion, anxiety, and attempts to find a way out of the bind. But because threat perceptions begin to ebb as costs of military effort flow, there is a tendency to slide back and forth between the horns of the dilemma. Congressional and public support for military competition with Moscow waxed after Eisenhower's defense-spending retrenchment as it has waned after Reagan's buildup pinched the economy. Frustration recurs because of the idealistic instinct that some finite and enduring configuration of stability exists, if only it can be found and fixed.

The most helpful change in the U.S. approach may thus be least manageable: fostering broader recognition that there is no nuclear teleology, no grail of stability that is both permanent and static, no plateau on which nuclear forces and doctrine can be brought to eternal rest—only the possibility of easing Sisyphus's trips up and down the hill, confining rather than resolving the incongruities that emerge from theoretical, technological, political, and diplomatic interactions. Much of the problem in managing the nuclear relationship has been the friction between ambitious American hopes for either superiority or radical arms control, Soviet desire for more compartmentalized restraints, and West European distaste for grappling with doctrinal difficulties. If U.S. doves and hawks can be dragged closer to the center and accept that in an era of tenuous parity, competitive and cooperative solutions to military stability can only be complements rather than alternatives, it will be easier to deal with both allies and adversaries.

6
Political Crises

ALEXANDER L. GEORGE

Competition for power and influence has always been inherent in the "anarchic" system of sovereign states. In the European balance-of-power system of the nineteenth century, competition was regulated and moderated by a shared commitment on the part of the great powers to maintain that system, by the cultural homogeneity of their elites, and by various norms and practices for moderating rivalry and preserving the balance. It will be useful to recall the diplomatic options employed by the great powers from time to time to regulate their global rivalry, since this will provide a benchmark for discussing possibilities for moderating U.S.–Soviet competition in the post–World War II era. These options included: (1) spheres of influence; (2) the principle of compensation whereby any significant augmentation of power by one great power had to be accompanied by appropriate increases in territory, population, and resources for the other great powers in the interest of preserving the balance; (3) arrangements for mutual and collective decision-making in matters affecting or threatening the balance; (4) careful delineation and definition by the great powers of their interests and/or areas of involvement in third areas; (5) agreements for communication and advance notification of unilateral actions to be taken in third areas; (6) agreements to avoid unilateral action in third areas and, if necessary, to intervene only via multilateral action by several great powers; (7) arrangements for localizing and restricting regional conflicts; (8) agreements to limit the flow of weapons to third areas; (9) arrangements for pacific settlement of disputes; (10) the creation of buffer states between great powers; (11) establishment of neutral states and zones and of demilitarized areas.[1]

One may regard these diplomatic practices for moderating great-power rivalry as constituting a complex regime for avoidance of dangerous crises and war. The nineteenth-century European model worked

This chapter draws on a more detailed study: Alexander L. George, *Managing U.S.–Soviet Rivalry: Problems of Crisis Prevention* (Boulder, Colo.: Westview Press, 1983), as well as other sources.

1. For more detailed discussion, see Paul Gordon Lauren, "Crisis Prevention in Nineteenth-Century Diplomacy," in George, *Managing U.S.–Soviet Rivalry.*

imperfectly, of course, and collapsed during World War I; but our purpose here is not to evaluate the performance of the nineteenth-century model or to explain its demise. Rather, we wish to identify some of the changes in the international system and in conditions affecting world politics since World Wars I and II that have accentuated great-power competition. It proved impossible after the breakdown of the European system during World War I to recreate a stable multipolar balance of power; abortive efforts to do so gave way after World War II to a bipolar configuration dominated by the United States and the Soviet Union. The ·emergence of powerful rival ideologies and new elites shattered the cultural homogeneity of the European ruling classes that had underpinned the balance-of-power system. Whereas the European great powers had attempted to base foreign policy on the criterion of national interest, detached as much as possible from sentimental or ideological considerations, the outlook on foreign policy and world politics of the two superpowers—the Soviet Union and the United States—that confronted each other after World War II was heavily influenced by their ideological differences.

The new bipolar configuration of power after World War II combined with sharpened ideological conflict to accentuate U.S.–Soviet rivalry in third areas and to handicap efforts to moderate it. The search for stability during these years has been further prejudiced by the process of worldwide decolonization that vastly expanded the number of states in the international system. These new states often experienced internal instability and rivalries of their own that interlaced with and exacerbated the global rivalry of the superpowers. Further complicating the search for regional and local stability in the post–World War II era has been the revolution in weapons technology and easy access to conventional arms. An additional dimension to the already difficult task the United States and the Soviet Union were experiencing in efforts to control the risks of their competition in third areas emerged when, after the Sino-Soviet split, the Soviet Union and the People's Republic of China began to compete with each other for influence with "national liberation" movements in third areas.

The emergence of new states from the colonies of the former imperialist powers, their vigorous assertion of nationalism and sovereign independence, their voice in international forums such as the United Nations, and the universal condemnation of anything that smacks of imperialism have meant that the two superpowers cannot employ some of the modalities available to the great powers in the nineteenth century for moderating their competition in third areas. Explicit spheres of influence that played an important role in regulating the global rivalry of the great imperial powers of the nineteenth century are not acceptable in the modern era. Even collaborative efforts by the two superpowers to settle regional conflicts (such as in the Middle East from time to time) or to map out ground rules for moderating their competition in third areas, even when undertaken to reduce the likelihood of possibly dangerous U.S.–Soviet confrontations, trigger fears elsewhere in the international community of a superpower condominium harmful to the interests of other states.

Counterbalancing these various changes in the international arena that exacerbate superpower rivalry is another historical development—the emergence of nuclear weapons—that has powerfully reinforced the incentives of the two superpowers to prevent their conflicts of interest and rivalry from leading to a possibly disastrous war. The fear of a thermonuclear holocaust is undoubtedly the major factor that accounts for the success which the two superpowers have achieved in managing a series of diplomatic crises and tense confrontations since the beginning of the cold war. On the other hand, while the danger of such a war has undoubtedly contributed to dampening the escalation potential inherent in U.S.–Soviet competition, it has not prevented the occurrence of dangerous confrontations and lesser crises that have damaged the overall Soviet–American relationship.

The success of the two superpowers thus far in managing their crises without war cannot be explained solely with reference to their shared fear of thermonuclear war. The United States and the Soviet Union quickly grasped the requirements for managing crises. Fortunately these requirements are more easily recognized and applied than the principles for crisis prevention. To be sure, crisis management requirements must be operationalized and tailored to the special configuration of any particular situation, but these requirements remain the same, generally speaking, from one situation to another. Not only is crisis management easier to learn than crisis prevention, but the learning experiences are more easily accumulated and transferred to management of subsequent crises. Then, too, domestic politics generally are less intrusive in the management of existing crises than they are in policymakers' efforts to avoid them.

In contrast to crisis management, crisis prevention is a more amorphous objective and is not one that both superpowers are equally committed to in every situation. There are different kinds of crises in U.S.–Soviet relations, some more dangerous than others. Not only are some crises more acceptable (to one side if not both) because they are thought to carry with them a lesser, controllable risk of war; in the era of thermonuclear weapons some crises have become a substitute for war. That is, crises may be deliberately initiated or tolerated by one side in the hope of catalyzing desired changes in the status quo. Viewed in this way, crises offer opportunities for achieving foreign policy goals even though they may represent threats to important values.

Crisis prevention is more complicated than crisis management also because there is no single, prototypical set of requirements or strategy for preventing U.S.–Soviet competition in third areas from developing into a confrontation. Thus, crises can be avoided by a variety of *unilateral* policies undertaken by either superpower—for example, deterrence; economic, military, or political assistance to reduce instability in a third country or region that might otherwise provide tempting opportunities for encroachments by the other superpower or its proxies; decisions by one superpower not to compete with the other superpower in a given third area.

Crises can also be avoided through *initiatives by third parties* (e.g., the United Nations, the Organization of American States, the Organization of African Unity, or other regional actors) to mediate or resolve local disputes.

Finally, there are various ways in which the United States and the Soviet Union can *cooperate,* or coordinate their policies, in order to moderate competition and avoid being plunged into a crisis. I shall discuss in detail later in this chapter several different modalities for U.S.–Soviet cooperation in crisis prevention.

Given these important differences between crisis management and crisis prevention, it should not be surprising to learn that the United States (indeed, the Soviet Union, too) quickly learned how to manage crises with its major cold war opponent and that developments during the era of détente reinforced and further strengthened crisis-management capabilities. The principles of crisis management and the operational requirements that go with them are now not only well understood but are much more explicitly formulated than they were during the early cold war. There can be no guarantee, however, that crisis management will be successful in confrontations with the Soviet Union that may occur in the present era of renewed hostility. Not only is the danger of a fateful misperception and miscalculation, by one or both sides, ever present in a crisis; one or another of the requirements for crisis management may be inadvertently or deliberately ignored and a direct military clash—such as has not yet occurred—between U.S. and Soviet military forces may take place which, on however limited a scale initially, may generate pressure for escalation that may be difficult to control.

CRISIS MANAGEMENT

It is well to begin our discussion by taking note of a basic paradox or dilemma: crises can be easily managed and terminated—indeed, avoided altogether—if only one side is willing to forego its objectives and accept damage to the interests at stake. It is only because there is a conflict of interests in a given situation, because each side mobilizes or alerts its forces and makes threatening moves to demonstrate resolution in order to coerce the other side, and because, having become committed or engaged in some way, neither side is initially willing to back down that a crisis poses the danger of war. If escalation toward actual use of force is to be avoided under these circumstances, both sides must cooperate in crisis management.

Analysis of U.S.–Soviet crises, and others as well, indicates that peaceful resolution of such confrontations has required that one or both sides modify either the *objectives* they are pursuing—namely, be willing to settle for less—and/or limit the *means* they will employ in pursuing those objectives. In the Berlin blockade crisis of 1948–49, to be sure, the Soviets did pursue ambitious objectives—they attempted a blockade of Allied ground access to West Berlin in order to coerce the Western powers into altering their policy in West Germany—but Moscow also carefully limited the means employed to this end, being unwilling to interfere seriously with the Allied airlift to West Berlin for fear of creating incidents that would trigger a military response. President Truman, in turn, would not abandon the new policies that the Allies had adopted in West Germany, nor would he accept the suggestion of some of his advisers that the Allies leave West Berlin. But he also rejected advice to use military force to test and break the blockade, choosing instead to see whether the less dangerous option of trying to supply West Berlin via an airlift might be successful. In other words, Truman avoided an escalation of the conflict, accepting instead a test of capabilities within very restrictive ground rules that initially favored the Russians. At first the Allied airlift was intended merely to buy time for negotiations, which, however, failed to resolve the dispute. In time, the airlift was unexpectedly transformed into an effective weapon for breaking the blockade of ground access by dint of skill in improvisation and the mustering of increasingly larger resources for the airlift. Thereby the Western powers succeeded in reversing the expected outcome of the test of capabilities within the existing pattern of ground rules and transferred back to the Soviets the onerous decision whether to engage in a risky escalation or to accept defeat. (Essentially the same strategy was employed by the Eisenhower administration—again successfully—in the Quemoy crisis of 1958 to "break" the Chinese artillery blockade; with indirect, limited U.S. naval assistance, the Chinese Nationalist navy was finally able to resupply the Nationalist garrison on Quemoy. The next move was up to the opponent, who decided to curtail the artillery shelling rather than to escalate the level of violence.)

Unlike Truman, who did not resort to coercive threats to pressure the Soviets to give up their blockade of Berlin, in the Cuban missile crisis Kennedy employed the strategy of coercive diplomacy—relying initially upon a naval blockade to which he later added an ultimatum coupled with the threat of escalation—to induce Khrushchev to remove the missiles. Confronted by the unexpected deployment of missiles into Cuba, Kennedy limited both the objective and the means of his response in the interest of managing the crisis without war. Contrary to the suggestions of important advisers that the United States should respond to the crisis by attempting to eliminate the Castro regime or, at least, Soviet influence in Cuba, Kennedy decided to limit the objective to securing the removal of the missiles. And, in order to give diplomacy a chance to secure a peaceful resolution of the crisis, he chose the weaker blockade option as his initial response rather than the air-strike or invasion options. Moreover, to facilitate Khrushchev's agreement to withdraw the missiles and to reduce the possibility that the United States would have to carry out its threat of escalation, Kennedy coupled his ultimatum with an indication that in return for the withdrawal of the missiles he would be willing to give assurance that the United States would not invade Cuba in the future. And, while engaged in coercive diplomacy, Kennedy showed a keen awareness of the operational requirements for crisis management that will be discussed shortly.

The successful management of crises requires that some way of terminating them be found that is mutually acceptable. The Berlin blockade ended with a tacit admission of failure by Stalin that was barely glossed over by face-saving diplomatic language. Khrushchev's forced retreat in the Cuban missile crisis was ameliorated, if not also made possible, by the quid pro quo offered by Kennedy, which was certainly much more than a mere face-saving concession. The Berlin crisis of 1961 was terminated in still another way, with each side gaining its most important objective and conceding the same to its opponent—the Western powers managed to maintain their position in West Berlin; the Soviets succeeded in closing off the flood of East Germans to the West by erecting a wall between East and West Berlin.

The task of crisis management takes on additional dimensions when the superpowers are drawn into a regional conflict involving their allies or client states. In the Middle East wars of 1967, 1970, and 1973, each superpower was confronted by a policy dilemma: how far to go in assisting its local ally without risking a dangerous confrontation or war with the other superpower. This policy dilemma was eventually resolved in each crisis without a military clash between U.S. and Soviet forces, although not before they were drawn into tense confrontations in 1967 and, even more so, in 1973. A common pattern can be seen in these three crises. After war broke out between the Arab states and Israel, the superpowers were drawn into efforts to arrange a cease-fire. They were initially unable to agree on the timing and nature of a cease-fire: whether it should be initiated at a time when the battlefield situation clearly favored one of the local combatants, and whether it should be a standstill cease-fire or one that required a return to the status quo ante. Each superpower, predictably, was reluctant to support a cease-fire proposal distinctly disadvantageous to its local ally. Accordingly, the two superpowers found it difficult to cooperate effectively in bringing about a cease-fire or in assuring that it would not be violated by their ally on whom it was imposed.

In this situation, and given Israel's establishment of military superiority in each of these three wars, it became necessary for the Soviet Union to threaten military intervention in order to obtain a cessation of hostilities before its Arab client suffered a catastrophic setback. In 1967 and again in 1973 the Soviet threat of intervention was quickly countered by U.S. deterrence measures—President Johnson moved the U.S. Sixth Fleet toward the Syrian coast as a signal that the United States was prepared to resist Soviet intervention; President Nixon put U.S. military forces on alert in answer to Brezhnev's threat and Soviet preparations for intervention. During a critical time during the War of Attrition in early February of 1970, the Soviet Union issued a somewhat ambiguous warning that it would not remain idle in the face of the Israeli deep-penetration air raids that were threatening to topple Egyptian president Nasser. The Soviet warning was not correctly interpreted or taken seriously by Washington, and therefore it neither undertook strong deterrence measures to dissuade the Soviets from implementing their threat nor pressed the Israelis to curtail their deep-penetration air attacks.

In this connection it should be noted that in 1967 and 1973, in contrast to 1970, U.S. leaders promptly countered Soviet intervention threats and *also* pressured Israel to accept a cease-fire, thereby removing the necessity or excuse for Soviet intervention. In a sense, therefore, Soviet intervention threats in these two crises achieved their purpose: the United States was induced to curb its ally, something which it had been unable or unwilling to do prior to the Soviet threats of intervention. Soviet–U.S. interaction during these two crises can be characterized, therefore, as a pattern of last-ditch, "coerced cooperation" in crisis management and crisis resolution. Developments in the War of Attrition crisis of February–March 1970 took a different course which, however, is not inconsistent with this interpretation. When the United States failed either to curb the Israeli deep-penetration raids against Egypt or to deter Soviet intervention, the Soviets gradually introduced major air-defense forces of their own to defend Egypt—a development which U.S. policymakers accepted and, however reluctantly, tacitly acknowledged as legitimate under the circumstances.

The two superpowers avoided direct involvement in the case of the Syrian tank invasion of Jordan in 1970 and the Indo-Pakistani war of 1971. In both cases Washington exerted coercive pressures on behalf of the side which it favored but no confrontation with the Soviet Union occurred. In the Vietnam War the Soviet Union continued to provide military supplies to Hanoi and took no military countermeasures when U.S. planes mined Haiphong harbor in the spring of 1972. Moscow's interest in developing détente with the United States probably accounted for its quiescence on this occasion, as well as for whatever pressure it subsequently exerted on Hanoi to induce it to terminate the war.

However important limitation of objectives and/or of means employed are for crisis management, they do not suffice. Beginning with the Berlin blockade of 1948–49 and in subsequent crises, U.S. policymakers became aware that a number of more specific operational requirements had to be met in order to control the risk of escalation. The learning experience was rapid, cumulative, and thorough; the only serious failure to comprehend and to apply the operative requirements of crisis management occurred after the Chinese intervention in Korea in November 1950.

Seven general operational requirements for effective management of crises have been identified. We cannot trace here the way in which the two sides adhered to these crisis-management principles in each crisis. That all seven requirements were important was plainly evident during the Cuban missile crisis; both Kennedy and Khrushchev gave every indication of understanding these requirements and regulating their behavior accordingly, even while attempting at the same time to coerce each other.[2] As already noted, by 1962 the two superpowers had acquired considerable experience in controlling and managing tense situations, particularly in Berlin. It is nevertheless essentially correct to say that before Cuba there was little in the way of an explicit theory of crisis management to guide policymakers who wanted to safeguard important national interests in a diplomatic confrontation without becoming involved in a war.

Here, then, are the seven operational requirements for crisis management:

1. Each side must maintain top-level civilian control over military options—any alerts, deployments, and low-level actions, as well as the selection and timing of military moves.

2. The tempo and momentum of military movements may have to be deliberately slowed down and pauses created to provide time enough for the two sides to exchange diplomatic signals and communications, and to give each side adequate time to assess the situation, make decisions, respond to proposals, etc.

2. For discussion of crisis management in the Cuban missile crisis, see A. L. George, "The Cuban Missile Crisis, 1962," in A. L. George, D. K. Hall, and W. E. Simons, *The Limits of Coercive Diplomacy* (Boston: Little, Brown, 1971), pp. 86–143.

3. Movements of military forces must be carefully coordinated with diplomatic actions as part of an integrated strategy for terminating the crisis acceptably without war.

4. Movements of military forces and threats of force intended to signal resolve must be consistent with one's limited diplomatic objectives.

5. Military moves and threats should be avoided that give the opponent the impression that one is about to resort to large-scale warfare, thereby forcing him to consider preemption.

6. Diplomatic-military options should be chosen that signal, or are consistent with, a desire to negotiate a way out of the crisis rather than to seek a military solution.

7. Diplomatic proposals and military moves should be selected which leave the opponent a way out of the crisis that is compatible with his fundamental interests.

Mere awareness of these requirements by no means assures their effective implementation. To use these seven principles successfully requires appropriate military capabilities, doctrines, and options; effective command and control from top-level authorities not only to the theater commander but also to tactical units under his command; intimate interaction between civilian officials and military planners in order to design usable options compatible with crisis-management requirements; skill and flexibility in adapting existing contingency plans to unexpected developments as a crisis unfolds.

During the détente era some improvements were made in the U.S.–Soviet crisis-management regime. In addition to indirect signaling, the two superpowers now engaged more frequently in direct communication.[3] After the Cuban missile crisis, Kennedy and Khrushchev moved quickly to set up a direct communications link, the "hot line," between Washington and Moscow. It was used by President Johnson, apparently for the first time, during the Middle East war of 1967, to avoid Soviet misapprehensions as to U.S. intentions after he ordered U.S. aircraft to search the waters near Egypt for survivors of an American vessel that had been sunk by Israeli planes. The hot line could be used, of course, not only to clarify ambiguous situations in order to avoid superpower confrontations, but also during such crises to assist in their management and termination. However, the hot line is not a panacea; direct communication between heads of state over a hot line is no substitute for carefully prepared, more formal diplomatic communication. During the détente period, which President Nixon heralded on one occasion as the era of negotiation, direct communication between Soviet and U.S. leaders increased in

3. Dan Caldwell, *American–Soviet Relations: From 1947 to the Nixon-Kissinger Grand Design* (Westport, Conn.: Greenwood Press, 1981), pp. 36–44, 66–70, 127–37.

many other ways as well. The Dobrynin-Kissinger "back channel" played an important role not only in preparing for various agreements; it also served as a vehicle for serious diplomatic communication during crises such as the Syrian invasion of Jordan in 1970 and incipient crises such as the building of a base for Soviet submarines in Cuba in 1970. One of the most dramatic instances of direct communication in the interest of crisis management occurred during the Middle East war of October 1973, when Brezhnev invited Kissinger to Moscow to work out the details of a cease-fire.

Finally, mention should be made of recent proposals for setting up a joint U.S.–Soviet command post of some kind for quick monitoring and evaluation of ambiguous indicators of missile launches and of other events that might accidentally trigger nuclear war.

CRISIS PREVENTION

During the era of the cold war, the United States relied largely upon the various instruments of its containment strategy—deterrence, alliance commitments, military and economic aid—to prevent challenges to the Free World that could result in tense diplomatic crises, if not also war. The problem of how the United States and the Soviet Union might moderate their rivalry and competition to avoid dangerous confrontations received much less attention than problems of deterrence, crisis management, coercive diplomacy, preventing limited conflicts from escalating, and arms control. The great gulf that divided the United States and the Soviet Union appeared to make it futile to utilize classical diplomacy and negotiation to resolve or moderate conflicts of interest between the two superpowers. Even during the cold war, however, the two superpowers occasionally found ways of limiting the potential conflict in their relationship. In Europe the wartime agreement for dividing Germany into occupation zones was gradually transformed into a tacit, if also somewhat ambiguous and uneasy, sphere-of-influence arrangement. Despite the Eisenhower administration's moral support of the "captive peoples" of Eastern Europe and its talk of "liberation," he acted with great prudence when crises erupted in that area which challenged Soviet control. Washington stood aloof when the East German rebellion was crushed in 1953. A noninterventionist policy was articulated by Secretary of State John Foster Dulles during the Polish crisis of October 1956, and it was adhered to again by the Eisenhower administration during the Soviet invasion of Hungary in 1956 and by President Johnson in the face of the Soviet invasion of Czechoslovakia in 1968. In the recent Polish crisis as well, both the Carter and Reagan administrations clearly indicated that the United States did not have any military option.[4]

Washington's acceptance of Soviet primacy in Eastern Europe during the cold war was consistent, of course, with Roosevelt's and Truman's earlier decisions to recognize the special security interests of the Soviet Union in Eastern Europe while at the same time engaging in abortive efforts to couple that recognition with insistence on self-determination and free elections in the countries liberated from the Nazi yoke.

Other instances of unilateral actions or coordination of policies in the interest of crisis prevention can be found during the cold war. The Soviet Union withdrew from northern Iran under U.S. pressure in 1946 and, soon thereafter, in the face of U.S. opposition, gave up its demands on Turkey for guaranteed passage of Soviet vessels through the Straits of Bosphorus. There were also instances of U.S.–Soviet cooperation that harked back to some of the practices that the great powers had utilized from time to time during the nineteenth century to reduce sources of potential conflict. Thus, in 1955 prolonged negotiations between the Western powers and the Soviet Union finally resulted in the Austrian State Treaty, which created a neutral buffer state and removed it from the ongoing competition between the two sides in Europe. Another instance of U.S.–Soviet cooperation of this kind occurred during 1961–62 when President Kennedy, determined to de-commit the United States from its involvement in Laos, induced Khrushchev to help bring about a cease-fire there as a prerequisite to American participation in a reconvened Geneva conference on Laos. At their Vienna summit talks in June 1961, Kennedy and Khrushchev agreed that what was at stake in Laos was not worth the risk of a superpower confrontation and, in the year that followed, they cooperated to bring about a cease-fire and the Declaration on the Neutrality of Laos.[5]

As these examples from the cold war period demonstrate, the goal of crisis prevention in the U.S.–Soviet relationship can be pursued—either via unilateral policies or through cooperative actions—even in a period otherwise marked by acute mutual hostility and distrust. The avoidance of dangerous superpower confrontations is in the interest of both the United States and the Soviet Union also in the present era of renewed

4. For an analysis of U.S. responses to crises in Eastern Europe, see Jiri Valenta, "Toward Soviet–U.S. Prevention of Crises at the Soviet Periphery," paper presented at the International Political Science Association, 12th World Congress, Rio de Janeiro, August 9–14, 1982.

5. David K. Hall, "The Laotian War of 1962 and the Indo-Pakistani War of 1971," in Barry M. Blechman and Stephen S. Kaplan, eds., *Force without War: U.S. Armed Forces as a Political Instrument* (Washington, D.C.: The Brookings Institution, 1978), pp. 135–221.

hostility. The confrontational relationship, or new cold war, that has emerged since the demise of détente need not exclude unilateral and joint actions in the interest of avoiding dangerous crises.

One might assume that the goal of crisis prevention would have been facilitated when the relationship between the United States and the Soviet Union was marked by détente. Our necessarily brief review of this period, however, reveals a mixed picture of major disappointments as well as of important achievements. There are important lessons to be learned from this experience, not only from the flawed experiment in détente but also from the abortive experiment in cooperation in crisis prevention that accompanied and was indeed an important part of the détente package.

The onset of détente following the Cuban missile crisis reached its apex during Nixon's first administration. New opportunities emerged for reducing the conflict potential in U.S.–Soviet relations, for now there was a shared disposition to utilize negotiation and accommodation to settle some of the long-standing conflicts of interest that had been bones of contention during the cold war, particularly in Europe where the vital interests of both sides were engaged. Agreements were signed stabilizing the situation in Berlin, recognizing the existence of the two German states, and tacitly formalizing the division of Europe that had emerged following World War II.

Europe was an area in which both of the two superpowers had vital interests, a fact that facilitated cooperation in crisis prevention. The two sides were less successful in making arrangements for moderating their competition in the Middle East, Africa, Asia, and other third areas—areas characterized either by low-interest symmetry or by disputed or uncertain symmetry of U.S.–Soviet interests.

The new relationship that Nixon and Brezhnev set out to create between their countries was burdened from the start by crucial ambiguities and latent disagreements on important issues that created mutually inconsistent expectations regarding the benefits each side hoped to derive from the détente process. We cannot examine all aspects of these developments and shall focus on those most directly relevant to the task of managing their rivalry in third areas.

The Basic Principles Agreement (BPA) which Nixon and Brezhnev signed at their first summit meeting in Moscow in May 1972 was regarded by them as a "charter" for détente. In this document the two sides agreed to hold periodic high-level meetings, to continue their efforts to limit armaments, and to develop economic, scientific, and cultural ties. The document also included general principles that committed the United States and the Soviet Union to avoiding dangerous crises and the outbreak of nuclear war. However, the available historical record indicates that the two sides did not discuss and clarify what their interests were in different parts of the world, did not attempt to assess how serious their conflicting interests might be, and did not set into motion an agenda or procedures for determining how their conflicting interests might be accommodated in the future. The BPA, however, did commit the two sides to the development of normal relations "based on the principles of sovereignty, equality, noninterference in internal affairs and mutual advantage." Nixon and Brezhnev also stated that they would be prepared "to regulate and settle differences by peaceful means" and that negotiations on outstanding issues would be conducted "in a spirit of reciprocity, mutual accommodations and mutual benefit." The document went on to state that the prerequisites for strengthening peaceful relations between the two countries were "the recognition of the security interests of the parties based on the principle of equality and the renunciation of the use or threat of war."

What can be said about this effort to formulate general principles that would serve to moderate competition between the two superpowers and articulate their seemingly parallel interest in crisis prevention? In the first place, not only were these general principles extremely abstract, the agreement to cooperate in crisis prevention itself was, in important respects, a pseudo-agreement. Article 1 of the BPA contained the Soviets' favored formulation that "in the nuclear age there is no alternative to conducting . . . mutual relations on the basis of peaceful coexistence." Earlier, when preparations for the Moscow summit were under way, Nixon had instructed Kissinger to state clearly and explicitly to the Soviet leaders that the United States could not accept either the Soviet concept of "peaceful coexistence" or the "Brezhnev Doctrine," whereby the Soviet Union claimed the right to support "national liberation" movements all over the world and the right to intervene militarily in East European countries that deviated from the path laid down by Moscow. For reasons we need not go into here (which have to do mainly with the desire to obtain Soviet help in seeking a Vietnam settlement), Kissinger did not follow Nixon's directive; nor did Nixon himself pursue the matter at the Moscow summit. Instead of opposing the inclusion of "peaceful coexistence" in the BPA or insisting that the document include a statement of their disagreement with the Soviet concept, Nixon and Kissinger contented themselves with introducing elsewhere in the BPA (Article 2) language that reflected their long-standing exhortation to the Russians to forego "efforts to obtain unilateral advantage" at the expense of the West and to "exercise restraint" in their foreign policy.

By obscuring their fundamental disagreement on this important issue, the BPA gave the erroneous impression that the Soviet Union and the United States were in substantial agreement on the general rules of the game and the restraints to be observed in their competition in third areas. Thereby Nixon and Kissinger contributed to what their domestic critics were later to refer to as the "overselling" of détente.

As subsequent events were to make clear, each side read its own hopes and desires into the language of the general crisis-prevention principles of the BPA (and of the more specific Agreement on Prevention of Nuclear War signed at the second summit a year later). In the first place, Washington and Moscow had rather different conceptions of the "dangerous crises" that these two agreements were supposed to help avoid. Soviet leaders were interested primarily in using the general principles to avoid crises carrying the danger of nuclear war with the United States. Nixon and Kissinger were interested, in addition, in using the agreements (together, of course, with positive inducements offered to Moscow for good behavior) to moderate Soviet efforts to make gains in third areas at the expense of the West, whether or not such assertive Soviet behavior should lead to dangerous crises of the kind feared by the Soviets. But for Moscow the virtue of U.S. adherence to the concept of peaceful coexistence was precisely that it should make it more acceptable and safer for the Soviet Union to engage in low-level, controlled efforts to advance its influence in third areas.

For the Soviets, the notable achievement of having U.S. leaders accept peaceful coexistence as the basis for their relationship in the future was reinforced by what they regarded as a formal acceptance by Nixon of the political equality of the Soviet Union with the United States. For Moscow the value of Article 1 of the BPA was that it committed the United States to developing "normal relations" with the Soviet Union on the basis of the principle of "equality." Article 2 further committed the United States to the principle that peaceful relations require recognition of Soviet "security interests . . . based on the principle of equality." Although the language of these articles was phrased as applying to both sides, it had special significance for Soviet leaders as constituting an acknowledgment by the United States that Soviet achievement of strategic military parity entitled the Soviet Union to be treated by the United States as a political-diplomatic equal as well.

From Moscow's perspective, strategic parity marked the emergence of the Soviet Union as a superpower in political as well as in military terms. This, in turn, entitled the Soviet Union to participate as an equal with the United States in settling all international problems that, in Moscow's view, affected its security in areas such as Europe, the Middle East, and, to a lesser extent, Northeast Asia in geographical proximity to the Soviet Union. Foreign Minister Gromyko had already given voice to this claim at the 24th Congress of the CPSU in 1971 when he observed that "there is no question of any significance which can be decided without the Soviet

Union or in opposition to it." Moscow saw in the acknowledgment of equality in the BPA a confirmation of this aspiration, an acceptance by the United States of the fact that the Soviet Union's status as a superpower entitled it to assume a global role.[6]

Consistent with this, in the Soviet view, was the apparent fact that the Nixon administration was already working together with the Soviet Union, however unsuccessfully thus far, to develop general principles for a Middle East settlement. To the Soviets this constituted practical recognition by the United States of Soviet security interests in the Middle East and an acceptance by Washington of the necessity to act jointly with the Soviet Union in settling the Arab–Israeli conflict.

As a matter of fact, however, this was a gross misperception of the American attitude on Moscow's part and an incorrect appraisal of the Middle East policy Nixon and Kissinger were actually pursuing. As with regard to "peaceful coexistence," the concept of superpower "equality" and whether the two sides shared a common understanding of its implications for their foreign policies was not discussed at the summit or thereafter. It would appear that Nixon and Kissinger believed that, while they were indeed recognizing Soviet achievement of strategic military parity, they were according to Moscow only a symbolic form of political equality. There is no indication that U.S. leaders were aware of the special significance their Soviet counterparts attached to the reference to "equality" in the BPA. This is not to say that Kissinger failed to perceive Brezhnev's sensitivity on the subject of "equality," but he appears to have misinterpreted it as a sign of the Soviet leader's psychological insecurity. In Kissinger's account of his secret trip to Moscow in April 1972, he recalls, with a trace of disparagement, that "equality seemed to mean a great deal to Brezhnev. It would be inconceivable that the Chinese leaders would ask for it. . . . To Brezhnev it was central. . . . What a more secure leader might have regarded as a cliché or condescension, he treated as a welcome sign of our seriousness."[7] Even at the time he wrote his memoirs, Kissinger still failed to understand the significance that Soviet leaders attached to the status of equality and the hopes and expectations generated thereby.

As for the Middle East, even while going through the motions of trying to work out a basis for a joint U.S.–Soviet approach, Nixon and Kissinger had in fact embarked on a concealed policy aimed at removing the Soviets from the area. As Kissinger reveals in his memoirs: "To some

6. Coit D. Blacker, "The Kremlin and Détente: Soviet Conceptions, Hopes and Expectations," in George, *Managing U.S.–Soviet Rivalry.*
7. Henry Kissinger, *White House Years* (Boston: Little, Brown, 1979), p. 1141.

extent my interest in détente was tactical, as a device to maximize Soviet dilemmas and reduce Soviet influence . . . in the Middle East."[8]

Far from providing solid norms of restraint on which to base the further development of the détente relationship, the general principles of the BPA were viewed by each side as a vehicle for imposing constraints on the foreign policy of the other side, not on its own. Given the generality and ambiguity of the principles and the fact that they were in no sense self-enforcing, they were bound eventually to provoke charges and countercharges of nonfulfillment and thus to generate disillusionment and additional friction in U.S.–Soviet relations.

Developments leading to the Arab–Israeli war of October 1973, just a few months after the signing of the Agreement on the Prevention of Nuclear War (APNW), provided the first test of the nascent U.S.–Soviet crisis-prevention regime. The Soviets did not go as far as they might have (or as far as they ought to have gone, according to one interpretation of their responsibilities under the BPA and APNW) to prevent the Arab attack or to consult adequately with the United States to enlist its cooperation to this end. However, at their second summit meeting in Washington in June 1973, Brezhnev strongly warned Nixon about the danger of war in the Middle East. Brezhnev's warning, however, was of a general character. He did not state that Sadat had definite, firm plans for an attack. Washington dismissed Brezhnev's warning as scare tactics designed to pressure the United States to change its Middle East policy. But it is also possible that the Soviets attempted to give indirect warning of the Arab attack a few days before it occurred when they suddenly ordered the evacuation of Soviet civilian personnel from Egypt and Syria. For various reasons, however, U.S. leaders did not regard this as an indication that Soviet leaders knew that an Arab attack was imminent.

The origins of the October War reveal the difficulties of implementing the APNW provision for urgent U.S.–Soviet consultations to head off the development of dangerous situations carrying with them the threat of war. The Soviets were caught in a situation in which honoring the requirement for consultation conflicted with their responsibilities to their Arab allies. Viewed more broadly, the origins of the October War, if analyzed in more detail than is possible here, would reveal the complexities of the

8. Ibid., p. 1255. It may be noted that neither Moscow nor Washington attempted to engage the other in follow-up conversations after signing the Basic Principles Agreement and the Agreement on Prevention of Nuclear War in order to consider the operational implications of the agreements for cooperation in crisis prevention. Nor did the two sides attempt to set up institutionalized procedures for periodic meetings to discuss how the general principles would apply to countries and regions of potential crisis. Neither did the U.S. government initiate any policy-planning studies to consider the implications of the agreements or to devise procedures for making effective use of them.

Middle East situation that made it a particularly severe test of détente and the crisis-prevention agreements. After an initial effort during the first year or two of the Nixon administration to find a basis for diplomatic cooperation with the Soviet Union in settling the Arab–Israeli conflict, first Washington and then Moscow pursued divergent objectives and strategies in the Middle East that in effect ruled out cooperation between them in the interest of crisis prevention. Even while ostensibly seeking a cooperative solution, each superpower covertly pursued a self-seeking unilateral policy of its own toward the Middle East conflict—the United States seeking to bring about a reversal of alliances that would exclude Soviet influence in Egypt, the Soviet Union arming Egypt and Syria and condoning their resort to war.

The competition and diplomatic disunity of the superpowers gave Egypt, the local actor most dissatisfied with the status quo, an opportunity to maneuver and to use force to pursue its own policy objectives. This case is a reminder, therefore, that prevention of crises is not under the exclusive or reliable control of the two superpowers. Competition between them in third areas may allow highly motivated local actors to play one superpower off against the other and to pursue their own interests in ways that generate crises into which the superpowers are then drawn.

In the aftermath of the October War the interests of the two superpowers collided even more sharply in the Middle East, and soon in Africa as well, in ways that exposed the ambiguities and shallowness of the general principles to which Nixon and Brezhnev had ostensibly subscribed. As soon as the cease-fire between Egypt/Syria and Israel was firmly fixed, Kissinger moved quickly to establish himself at the hub of diplomatic efforts to bring about a disengagement of forces. With Egypt now looking to the United States and with Israel as dependent as ever on Washington, Kissinger was able to exclude Moscow from the real negotiations, forcing it to be content with symbolic equality as co-chair with the United States of the Geneva Conference. The hopes generated in the Kremlin by the 1972 summit that it would participate as an equal in the search for a solution to the Arab–Israeli conflict were now clearly dashed. The Soviet leaders found themselves outmaneuvered and, indeed, deceived by Kissinger. Their repeated complaints at being excluded were to no avail, but the damage to détente was considerable.

By January 1975, when the United States and the Soviet Union entered into covert competition to influence the internal struggle for power in Angola, many of the expectations and hopes generated in the Kremlin by the Basic Principles Agreement of 1972 had turned sour. Kissinger's success in excluding the Soviets from meaningful participation in Middle East negotiations was itself a source of deep frustration, being viewed as contradicting the principles of "equality" and "reciprocity" that were to have governed superpower relations in the era of détente. Moreover, the promise that détente would yield the Soviet Union substantial trade and credits had foundered on Washington's inability either to moderate Senator Henry Jackson's determined effort to link trade with Moscow's policy on emigration of Jews or to forestall Senator Adlai Stevenson's amendment that sharply limited credits to Moscow. By early 1975, moreover, prospects for a SALT II agreement had dimmed as a result of increasing controversy over its merits within the United States that extended to the highest levels of the Ford administration itself.

As a result of these developments, Soviet leaders were hardly disposed to withdraw from the competition in Angola when, in January-February 1975, Washington showed a notable lack of interest in the efforts of the Portuguese authorities, backed by the Organization of African Unity, to set up a transitional government in Angola composed of representatives of the three indigenous independence movements, and decided instead to give covert assistance to one of the anti-Marxist movements. Developments in Angola during the remainder of 1975, it is generally agreed, constitute a particularly important instance of the failure of the United States and the Soviet Union to manage their rivalry in third areas so as to avoid a diplomatic confrontation. One emerges from a study of the origins and development of the Angola crisis with the conclusion that a superpower confrontation there was not preordained and might have been avoided. Neither Washington nor Moscow foresaw or planned the scenario that unfolded in 1975. U.S. policy in Angola developed incrementally through a series of improvisations and adjustments to unexpected developments. It was fundamentally flawed in underlying premises, conceptualization, and implementation. At the outset and for some months thereafter, Kissinger appears to have believed that covert assistance to the anti-Marxist forces would suffice to ensure a favorable outcome. He erred in believing that the Soviets would have neither the incentive nor the leverage to give effective support to the pro-Marxist side. Later, by condoning—if not tacitly encouraging—intervention by South African military units, Kissinger made it possible for the Soviets to legitimize, and to assist, large-scale Cuban military intervention. The South African intervention, which for a while seemed to tilt the outcome of the internal struggle in favor of the anti-Marxist forces, succeeded in alienating other African states whose support Kissinger would desperately need later when, faced with imminent defeat in Angola, he sought a last-minute compromise diplomatic solution to the civil war. Toward the end of 1975, Kissinger attempted to apply diplomatic pressure on the Soviets to induce them to cooperate in a compromise settlement of the war. To obtain leverage for this purpose the administration attempted to obtain congressional approval of $28 million for additional military assistance to the anti-Marxist forces in Angola. The request boomeranged and resulted in a congressional cutoff of any additional covert aid to Angola.

Kissinger's policy in Angola has been justly criticized for its insensitivity to local and regional realities and for his insistence, when the Soviets chose to compete, on defining the stakes in Angola in global terms. In mid-1975 Kissinger turned aside the timely warnings and advice of his area specialists, opting instead for a substantial increase in covert assistance. Expecting that the anti-Marxist movements would be successful, Kissinger waited too long to approach the Soviets with a view toward working out a compromise settlement. He gambled—and assured congressional committees—that U.S. assistance would remain covert and would suffice. When the Soviet-assisted Cuban intervention unexpectedly created a desperate battlefield situation in Angola, Kissinger found that it was too late quietly to accept the failure of his covert policy and put an end to U.S. involvement. Instead, he now openly defined the stakes in terms of a compelling need for containment of the Soviet Union, denounced its behavior in Angola as contrary to the Basic Principles Agreement, and, when Congress did not respond with additional funds for Angola, blamed it for depriving the administration of the means for achieving an acceptable compromise settlement in Angola. Despite Kissinger's belated efforts to limit the damage to American foreign policy, to détente, to the Ford administration, and to his own professional reputation, the costs of his failure in Angola in all respects were substantial.

The Ogaden war of 1977–78 led to another Soviet-Cuban intervention in an African conflict and resulted in further damage to what remained of the détente relationship. As in Angola, the general principles for crisis avoidance agreed to in 1972 and 1973 seemed entirely irrelevant and ineffectual for preventing development of superpower competition in the Horn of Africa. And again, as in Angola, U.S. policymakers were unable to improvise ways of deterring or otherwise inducing the Soviets to act with restraint. In the early stages of the war, when it appeared that Somalia would win, Washington lacked incentives to limit the conflict. A Somali success was not unwelcome, since it might help to undermine the Soviet position in the strategic Horn of Africa. Neither were diplomatic efforts to induce Moscow to use its influence with Ethiopia to bring about a cease-fire a wholly attractive option, since this would tend to legitimize a Soviet role in the area. It was only after Soviet-supported deployment of Cuban troops to Ogaden reversed the local balance that Washington overcame its reluctance to engage Moscow in direct talks with a view to limiting and terminating the conflict. Soviet readiness to use force was encouraged by several aspects of the situation over which Washington had little leverage. Moscow could justify its support for Ethiopia as legitimate assistance to the victim of unprovoked aggression by Somalia, a position which many African states found persuasive. Moreover, whatever the risks of Moscow's intervention, they were reduced by the domestic constraints on U.S. policy occasioned by Vietnam, Watergate, and revelations of CIA activities. On the other hand, while the United States was unable to prevent the Cuban-Ethiopian counterattack from retaking Ogaden, Washington was more successful in discouraging any temptation Moscow might have felt to support an invasion of Somalia itself. Diplomatic exchanges between the two superpowers eventually resulted in a formula whereby the United States agreed not to carry out its threat to arm Somalia in return for a Soviet-Ethiopian pledge to stop the Cuban-Ethiopian advance into Ogaden at the Somalian border.[9]

What Angola, Ogaden, the Middle East, and other cases as well, demonstrate is that both superpowers are generally unwilling to forego perceived opportunities to advance their own interests at each other's expense *unless and until the threat of a dangerous confrontation appears to be imminent.* This makes one or both sides reluctant to initiate timely diplomatic consultations to work out an ad hoc understanding for avoiding or limiting their competition in any particular third area. As a result, the history of U.S.–Soviet relations in past decades reveals what appear to be many "missed opportunities" for working out in advance specific arrangements for avoiding competition that carries the risk of eventual confrontation.

The general norms of restraint embodied in the Basic Principles Agreement and the Agreement on Prevention of Nuclear War need to be supplemented by procedures for timely consultation to clarify ambiguous situations and to head off incipient superpower competition that, once under way, carries with it the possibility of escalation to the level of open confrontation. The two superpowers lack explicit "rules of engagement" to regulate their competition. Rules of this type should be much more specific than the existing general principles in indicating various types of intervention permitted or forbidden in different types of situations that emerge in third areas. However, it is most unlikely that U.S. and Soviet leaders would agree to specific rules of engagement intended to apply across the board to all third areas. The relative interests of the two superpowers vary in different geographical areas, and it would be difficult for this reason to formulate general rules of engagement that took into account these variations in relative U.S.–Soviet interests in different parts of the world.

One alternative is to rely on tacit norms, or patterns of restraint, that

9. Larry C. Napper, "The Ogaden War: Some Implications for Crisis Prevention," in George, *Managing U.S.–Soviet Rivalry.*

have emerged from historical experience. Sometimes experience yields a fairly explicit norm that may even take the form of a quasi agreement, as in the case of the quid pro quo that ended the Cuban missile crisis, when Kennedy indicated that the United States would agree not to invade Cuba in the future in return for a Soviet pledge to remove the missiles and not to reintroduce offensive weapons there. This understanding indeed provided the reference point for settling the disagreement that arose in 1970 over the construction of a Soviet submarine base in Cuba. Such norms or patterns of restraint, however, are subject to erosion over time. Moreover, they tend to be area-specific in content and coverage, and therefore are either irrelevant for regulating other types of competition or in any case do not apply automatically or reliably to the other third areas.

In the absence of either comprehensive rules of engagement or patterns of restraint that have evolved in specific areas, the two superpowers are left with the necessity either to agree in advance upon arrangements to avoid or regulate their potential competition in a particular third area, or to improvise ad hoc ground rules for escalation control after they have entered into competition in a given locale. Improvising ground rules to control escalation of an ongoing competition is highly problematic, though not impossible. The two sides succeeded in doing so eventually in the Ogaden case but failed to cooperate in controlling the escalation potential of their competition in Angola. In cases of this kind, timely diplomatic consultations are essential for the purpose of exploring, and, if possible, capitalizing upon opportunities to limit competition before the dynamics of escalation take hold. Even in situations as complex as Angola undoubtedly was in 1975, had Washington and Moscow consulted as soon as the Alvor Accord was signed, and had they jointly supported from the beginning efforts on behalf of the Accord made by the Organization of African Unity, they might have agreed to severely limit their own involvement as well as discouraging that of other states such as Zaire, China, South Africa, and Cuba.

Paradoxically, development of patterns of restraint and ad hoc rules of engagement has encountered special difficulties in so-called gray areas—countries and regions where neither superpower has vital interests and where, therefore, it might be expected that it would be easier for them to moderate and regulate their competition. Various factors help to explain this paradox. Precisely because vital U.S. interests are not at stake in many third areas, the Soviet Union may feel it is safer to strive for advantage and increased influence in these areas at the expense of the West. Besides, in the Soviet view, détente with the United States and Washington's acceptance of "peaceful coexistence" in the Basic Principles Agreement meant, if anything, acceptance of the Kremlin's view that it was entitled to compete for increased influence in such areas.

In other third areas, for example in the Middle East and the Persian Gulf area, Moscow and Washington do not agree on the state of their relative interests. It is often said, with some justification, that the United States and the Soviet Union can reduce the risk of confrontations in areas of disputed or uncertain symmetry of interests, as well as in "gray areas" of mutual low interest, by clarifying their interests and intentions in a timely fashion in order to avoid being drawn into low-level escalating competition. However, in many situations of this kind, U.S. and Soviet leaders experience difficulty in achieving mutual clarification of interests and intentions. Diplomatic communications and signaling often lack clarity and/or credibility. The danger of misperception and miscalculation is particularly serious when one superpower—typically the Soviet Union—intervenes cautiously and on a low level in a local situation, probing to test the other superpower's reaction and, when receiving no response, then decides to escalate its involvement. Failure to grasp that the opponent is conducting a carefully controlled probe and is engaged in a subtle asking of a question regarding the other side's intentions can easily abet miscalculation and set into motion escalation leading to confrontation.

Specialists on Soviet foreign policy behavior believe that miscommunication of this kind has occurred repeatedly in the history of U.S.–Soviet relations. Testifying in the Senate hearings on Angola, Soviet specialist Leon Gouré, for example, observed that this case illustrated the chronic tendency of American policymakers to overlook or discount initial Soviet probes and signals. As a result, after "the Russians have committed themselves to some course of action, have really become involved and are successful, we then begin to object. By that time it is late, they are in there. Retreat involves a matter of prestige, all kinds of political costs for them and they feel essentially that we have misled them."[10]

The problem of timely, unequivocal clarification of interests and intentions is not one, however, that can be easily corrected. In recent years Soviet and American leaders seem to have become increasingly reluctant in many situations to define and delimit their interests lest they "give away" a third area or encourage the other side to proceed with its efforts to consolidate or increase its influence by allowing it to assume that such efforts will not risk a strong response.

This trend has been strengthened as détente has eroded and been replaced by an era of renewed hostility. On the one hand, Moscow's conception of its foreign policy "interests" has expanded or become more elastic with the Soviet Union's emergence as a global power, its claim to a superpower status of "equality" with the United States, its interpretation

10. *Hearings, Subcommittee on African Affairs,* Senate Committee on Foreign Relations, 1976 (Washington, D.C.: U.S. Government Printing Office, 1976), p. 113.

that its new status entitles it to have a say in shaping events and outcomes in many parts of the globe where Soviet influence was more restricted in the past. As for the United States, the return to a more confrontational relationship with the Soviet Union since the demise of détente has been accompanied by the reemergence not only of a hard image of the Soviet Union's intentions but also an image of the international system as being highly unstable. According to this perception, the parts of the international system are tightly interlocked, so that a gain anywhere for the Soviet Union is not only automatically a setback for the United States but is also likely to have a "billiard-ball" effect, threatening to destabilize other parts of the system and lead to further challenges to U.S. interests elsewhere as well. While members of the Carter administration attempted to moderate this global, geopolitical approach in favor of a regional perspective on problems of the Third World, the continued erosion of détente and assertive Soviet foreign policy forays made the new approach increasingly controversial, even within the Carter administration, and it was abandoned after the Soviet invasion of Afghanistan.

Clarification of U.S. interests in third areas often encounters another obstacle as well. Responsible policymakers are not always able to define or anticipate the full extent to which U.S. interests are engaged before competition in a particular area has escalated. Often it is only when a situation has deteriorated or is on the verge of serious deterioration—for example, as a result of the unexpected Soviet-assisted Cuban intervention in Angola—that the broader ramifications for American interests or for the domestic political standing of the administration become evident in Washington, forcing consideration of a strong response. This dilemma cannot be avoided merely by enjoining policymakers to define their interests in advance, for in many situations what is at stake for the United States or for the administration increases substantially and somewhat unpredictably as a result of actions by the Soviet Union, its allies or proxies, or through internal developments within a third area.

DOMESTIC AND INTERNATIONAL CONSTRAINTS

The ability of policymakers to implement the requirements for crisis avoidance and crisis management can be jeopardized by various domestic and international political constraints. Particularly in democracies such as the United States, policymakers are subject to pressures from the legislative branch, the media, organized interest groups, and public opinion. In addition, alliance partners often generate additional constraints on Washington's ability to pursue what it regards to be optimal strategies and tactics for avoiding or managing crises.

Let us consider first the impact of such constraints on the employment of deterrence strategy, one of the principle means utilized for avoiding crises. As noted by Thomas Schelling many years ago,[11] deterrence strategy contains a fundamental paradox; for to deter an opponent from undertaking actions harmful to our interests we often find ourselves obliged to make threats we would rather not have to carry out. As a result, the credibility of deterrent threats may be called into question, at times so severely as to render them of questionable value either for deterring the opponent or for reassuring allies who are supposed to be protected by the U.S. deterrence commitment.

This fundamental paradox of deterrence enters into the consciousness of the public and of allies whenever they are forced to contemplate what would happen if deterrence were to fail, as was the case, for example, during the various crises over Berlin. The ability of U.S. policymakers to reinforce deterrence and to respond effectively to low-level Soviet probes in these cases was constrained by allied and domestic anxiety over the rising danger of war and by the difficulty of developing joint plans with our NATO allies for responding to low-level Soviet encroachments and threats of escalation. When the 1948 Soviet blockade of allied access to West Berlin galvanized the West into action, Moscow learned from that experience. Thus, in subsequent crises over Berlin, Moscow found it more useful to limit itself to the threat of a blockade, thereby activating fear of war among Western publics and encouraging allied disunity in how best to deal with the Soviet threat.

In the United States itself past experience indicates that Congress and the public are often much more willing to support presidential efforts to reinforce deterrence in certain geographical areas by means of formal verbal declarations than to support the Executive in taking actions to implement such deterrence commitments. Thus, in 1955 President Eisenhower had little difficulty in persuading Congress to pass the Formosa resolution, which announced a conditional commitment to help defend the offshore islands as well as Formosa itself. It was hoped that such a formal indication of congressional support would strengthen deterrence. A few years later, however, when Chinese Communist artillery began shelling the offshore islands of Quemoy and Matsu, Eisenhower's efforts to assist the Chinese Nationalist forces to hold those islands encountered extremely strong criticism in Congress and among the public, which imposed severe constraints on the means Washington could employ for this purpose.

In 1964, after the Tonkin Bay incident, Congress responded almost unanimously to President Johnson's request for a strong resolution re-

11. Thomas C. Schelling, *The Strategy of Conflict* (Cambridge, Mass.: Harvard University Press, 1960).

affirming the U.S. commitment to South Vietnam and warning North Vietnam against additional provocations. When Johnson used the Tonkin Bay resolution as a basis for introducing increasingly large American military forces into the Vietnam War, both Congress and the public gradually began to withdraw support and to question the wisdom of the passage of the resolution.

The debacle in Vietnam led to strong, persistent public and congressional constraints on presidential efforts to employ deterrence strategy or to use military deployments and threats of any kind on behalf of crisis-management objectives. In Angola, as we have already noted, the Senate voted to cut off further funds for any covert U.S. operations in that country when Ford and Kissinger attempted to cope with the imminent defeat of the side they were backing in the civil war as a result of the Soviet-assisted Cuban military intervention. More recently, during the first months of the Reagan administration, its resort to coercive threats to restrict outside aid to the rebels in El Salvador so aroused public and congressional concern over the possibility of American military involvement that the administration was forced to soften its rhetoric and to offer reassurances that intervention by U.S. forces was not contemplated.

Thus far, the ability of U.S. policymakers to manage crises involving the Soviet Union has not been unduly affected by domestic and allied constraints. In the Cuban missile crisis, domestic and congressional pressures were not powerful enough to push the president into taking stronger military initiatives. Congressional leaders who were briefed by President Kennedy just before he announced the blockade felt it was too weak a response and urged an air strike against the missile sites, a suggestion that Kennedy turned aside even though it had powerful supporters within his advisory group. Later in the crisis, when it seemed to be getting dangerously out of control and pressure for an air strike was mounting, the president preferred to convey an ultimatum to Khrushchev and coupled it with the offer of a quid pro quo, which fortunately was quickly accepted by the Soviet premier. Interestingly, the Cuban missile crisis ran its course so quickly that the widespread, intense fear of war it generated within the public did not have an opportunity to crystallize into pressure upon the president that might have weakened his hand in dealing with Khrushchev.

Generally speaking, it would appear that the longer a crisis lasts, especially when it is accompanied by rising tension between the adversaries, the greater the likelihood of strong public and congressional pressures being exerted on the president to make concessions in order to terminate the crisis before it results in war. Consistent with this generalization is the tense but short-lived confrontation between the two superpowers during the Arab–Israeli war in October 1973, when Washington responded to

Brezhnev's threat of unilateral military intervention by alerting U.S. forces, an action that aroused keen apprehension and immediate criticism of the administration. However, the crisis was so quickly brought under control and terminated that public and congressional pressure was cut short and had no impact on the administration's management of the crisis.

On the other hand, other aspects of the October War provided an ominous warning of the fact that the ability of the United States to preserve its interests in a crisis of this kind can be gravely impaired by constraints imposed by allies who either disapprove of the policy the United States is pursuing or do not want to risk being drawn into it. Thus, during the October War when the United States felt obliged to engage in a massive time-urgent aerial resupply of the Israeli forces, Washington had difficulty obtaining air transit rights from some of its European allies.

Some strategies for crisis avoidance, it should be noted, are also vulnerable to domestic and/or allied constraints. The very idea of cooperative U.S. arrangements with the Soviet Union to moderate rivalry and avoid dangerous crises triggers suspicions in other countries of the formation of a superpower condominium at their expense and arouses fears of old-fashioned spheres of influence.

We noted earlier the suggestion often advanced that Washington and Moscow might reduce the risk of confrontation with each other in some third areas if they were to clarify their interests and policy intentions in a timely fashion so as to avoid entering into escalating competition. Various difficulties that stand in the way of achieving mutual clarification of interests and intentions have already been noted. Here we should note that domestic politics and sensitive allies often operate to make it particularly difficult for the United States to clarify or delimit its interests in some third areas. Washington often finds it difficult to discount the importance it attaches to a particular area from the standpoint of U.S. national interests. There is the ever-present likelihood that someone in the executive branch, in Congress, or among vocal interest groups will be quick to charge that the administration is insufficiently attentive to the need to protect American interests abroad.

PROSPECTS FOR CONTAINMENT WITHOUT CONFRONTATION

Continuing and deepening the drift toward a confrontational relationship that began in the latter part of the Carter administration, the Reagan administration has not yet developed a coherent view of the kind of long-range relationship with the Soviet Union it regards as desirable and feasible. Important disagreements persist within the administration on this fundamental question that have not been resolved; these disagreements, in turn, reflect the diversity of views and images of the Soviet Union within the public and in Congress. At the same time, while undertaking a strengthening of American military forces and adopting a tough posture and rhetoric in its foreign policy, the Reagan administration also occasionally expresses an interest in a more stable, less conflictive relationship with the Soviet Union. On September 22, 1981, for example, Reagan wrote to Brezhnev saying that the United States was interested in developing "a stable and constructive relationship with the Soviet Union." Continuing in language reminiscent of the rhetoric of détente but without mentioning that word, Reagan added that such a relationship, however, must be built upon "restraint and reciprocity," elements that have been "missing from many Soviet actions in recent years." As examples of such Soviet behavior, Reagan mentioned "the USSR's unremitting and comprehensive military buildup over the past 15 years" and its "pursuit of unilateral advantage in various parts of the world—through direct and indirect use of force in regional conflicts." In this context, Reagan added that the role played by Cuba in Africa and Latin America was particularly disturbing and also referred to developments in Poland, Afghanistan, and Kampuchea. He ended by expressing the hope that the two sides can succeed in establishing "a framework of mutual respect for each other's interest and a mutual restraint in the resolution of international crises."[12]

Although earlier in 1981 Secretary of State Haig had on several occasions spoken of the need for new "rules of conduct," the president's letter to Brezhnev evidently did not. Neither, apparently, did Reagan refer to the Basic Principles Agreement of 1972. Left ambiguous for the time being, therefore, is the administration's attitude toward the Basic Principles Agreement. Also lacking in the Reagan administration's policy is a more specific indication of the contributions it would be willing to make to the overall relationship with the Soviet Union under certain conditions, with respect to such matters as trade, credits, scientific and cultural exchanges, and so on. In other words, while urging the Soviet Union to adhere to the norm of "reciprocity," the Reagan administration has not advanced a definition of this norm, nor has it indicated what obligations "reciprocity" would impose on the United States as well as the Soviet Union. Similarly, while enjoining the Soviet Union to behave in the world in accordance with the norm of "restraint" and while giving concrete examples of Soviet actions regarded as inconsistent with such a norm, the Reagan administration has not given a very clear indication of what "restraint" would imply for its own foreign policy behavior.

12. *The New York Times*, September 23, 1981. The verbatim text of President Reagan's letter was not released. The quoted material is from the summary statement issued by the State Department. Reagan repeated his hopes for "a more constructive relationship" with the Soviet Union in a commencement address at Eureka College on May 9, 1982.

Since one of the major lessons that emerges from analysis of why détente failed is that the two superpowers operated with divergent interpretations of the norms of reciprocity and restraint,[13] it is all the more important to address this problem explicitly in considering what kind of new "stable and constructive relationship" with the Soviet Union we are trying to achieve.

Given the greater prominence that deterrence strategy is assuming once again as the major backup for the administration's effort to develop a new containment policy, it behooves us to take stock of its uses and limitations. A strengthening of the U.S. military posture is essential given the failure of détente and the continued buildup of Soviet forces. Under present and foreseeable world conditions there is no substitute for a strong, clear, articulate deterrence posture. But at the same time it is incumbent on American policymakers, Congress, and public opinion to understand that strengthening military capabilities cannot be a substitute for a well-conceived, realistically grounded foreign policy. Creating a "position of strength" or a more favorable balance of forces is only a means to an end. The end itself—namely, the kind of relationship with the Soviet Union that the strengthening of the U.S. military posture is designed to help achieve—must be clarified and a comprehensive strategy for developing that kind of relationship must be formulated.

Beginning with President Ford and continuing with his successors in the White House, the United States has gradually returned to a greater emphasis on containment alone as the basis for policy toward the Soviet Union. Yet many of the conditions which made containment possible during the cold war are lacking in the contemporary era. Collective security arrangements with allies in Europe and elsewhere are much more difficult to arrange or to bring into play as instruments for containment today than in the late 1940s, 1950s, and 1960s. Even heavy military expenditures will not create a position of strength that can be easily converted into appreciable diplomatic dividends. Strengthening of the U.S. military posture may be a necessary condition, but it is certainly not a sufficient condition for achieving the limited objective of "containment without confrontation" in our relations with the Soviet Union.

We must not forget the hard-learned lessons regarding the limited utility of deterrence for preventing encroachments on U.S. interests in third areas during the cold war.[14] Although deterrence was an essential and useful part of containment during that period, it became increasingly evident that deterrence was an unreliable, imperfect strategy at middle

13. Cf., for example, George W. Breslauer, "Why Détente Failed: An Interpretation," in George, *Managing U.S.–Soviet Rivalry*.

14. Alexander L. George and Richard Smoke, *Deterrence in American Foreign Policy: Theory and Practice* (New York: Columbia University Press, 1974).

and lower levels of conflict. An opponent who is dissatisfied with a given situation or sees an opportunity to advance his interests can usually find some way of challenging the status quo, even in the face of a commitment by the United States that is backed by a deterrence posture of some kind. As was evident during the cold war, it was difficult for the United States to devise a comprehensive strategy that deterred all of the options available to an opponent. This "gap" in deterrence is even greater in today's world, and it is evident particularly in situations characterized by low-level conflict, internal instability, "national liberation" struggles, indirect and limited involvement by outside powers, use of proxies, and so on.

Even when U.S. deterrence strategy is successful, it is often best to regard it as no more than a *time-buying* strategy. Successful deterrence seldom eliminates the underlying conflict of interest or the causes of instability. The motivation of other actors to change the status quo in a third area usually persists in the face of deterrence and may become even stronger. The dissatisfied actors may simply create or await more favorable circumstances to renew their challenge. But successful deterrence does at least provide time for the two sides to use, if they will, to work out ways of reducing the escalation potential of the situation. It is often the better part of wisdom to regard deterrence, therefore, as an aid to other conflict-resolution methods that make greater use of diplomacy and negotiation.

Finally, one must ask whether it is realistic to expect of American foreign policy that it prevent *any* further extension of Soviet influence or that it induce Soviet leaders to forego this aim altogether. Rather, it must be expected that the Soviet Union will continue to seek to enhance its position in the world, winning on some occasions and losing on others. What U.S. policy can hope to do is to compete more effectively itself where it can; to act to limit expansion of Soviet influence particularly in areas of high interest to the United States; and to induce Soviet leaders by a variety of means, however imperfect, to moderate their behavior.

7

Economic Relations

MARSHALL GOLDMAN AND RAYMOND VERNON

Special difficulties hamper the United States in any effort to formulate a set of effective economic policies toward the USSR. One set of problems arises from the intimate tie in our relations with the Soviet Union between economic policies on the one hand and political or security policies on the other; whereas in relations with most other countries, these fields of policy can be somewhat insulated from one another, in relations with the USSR that distinction has proved in practice impossible to maintain. Another set of difficulties has been due to the profound incompatibility of the Soviet system of trade and payments with the open global system that U.S. interests would like to see maintained and strengthened; an expansion of trade with the USSR encourages the growth of trading practices that threaten the system. Moreover, the controls the USSR maintains over its trade open up the possibility that the gains from trade will be captured mainly by the Soviet Union. Whereas in relations with most other countries, such differences usually can be accommodated within the existing world system of trade and payments, in the case of the USSR those differences are so vast as to pose special problems of vulnerability for countries that maintain a market economy. Finally, there are the well-known differences in political institutions and processes between the two countries—differences that have pitted a closed and controlled political process against one that is fractionalized, diffuse, and open.

THE POLICIES REVIEWED

Partly as a result of these factors, U.S. policy toward the Soviet Union has appeared vacillating and complex, shifting among a number of different goals. These have been pursued singly or in combination, changing their identity and their weights according to shifts in U.S. political and military policy, and according to the needs of domestic politics.

The Stalinist Era

The end of World War II marked the end of a decade in which U.S. policy toward the USSR had gone through a number of extreme stages, from

159

cautious contact in the early New Deal days, through implacable hostility over the Finnish invasion and the Hitler–Stalin partnership, to wartime support and alliance.

With the onset of the cold war in 1948, the U.S. government instituted a special set of controls over transactions with the Soviet Union and Eastern Europe. Some were aimed at curbing Soviet growth and limiting its supplies of hard currency in order to restrain Stalin's war-making potential; some were smuggled into U.S. law for domestic protectionist purposes. When the Soviet Union emerged as North Korea's supporter in the Korean war, the U.S. Congress responded by including a provision in the Trade Agreement Extension Act of 1951 that denied most-favored-nation (MFN) tariffs to Soviet imports. As a result, Soviet exports to the United States became subject to the very high tariffs enacted under the Smoot-Hawley Tariff Act of 1930, making such exports relatively unprofitable. At the same time, imports of some products, such as various furs and crabmeat, were banned from the United States entirely.

U.S. exports to the USSR were similarly encumbered. Under the terms of the Export Control Act of 1949, prospective exporters of most strategic goods to the Soviet Union were required to obtain licenses from the American government. At the time, Western Europe and Japan were still recovering from the war's destruction, and the United States was the undisputed industrial and technological leader of the noncommunist world. U.S. restrictions on the sale of technologically sophisticated goods to the Soviet Union therefore carried a considerable bite. In addition, most of the countries of Western Europe joined the United States in 1949 to form the Consultative Group Coordinating Committee (COCOM); Japan would join a few years later. COCOM was charged with the task of coordinating the embargo of strategic goods to the Soviet Union. Although exports from the Soviet Union to Western Europe were not subject to similar controls, these were inhibited by the import restrictions that most countries in Western Europe had adopted in order to strengthen their own foreign-exchange positions.

These early measures restricting transactions between the United States and the USSR were probably more important for their symbolic import than for their direct substantive effect. It is not at all clear that during this period the USSR was much interested in increasing its imports and exports with the West; under Stalin's orders, there was a marked shift in the trade flows of Eastern Europe and the Soviet Union away from Western Europe and toward one another. In any event, the denial of Western markets, products, and technology during the Stalin era did not seem to affect Soviet economic and military growth. The late 1940s and early 1950s were years of very rapid growth for the USSR.

With the death of Stalin, political relations between the two countries took a turn for the better. But with the legacy of the cold war still strong, most Americans approached the period of détente with an understandable wariness. Trade with the Soviet bloc had never been of much importance to the U.S. economy. Accordingly, very few champions were to be found in the United States prepared to fight for a less restrictive set of trade policies toward the USSR.

An Initial Opening

Nevertheless, as the years passed, the Western attitude toward the Soviet Union and the Soviet attitude toward the West did begin to change. In part this was because Khrushchev in 1958 embarked on a program designed to liberalize the Soviet Union from within and to increase interaction with the outside world.

For the first time in the postwar era, the Soviet Union seemed to be seriously interested in making significant purchases of industrial machinery from the West. Khrushchev's effort to increase the productivity of Soviet agriculture required greatly increased use of chemical fertilizers. However, the Soviet Union had almost no chemical industry and no industry that built chemical process plants. Between 1959 and 1961, the Soviet Union ordered approximately fifty chemical plants from abroad. This resulted in a brief surge in machinery exports from Western Europe, a surge that ended in 1963; at that time, a particularly disappointing grain harvest obliged the USSR to divert its foreign exchange to grain purchases, while Khrushchev's ouster brought an end to some of his liberalizing policies.

Even in the brief period of expanded Soviet trade, however, the volume of Soviet purchases of foreign goods was still small, not great enough to interest U.S. manufacturers. Exports from West Germany, for instance, totaled only about $200 million a year, and those from the United Kingdom, France, Italy, and Japan amounted to even less. Not surprisingly, the main characteristic of American economic policy toward the Soviet Union continued to be restraint. Surveys among American businessmen at the time indicated a continuation of the cautious attitude toward trade with the Soviet Union.[1]

In the mid-1960s, however, more changes of atmosphere occurred. In April 1966, Premier Aleksei Kosygin announced that, in an effort to speed up economic growth, the Soviet Union would henceforth increase

---

1. *East–West Trade*, U.S. Senate Committee on Foreign Relations, 88th Cong., 2d sess., pts. 1, 2, 3 (Washington, D.C.: U.S. Government Printing Office, 1964); Marshall I. Goldman and Alice Conner, "Businessmen Appraise East–West Trade," *Harvard Business Review* 44, no. 1 (January/February 1966): 6.

significantly its purchases of foreign technology and machinery.[2] This policy declaration was followed in August 1966 by the signing of a contract with Fiat to build a $1.5 billion automobile plant in the USSR. Soon thereafter, the USSR unveiled a shopping list of major industrial projects whose import components would come to approximately $5 billion in 1969 prices. That the USSR was serious at the time is reflected by the fact that almost all the plant imports that were then listed were actually realized in later years.

With the accelerated pace of Soviet imports, the interest of U.S. businessmen quickened. By 1968, West Germany doubled its 1962 exports to the USSR, raising the total to over $400 million, and the Japanese and the Italians were not far behind. Observing these lost opportunities, members of the American business community and Congress began to reexamine the effectiveness and wisdom of existing policy.[3] Gradually, the mood changed from one of restraint in the approach to Soviet trade to one of outright encouragement of such trade.

The shift in the position of U.S. businessmen and the Congress at this stage raises the usual question of whether profit once more had managed to rise above principle. That conclusion, however, would be too simple. As other essays in this volume point out, after 1963 the prevailing mood in East–West relations was one of détente. The new mood was exposed to considerable stress in 1968, with the Soviet Union's invasion of Czechoslovakia and its continued support of North Vietnam. Factors such as these served to postpone the time when the quickened interest of U.S. business in Soviet trade would actually be translated into a less restrictive U.S. policy, demonstrating that political factors still played a major role in determining such matters. Finally, in 1972, the switch to a liberalized policy occurred, generated at least in part by the interest of U.S. businessmen in sharing in a growing Soviet market.

An Era of Linkage

As the mood toward trade with the Soviet Union began to change, the U.S. government acknowledged the change by drastically relaxing its controls over East–West trade. But the relaxation was not unconditional; instead it was linked to Soviet political behavior. "Linkage," as Secretary of State Henry Kissinger came to call his policy, tied the liberalization of restrictions on trade, technology, and credits to the Soviet Union's demonstrating a commitment to restrained international conduct, a willing-

2. *Pravda*, April 6, 1966, p. 7.
3. *East–West Trade*, U.S. Senate Committee on Banking and Currency, 90th Cong., 2d sess. (Washington, D.C.: U.S. Government Printing Office, 1968).

ness to help settle concrete issues including those of Vietnam, Berlin, and the Middle East, and a willingness to negotiate a SALT treaty.[4]

It is difficult to assess how much the USSR actually modified its foreign policy in response to these trade pressures during the few years in which linkage was practiced. Henry Kissinger, who was the president's assistant for National Security Affairs in 1972, was of the view that the Soviet Union tempered its behavior in the Middle East at the time and made other small concessions in response to the linkage policy. However, other articles in this volume, such as those by Talbott and Simes, reflect a sense of uncertainty on this critical point. On the other hand, the USSR did respond in substantial ways to U.S. pressures in the human rights field, directed mainly at changing internal Soviet practices.[5] *Refuseniks* who had been imprisoned for seeking to emigrate were sometimes released from jail, and a large percentage of those for whom emigration was requested were allowed to leave. Similarly, a repugnant education tax levied on emigrants was removed. In much the same way, pressure from the West Europeans pushed the Soviets into agreeing to a human rights clause in the 1975 Helsinki Agreement; this later became the source of considerable embarrassment for the Soviet Union.

Concurrently, the U.S. government shifted its emphasis from hampering trade to promoting it. Under the terms of the U.S.–USSR trade agreement of October 18, 1972, the two countries agreed to take specific measures to facilitate a sharp increase in trade between them. For instance, the American side agreed that the president would go to Congress to seek a change in the 1951 Trade Agreement Extension Act which denied MFN treatment to Soviet goods. As part of the same package, the Soviet Union for its part agreed to resume payment of its lend-lease debt incurred during World War II; it undertook to make three token payments totaling $48 million between October 1972 and July 1975. Future annual payments would be made contingent on the restoration of MFN status by the United States. As a byproduct, with the resumption of lend-lease payments, the Soviet Union would again become eligible for loans from the United States Export-Import Bank. Under the trade agreement, the United States also agreed to the formation of the U.S.–USSR Commercial Commission, consisting of senior government economic officials, to ensure that there would be high-level attention paid to any trade problems that might arise.

In accordance with the spirit of the détente era, the United States did what it could to facilitate the sale of grain in 1972 and again from 1975 to 1979, after the U.S.–Soviet grain agreement was signed. In the same

4. Henry Kissinger, *Years of Upheaval* (Boston: Little, Brown, 1982), p. 247.
5. Kissinger, *Years of Upheaval*, pp. 204–05, 247, 252, 995–96.

spirit, U.S. laws governing export controls were altered so that the burden of proof no longer lay with the American exporter to explain why such trade should be allowed. Instead, export controls were not to be applied unless the Department of Commerce could show that the sales of such goods would threaten American national security or that similar goods were unavailable in the West or in Japan.[6]

It was during this period that some of the incompatibilities generated by the differences in the trading systems of the two countries began to surface. All foreign trade of the USSR is conducted by the state, operating through designated foreign trade organizations. We shall shortly be exploring some of the implications of that arrangement; but it is sufficient at this point to observe that the Soviet government acts as a monopsonist when it buys from foreign sellers. At times, that power is ineptly used. But in 1972 the USSR was able to complete one of the largest grain purchases in history up to that time without causing a noticeable increase in the price of grain. Only after the Soviet purchasing agents had completed their mission did word of what had happened reach the market; then the prices tripled. It turned out that officials in the U.S. Department of Agriculture were informed of what was happening but did nothing with the information. The incident had considerable impact on the U.S. public, contributing to the souring of the trading atmosphere that was to follow.

A Return to Tension

The period of a positive U.S. trade policy toward the Soviet Union was relatively short-lived, covering only three or four years. While it is hard to assess blame, the Soviets argue that the U.S. government did not live up to its agreement to provide MFN treatment and access to Export-Import Bank credits. Led by Senator Henry Jackson and Congressman Charles Vanik, the U.S. Congress not only refused to revoke the 1951 Trade Agreement Extension Act which denied MFN treatment to Soviet goods, but it passed the so-called Jackson-Vanik Amendment to the Trade Act of 1974, which only granted the extension of MFN status on the condition of Soviet willingness to allow a substantial flow of immigrants from the Soviet Union. Continued Soviet harassment of potential immigrants and dissidents plus the arrest in 1978 of J. Crawford, a Moscow representative of International Harvester, ensured popular as well as congressional support for such punitive legislation. In the years to follow, the United States would complain about Soviet expansionism in Africa, the invasion of Afghanistan, interference in Poland, and the shooting down of a Korean

6. Franklyn D. Holzman, *International Trade under Communism* (New York: Basic Books, 1976), pp. 151, 159.

commercial aircraft. Unlike the containment era of the 1940s and 1950s, however, the post-1975 restraints on trade with the Soviet Union were made by selective denials of export licenses for critical items rather than by more sweeping prohibitions.

During this period, the U.S. government received constant reminders of its own limited capacity to act effectively unless there was collaboration from other industrialized countries. The perennial competition of exporting countries to sell their machinery to the USSR kept generating frictions. Cases commonly arose in which the U.S. government was prevented from denying the USSR some useful technology, simply because the same technology or something very much like it could be obtained from other sources. In the most spectacular effort of the U.S. government to impose such a denial—the case of turbines for the Soviet gas pipeline to Germany—the limitations of the U.S. capacity to prevent such purchases became palpable.

The competition for sales to the Soviet Union also led Western exporters to undercut one another by offering heavily subsidized credit terms. Periodically, the exporting countries would agree to place a floor on interest rates charged the USSR, and just as often the agreement would be violated. The most recent attempt at credit restraint was made in 1982, with uncertain results.

The Policies Reviewed

Looking back on the three-and-one-half decades in which the U.S. government has shaped and reshaped its economic policies toward the USSR, one can discern a number of different approaches, never fully juxtaposed or reconciled, that have motivated U.S. actions. At one extreme has been the view that transactions with the USSR should be held to an absolute minimum, in the hope of increasing the general stress on the Soviet economy; such increased stress, according to extreme versions of this view, might eventually change the nature of the Soviet system and reduce its warlike potential. A second view has been more restrained in its objective, which has been to retard the Soviet Union's buildup of its military capability by selectively denying it strategic materials, hoping thereby to maintain or widen the U.S. lead. A third view has been to use economic restrictions as a way of punishing or rewarding the USSR hoping thereby to modify its aggressive behavior. And a fourth, in various degrees and variations, would positively encourage economic contacts with the USSR, in the hope that its people will develop a taste not only for Western products but also for Western ideas.

Although U.S. government policy has vacillated among the various objectives, its behavior has been consistent in certain basic respects.

One consistent characteristic has been the deep-seated ideological preference of the United States to hold down the direct transactional role of government in trade and investment. In spite of the importance that the U.S. government has attached at times to the management of its economic relations with the USSR, the government's direct transactional role has been kept to a minimum: the introduction of new economic initiatives and the execution of economic transactions have by and large been left to the private sector, to a degree unmatched by other countries.

Another characteristic of U.S. policy has been the tendency to use general rules, formal procedures, and publicized decisions in the administration of its various policies toward the USSR, once again in sharp contrast to the approaches of other countries. Here, too, the style of the U.S. government has been typical of the application of its governmental powers in general.

A third characteristic, noted also in the Destler and Bowie chapters in this volume, reflects the fact that governmental powers over foreign economic policy are widely diffused within the U.S. government. Numerous studies have emphasized the point that the U.S. decision-making process is almost unique among nations in the extent to which such governmental powers are shared among the various units of government. Within the executive branch, the defense establishment is constantly at odds with the State Department, while Commerce and the White House provide added points of view. Moreover, as the various studies indicate, each of these units as a matter of course makes complex alliances with congressmen and their staffs in an effort to carry their positions in the executive branch. To add to the complexities, both the president and the Congress are obliged at times to bow to the courts, as individuals and groups exercise their rights of judicial initiative and appeal.

With a structure of that sort, policy initiatives and actions to block policy initiatives can come from a dozen different quarters. Where special interests are concerned, therefore, the U.S. process offers a picture of frenetic activism, with results that are often both unpredictable and inconsistent in direction; the export restrictions relating to the Soviet gas pipeline and the offers to sell grain to the USSR are only the latest illustrations of such contradictions. As a result, it has been especially hard for the Executive to conduct a policy of linkage in relations with the USSR; neither the Executive's power to punish nor its power to reward has been secure.

All these characteristics promise to some extent to typify U.S. behavior in the future. That prospect obviously places some powerful restraints on the kinds of policies that realistically can be considered.

THE MERITS OF U.S. POLICIES

Deciding on the right U.S. policy for East–West trade relations turns not only on what is feasible but also on what will produce the appropriate benefits. To calculate the costs and benefits of various policies, however, entails some difficult judgments. In the first place, how will restrictions on the export of strategic goods and technologies affect the behavior and performance of the USSR and its COMECON partners? A second group of questions addresses the noncommunist countries and the enterprises within their borders. Are there common policies with which these countries can be expected to agree? In the absence of agreement, how can they and the industries within their borders be expected to behave toward the USSR and Eastern Europe? Finally, there are the judgments relating to the United States: what economic difference will the presence or absence of restrictions have on the U.S. economy?

Judgments of this sort are difficult in any case, requiring not only an estimate of the existing situation but also estimates of various counterfactual possibilities; and not only estimates of the immediate impact of any given restraint but also estimates of the adjustments that the USSR might ultimately undertake. If the question, for instance, is whether to deny the Soviet Union some important U.S. export, such as blades for the turbines of giant gas compressors, it is not enough to establish the fact that the denial will be painful to the USSR; it is necessary also to determine if, after the USSR has made its various adjustments to the embargo, it will be in a better or a worse position than if the denial had not occurred. By the nature of the question, exploring the consequences of any policy becomes an exercise in projection far beyond the point at which hard data are still relevant. It demands an extensive understanding of how the economy of the USSR is structured and how it operates under stress. Judgments such as these rest on fact and speculation that extend far beyond the individual case, requiring generalizations about the Soviet system as a whole.

Increasing the Stress

Perhaps the most important judgments regarding the wisdom of the West's export restrictions have to do with their overall effects on the strength of the USSR and its COMECON partners. Those who would limit economic contacts with the USSR to an absolute minimum usually see the added costs as likely to create a more restless and less governable Soviet populace. With more difficulties at home, according to this set of views, Soviet leaders are likely to be less adventuresome abroad. Those

who support more contact also hope to reduce the aggressiveness of the
USSR by such a policy.

The two views are not necessarily contradictory; both could be right.
The important point to recognize is that propositions such as these are
altogether conjectural; no hard data exist as a basis for choosing between
them.

Yet one must realistically admit that, right or wrong, it is certain that
our allies will not buy the restrictive approach. The long history of the
differences between the United States and Europe on this issue is touched
on in the chapters by Hoffmann and Huntington in this volume. The gulf
between the United States and Europe on the subject has been very wide
at times in the past few years, particularly because of the disputes over the
gas pipeline from the Soviet Union. And as long as the United States
pursues highly restrictive policies based primarily on political and security factors, the prospects of finding a working consensus with the
Europeans on this basic subject seem close to zero. And without the support of Europe, a U.S. effort to curtail economic contact with the USSR is
almost meaningless. The U.S. government's choices, therefore, are more
limited, ranging from a policy of aloofness and selective denial to one of
the aggressive promotion of contact between the two camps.

Restraining a War-Making Capacity

To restrain the USSR's capacity to make war, U.S. analysts regularly
identify products and technologies that the USSR would have difficulty in
providing for itself and seek to withhold such products or technologies.
The object has been to exacerbate the bottlenecks in the system and place
obstacles in the way of the Soviet learning process in order to create or
protect a U.S. technological lead in the short run, and perhaps cumulatively, to enlarge the lead in the longer term.

After thirty-five years of pursuing such a policy with varying degrees
of intensity, however, there is no hard evidence that on balance it has had
its intended effect. The difficulty with such a policy is obvious. In the
short run, to be sure, it does stand a chance of producing its intended
effect, creating or producing a technological lead. The longer-run effects, however, are much less certain. Sometimes denial slows up forward
movement; sometimes it stimulates its target to find effective substitutes
or to find ways of doing without. In the Soviet case, there are instances in
which it is reasonable to assume that restriction has slowed the growth of
Soviet capabilities, but also instances in which it is reasonable to assume
the opposite. As a result, we cannot exclude the possibility that the extensive control system of past decades in some respects may actually have
improved the Soviet Union's present capacity to make war.

At first blush, these conclusions may seem to go against one's intuitions. But a little reflection will indicate why they are quite consistent with similar conclusions regarding the effects of restrictions in somewhat analogous situations. Consider, for instance, the industrialization processes of developing countries. A number of such countries have deliberately refrained from importing technologically advanced products from more industrialized countries, aware that their action would probably handicap their economy in the short run. Their hope has been, however, to stimulate their own enterprises over the longer run to master difficult production problems; India's outstanding success in the field of large-scale electrical generators and Brazil's equally striking success with the manufacture of executive aircraft illustrate the strategy.[7]

In the case of the Soviet Union, there are special reasons for supposing that U.S. denials of strategic products may galvanize the country to overcome its vulnerabilities over the longer run. To understand the basis for that conclusion, one has to begin with some appreciation of the sluggishness and insensitivity of the Soviet planning process. Exceedingly strong signals are needed for a significant redirection of resources on the part of the system. Every so often, vast elephantine shifts do occur: a movement to rural electrification, to the use of chemical fertilizer, to the mechanization of agriculture, to the development of gas reserves. But these initiatives are a reaction to visible failings in the system too obvious to be disregarded.

Picture a situation in which the USSR is unequivocally vulnerable with respect to some critically important item—vulnerable in the sense that its supplies come from foreign sources, that the sources could conceivably be cut off for political reasons, and that the development of replacement sources would take considerable time or entail considerable cost. As long as such vulnerability continues, the supplier country does have some capacity to disrupt the USSR's economy.

Our judgment is that modest vulnerabilities of this sort can be created and maintained for some period of time, provided their existence is not drawn to the attention of the upper planning echelons of the USSR. The original decision to import is generally made at lower levels of the Soviet hierarchy, the upper levels usually being involved only on high-priority matters. As long as the critical supplies are small in amount and as long as they continue to be available from foreign sources without interruption,

7. For the Indian case, see Ravi Ramamurti, "Strategic Behavior of Effectiveness of State Owned Enterprises in High-Technology Industries: A Comparative Study in the Heavy Engineering Industry in India" (D. B. A. thesis, Harvard University, 1982), chap. 6. For the Brazilian case, see "Airlines Have 1100 Planes on Firm Order: U.S. Hold on Market is Slipping," *Air Transport World*, vol. 18, no. 3, March 1981, pp. 64–65; "Brazil Seeking New Aircraft Markets," *Aviation Week and Space Technology*, June 27, 1977, pp. 63–65.

the vulnerability can go "uncorrected" for extended periods of time. Indeed, managers in the USSR that rely on such imported goods as inputs generally have strong incentives not to interrupt the flow, inasmuch as any shift to domestic sources will introduce new uncertainties over their plan fulfillment.

In this kind of system the U.S. export restriction lists can serve the Soviet planning authorities as a convenient monitoring device, a dry run on their vulnerabilities. Soviet authorities hardly need such a list to tell them that they are still incapable of producing satisfactory mainframe computers, large aircraft engines, or oversized steel pipe. But for hundreds of less obvious deficiencies, the U.S. export restriction lists can serve at times to bypass the clogged lines of internal communication, to stimulate the Soviet planning process, and to speed up the reaction time of the USSR to its strategic weaknesses. Given the sluggish character of the Soviet planning process, one cannot be sure that even such a stimulus will induce a corrective reaction; but evidence of such a reaction has occasionally appeared. For instance, the CIA report of the middle 1970s that the Soviet Union and its allies would become importers of large quantities of petroleum by 1985 appears to have galvanized the Soviet planning authorities into action. After having ignored the repeated appeals of their own specialists for increased investment in the Soviet petroleum industry, Soviet political leaders finally bestirred themselves after the issuance of the CIA report.[8]

To be sure, the USSR will not always find an acceptable replacement for a foreign product that has been denied it. For instance, it was shaken by the U.S. denial of spare parts for its Kama River truck plant following the invasion of Afghanistan and by the U.S. denial of various products required for its gas pipeline projects. But even in these cases, U.S. denials have prodded Soviet planners into attempting to overcome vulnerabilities at a time when the burden of the adjustment could reasonably be met. It is in this sense that U.S. denial efforts give the USSR a dry run on its vulnerabilities and a chance for substitution and learning, thus reducing rather than increasing U.S. capacity to squeeze the country into an acute emergency.

The dangers of advertising Soviet vulnerabilities well in advance of the outbreak of hostilities are apparent, and the potential costs of such advertising are obvious. The hope of those who press for a strict system of restrictions is that the retarding and bottleneck-creating effects of such restrictions will more than offset their stimulative and learning effects. There is no doubt that individual cases exist in which the costs of

8. See Marshall I. Goldman, *Enigma of Soviet Petroleum: Half Empty or Half Full?* (Boston: George Allen & Unwin, 1980), p. 178.

developing a substitute source for an embargoed product or the costs of doing without such a product impose a burden on the Soviet economy. But the assumption that the aggregate costs to the USSR generated by the restrictions are enough to offset the advantages that the Soviet Union gets from them is no more than a guess. And certain characteristics of the Soviet economy suggest strongly that the guess may be wrong.

The strength of a policy of denial depends on its ability to create bottlenecks and scarcities. In the USSR, there is no doubt that acute bottlenecks do exist from time to time, often for reasons that have little to do with the U.S. denial policy. For instance, the absence of chemical machine-building equipment, machine tools used to produce miniature ball bearings, ammonia plants, geological exploration systems for petroleum, sophisticated drill-bit plants, pipe-laying equipment, and computers has retarded Soviet economic and military growth. However, by far the more common problem for Soviet planners is not the lack of capital and human resources but their misapplications throughout the system. Foreign technology and foreign machines sometimes help break bottlenecks; but they are commonly misplaced and misused, sometimes putting off the development of more appropriate solutions.[9]

The same tendency toward lack of coordination and misapplication in the system means that equipment and labor are underutilized, while industrial materials are wasted. For example, because of various wasteful practices, the expenditure of fuel per ton of open-hearth steel is considerably higher in the Soviet Union than it is in the United States and Japan. Similarly, the expenditure of fuel per kilowatt of electricity generated is higher in the Soviet Union than it is in the United States. The Soviet Union also uses more metal per unit of engine power than is used in comparable engines in the United States.[10] These results are mainly due to inadequate incentives and coordination, and they generate a level of factor productivity for the Soviet economy that is about one-half that of the United States.[11]

In our judgment, the poor coordination and wasteful use of resources that typify normal Soviet industrial performance provide a cushion for Soviet planners when the upper levels of the bureaucracy have been alerted to the need to correct some specific vulnerability in the economy. If the priority is high enough and the goal narrow enough, some of the

9. Thane Gustafson, *Selling the Soviets the Rope? Soviet Technology Policy and U.S. Export Controls* (Santa Monica, Calif.: The Rand Corporation, April 1981), p. 6.

10. T. Khachaturov, "Prirodnye resursy i planirovanie narodnogo khozyaistva" [Natural resources and national economic planning], *Voprosy ekonomiki*, no. 8 (August 1973), p. 25.

11. Abram Bergson, *Productivity in the Social System—The USSR and the West* (Cambridge, Mass.: Harvard University Press, 1978), p. 101.

slack resources that are to be found throughout the system can be mobilized to overcome the difficulty. In some cases, to be sure, the effort may be slowed down because the problems are too vast (as in the case of agriculture) or because critical technological inputs are missing (as in the case of some advanced electronics applications). But more generally, engineers and technicians can be rounded up for the relatively uncomplicated task of cutting, pasting, fitting, and testing that comprises much of the activity associated with imitative industrial innovations. (Indeed, the number of persons classified in the USSR as scientists and engineers is about twice that of the United States, suggesting slack in this category as well.) Specialized materials that are being stockpiled or used in the civilian economy, once they are located, can readily be diverted to the higher-priority projects. This capacity to draw on slack resources, we believe, is why the USSR has been able to produce extraterrestrial satellites, submarines, nuclear reactors, and high-performing fighter aircraft, all with considerable speed and of acceptable quality, as the need has arisen.

The effectiveness with which the USSR responds to the information it gains from U.S. denial lists depends in some cases on the country's ability to produce the needed products from domestic resources that previously had been improperly utilized; but it depends in other cases on the country's ability to find other foreign suppliers of the proscribed technologies or products. Judgments on the ineffectualness of U.S. embargoes come mainly from unsystematic and anecdotal evidence. But cumulatively the evidence is persuasive. And it points to several key conclusions.

Since World War II, the technological links between the U.S. economy and facilities located in foreign countries have been growing at a quite staggering rate. There has been a rapid growth in the number of foreign subscriptions to technical journals in the United States, as well as a rapid increase in the number of foreign graduate students enrolled in technical fields in U.S. universities. In addition, there has been an extensive internationalization of U.S. engineering and other technical firms, partly through licensing agreements with independent producers outside the United States, partly through the creation of foreign subsidiaries by U.S. firms. The number and intimacy of the foreign technological links that the U.S. economy has created suggest that efforts to restrict the flow of technology are highly vulnerable and that they are getting more so. U.S. technology has become increasingly accessible in foreign jurisdictions, sometimes through channels that are quite legitimate in character, sometimes by illegal means. And as the U.S. government has pressed its efforts to embargo strategic items, the USSR has acquired increasing experience in the art of ferreting out alternative sources of supply.

Besides, even when the United States can guard the precise specifications needed to duplicate a new technological capability, it has much greater difficulty concealing the fact that the capability exists. Often, the knowledge that the capability has been achieved is enough; the history of scientific research and industrial innovation suggests that once scientists and engineers are aware that a given capability has already been achieved, they proceed in their search with a much higher expectation of success. Accordingly, where the flow of technological information is concerned, restrictions applied at the U.S. border have lost a considerable part of their meaning.

In addition to the fact that the U.S. border has grown more porous, there is also the fact that in many of the industries that encompass crucial technological areas, U.S. technology no longer enjoys a commanding lead. Accordingly, the technology originating in other nations is often quite good enough to serve Soviet needs.

Agreement among the industrialized countries, therefore, is necessary for any serious effort at denial; when other industrial countries fail to go along with a U.S. attempt to withhold technology or products, the likelihood that the U.S. effort will have much effect is considerably reduced. But such agreements unfortunately entail a cost for the United States. Over the years, justifiably or not, other countries have come to think of these agreements as something that the Americans want and that the other countries concede; the United States is seen as securing the benefits of the undertakings while the other countries assume the burdens. Just how divisive the issue can be has been amply demonstrated in the battle over the building of the Urengoi natural gas pipeline. To the West Europeans, the pipeline not only meant an additional source of energy supply, but exports and jobs in a recession. To U.S. policymakers, however, the pipeline was seen as an example of selling the hangman a rope: a case in which the West finances the Soviet export of a crucial commodity that provides the Soviet Union with badly needed hard currency and that someday may be used for political blackmail. In the end, the U.S. government lamely modified its ineffectual restrictions. The result of the quarrel was that the United States managed to convert what should have been an East–West issue into a West–West issue, in which the only clear winner was the Soviet Union.

The difference in view between Europe and the United States stems partly from the fact that U.S. interests have had relatively little economic stake in the maintenance of East–West trade. Only in 1975 and 1976 did U.S. machinery exports to the USSR substantially exceed a half-billion dollars. For the most part, therefore, the United States is not giving up much when it urges an embargo on machinery exports to the Soviet Union. As a consequence, the United States has jockeyed itself into a position of appearing to impose undue costs on the rest of the alliance while escaping similar costs for itself. This is made all the more apparent by the fact that the United States, which does have a major stake in agricultural exports to the Soviet Union, has awarded itself an exception from its own policy of denial. To add insult to injury, the exception is justified by a transparently feeble rationalization—namely, that the USSR's purchase of the grain will reduce its economic strength by reducing its foreign exchange resources.

It will be objected, of course, that the reaction of the other members of COCOM to U.S. proposals for strategic export controls is unreasonable, that the U.S. desire to enforce a web of COCOM restrictions is intended for the benefit of all the alliance members. The others have characteristically replied, however, that their desire for security against the Soviet threat is no less than that of the United States; that if they thought the sale of technology and goods to the USSR or the purchase of goods from the USSR weakened the relative position of the West, they would be foolish to allow it; and that their ability to make such judgments is at least as good as that of the United States. Irrespective of the merits of the debate, the strains that it places upon the unity of the West are considerable.

All told, therefore, the efforts of the United States to restrain the USSR's war-making capacity by restricting exports are having consequences that are altogether uncertain; they may even be having the opposite of their intended effects. By strengthening the USSR's autarkic capabilities and by weakening our NATO ties, the effort could be tipping the war-making scales in favor of the USSR.

Signaling Displeasure

More difficult to evaluate is the question whether it is useful to use trade restrictions from time to time as an expression of disapproval of the political or military behavior of Eastern countries, such as on the occasion of the Afghanistan invasion.

The objectives of the U.S. government in expressing displeasure over some objectionable policy of the USSR are usually quite complex. One purpose—perhaps the most important one—is simply to find some vent for U.S. frustration in cases in which the U.S. government has no way of striking back. Barely distinguishable from that motivation is the desire of U.S. leaders to signal their U.S. constituencies in some cases that they are not indifferent to Soviet policies. Another objective, however, is to stiffen the backs of groups outside the United States—of the victims themselves, or of third countries. And yet another is to try to persuade the USSR to change its policies.

There is a respectable case for the view that the USSR is sensitive to manifestations of displeasure. We have already observed that it was prepared to go a little way to meet U.S. demands during the linkage period. Moreover, the world's outcries after the Afghanistan invasion, some contend, have been partly responsible for the USSR's seemingly ineffectual pursuit of Afghan guerrillas, as well as its muted role in Poland and the Middle East.

But these cases suggest that manifestations of displeasure on the part of the United States will only work in some cases: if they are attached to some quid pro quo, as in the case of the linkage era; or if they are reinforced by a large number of other countries. But as the Destler chapter suggests, the capacity of the United States, under its diffuse system of governance, to manage a policy of linkage is very limited; that was amply demonstrated by the disruptive impact of the Jackson-Vanik Amendment on Secretary Kissinger's linkage policy. And the ability of the U.S. government to secure the cooperation of other countries on any set of strongly restrictive measures is also limited.

In practice, therefore, there will be only a very occasional instance in which the signaling device will produce results.

Protecting the Western Trade Regime

One type of threat to the West that is associated with the growth of East–West trade is mentioned only infrequently—the possibility that such growth may help to weaken the existing trade regime within the West itself. Operating mainly through the rules of the General Agreement on Tariffs and Trade (GATT) and the European Community, the Atlantic alliance countries have managed over the past thirty-five years to create a remarkably open system among themselves for the movement of industrial goods. The system is, of course, riddled with exceptions: limitations on the movement of steel, automobiles, and textiles are illustrative. Still, the system is remarkable for its vitality, and it presumptively produces major economic gains for the West.

Trade with the East, on the other hand, is conducted along the lines that centrally directed economies require, which differ profoundly from the Western system in two important respects. First, as noted earlier, the Eastern authorities begin with a principle that is the obverse of the Western rule. Whereas the West assumes that all trade is permitted unless the state intervenes, the East assumes that no trade occurs until the state initiates it; that is why the state can act as a monopsonist in the acquisition of technology and grain. But it is the second principle that creates the real source of conflict. Authorities of the Eastern countries typically try to set up their trade arrangements in a way that guarantees a balance between their imports and their exports in each separate segment of their trade. West Germany sells the steel and related equipment for gas pipelines and is paid off eventually in deliveries of gas; Pepsico trades soft drinks for vodka; and so on.

From the viewpoint of the West, a system that forces a balance between imports and exports in the trade of every country or every firm undermines the trade regimes developed in the West under the GATT and the European Community. In order to achieve the required bilateral balance, each country or each firm is obliged to take the goods of the other in amounts sufficient to bring about balance. The countries participating in the GATT or the European Community will be obliged to reserve corners of their national markets for the products of their Eastern partners, irrespective of the competitive quality of products being offered by trading partners in the West. The economic gains from trade for the West are accordingly sharply reduced.

This fundamental incompatibility between the East's trading system and that of the West has always existed. But East–West trade has been sufficiently limited in amount up to now so that the occasional awkwardnesses created by such a requirement could be handled as special cases. Accordingly, the aborted trade agreement between the United States and the USSR that was negotiated in 1972 contained an ambiguous clause that simply allowed each party to ban imports from the other whenever it felt that such goods would "cause, threaten or contribute to the disruption of the domestic market." At present levels of East–West trade, Western governments could presumably go on, without great loss, sweeping problems of this sort under the rug. But if there were ever a substantial increase in such trade, it would place new stresses on the existing trade arrangements within the West, imperiling the substantial economic and political advantages that have been derived from the present system.

Problems such as these suggest a need for a more effective set of economic policies toward the USSR. But the policies appropriate for dealing with this problem, although they might entail restrictions in some circumstances, would be quite different in objective from the restrictions embodied in the present U.S. system of security export controls, and could readily be distinguished from such controls.

Capturing the Gains from Trade

There is a related area in which worries over economic interactions with the USSR do seem to be based on solid considerations. Overall, present patterns of trade between East and West probably generate gains for both sides. But given the present institutional structures and ground rules under which East–West trade is conducted, the odds seem overwhelming that the East captures most of the gains from trade. Indeed, the possibility is not to be excluded that, when measured in social welfare terms, there is a significant volume of transactions in which the gains to the West are negative.

The tilt in that direction is suggested by a number of different factors. One factor pointing to the likelihood that the East captures the bulk of the gains is the fact that, apart from the items subject to security controls, the level and composition of the trade between East and West are determined by the official policies of the East, not by those of the West. In principle, unless the appropriate authorities in the East have determined that there are gains to be made for their economies from a given transaction, the transaction does not take place.

On the Western side, on the other hand, no similar screening occurs; any proposal from the East that a private buyer or seller in the West wishes to pursue can presumably take place unless it is blocked by security controls. Besides, no effective coordination of buying or selling power takes place on the Western side. There may be occasional coordination among the buyers or sellers of a single nationality, such as the French or the Japanese; but there is rarely collaboration of buyers or sellers of different Western nationalities such as the gas-pipeline deal produced.

If private gain were the equivalent of social gain, the fact that the judgment was in private hands rather than in the hands of government authorities might not matter a great deal. But discrepancies between the two are common, especially in East–West trade.

One source of the discrepancy is the role played by public subsidies in such trade. Grain figures heavily in the West's exports to the USSR; and grain production is subsidized to some degree by agricultural research and extension services, by price support programs, and by government loans. Another part of the eastward flow is capital equipment. Such equipment is commonly financed by the East through long-term loans offered by the West; and these loans are typically subsidized by Western governments. In addition to capital equipment, the East also imports considerable quantities of technology from the West; these too are subsidized heavily by Western governments.

The fact that the East can exert some means of monopsony or monopoly power in its transactions with Western enterprises adds to the risk that the East may be seizing an undue share of the gains. In the case of most products, to be sure, the gains that the USSR can eke out from its monopsony or monopoly power are probably not very large.[12] But there are important exceptions to that generalization, including notably sales of technology. A Western seller of technology, when selling to a centrally

12. M. M. Kostecki, ed., *Soviet Impact on Commodity Markets* (London: Macmillan Press, 1983).

directed economy, does not have any of the usual alternatives that normally exist in the foreign markets of the West: failing to license the technology, the Western seller does not have a substantial possibility of exporting products to Eastern markets that incorporate the technology; nor does the Western seller have the ready possibility of setting up a producing subsidiary in the East. From the seller's viewpoint, therefore, if there is to be any profit from the use of the technology in Eastern economies, the license is usually the only alternative. And because the technology is already in existence, any licensing fees received from the East represent almost clear profit. With the bargaining conditions set up in this way, Eastern buyers will almost certainly manage to extract a much better price for the technology than a Western buyer with the same information.

The Key Lessons

Some fundamental propositions are suggested by this analysis that should be governing in the development of East–West economic relations. First, the relationship of the United States to other noncommunist industrial countries must be a central consideration in the choice of policy. Without joint actions, the U.S. capacity to develop an effective trade policy toward the Soviet Union is quite limited; this conclusion applies both to the U.S. efforts to deny the Soviet Union goods that are useful for its military potential and U.S. efforts to generate gains from trade with the Soviet Union. Second, the advantages that the United States gains from holding back strategic goods are advantages of uncertain value; indeed, there is a substantial risk that they are actually counterproductive. By giving the USSR a dry run on its vulnerabilities and by reducing its dependence on external resources for critical items, the restrictions produce complex results whose net effects on Soviet war-making capabilities are uncertain.

MANAGING EAST–WEST ECONOMIC RELATIONS

The National Context

In developing its economic policies toward the Soviet Union, the United States is unlikely to stray very far from the fundamental constraints imposed by its ideology and its institutions. Its preference for limiting the direct transactional role of the U.S. government in trade and investment will surely continue, leaving such activities largely to the private sector. Moreover, consistent with the U.S. preferences for restraining the role of government, U.S. policies will continue to lean toward developing rules of the game that are nonselective in application, such as the nondiscriminatory application of tariffs and the mechanistic application of quotas pursuant to explicit transparent formulas.

And despite those preferences at the level of principle, the U.S. system will continue to leave plenty of room for narrower interests in the country to attempt to improve their positions within any general program that the government may devise. These enduring characteristics are likely to shape any policies that the U.S. government may adopt.

Relations with Third Countries

Where the U.S. government has been at its best in the development of effective economic policies has been in promoting general regimes among nations that limit the direct operational role of government. That kind of regime has governed relations between the United States and its principal allies since the end of World War II. It was noted earlier that any considerable increase in trade with the USSR under the rules of the game that the USSR prefers would weaken such a regime. An important corollary is that the weakening of the existing regime—epitomized in GATT and by various other agreements in support of an open competitive market—will concurrently increase the willingness of those countries to accept the USSR's terms for doing more business. The German gas deal, for instance, can be seen in part as the country's response to the fact that it could not rely on economic arrangements outside the Soviet bloc to assure supplies of energy, as well as to the more pervasive fact that the existing system was not producing full employment for Germany. If the GATT system weakens much further and if the open-market system which the United States has promoted begins to falter, the ability of the United States to frame effective economic policies toward the USSR will weaken as well.

Practically speaking, for those who are concerned with maintaining an effective set of economic relations toward the USSR, U.S. efforts to strengthen an open trading system for the world offer the most feasible area for action. Restrictive provisions designed explicitly to deal with the USSR seem much less promising, given the characteristics of the U.S. system of governance, because they constantly require the U.S. side to address individual cases in a context that is highly politicized and involves strong special interests, and in a context that demands the active cooperation of other countries to support individual cases.

Bilateral Policies

If a special restrictive regime toward the USSR is unfeasible or ineffectual, are there other possibilities for special policies toward it that might produce constructive results? One possibility suggested earlier was that of deliberately expanding our economic contacts with the USSR in the hope that increased contacts will have the effect of reducing the Soviet Union's ability and propensity to engage in destructive foreign policies. That line of policy may be worth pursuing. If it were followed, however, a number of important points would have to be taken into account in its implementation.

First, the principal advantage by far to be gained from such a policy is that it would reduce the gap between the United States and its allies and therefore increase the probability of cooperation and joint actions over the forms and limits of increased contact with the USSR.

Second, the spirit in which the United States invites increased economic contact with the USSR is of crucial importance. On this point, Khrushchev's formula for justifying increased East–West contact could conceivably be adapted for U.S. use. In seeking an expansion of economic contacts, we should be expressly and openly seeking an opportunity to compete. And we should be voicing the confident expectation that in the competition the Soviet system will be beaten.

If that approach could be adopted and maintained, it would have several major advantages for the United States. If the Soviet Union held back, as it very well might, the advantage would lie with the United States. If the Soviet Union did not hold back, the U.S. position might help to explain to an uncertain or resistant U.S. Congress and U.S. public why increased economic contacts between the two countries are desirable even though political hostility remains high. Accordingly, it might reduce the domestic pressures that have derailed U.S. policies toward the Soviet Union in the past. It would reduce the risk that the president might be obliged to use unproductive trade restrictions as a gesture of the country's displeasure whenever the USSR engaged in some unfriendly act. And it would reduce a risk of quite another sort—the risk that an increase in the level of trade might be misinterpreted in the United States as a decline in the level of military risk.

Third, in the exceptional case in which a U.S. transaction would contribute directly to the military capabilities of the USSR for conducting large-scale hostilities, we should not hesitate to restrict the export. But such controls must be used sparingly and with great selectivity. Where military objectives are concerned, the cases that would best merit such controls are those that satisfy two conditions: that the USSR is already fully alert to its military vulnerability and will not profit from the U.S. denial signal; and that the USSR's efforts to fill its lack from alternative sources will entail considerable delays or high costs in terms of military capabilities. A limited number of such cases clearly exists; but any effort significantly to enlarge the list would be a threat to the policy as a whole.

Finally, if the objective were to increase economic contact with the

USSR, we could not altogether overlook the risk that the USSR might continue to capture the lion's share of the gains from trade between us. Accordingly, measures that might help to redistribute those gains should be considered, such as those mentioned below.

Realistically, it must be recognized that any steps to redistribute the gains from trade would be difficult to implement. U.S. controls over trade with the USSR have for so long been determined by strategic military considerations and domestic politics that it would be difficult at first for the United States to establish the critical fact that it intended thenceforth to be guided primarily by economic objectives. Recognition that such a shift had occurred could not be achieved by any single presidential pronouncement nor over a short period of time. The spirit in which the necessary measures were sought and carried out, therefore, would probably be as important as the substance; particularly important would be a constant sensitivity to the point that the cooperation of other friendly countries is indispensable. Some joint curbs would be needed on the use of countertrade and other bilateral balancing devices, along with joint limits on the use of subsidies. The countries of the West would also have to agree on a process for fixing upset prices in exceptional transactions, in order to prevent excessive discriminatory pricing in favor of the USSR by Western exporters; and the U.S. government would have to arm itself with the powers and procedures for participating in such a process. That power would prove especially important in selected transactions involving the sale of technology.

As befits measures intended for the economic improvement of the Western position, however, it would be important to ensure that the needed coordinating machinery did not have the furtive and clandestine quality of COCOM undertakings; if it retained that quality, it could not escape being regarded as existing primarily for security purposes. The coordinating process would have to be overt and nonconspiratorial, a simple effort to redress a balance in negotiation brought about by institutional differences between the two systems. There may even be a time when the USSR can be invited jointly with the West to explore the problem of the institutional imbalance, possibly with a view to reaching joint solutions.

In the end, such efforts could fail. Even if they did not, the U.S. government could well find that its endemic inability to conduct a program that demands consistency and subtlety in the handling of individual cases had prevented its following an effective policy especially designed for the USSR relationship. In that case, we might be pushed back to the one remaining line of policy that offers some hope—the task, difficult enough in its own terms, of building the most effective possible system for the economic linking of the noncommunist market economies.

8

Social Issues

STROBE TALBOTT

The United States and the Soviet Union are more than adversaries: they are fundamentally alien to each other. Their political systems are so different that the two countries are forever confounding and alarming one another, not just in what they do in the international arena, but in the way they function internally. The sheer dissimilarity of the two systems has exacerbated virtually every aspect of their relations over the past sixty-five years, and never more so than when one superpower has sought to manipulate the inner workings of the other.

A vague but earnest desire to see the Soviet Union mend its repressive, often brutal ways has been constant in American public opinion and official rhetoric from the days of Vladimir Lenin through these of Yuri Andropov. But attempts actually to make that happen have been as sporadic as they have been unsuccessful. When changing Soviet society has, from time to time, become an objective of U.S. policy, it has usually been an adjunct to some other broader goal, such as the containment of international communism or the championship of human rights around the world. American efforts to transform the Soviet system have rarely been based on a coherent concept of how that system works. Partly for that reason, the targets at which the United States has taken aim over the years have seemed always to be changing. Should American influence be concentrated on coaxing gradual evolution, prompting rapid reform, or triggering revolution? Should it be conducive to economic trends that will make the system more responsive to the needs of the average citizen or to ones that will bring it grinding to a halt? Is the goal a slow but steady increase in emigration, a quota of emigrants in a given year, or the release of one political prisoner whose case has become a cause célèbre? The answer, over the years, has been sometimes none, sometimes all, of the above.

The variety of targets has been matched by a dizzying array of weapons that the United States has used, and misused: trade and propaganda, quiet diplomacy and noisy crusades—a grab bag of carrots and sticks. The wide choice of instruments available has never been matched by coordination in their application.

The American political system, with its lively interplay of special-interest groups, contesting ideological camps, and ethnic constituencies, has proved ill suited to steady, relentless, effective interaction with the USSR. If nothing else, that hidebound country is very well suited indeed to withstanding the fits and starts of American policy. In one episode after another, an all-too-resistible force has met an object which, if not immovable, moves in ways that continue to mystify, frustrate, and frighten many Americans, notably including their leaders.

In 1917, when Woodrow Wilson cast an eye in the direction of Russia, he saw "wonderful and heartening things" happening. Russia, he said, "was always known by those who knew it best to have been always in fact democratic at heart." Long after it became apparent that Russia had shed one tyranny for another, the hope persisted in the United States that Wilson's basic assertion might someday still be vindicated.

Early in his presidency, in 1981, Ronald Reagan assured the graduating class of the University of Notre Dame that "the years ahead are great ones for this country, for the cause of freedom and the spread of civilization." One reason for his optimism, he said, was that "the West won't contain communism, it will transcend communism. It won't bother to denounce it; it will dismiss it as some bizarre chapter in human history whose last pages are even now being written."

Yet on numerous other occasions, Reagan has denounced Soviet communism with great frequency and vehemence; he has portrayed the USSR as posing a mortal danger to the very survival of the West, and he is determined to devote an unprecedented portion of the nation's resources precisely to the task of doing what he told the Notre Dame seniors was unnecessary: containing Soviet communism. History helps those who help themselves, and the West, in Reagan's view as expressed in his policies as opposed to commencement speeches, needed all the help it could get in holding the Soviet challenge at bay.

Nor was Reagan the first American leader to find himself caught in this tug-of-war between self-confidence in the face of Soviet weakness and apprehension in the face of Soviet strength. There has been a manic-depressive quality in the attitude of every administration since Wilson's toward the Soviet Union. The symptoms have been particularly pronounced since World War II, and even more so in the past decade, when Soviet military power and global adventurism have grown by an order of magnitude. But the ambivalence has been there all along.

From the very beginning, the United States tended to draw back from the Soviet Union, waiting to see what it would turn out to be, rather than engaging it head-on. Woodrow Wilson soon realized that communism was a blueprint for revolutionizing not one society but all societies, and that the no longer wonderful and heartening things happening in Russia carried the menace of expansionism. But even then his concern was with preventing the spread much more than eradicating the threat at its source. Wilson refused to recognize the new Soviet regime because he believed it was important to deny the Bolsheviks legitimacy. If the Soviet leaders were acknowledged to be the rightful rulers of their own people, they would be that much closer to pressing their internationalist claims of championing peasants and workers in other societies. The Soviet system was of concern to the United States first and foremost because of the inimical foreign policy interests it was believed to pursue.

In the 1920s, a number of official statements from Washington made clear that while perhaps the United States could force changes for the better inside Russia by refusing to have anything to do with its regime, the primary purpose for the nonrecognition of bolshevism was to protect those war-weakened societies of Europe that were susceptible, but had yet to succumb, to the "Red virus." The medical metaphors favored by politicians and policymakers in the West implied an epidemic that must be quarantined. There was not much talk—and even less action—about actually curing the patient already stricken. The Soviet people were to be left in an isolation ward. If, over time, the revolutionary fever subsided and they returned to political health, so much the better. But that goal was by no means the main objective or responsibility of the West.

Franklin D. Roosevelt's decision in 1933 to end the quarantine and finally extend recognition to the USSR was one of the first in a series of zig-zags that has been the pattern of American policy toward the Soviet Union. The United States, with its impatience for quick results, its penchant for improvisation, and its relatively frequent turnovers in administrations, has by nature tended to deal erratically with problems as stubborn and obscure as those posed by the Soviet Union.

Nonrecognition had failed to alter either the internal or foreign policies of the USSR, much less bring the regime there tumbling down. As holding the Soviets at arm's length hadn't worked, America decided to try an embrace. Once relations were established, there was a brief burst of self-delusion among the Americans involved that perhaps they could work some moderating magic on the Soviets. But even in the early 1930s, underlying the wishful thinking, there was still more anxiety about what harm the Soviet Union could inflict on the United States and its interests than there was hope about what good the United States could do for the Soviet people. In a letter to Foreign Minister Maxim Litvinov reviewing the terms of recognition, Roosevelt stressed the assurance he had already received that the Soviet Union would not interfere in *American* domestic politics.

For all its moralism, American policy abroad—and, indeed, American public opinion on which that policy rests—have not been distinguished by great sensitivity to the crimes of foreign rulers against their subjects. The two most monstrous such outrages in this century have been Hitler's Holocaust and Stalin's Great Terror. In neither case did the United States display gimlet-eyed perspicacity. Even less did it act boldly on whatever awareness it had. In the 1930s, there was a widespread inclination in the United States to judge Stalinism far less harshly than Nazism; and that judgment was based on the comparative threats to Western interests which the two tyrannies posed. Clearly, Hitler was explicitly bent on territorial expansion. Stalin, on the other hand, was busily pursuing the goal of Socialism in One Country. Fine. Never mind what he was doing to the people of that one country in the name of socialism. Once World War II was raging, with the USSR drawn in as the enemy of America's enemy, there was even more willingness to tolerate "Uncle Joe" as the lesser of two evils.

As the end of the war drew near, there was a flicker of hope on the part of many Americans that if the United States could just get Stalin involved in the United Nations, the Soviet leaders would join the community of nations and eventually, perhaps even quite quickly, be transformed into folk who were easier to get along with. Only very incidentally was there much concern about how that hoped-for mellowing would affect the Soviet people. "If Russia wants a Socialist state," wrote Harry Hopkins, "that is surely their own business." It was a premise of American policy that the United States would not quarrel too loudly with the way Stalin ran his own country as long as he refrained from trying to run other countries the same way.[1]

CONTAINING THE THREAT

Not until Stalin launched his nation on a course of postwar expansionism did the American leadership adopt the goal of forcing a transformation in the Soviet regime. The decisive events were the Soviet Union's conquest of Eastern Europe, its occupation of northern Iran, its maneuvers against Greece and Turkey, and, later, the North Korean invasion of the South—an aggression that Americans were mistakenly convinced had been instigated by Moscow. Only in the face of these menacing international developments did American presidents and secretaries of state take the view that, contrary to Hopkins's bland tolerance for what Uncle Joe chose to do at home, communism was everybody's business.

Once again, as in the early 1920s, the metaphors of pathology and epidemiology were dusted off and applied to the tasks both of analyzing and of combatting the threat. And once again, the concern was with

1. For an excellent interpretive history of Soviet–American relations, see John Lewis Gaddis, *Russia, the Soviet Union, and the United States* (New York: John Wiley & Sons, 1978).

isolating the contagion rather than curing the illness at its source. "World Communism," wrote George Kennan at the end of his famous Long Telegram in 1946, "is like a malignant parasite which feeds only on diseased tissue."

Dean Acheson and John Foster Dulles both correctly understood that there was an intimate and pernicious connection between the Soviet Union's external behavior and its internal makeup (although there was, and remains, a good deal of uncertainty and disagreement over what exactly the connection is and how it works). In that sense, their view was an improvement on that of Roosevelt, who had been willing to give the Soviets the benefit of many doubts about their internal system as long as they abstained from thrusting communism upon others.

Nonetheless, two critical misreadings of the Soviet challenge underlay the thinking and writings of policymakers during the cold war: first, there was a presumption that the Soviet threat derived, in larger measure than was actually the case, from communist ideology as such, rather than from militarism, nationalism, and totalitarianism; and second, there was a tendency to exaggerate the dimensions of the threat. These two overestimations—of the ideological component in Soviet power and of Soviet power itself—have recurred from time to time until the present day, further complicating the already difficult task of understanding and dealing with the Soviet Union.

Kennan's Long Telegram and other cornerstone documents of the era, such as Paul Nitze's NSC 68 in 1950, examined the Soviet challenge largely (though by no means exclusively) in terms of the same ideological concepts that Soviet spokesmen themselves used in describing, defending, and glorifying their system: Marxism-Leninism, socialist internationalism, the class struggle, a new economic order. While Americans used those concepts to try to *elucidate* the nature of the Soviet system, the Soviets have been using them to *obscure* that truth.

Much American musing about how to change the Soviet Union was concentrated on the idea of changing its ideology. One way to do so would be to fight ideology with ideology, propaganda with propaganda. Kennan favored introducing into the Soviet Union as much information as possible about the United States so as to hold out to the Soviet people an attractive alternative to what they were hearing from their own government. That same year, 1946, President Truman's Special Counsel, Clark Clifford, wrote a report saying, in effect, that the way to get at the Soviet system was through a hearts-and-minds campaign.

John Foster Dulles advocated a more militant version of the same approach. He saw the world as a battlefield for the conflict between "the idea of freedom" and "the idea of slavery." NSC 68 contains a crystallization of that highly ideological, Manichaean view of the world: "The idea of slavery can only be overcome by the timely and persistent demonstration of the superiority of the idea of freedom. Military victory alone would only partially and perhaps temporarily affect the fundamental conflict. . . . Victory in such a war would have brought us little if at all closer to victory in the fundamental ideological conflict." Here, couched in tones reminiscent of what comes out of Moscow itself, is ringing expression of the belief that what the U.S. is really up against in the USSR, what the USSR is really all about, is a set of ideas. According to this view, the party theoreticians would be the real commanders on the enemy side. Soldiers, policemen, and *apparatchiks* would be clearly subordinate to ideologues.

The same belief in the preeminence of ideology has taken a less combative form in the recurring American hope that Soviet ideology would wither away by itself and thereby permit the internal and external behavior of the regime to change for the better. Roosevelt believed that the USSR was evolving away from Soviet communism in its original form toward a modified form of state socialism of the sort the United States was already familiar with, and on reasonably good terms with, in Europe. While American capitalism and Soviet communism would never meet, they might dramatically narrow the gap and approach each other. Stalin's mid-war decision to shut down the Comintern contributed to this impression that ideology was a transitory obsession with the Soviet leaders and that once they got over it, they would behave, both toward their own people and toward the world at large, in a more normal, less threatening way.

A latter-day variation of this theory—convergence, as it was often termed—was fashionable again in the 1960s, and by no means just on the left. Walt W. Rostow, Dean Rusk, and Zbigniew Brzezinski all, at various times and with various twists, were intrigued by the notion that the Soviet Union was experiencing "the end of ideology." If that were true, then perhaps with the demise of Marxist-Leninist dogmatism the Soviet leadership would become more pragmatic, more reasonable, less repressive toward its own people, and less aggressive toward the rest of the world.

So far, at least, the convergence theory has turned out to be a chimera. It stems from an overemphasis on ideology per se as a source of Soviet behavior. Too much Western attention to Soviet ideology has meant an inadequate realization of the extent to which communist doctrine is a largely cynical camouflage for cruder mechanisms and ambitions. Members of the Soviet leadership and power structure have, of course, been conditioned by their ideological upbringings. Their rhetoric and mindset, particularly in response to the outside world, draw heavily from the intellectual gimmickry of Marxism-Leninism. But the problem they pose to the world is not, in Kennan's phrase, so much "world communism." Nor is it, in the words of both Dulles and Nitze, "the idea of slavery." The

Soviet Union is not, above all or even mainly, an embodiment of "ideas" born of Marx and reared by Lenin. Rather, the Soviet Union is a sprawling, multinational state with a backward economy and an autocratic past that has continued nearly into the present; it has a large army, a ubiquitous police force, and a self-perpetuating elite that is dominated by one ethnic group and determined to establish, consolidate, and—wherever and whenever possible—extend its own power and that of the state. However, the fact that the Soviet system is not, in essence, an ideological phenomenon does not mean that it is any easier to deal with. Soviet Army commanders and KGB operatives are no more benign even if they privately ignore, or smirk over, their Marxist catechisms.

Ideology is important—for them, and for us—insofar as it is understood to provide pretensions and trappings with which to disguise the real dynamics of the system. And one of the critical features of the system is that it is designed to be resistant, if not immune, to fundamental change of any kind, but particularly to change imposed from the outside. The phrase "non-interference in the internal affairs of sovereign states" has enjoyed a special sanctity in the language of Soviet diplomacy. It has become a shibboleth in bilateral communiqués the USSR signs and in resolutions it sponsors in international fora. That, as the Russians like to say, is no accident. The principle of guarding against interference in its own internal affairs is a cardinal imperative of Soviet foreign and internal policy. It is an important part of the raison d'être of the KGB and the Soviet Army alike. Interference in other countries' internal affairs is, of course, quite another matter (and another important function of the KGB and Soviet Army). By other names, such interference is a key instrument by which the USSR advances its interests. It is a key part of the global offensive by which the USSR keeps various adversaries, notably the United States, on the defensive. No doubt in recent years that policy was the subject of many consultations between Yuri Andropov, in his earlier capacity as head of the KGB, and Defense Minister Dimitri Ustinov; the partnership between the two men was perhaps decisive in allowing Andropov to succeed Leonid Brezhnev in 1982.

MISMEASURING THE MONSTER

The other striking thing about Kennan's Long Telegram and NSC-68, besides their fixation with ideology, is their magnification of Soviet might. Both documents imply that the USSR is not just too unsavory to deal with, but that it is too strong to deal with; the United States would have to buy time, build up its own strength before it could tackle this monster. NSC-68 saw the Soviet Union as capable at any moment of overrunning most of Western Europe, launching air strikes against Britain and cutting allied sea-lines of communication in both the Atlantic and Pacific, and even attacking North America with atomic weapons. Yet this monster, in 1946 and still in 1950, had nearly bled to death from wounds suffered in the war and from self-inflicted ones as well. It had no deliverable nuclear power to speak of.

This inordinate American fear of the Soviet Union was an extension of the West's sense of its own weakness, of being in disarray as a result of devastation, disorganization, and demobilization after the war. It also reflected alarm over the rise of the Left in Western Europe. Stalin's aggressiveness was real enough, but his ability to indulge that aggressiveness was more severely depleted than the West, in its own weariness and apprehension, recognized. And his political appeal beyond the reach of his commissars and tanks was considerably exaggerated. In retrospect, the United States seems to have cast itself under an almost paralyzing spell as it contemplated the Soviet Union: all the U.S. and its allies seemed to believe they could do in the face of such an adversary was to try to hold it at bay.

The Containment Doctrine, as spelled out in Kennan's Long Telegram and then in his "Mr. X" article in the July 1947 issue of *Foreign Affairs* envisioned little opportunity for the United States directly to effect change within the Soviet Union. The most that could be hoped was that if the USSR's expansionist tendencies were contained, then, perhaps, over time—a great deal of time, most likely—some sort of chemical reaction would take place, denaturing the poisons. Kennan was careful to stress that the mellowing would be only indirectly a result of Western policy. The catalysts would be indigenous forces working slowly and, like everything else Soviet, mysteriously.

Four years after the Long Telegram, U.S. policy on the question of fostering internal change became more assertive. Instead of simply letting the Soviet Union stew in its own juices, the West should find ways of turning up the heat. In 1950, Nitze and his colleagues who produced NSC 68 were looking for systemic weaknesses and pressure points which, if properly exploited by the West, might bring the system down, or at least rein it in. There was no pretense in NSC 68 that the principal purpose of an "intelligent challenge by a strong outside force" to the inner workings of the USSR would be to benefit the Soviet people themselves. Rather, the purpose was to protect the West: the United States should seek "by all means short of war [to] so foster the seeds of destruction within the Soviet system that the Kremlin is brought at least to the point of modifying its behavior to conform to generally accepted international standards." In other words, make trouble for the Soviets at home so that they would cause less trouble abroad.

More than a quarter of a century later, Zbigniew Brzezinski speculated along similar lines, concentrating on the opportunities represented by the ethnic makeup of the USSR. Perhaps the tension between the centripetal force of Great Russian nationalism and the centrifugal forces of the non-Russian, particularly non-Slavic, minorities might work to the advantage of the West. "Some realistic encouragement of pluralism via nationalism and separatism may be our best answer to the Soviet challenge on the ideological front," Brzezinski told an interviewer.[2]

But how can the United States play on the indisputable structural flaws of a multinational police state in which one nationality jealously guards its supremacy? No American policy has succeeded in doing anything beyond identifying the goal.

ROLLBACK VERSUS BENIGN NEGLECT

Eastern Europe, too, has been an arena in which the United States has attempted varying and frequently contradictory theories and strategies for inducing changes in the Soviet system. Before he became a policymaker himself, Dulles advocated "rolling back" Soviet power in the satellite countries with an eye, ultimately, to shaking loose those forces at their very center and bringing about the liberation of the USSR itself. But like other slogans favored by critics of incumbent American administrations, rollback was quickly discarded once Dulles became secretary of state; his earlier advocacy of a vigorous counteroffensive gave way to the pursuit of something much more like Kennan's selective containment—"the adroit and vigilant application of counterforce at a series of constantly shifting geographical and political points, corresponding to the shifts and maneuvers of Soviet policy."

With the notable exception of Yugoslavia, Soviet policy toward Eastern Europe neither shifted nor maneuvered nor budged: it sat there, digging in. There was little opportunity for the application of American counterforce, adroit or otherwise. When the nations of Eastern Europe rebelled against the Soviet system that had been imposed upon them, it was the USSR itself that applied counterforce, brutally and decisively. Berlin 1953, Budapest 1956, and Prague 1968—each of those bloody episodes demonstrated that part of the premise of rollback was correct: Eastern Europe is made up of truly "captive nations," and their people do yearn for "liberation." But while the United States in the abstract wanted to help that cause, in reality it never felt able to do so. Moreover, in the soul-searching that went on in the West, and particularly among the watchdogs of Radio Free Europe, after Soviet tanks crushed the Hungarian uprising of 1956, there was a consensus that the best the United

2. An interview with Brzezinski conducted by G. R. Urban, published in G. R. Urban, ed., *Détente* (New York: Universe Books, 1975).

States could do to help the peoples of Eastern Europe achieve some mitigation of their captivity was to avoid provocative rhetoric and policies that might give the overlords in Moscow a pretext for cracking down. By subjecting Eastern Europe to a kind of benign neglect, perhaps America could make it easier for regimes to distance themselves—subtly, gradually, and selectively but still quite significantly—from the Soviet model.

One of Henry Kissinger's principal associates, Helmut Sonnenfeldt, ventured a version of this idea in what he thought was a private meeting with American diplomats in 1976. He pointed out that U.S. policy toward Eastern Europe was on the horns of a dilemma. The Soviet Union had both the military power and the political will to maintain its subjugation of Eastern Europe. For good reason, the West did not accept the legitimacy of Soviet hegemony, but it had neither the military nor the political wherewithal to do anything about it. Dramatic uprisings against the status quo within Eastern Europe had failed consistently and tragically. Only those who worked within the system seemed able to change it. Hungary was doubly a case in point, representing both the worst to be feared and the best to be hoped for. Imre Nagy had become a martyred hero in the eyes of the West, while János Kádár was for a long time regarded as a Quisling. But Nagy demonstrated that attempts to evict Soviet rule were answered by tanks and firing squads, while Kádár had succeeded in instituting free-market economic mechanisms, managerial decentralization, as well as personal and political freedoms considerably higher than those that prevailed elsewhere in the Warsaw Pact bloc. It was in the management of the Hungarian crisis and its aftermath that Yuri Andropov earned his spurs.

Sonnenfeldt and others concluded that anticommunist revolutions were probably doomed inside the Soviet sphere, at least for the foreseeable future, and nothing the West could do would give them a better chance. If there was to be any change in the system, it would have to be evolutionary. It was in that sense, as Sonnenfeldt put it in a phrase he would soon come to regret, that there was an "organic" relationship between Eastern Europe and the Soviet Union. A paraphrase of Sonnenfeldt's ruminations leaked to the press and fueled the right-wing attacks on détente. He—and, by association, Kissinger—were accused of selling out Eastern Europe in deference to Soviet sensibilities.

As has so often occurred in the action–reaction cycle of American politics, the next administration was inclined toward policies whose principal perceived merit was that they were repudiations of its predecessor's policies. In the Carter administration, the so-called Sonnenfeldt Doctrine, positing an organic relationship between Moscow and its satellites, was, naturally enough, a prime candidate for rejection. It was replaced by a "policy of differentiation." The brainchild of Zbigniew Brzezinski, this approach set about to gain leverage against the Soviet Union by building up America's bilateral diplomatic and commercial relations with other Warsaw Pact countries and thus straining their ties with the USSR.

There have been, however, at least two paradoxes in any American policy that has relied on tactics of splitting the bloc. One is the anomalous case of Romania. That nation has been on the receiving end of blandishments, bridge-building, and encouragement from successive American administrations. Most-favored-nation status and presidential visits bypassing Moscow have all come to Bucharest. Why? Because Nicolae Ceauşescu's Romania has indeed "differentiated" itself from the Soviet Union—by maintaining diplomatic relations with Israel, by avoiding polemics with the Chinese, by not allowing Warsaw Pact exercises on its territory. Yet its internal regime is one of the most Stalinist in the communist world, more so in some ways than that of the Soviet Union itself. Therefore, in practice, U.S. policy cannot claim to have made internal reform in Eastern Europe the sine qua non for the benefits of improved bilateral relations. The case of Romania suggests that the nastiness of life inside a country almost does not matter so long as its foreign policy gives the Kremlin fits.

The other problem with an explicitly anti-Soviet, bloc-splitting American policy is that it neither pleases nor encourages nor benefits the East European leaders themselves, notably including those who see themselves as reformers. To be perceived as having the blessing of American "differentiation" only complicates their lives and restricts their room for maneuver. It increases the mistrust and intolerance toward them on the part of their "friends and comrades to the East."

In both the Soviet Union itself and its colonies in Eastern Europe, internal conditions have tended to improve or deteriorate in direct correlation to the prevailing conditions in the international environment. When the United States had gone out of its way to convey an impression that it is bent on subverting the Soviet Union, the effect within the USSR itself has almost invariably been a marked increase in repression and a decrease in whatever incipient pluralism or liberalization might have been detectable.

For example, in the immediate postwar period, when Stalin was still regarded in the United States as more avuncular than demonic, there were some brief signs of loosening up in cultural and intellectual life. But with the onset of the cold war, starting in late 1947, dogmatists and chauvinists took the offensive against those they accused of ideological softness and "internationalism." The latter accusation could hardly have made clearer the complicity that the regime was so quick to allege between enemies at home and abroad. A few, very tentative signs of moderation gave way to those forces that brought about the Leningrad Purge, the

"Doctors' Plot" and other pogroms, the triumph of dogmatists and obscurantists in science, like the pseudo-geneticist Trofim Lysenko.[3]

The first glimmerings in the mid-1950s of what later became known as détente were accompanied by a relaxation of tensions in Soviet political and cultural life. That process of positive interaction between international affairs and life inside the Soviet Union might have begun as early as 1953. Stalin's death had left his heirs clustered nervously around his embalmed body, still frightened of his legacy, of his ghost, of each other, and certainly of the whole world. As they began to face up to the Soviet Union's massive troubles, they might have welcomed an end to the cold war. Sensing that, Winston Churchill urged a quick probe to see if what he had a few years before called the Iron Curtain might not be lifted just a bit, and if there might not be an opportunity for an opening to the post-Stalin leadership.

But Dulles opposed the idea. The United States first had to emerge from its own postwar insecurities. That finally happened in 1955. Only then did the West feel sufficiently self-confident to engage the Soviet Union on other than hostile terms. The result was the Big Four Summit in Geneva that year. It was Nikita Khrushchev's coming-out. It gave him the self-confidence and the pretext for initiating some important, lasting changes once he got home. Within months, Khrushchev had delivered his Secret Speech launching the de-Stalinization campaign. That initiative was largely a matter of Khrushchev's attempting to advance his own career and outflank his various rivals. De-Stalinization also represented a delayed decompression of the political and societal pressures, intolerable even for the Soviet Union, that had built up during the Stalin era. The Soviet Union has remained repressive, totalitarian, often brutal. But it no longer institutionalizes the homicidal paranoia and megalomania of one man. There is reason to hope that whatever partial rehabilitation of Stalin may take place around the edges of the Kremlin wall and in the odd history text or film about the Great Patriotic War, Khrushchev's repudiation of Stalinism in the late fifties and early sixties was irreversible. His Soviet Union is basically different from Stalin's, and so, therefore, is Brezhnev's. For that, both the Soviet people and humanity at large owe a debt to Khrushchev.

Khrushchev probably would not have given the Secret Speech, nor would he have released so many prisoners from the Gulag, nor could he have defeated the so-called Anti-Party Group (which he accomplished with the decisive backing of Marshal Georgii Zhukov, the personification

---

3. For a persuasive case that an incipient liberalization was nipped in the bud, see Werner G. Hahn, *Postwar Soviet Politics: The Fall of Zhdanov and the Defeat of Moderation, 1946–53* (Ithaca, N.Y.: Cornell University Press, 1982).

of the Soviet military-security complex) had it not been for the relaxation of East–West conflict after the Geneva summit of 1955. He simply would not have dared to ease up inside the country if its external enemies had been bearing down. The Khrushchev thaw was possible only in an international climate warmer than the one that had prevailed during the height of the cold war.

Thus the United States did its part in making some salutary changes possible. But it did so neither directly nor deliberately. It did so as a side effect of its management of international relations. And it did so with only the vaguest notion of what the consequences would be.

Even when that climate turned dangerously chilly again between 1958 and 1962, with the U.S.–Soviet confrontations over Berlin and Cuba, it was a period of hostility with an important difference from the earlier cold war: the Soviets were no longer responding to what they saw as provocations and threats of rollback and encirclement from the West. Instead, they were responding to perceived (or misperceived) opportunities and weaknesses on the part of the West. Recklessness had replaced paranoia. It was the period of Khrushchev's geopolitical self-confidence and derring-do. His brashness and willingness to take risks would soon be denounced by his comrades-turned-usurpers as "harebrained scheming" and would rank high on their bill of particulars against him when they threw him out. But however misplaced his confidence may have been, however close it may have brought him to the brink of war with the United States, and however fatal it may have been to his own career, it allowed him to continue, in his own bumptious, mercurial fashion, a certain amount of liberalization at home even as he was flexing his muscles and rattling his missiles abroad.

One change instituted by Khrushchev, and extended by Brezhnev, has had an effect on the inner life of the Soviet Union that is difficult to define and measure but is almost certainly important. In Stalin's day it was common for "enemies of the people" simply, silently to disappear. In the Khrushchev-Brezhnev eras, by contrast, dissident intellectuals and disaffected artists have been more likely to end up as exiles in the West, or as exiles within their own country who go on writing and speaking out, often on the Western radio stations that broadcast to the USSR. What has it done to the Soviet Union's sense of itself to have so many of its artists lionized abroad? Or to have Western scientists and advocates of détente celebrating the sixtieth birthday of Andrei Sakharov, in absentia but by no means incommunicado? What does it do to the morale and self-esteem of a society and a political system when so many of its best creators and performers seem to want to leave, and often do leave? These questions, however difficult to answer from afar, must nag at Soviets both inside the ruling elite and outside of it.

BUYING AND SELLING REFORM

The commercial dimension of the Soviet–American relationship has always reflected the more general inability of Americans to make up their
minds over the nature of the Soviet system and how to deal with it (see
chapter 7). When trade is at issue, policymakers have had to contend with
the generally indiscriminate American desire to do business wherever
and with whomever a buck can be made. Part of the motivation for ending
the diplomatic blockade of the Soviet Union in 1933 was that the Depression had increased the need for the United States to engage in foreign
trade. Commerce with the Soviet Union had been doing well enough in
the absence of recognition, but it was expected to do better with it. Thus,
in addition to all the other uncertainties and contradictions that have
plagued efforts to manage the relationship, the United States has had to
resolve a conflict between its mercantile instincts and its desire to tame the
Soviet beast. Taming the beast often means punishing it, depriving it of its
feed, and that in turn means sacrificing opportunities for doing business.
Such sacrifices do not come naturally to a capitalist democracy, and the
result has been sixty-five years of oscillation between two schools—the
free-traders and the boycotters.

For the last twenty years or so, officials managing the Soviet–American relationship in Washington have tried to harness these contradictory
impulses to a carrot-and-stick policy: "Cooperate with us politically," they
have, from time to time, intimated to the Kremlin, "and we'll let the free-
traders trade with you freely. Give us a hard time, and you'll have to
contend with the boycotters." The trouble, however, has been that American governments do not have sufficient control over their own body
politic to make either the threats or the promises entirely credible, or to
moderate and synthesize between the two schools of thought.

One school rationalizes unfettered Soviet–American trade on the
grounds that the gradual reform of the Soviet Union can be encouraged
by commerce and investment. Get them to drink our Pepsi, wear our
jeans, buy our ball bearings and computers and grain. They will get used
to the quality and availability of our products and will reorient their
economy accordingly from guns to butter. Trade with them a lot, it has
been argued by many businessmen and some government officials, and
slowly but surely, the Russians will become more like us.

The other school argues that *until* the Russians become more like us—
until they start behaving in a more civilized way toward their own citizens
and the other nations of the world—they do not deserve our products or
our credits. Besides, if they get our ball bearings, they will put them on
tanks; if they get our computers, they will only use them to track dissidents and ICBMs. Therefore, instead of bailing them out of their eco-

nomic mess, we should force them to come to terms with the inefficiency of their industry and the inadequacy of their consumer sector. The only way to get them to build fewer guns is to let them run out of butter, or grain, or whatever.

Neither school has won the argument. For one thing, neither approach has ever been applied long enough and skillfully enough to prove anything. That fact alone is telling. The United States is too undisciplined and erratic in its own policies to impose discipline on, or to foster gradual but consistent change in, the policies of the USSR. American diplomacy is simply too subject to pressures from its own private sector and special-interest groups for it to apply sustained economic pressure on the Soviet Union. A vivid example occurred during the Reagan administration. Sticking to his own campaign promise of the year before and responding to intensive lobbying by American farmers in 1981, Reagan decided to suspend his across-the-board anti-Soviet policies just long enough to end the grain embargo that the Carter administration had imposed as a punitive sanction against the Soviet Union for its invasion of Afghanistan. Then, in the fall of 1982, just as the Polish military regime was formally outlawing the Solidarity trade-union movement, a move that infuriated Reagan and led him to denounce the Polish authorities as "bums," his administration actually raised the level at which the USSR could buy in the American grain market.

What evidence there is suggests that neither carrots nor sticks have had much impact on Soviet policy, domestic or foreign. From the very beginning, the Soviet leaders have been vigilant against Americans bearing gifts or selling wares with political strings attached. During the 1921–22 famine, the United States was laudably forthcoming with humanitarian aid. Herbert Hoover, secretary of agriculture in the Harding administration, was put in charge of the project—a highly suspicious choice, as seen from Moscow. Hoover had earlier advocated using food as a political weapon against the revolutionary government of Béla Kun in Hungary and against the Bolsheviks in Russia after 1917. Lenin and his colleagues wondered if Hoover's taking the lead in the famine relief was not a giveaway that what the United States was actually up to was "bread intervention." The Soviet leaders have girded themselves against bread intervention ever since.

LETTING PEOPLE GO

The episode that most dramatically demonstrates how little leverage dollar diplomacy gives the United States over the Soviet internal order is the case of Jewish emigration. An attempt by the American government to make it possible for Jews to leave a closed society with a deeply rooted tradition of anti-Semitism would seem an almost perfect test case of how much, or how little, the United States can do if it puts its mind to it. The experience has been more instructive than encouraging.

The leaders in Moscow have recognized from the outset that Jewish emigration from the USSR is a more volatile, significant, and indeed exploitable issue in the context of *American* domestic politics than in their own. In the early 1970s, they knew that they could help Henry Kissinger fend off his more vociferous opponents of détente, particularly the late Senator Henry Jackson, by increasing the flow of emigrants. That way, Kissinger could claim, as he does in the second volume of his memoirs, that, thanks to his "quiet diplomacy" ("we sought action, not acclaim"), the number of Jews allowed to emigrate rose from only 400 in 1968 to 36,000 in 1973.[4] It was a spectacular increase indeed, but it was not so much a triumph of American efforts to manipulate Soviet internal politics as it was the other way around.

Then came the passage in 1974 of the Jackson-Vanik Amendment, which made the lowering of Soviet emigration barriers a precondition for the lowering of American trade barriers. Not only was this congressionally mandated linkage intolerable to the Soviets on grounds of what they have always liked to call "principle" (especially the principle of noninterference in internal affairs); the passage of the legislation signaled to the Kremlin that Kissinger and the executive branch had lost control over American policy. There was no longer any point in the Soviets helping Kissinger score points against his congressional opponents. For the time being at least, he had lost and they had won. So the Kremlin slammed the gate shut.

Many of the seventy-two members of Congress who cosponsored the amendment sincerely believed they were making the Soviet system more humane, more receptive to the moral concerns of international public opinion. What they were actually doing, however, was helping Jackson block the executive branch and torpedo détente. They were also stiffening the backs of the Soviet leaders, making them less receptive to Western pressure and more repressive toward their own people.

Since then, the numbers of Jews allowed to emigrate to Israel and the West have gone up and down, carefully calibrated to the Kremlin's assessment of how best to advance its broader interests. So have the figures for Soviet citizens of German background allowed to emigrate to the Federal Republic. Soviet emigration policy has never implied any willingness to relax internal controls or, in any meaningful sense, to open borders. It has

---

4. Kissinger deals with the Jewish emigration issue and the Jackson-Vanik episode at considerable length in the first volume of his memoirs, *White House Years* (Boston: Little, Brown, 1979).

been strictly an instrument of external relations, and the regime has been careful to accompany let-ups on exit visas with compensating crackdowns on those who have remained behind, just so that no one gets the wrong idea.

The Jackson-Vanik episode illustrates the more general failure of the United States to establish linkages between improvements in bilateral relations and improvements in the internal regime of the USSR. The United States has proposed such deals sporadically and pursued them ineffectually. The Soviets have rejected them firmly and consistently. In his negotiations with Litvinov over the establishment of diplomatic relations in 1933, Roosevelt suggested that the new relationship would be more profitable for the USSR if there were reforms of the Soviet domestic structure. Litvinov replied that his government was not about to ease up, or alter in any way, its internal regime for external rewards.

And so Litvinov's successors have been saying ever since. They have said it recently in their response to criticism that the USSR was not living up to the so-called Basket Three provisions of the 1974 Helsinki Accords on European Security and Cooperation. The Soviet leaders had no intention of ever implementing those provisions when they signed the accord. Nor is there any way the West can make them do so. In those few cases where the United States has, briefly, been able to define a policy of linkage, there has been little sign that it has actually worked.

Whenever the slogan of linkage has reared its head, it has, in the main, done far more to disrupt American politics and policies than to affect the Soviet system. Richard Nixon said in 1970, in a foreign policy report drafted by Kissinger, "The internal order of the USSR, as such, is not an object of our policy, although we do not hide our rejection of many of its features. . . . I cannot in good conscience recommend as a principle of American foreign policy that our entire foreign policy should be made dependent on [a] particular aspect of the domestic structure of the Soviet Union." It was a cautious, somewhat defensive statement, motivated in part by Nixon's and Kissinger's desire to express a more sophisticated view of the Soviet Union than the one asserted in NSC 68 and to distinguish their more modulated, subtle approach from the Acheson-Dulles version of containment. Nixon's foreign policy report was delivered well before détente was a dirty word, yet his comment on the relevance of the internal Soviet regime to American foreign policy was still highly controversial. It was criticized by conservatives and liberals alike as betraying a cynical willingness to abandon the Soviet people to their fate.

The Carter human rights crusade as applied to the Soviet Union was little more than a combination of symbolic gestures, such as Carter's writing a letter to Andrei Sakharov, and displays of anguish over dilemmas, such as whether Secretary of State Cyrus Vance should keep an appointment with Andrei Gromyko in Geneva to negotiate strategic arms limitation in the wake of a new persecution of Anatoly Shcharansky. Vance decided to go, fueling attacks from the right that the human rights policy was a paper tiger—as indeed it was, and could only be. But even if Carter's correspondence with Sakharov had blossomed, or Vance had succeeded, by delaying his trip to Geneva, in winning some mitigation in the plight of Shcharansky, the administration could hardly have claimed to have worked some basic transformation of the Soviet regime. Even less could it have claimed to have hastened the collapse of that regime. The achievements of the human rights policy in the Soviet Union, had there been any, would have been little more than cosmetic. They would have come about because the Soviet authorities decided to play a pawn or two as a gambit in a larger, more complicated strategy. They would have done so with a calculating eye toward American public opinion and Congress. As with Kissinger's "success" in increasing Jewish emigration, the Soviet Union was playing on the American system, not the other way around.

The debate over how to deal with the Soviet system and leadership has often been, at least subliminally, a debate over the virtuousness of America's own political system and the morality of its own leaders. Americans have traditionally wanted their foreign policy not only to do well—that is, to advance and protect American interests—but to do good—to advance and protect the interests of other, less fortunate peoples. This is a tall order, one that has often generated tensions, and policymakers have tended to resolve those tensions in favor of doing well rather than doing good.

Kissinger's critics on both the left and the right often attacked his realpolitik on the grounds that it was amoral and unworthy of American strengths and responsibilities. Carter sought to bring his human rights campaign to bear against the Soviet Union partly in order to establish that the United States as a nation and that *he* as a president were moral. There is something intellectually as well as emotionally appealing in the notion that the Soviet Union should not be allowed to trade, negotiate, or otherwise conduct "business as usual" with the United States while it is repressing dissidents or letting Jewish *refuseniks* starve themselves to death. No wonder, then, that linkage has been a slogan and a concept that congressional critics and opposition politicians love. It is handy for purposes of faulting an incumbent administration. On a loftier plane, it is a way of making Americans, who cherish the idea that theirs is a virtuous country, feel better about their government's dealing with the Soviet Union, which is, in so many ways, a manifestly villainous one. While they may pretend it is part of a political strategy aimed at the Soviet Union, linkage is actually more of a psychological exercise that Americans perform on themselves. It is a way for them to conduct business with the Soviet Union while overcoming their distaste at having to do so.

No wonder, then, that linkage has turned out to be a sticky, unwieldy instrument when it is thrust into the hands of those who must actually formulate and implement policy. Ronald Reagan, for example, became suddenly and markedly less enthusiastic about linkage—and certainly less confident and categorical about his intention to apply it—once he made the transition from candidate to president.

GETTING INSIDE THE KREMLIN

Thus, the Reagan administration learned, rather quickly and rudely, that it is extremely difficult for American diplomacy to establish mechanistic connections between different areas of Soviet behavior. But in another respect, the administration persisted well into its term in an unprecedented self-delusion about America's ability to effect crucial changes at the very core, and at the very top, of the Soviet system. The Reagan administration believed, for a long time, that it could influence the composition and orientation of the post-Brezhnev leadership. It felt it had an opportunity to play Kremlin politics, and it had a theory for beating the system.

The opportunity—an "historic" one, declared Secretary of State Haig—was Brezhnev's obvious failing health and the superannuation of the collective leadership. The theory was that there were two camps vying for eventual control of the USSR. One was the "Old Guard," the internationalist-militarists, who sought to establish the legitimacy of their rule and make up for the failures of the economy by pursuing the prestige, territorial gains, and natural resources that would come with foreign adventures and expansionism. The other camp was made up of the "Young Turks," the nationalist-modernizers, who believed that the USSR had to stop squandering resources and risking war abroad; that it had to turn inward and set about salvaging the economy, society, and political structure from their systemic weaknesses. Some in the administration felt that the goal of U.S. policy should be to encourage and strengthen the latter camp against the former, increasing the chances that, in the long run, the Young Turks would prevail. Just as Kemal Atatürk modernized and, in the grateful view of his contemporaries, saved his country by forswearing what was left of the Ottoman Empire after World War I and drawing back to the Anatolian mainland, so these up-and-coming Soviet nationalists might give up their predecessors' imperialistic ways and build up Russia itself.

There were two ways for the United States to influence the outcome of this putative struggle taking place inside the Soviet elite. Both were based on the thesis that since the Soviet system was in a state of terminal crisis, the United States, by applying pressure, could assure that the crisis resolved itself in a way favorable to Western interests. First was to step up

American military competition with the USSR and thereby increase the costs and risks entailed by the policies favored by the Old Guard; second was to use boycotts, blockades, and other commercial sanctions to hasten the moment of reckoning in the Soviet economy. In short, an American hard line was envisioned as the best way of inducing a Soviet soft line.[5]

The trouble with this diagnosis and prescription was that, like so many other causal models of Soviet behavior, this one was essentially an abstraction, and a rather implausible one at that. While there are almost certainly conflicts in philosophy as well as personality beneath the surface of the collective leadership, the idea that those disputes break down into clearly defined factions is without substantiation and strains credulity. Moreover, even if there were identifiable good guys and bad guys vying with each other for ultimate power, the idea that confrontational, punitive policies and pressure tactics on the part of the United States would help the good guys prevail is even less credible. What historical experience there is, and what little is known about the way the Soviet Union operates, suggest just the opposite.

Hard times breed hard lines. And hardliners in Washington, whatever they may think they are doing, actually tend to vindicate hardliners in Moscow.

In fact, that proposition seems to work both ways. The Soviets have had their own significant, albeit indirect, certainly unintended and unwanted, effect on the inner workings of American politics. It is quite possible that Ronald Reagan would not have become president in 1981 if the Soviets had not sent proxy troops to Africa in the mid-1970s, thus giving Reagan a powerful issue on which to mount an impressive challenge against Gerald Ford in 1976, and if they had not invaded Afghanistan in late 1979, thus making Jimmy Carter's foreign policy all the more vulnerable to a conservative backlash the following year.

---

5. The principal theoretician for this view was Richard Pipes, a distinguished historian of medieval and prerevolutionary Russia who, by way of the Committee on the Present Danger and the neoconservative opposition to détente and SALT, came to be a senior staff member of the National Security Council. Pipes was not a particularly influential figure in the very lively and often acrimonious bureaucratic politics of administration foreign policy, nor was he very often permitted to serve as a public spokesman (he had a propensity for talking about nuclear war as an unpleasant but perhaps unavoidable fact of life, a view that others in the administration shared but did not want to advertise quite so candidly).

Nonetheless, as an ideologue Pipes made a significant mark on the administration. His perception of Kremlin succession politics and his recommendation of how the United States might, in a constructive way, interfere in those most secret, sensitive, and critical of all Soviet internal affairs found sympathy with Reagan himself, reverberated in some of the presidential pronouncements on the Soviet challenge, and was even embodied in a classified presidential directive later revealed in the press. Pipes returned to his post as a professor of history at Harvard early in 1983.

In any event, the Reagan administration was surely deluding itself to think that it was doing either the Soviet people as a whole or closet liberals in the Soviet elite any favors by laying siege to a country many of whose problems and more troublesome habits stem precisely from the fact that it feels constantly besieged.

In times of imminent or actual transition within the Soviet elite, the United States should not waste time backing phantom horses in phantom races. Nor should it dither and vacillate while waiting to see how the succession comes out. Instead, it would be better advised to make sure that it has in place and in train policies and initiatives that will provide some momentum to the relationship and thereby, in effect, point the next generation of Soviet leaders in a direction that the United States wants to go.

LESSONS

Partly because of its own pluralism and partly because of the opacity of the USSR, the United States has never been able to decide what exactly it is up against; it has never been able to figure out the system it would so like to change. Like an inkblot in a Rorschach test, the image of the USSR in the American mind has flickered with vivid but confusing, often antithetical associations, the result more of ignorance and anxiety than of knowledge, insight, and analysis. Moreover, some of the chronic American confusion about the nature of the Soviet political system is a function of the nature of American domestic politics. The foreign policy of a pluralistic democracy is inevitably, but sometimes unfortunately, prone to tugs and pulls from within, particularly when the preconceptions and prejudices of ethnic groups come into play. Any American government must answer to a constituency that includes large, articulate, and activist minorities of first- and second-generation immigrants from the Soviet Union and—to use a cold war cliché that also happens to be true—the "captive nations" of Eastern Europe. For many of them, the Soviet system is not so much a challenge to analysis and diplomacy as it is an absolute evil that they take, often with good reason, very personally and passionately.

It is hardly surprising, then, that direct, deliberate American attempts to foster reform in Soviet domestic policies or to tinker with the mechanisms of Kremlin politics have almost always failed, often backfiring in the process. This has been particularly true when the United States has sought to effect major, systemic change using specifically designated instruments of policy, be they carrots or sticks or combinations of the two, or to induce immediate and profound change inside the USSR against the fundamental interests of the Soviet elite by meddling or pressure tactics. Soviet resistance has always been more coherent, sustained, and, in its own terms, more successful than the application of various—indeed, constantly varying—forms of American political warfare. Moreover, when the United States has concentrated its energies on wringing concessions out of the Kremlin, it has often forced the old men who preside there to prove their manhood by resisting not only on the contended issue at hand but by being all the more vigilant against more gradualistic, generalized influence that the United States might otherwise have.

Whatever lasting influence the United States has had on Soviet internal affairs has for the most part been painfully, sometimes imperceptibly, gradual—almost subliminal. It has been the kind of osmotic change that even as thick-skinned a system as the Soviet one would undergo—despite literal and figurative jamming—after decades of permeation by Western, and particularly American, culture. This kind of change is immensely difficult to gauge. Its ramifications for Soviet officialdom are even harder to judge or to anticipate. After all these years of listening to Radio Liberty and the Russian-language service of the Voice of America, after developing a taste for jazz and rock and country-and-western music on the VOA's "Breakfast Show," after lining up to visit American exhibitions of education or outdoor sports, after clustering around visiting exchange scholars or tourists, whether to pick their brains or buy their blue jeans, the Soviet people must have developed attitudes and behavior of which neither their founding fathers nor their current leaders would approve. But have the attitudes and behavior of the leaders themselves been altered by this interaction? Marginally, perhaps.

There have been moments when the United States seems to have had a beneficial effect on the external circumstances under which the Soviet internal regime has gone about its glacially slow evolution and its occasional, very tentative experiments with reform. But such positive influence as the United States may have had has usually been as an indirect and unintended consequence of the way American policy has affected the climate in which the USSR conducts its own foreign relations.

Evidence about the innermost workings of the Soviet system and the most deep-seated motivations of Soviet behavior is sparse and not always reliable. It lends itself more to speculation than to hard-and-fast conclusions. But what evidence there is does indicate that the Soviet system seems to tolerate relative liberalization in response to the relaxation of tensions with its external adversaries, and, conversely, that the system seems to turn all the more repressive in response to adverse international developments. That pattern has prevailed in the post–World War II period. Stalin cracked down on the instigators of a very tentative postwar moderation at least in part because of the onset of the cold war. Khrushchev was able to embark upon his thaw at least partly because there was a willingness in both East and West to give peaceful coexistence a chance.

He then felt able to continue the thaw even as he bore down on the pressure points of the West, Berlin and Cuba, because the East was not applying much pressure against the Soviet Union during that period. But Khrushchev was first embarrassed by the U-2 overflights, then humiliated in the Cuban missile crisis. The Soviet leadership began to suspect that it was getting something less than a good deal out of peaceful coexistence. Khrushchev's comrades not only dumped him; they launched a prodigious military build-up and tightened the screws on cultural and intellectual life.

Insofar as pronouncements and policies originating from Washington have had any effect on the Soviet home front—and insofar as those policies and pronouncements have stressed confrontation and the determination of the United States to defeat and destroy the Soviet Union—life for the average Russian, and certainly for the more free-thinking one, has gotten worse. It could be argued that worse in the short run is better in the long, that the more the Soviet regime cracks down on its citizenry, the sooner will come the day when the people will rebel. But that is a line of argument favored more by nineteenth-century Russian anarchists and twentieth-century terrorists than by statesmen and political scientists. It has never enjoyed much respectability among American specialists on Soviet affairs or among policymakers. Nor should it.

What emerges, and what matters, in a review of the interaction between the Soviet and American systems is the conclusion that only at those moments when they have felt less threatened by their external enemies have the Soviet leaders decided that they could be more lenient toward potential and imagined enemies within—namely, toward their own people and particularly the intelligentsia. Only in such moments have they been able to tolerate cultural innovations, economic experimentation, and some very rudimentary political pluralism. The possibility that the United States can contribute to the amelioration of the Soviet system by the reduction of Soviet–American tensions is one of the few positive lessons for the future that emerges from the otherwise erratic, perplexing, and rather dismal history of the relationship.

PART III

The Historical Record

Having looked at the key actors and key issues involved in managing the U.S.–Soviet relationship, it is now time to fit the pieces together chronologically in order to gain a third perspective on how we have shaped our policies toward our principal adversary. How has the game been played in the past? The first three chapters in this section describe the domestic process in the three main periods of our postwar policy: the cold war; détente; and the period of renewed hostility. Finally, as a counterpoint and check against this presentation of the chronology from the point of view of American domestic politics, the final essay surveys the history of the postwar period from the perspective of Soviet actions and behavior.

A consistent theme running through all three periods, despite their different political climates, is the tendency to exaggerate—whether it be the degree of Soviet threat in the 1950s or the Soviet conversion to a "new structure of peace" in the early 1970s. Ernest May points out that the need for the executive branch to recruit public support and overcome the institutional separation of powers presses presidents to feel that the issues must be oversimplified or exaggerated. One of the ironies of the historical record is that, while public opinion has appeared to support a two-track policy of peace and strength, presidents have found it difficult to formulate and implement strategies that appeared to the public to be effectively pursuing both goals at the same time. Policy was tugged toward one or the other pole, though, as Stanley Hoffmann shows, the tug toward the peace and détente pole was generally briefer and weaker.

Looking at the ebb and flow of the waves of public opinion regarding Soviet policy, Samuel Huntington argues that the winds of Soviet adventurism and domestic conservatism that gave rise to the latest wave of renewed hostility may be abating. If so, the question for the future is whether political leaders and improvements in the political process can establish American policy on a more stable course, or whether nothing can be done about the tendency of American opinion to oscillate between extremes. At the same time, looking at the entire period from the perspective of the Soviet Union, Dimitri Simes cautions against any illusions that the basic rivalry will soon be overcome. After studying the historical record in this section, we shall return to the tensions between American democracy and Russian reality in Part IV, on policy conclusions.

9

The Cold War

ERNEST R. MAY

After the Second World War, the United States and the Soviet Union were doomed to be antagonists. Though books and articles debating the origins of the cold war now cover several running yards on library shelves, with "traditionalists" blaming Russia, "revisionists" blaming America, and "postrevisionists" scattering condemnation evenhandedly, there probably never was any real possibility that the post-1945 relationship could be anything but hostility verging on conflict. Even in czarist times the two states had gotten along poorly. After the 1917 revolution, ideological enmity compounded national differences. Almost every American political leader abhorred the Soviet economic and political system. (Vice President Henry Wallace was no exception. Until captured by Communists in the 1948 presidential campaign, he was isolationist, not pro-Soviet.) According to Gallup polls, a substantial fraction of the public remained distrustful of Russia even at the height of cooperation in the war against Hitler; by the end of 1945 the proportion holding an unfavorable view had returned to levels of Nazi–Soviet Pact days.[1] In the eyes of Soviet leaders, the United States in many respects symbolized evil. Not even Maxim Litvinov and Ivan Maisky could conceal a fundamental abhorrence for the private enterprise system, open elections, an unregulated press, and their concomitants.[2]

After the defeat of Italy, Germany, and Japan, incompatible nations found themselves with common but impermanent frontiers. Occupied and liberated territories, many in ruins and almost none with a local government of unchallengeable legitimacy, inevitably became subjects of competition. Given the ideological antipathy and the course of previous history, it is hard to imagine any arrangements which could at the time have seemed mutually satisfactory. While Americans were in retrospect to think well of the communist/non-communist coalition system which ob-

1. See Ralph B. Levering, *American Opinion and the Russian Alliance, 1939–1945* (Chapel Hill: University of North Carolina Press, 1976).
2. See Stephen P. Gibert et al., *Soviet Images of America* (London: Macdonald and Jane's, 1977).

tained in Czechoslovakia from 1945 to 1948, Czechoslovakia was originally deemed "communist-dominated," and men in the State Department
who championed a tough line toward the Soviets applauded Secretary of
State Byrnes's decision to treat it as an unfriendly state and deny it American war surplus supplies.[3] Similarly, on the Soviet side, the non-communist but scrupulously sensitive regime of Finland came to be an object of
praise only in the 1950s. In the early postwar period, the Soviet press
classified it as "fascist."[4] Postwar political arrangements were either-or
issues for both sides.

Domestically, furthermore, both governments had reasons for making the contests visible and sharp. American leaders remained fearful for
years lest congressional and public opinion revert to the isolationism of
the 1930s. In order to secure appropriations for the UN and other international bodies, for relief and reconstruction abroad, for objectives such
as the rebuilding of the British economy, and for military forces possibly
needed to preserve collective security, it seemed useful—sometimes necessary—to point to a source from which a future threat to world order and
world peace might stem. The utility of the Soviet Union for such a purpose increased as it became more evident how completely devastated were
the former wartime enemies and as the elections of November 1946 swept
into control of both houses of Congress a Republican majority, many
members of which had, along with many Democrats, campaigned as anti-
communists. Soviet leaders had a stronger comparable need; for belief in
capitalist encirclement, counterrevolutionary intrigue, and the like had to
be revived if the dictatorship of the proletariat and democratic centralism
were to be restored, and if a disciplined populace were to make the
sacrifices requisite for fulfilling the goals set forth in the postwar five-year
plan. Traditions, belief systems, propinquity, and convenience thus all
combined to stimulate antagonism, and almost no factor operated in
either country to hold it back.

Though some type of cold war was inevitable, it nevertheless did not
follow that every feature of the actual cold war was equally predeter-
mined. The United States early adopted the objective of "containment."
Though the phraseology and logic were best developed in George Kennan's "Long Telegram" of February 1946 from Moscow and his subsequent "X" article in *Foreign Affairs,* some such aim inspired the drawing of
a line across Venezia Giulia in April 1945 and the hasty occupation of
southern Korea four months later. The defining of a general policy of
containment, adaptable to changing circumstances, was nevertheless a

3. U.S. Department of State, *Foreign Relations of the United States* (hereafter cited as
FRUS), 1946, 6: 216–17; 7: 223 (Washington, D.C.: U.S. Government Printing Office).
4. Eino Jutikkala and Kauko Pirinen, *A History of Finland* (New York: Praeger, 1974),
pp. 284–86.

slow, painful, and frequently confused endeavor continuing from 1945 on at least through the 1960s.[5]

For the United States, the essential questions regarding containment were: (1) where? (2) how? and (3) at what risk? They were seldom separable. Broadly speaking, they *seemed* to be answered differently before and after the onset of the Korean conflict in 1950. Before, the Truman administration *seemed* to reply: (1) Western Europe and Japan and some other islands off the Asian mainland; (2) primarily, though not exclusively, through political support and economic aid; and (3) at risk of a general war if the Soviets resorted to open aggression. After mid-1950, the Truman, Eisenhower, Kennedy, and Johnson administrations, though with steadily diminishing stridency, *seemed* instead to respond: (1) almost anywhere not already within the iron curtain; (2) primarily through use or threat of use of military force; and (3) at risk of a devastating nuclear exchange certainly in the event of open aggression by the Soviet Union or a satellite, possibly in the event of successful communist subversion of a noncommunist state. Emphasis is placed on *seemed* because, in the first place, the actual behavior of the U.S. government did not change a great deal. It was as cautious in the Berlin crises of 1958 and 1961 as in that of 1948–49, and it accepted Communist success in Cuba in 1959–60 much as it had accepted the Communist successes in Eastern Europe in 1945–48. In the second place, such documents as are now available suggest that thinking inside the government actually followed a contrary trend. Within officialdom, there was *more* inclination in the early period to think ambitiously of containment (indeed, to define it as pushing the Soviets back, not just holding a line) and to contemplate large-scale war as a means of implementing the policy. Later, when the posture and rhetoric of the United States appeared significantly more militant, the policy documents being written inside the government exhibited relatively more cautiousness concerning American objectives and more doubt as to whether they could be attained by military means. In a study focusing on United States management of relations with the Soviet Union, it is important to note how the disparity between appearances and realities developed and to speculate on the reasons why.

In the early stages of the cold war, Europe was divided along the line that Churchill characterized as "the iron curtain." The question of whether and how the United States might try to contain further extensions of Soviet influence rose first in connection with Iran. Under wartime agreements, Western and Soviet troops were to be withdrawn from

5. The clearest, most valuable analysis of the evolution of the policy is by John L. Gaddis, *Strategies of Containment: A Critical Appraisal of Postwar American National Security Policy* (New York: Oxford University Press, 1982).

that country. The Soviet troops did not leave on schedule. According to Iranians and Americans on the scene, the Russians were making preparations for virtual annexation of the province of Azerbaidzhan and perhaps for seizing control of the whole country. The U.S. government took a firm diplomatic stance, telling Moscow that if the Iranians took a complaint to the UN the United States would have to back them. While the consequences of a confrontation in the UN were not altogether foreseeable, people in the U.S. government seem to have been assuming that, if the Soviets stood fast, the most likely result would merely be a further chilling in diplomatic relations. A memorandum from the State Department to the State-War-Navy Coordinating Committee (SWNCC), a predecessor of the National Security Council (NSC), asserted that diplomacy was the only weapon available to the United States unless the Soviets were to seize "regions in which the power of the Soviet armies can be countered defensively by the naval, amphibious and air power of the U.S. and its potential allies," and the Joint Chiefs, asked to comment specifically on Iran, classified it as "important" but not "vital" and indicated that they could contemplate military operations there only if there were mobilization for general war.[6]

Internally, within the executive branch, this cautious attitude toward containment quickly disappeared. Later in 1946 and on into 1947, the U.S. government had to assess the extent of its interest in containing Soviet expansion into the eastern Mediterranean region. Turkey had remained neutral during World War II. No outside power had occupying forces there. According to Turkish officials and the American mission in Ankara, the Soviet government, consistent with czarist precedents, was pressing Turkey to cede control over the Turkish Straits and, for practical purposes, to become a protectorate. President Truman's advisers viewed this prospect, together with that of the Soviet Union's possibly gaining control of Greece, as more threatening to the United States than Soviet actions in Iran had been. Meeting with the president in mid-August, Under Secretary of State Dean Acheson, Secretary of War Robert Patterson, and Secretary of the Navy James Forrestal joined in declaring protection of Turkey to be "in the vital interests of the United States" and recommending a decision to "resist with all means at our disposal any Soviet aggression and in particular, because the case of Turkey would be so clear, any Soviet aggression against Turkey." At least with regard to the Turkish case, Truman said he agreed and would pursue the policy "to the end."[7] To the Turkish and Soviet governments, the administration committed itself to containing the Soviet Union behind the existing Russo-

6. *FRUS, 1946,* 1: 1165–69; 7: 529–32.
7. Ibid., 7: 540–41.

Turkish frontier, but to the extent that anything ever remains secret in Washington, the action took place behind closed doors. Press rumors, in other words, were not officially confirmed.[8]

In 1947, the famous Truman Doctrine message and legislation enacted by Congress in response to it constituted public notice that the United States proposed to check Soviet influence at the frontier of Greece as well as that of Turkey. Truman's expansive language, together with publication of Kennan's "X" article, suggested that the government might be prepared to block the Soviets at any and every frontier. Administration spokesmen, however, took pains to assure Congress and the public that not even the obligations to Turkey and Greece were open-ended. Reporting to the Senate regarding the aid program, the Foreign Relations Committee said: "It is proposed solely to help these governments help themselves. There is no plan to send to Greece or Turkey combat troops of any nature."[9]

The years 1948 and 1949 saw the United States mark a definite military boundary around Western Europe. The Soviet rejection and condemnation of the Marshall Plan, increasingly violent efforts by West European Communists to frustrate the success of that plan, the Czech Communists' coup in February 1948, and the Berlin blockade, stimulated fear in Europe. In a pattern that would repeat itself, the United States became foster parent for what was originally a European initiative. British Foreign Secretary Ernest Bevin promoted formation of a defensive alliance linking Britain, France, and the Benelux countries—the Brussels Pact of March 1948. The U.S. government initially discouraged the project, arguing that efforts for closer economic collaboration should come first. Similarly, the American government at first resisted Bevin's proposal that the United States in some way associate itself with the pact. The decision to explore doing so rested in part on feeling that it would help along economic negotiations, in part on an assumption that nothing could actually be done before 1949, when the Dewey administration was expected to take office. Once engaged, however, the U.S. government quickly found itself in the real or apparent position of shaping the terms of the alliance and prodding the Europeans.

In part, this resulted from the executive branch's drawing in the legislative branch. Robert A. Lovett, George Marshall's under secretary of state, started negotiations with Senator Arthur Vandenberg, the senior

8. See Bruce R. Kuniholm, *The Origins of the Cold War in the Near East: Great Power Conflict and Diplomacy in Iran, Turkey, and Greece* (Princeton: Princeton University Press, 1980).

9. See *FRUS, 1947*, 4: 577–79, and U.S. Senate, Committee on Foreign Relations, *Historical Series, Hearings in Executive Session: Legislative Origins of the Truman Doctrine* (Washington, D.C.: U.S. Government Printing Office, 1973).

Republican on (and therefore for the time being chairman of) the Senate
Foreign Relations Committee, and Vandenberg began to set terms to
which the Europeans would have to agree if the Senate were to be won
over. And this process, which in 1949 would result in the North Atlantic
Treaty and therefore the definitive American commitment in Western
Europe, also produced an extension of the area where containment was
unquestionably to apply; for Vandenberg insisted on bringing in Scandinavian countries because, as he said, "that had great vote appeal in the
Senate because of the considerable areas of the country involving high
proportions of Scandinavian voters."[10]

Nevertheless, the adoption of the North Atlantic Treaty involved a
comparatively restrained definition of the obligations of containment.
The State Department's missions and desk officers wanted guarantees
extended to Italy, Greece, and Turkey, and Senator Vandenberg was
amenable, saying only that he would object to embracing Iran on the
ground that "there was little or nothing we could do to help Iran."[11] It was
in this instance Secretary of State Marshall and the Joint Chiefs who
applied a rein, Marshall commenting to Lovett, "it tends to spread our
sphere of activity over far too widespread an area. . . . I see no compelling
reason for being pressured into dangerous efforts," and the Chiefs arguing that the United States did not have forces adequate to defend
Greece.[12] Despite warnings that any exclusions might be interpreted by
the Soviets as identifying fair game for them, the actual treaty of 1949 was
limited to the United States, Canada, the Brussels Pact five, Denmark,
Norway, Iceland, Italy, and Portugal.

On the other side of the world, the apparent commitment by the
United States was even more guarded. Under pressure from Congressmen who believed containment should apply equally or more in Asia, the
administration agreed to a $400 million appropriation for aiding Na-
tionalist China as part of the price for full funding of the European
Recovery Program, but the administration and congressional leaders cooperated to ensure that the United States was not even as much committed as to Greece and Turkey. The China Aid Act asserted that "assistance . . . shall not be construed as an express or implied assumption
by the United States of any responsibility for policies, acts, or undertakings of the Republic of China or for conditions which may prevail in
China at any time."[13]

10. *FRUS, 1948*, 2: 104–06.
11. Ibid., 3: 92–96.
12. Ibid., 1 (pt. 2): 564–67; 2: 103.
13. Public Law 472, Title 4. See Ernest R. May, *The Truman Administration and China,
1945–1949* (Philadelphia: J. B. Lippincott, 1975).

Similar caution was apparent in American policy concerning Korea. There, as in Germany, the Soviet Union and the United States had moved toward setting up separate Communist and non-Communist regimes. In August 1948 the United States transferred sovereignty over Korea south of the 38th parallel to a new Republic of Korea headed by Syngman Rhee. The attitude of the military establishment had been expressed in an extraordinary document of May 1947 in which the Joint Chiefs argued that, while the United States might lose something if all Korea were taken over by the Communists, it might actually have its "prestige . . . enhanced if a survey of our resources indicated we could not afford to resist our ideological opponents on all fronts and we publicly announced abandonment of further aid to Korea in order to concentrate our aid in areas of greater strategic importance."[14] Though no such ruthless policy was adopted, Truman and his newly created National Security Council did twice review the question of whether the objective of containment necessarily entailed defense of South Korea. The answer seemed to be no. In NSC documents of 1948 and 1949, Truman agreed to the proposition that "the U.S. has little strategic interest in maintaining its present troops and bases in Korea" and accepted advice that while Communist success in Korea might be a severe setback, the United States should not "guarantee unconditionally the political independence and territorial integrity of South Korea" or "commit the U.S. to continued direct political, economic and military responsiblity in Korea."[15]

In East Asia, the administration for practical purposes drew the containment boundary through blue water. As Marshall's successor, Secretary of State Dean Acheson, proclaimed in a long-remembered early 1950 speech to the National Press Club, the American defense perimeter included Japan and the Philippines but no part of the mainland and no near-in islands. As of 1950, therefore, the containment line seemed to have been very circumspectly drawn.

The question of how to effect containment had meanwhile come under debate. Truman had imposed tight ceilings on the military establishment during the postwar transition years. After being elected in his own right in 1948, he had shown determination to push those ceilings still lower and to shift expenditures to domestic programs of his "Fair Deal." In July 1949, having overridden Pentagon objections and held the Fiscal 1950 defense budget to $14.5 billion, he announced his Fiscal 1951 target to be $13 billion. His economic program had been rescued from sharp cuts in 1948 by congressional reaction to the Czech coup. (The event was

14. *FRUS, 1947*, 1: 744.
15. *FRUS, 1949*, 3: 969–78. See William Whitney Stueck, Jr., *The Road to Confrontation: American Policy toward China and Korea, 1947–1950* (Chapel Hill: University of North Carolina Press, 1981).

so appropriately timed that an imagination of the kind that reconstructs Kennedy assassination plots could suppose Stalin to have been influenced by a Western "mole.") In 1949 and 1950 opposition had been stronger, despite there now being Democratic majorities in both houses. Emphasis had shifted somewhat toward military assistance, with the State Department and the Economic Cooperation Administration trying to win votes by putting the Joint Chiefs "in the forefront." By the spring of 1950, supportive Congressmen such as Christian Herter of Massachusetts were warning Acheson of growing congressional feeling that the dollar cost of the cold war had become far too high.[16]

In both State and Defense, however, there was a steadily mounting sense of strain. In part, it was a product of intelligence surprises—not only the 1949 discovery that the Soviets had tested a fission device, but a combination of indications pointing to a massive buildup of Soviet capability for strategic bombing operations against Western Europe and the United Kingdom. In May 1948, Western agents had sighted the first Soviet TU-4, a copy of the U.S. B-29 bomber aircraft. Other sightings, together with testimony by a defector from the Soviet Long Range Air Force, led the American intelligence community by the spring of 1950 to ascribe to the Soviets a large and rapidly growing operational force of TU-4s.[17] Given the fact that the Long Range Air Force had been a neglected stepchild of the Red Army during World War II, these numbers could be interpreted as signs that the Soviets were preparing to threaten or actually to conduct a strategic offensive against Western Europe and the British Isles.

The temperature of debate and the level of alarm rose during the winter of 1949–50 because of the issue of whether or not to move urgently toward developing a hydrogen bomb. After a protracted review of the evidence and the pros and cons, Truman ordered that work proceed. Though doubt remained as to whether the bomb would ever materialize, there was clearly some prospect of thermonuclear weapons of orders of magnitude more powerful than the Hiroshima and Nagasaki bombs, and there was in any case an almost certain prospect of boosted fission bombs with yields measurable in hundreds of kilotons.

For those occupied with foreign and military policy, developments in the nuclear field doubled concern about the diminishing defense budget; for the services, in part responding to congressional preferences, had put increasing proportions of their procurement funds into weaponry designed for strategic operations. The air force was building up its Strategic

16. *FRUS, 1949*, 1: 377; *1950*, 1: 206.

17. John Prados, *The Soviet Estimate: U.S. Intelligence Analysis and Russian Military Strength* (New York: Dial, 1982), pp. 38–39.

Air Command; the navy was flying clumsy but nuclear-capable Neptunes off carrier decks and declaring that all carrier aircraft were eventually to have strategic nuclear missions. The army was investing in antiaircraft missilery. With most troops assigned to occupation duty, the army doubted its capacity for defending even Alaska.[18]

Increasingly, therefore, the sanction behind actual and possible American containment guarantees consisted of strategic nuclear weaponry and nothing else. This fact alarmed many officials. Kennan reacted by writing Acheson, "we should act at once to get rid of our present dependence . . . on the atomic weapon. . . . I should think it entirely possible that this would require a state of semimobilization."[19] Men more sensitive than Kennan to the constraints of domestic politics did not see permanent mobilization as a feasible alternative. Leading an organized State Department–professional military conspiracy to subvert the president's budget ceilings, Paul Nitze, Kennan's successor as head of the Policy Planning Staff, consulted with a number of such men. Out of his effort came the now famous document, NSC 68, which answered one expert's appeal for a "gospel which lends itself to preaching" while at the same time making a cogent case for significantly increased spending on nonstrategic, nonnuclear forces.[20]

NSC 68 did not specify how much more should be spent or even on what. While it was being drafted, a mood of crisis was developing in the country. Some members of Congress reported their constituents as calling for preventive war. Others said the people wanted some grand negotiation.[21] In any case, there seemed a widespread desire for the government somehow to finish off the cold war. J. Robert Oppenheimer attributed it to delayed reaction to the Soviet nuclear device and the H-bomb debate. The most bizarre symptom of anxiety was the wide publicity and credulous reception accorded to Senator Joseph R. McCarthy's speech in Wheeling, West Virginia, alleging that Communists controlled the State Department. Though Truman reviewed NSC 68 and ordered that it (a) be kept completely secret and (b) be studied by the unfriendly eyes of the Treasury and the Bureau of the Budget, there appeared to be

18. U.S. Senate, Committee on Armed Services and Committee on Foreign Relations, 82d Cong., 1st sess., *Military Situation in the Far East*, pt. 1, p. 382 (Washington, D.C.: U.S. Government Printing Office, 1951).

19. *FRUS, 1950*, 1: 164–65.

20. Ibid., 1: 234–92. In the large literature on NSC 68, the signal works, other than Gaddis's *Strategy of Containment*, are Paul Y. Hammond, "NSC 68: Prologue to Rearmament," in Warner R. Schilling et al., *Strategy, Politics, and Defense Budgets* (New York: Columbia University Press, 1962), pp. 267–378, and Samuel F. Wells, Jr., "Sounding the Tocsin: NSC 68 and the Soviet Threat," *International Security* 4, no. 2 (Fall 1979): 116–38.

21. *FRUS, 1950*, 1: 140.

a developing consensus within the executive branch that some adjustment was probably needed in the extent to which containment depended on the nuclear threat. Asked by Harvard President James Bryant Conant what line the United States should seek to hold, and why, Nitze spoke in March 1950 only of the North Atlantic Treaty and Turkey and said, "What we were trying to do was to buy 30 years of peace."[22]

Before 1950 ended, the United States had commenced a full turn in its apparent position—from comparatively selective to comparatively non-selective containment, combined with a display of ready military power beyond anything foreshadowed earlier but, paradoxically, with no diminution in dependence on strategic nuclear weaponry.

Since documentation peters out after 1951, subsequent developments can only be sketched. The North Korean attack on South Korea constituted the point of transition. Interpreting the attack as a deliberate challenge by the Soviets, a counterpart to tests of Western will by the Axis powers in the 1930s and a possible harbinger of an East German attack on West Germany, President Truman abruptly reversed himself with regard to Korea. The United States committed itself to maintain the boundary separating South from North Korea, almost regardless of cost. In the actual clamor of battle, the U.S. government attempted to push that line northward, liberate North Korea, and thereafter contain communism at least at the Yalu River. Communist Chinese intervention, however, inspired a fresh review which ended in a return to the more limited objective. After an armistice in 1953, the United States pledged itself through a bilateral treaty to defend the South Korean frontier as if it were its own.

Elsewhere in Asia the United States made comparable pledges, formalizing undertakings to defend a freshly independent Japan, the Philippine Republic, Australia, and New Zealand. With regard to Taiwan and associated islands, where Chiang Kai-shek continued to rule, Truman announced in 1950 that the United States would provide defense against an attack from the mainland. By 1954 the Eisenhower administration had first "unleashed" Chiang, declaring that it would not interfere with a Nationalist attack on the mainland, then made the Republic of China a full ally. Regarding Southeast Asia, the United States ceased distancing itself from the French and provided increased aid for their war against the Communist-led Viet Minh. In 1953–54 the Eisenhower administration did its utmost to discourage the French from giving up. After this effort failed, it signed a Southeast Asia Treaty which, though in language more guarded than that of the North Atlantic Treaty, engaged the United States to protect Thailand, Pakistan, South Vietnam, Laos, and Cambodia against "Communist aggression."

22. Ibid., 1: 181.

In Europe, Greece and Turkey were formally added to the North Atlantic Treaty Organization (NATO). After exploring the possibility of also adding Spain, but finding the Europeans resistant, the U.S. government signed bilateral understandings for establishing American military bases in Spain and providing military aid to the Spanish government. Similar understandings concerning bases and military aid linked the United States with newly independent states in North Africa.

Regarding the Middle East, the United States urged establishment of an American-French-British-Turkish-Egyptian unified defense command pledged to mutual protection and to defense of the region as a whole. When that failed to materialize, owing to Egyptian hesitancy, the American government fostered a Baghdad Pact uniting Britain, Turkey, Iraq, Iran, and Pakistan for such an objective. Though not itself a formal signer, the United States endorsed and underwrote this alliance. In 1957, President Eisenhower then proclaimed as the "Eisenhower Doctrine" that "the United States regards as vital to the national interest and world peace the preservation of the independence and integrity of the nations of the Middle East" and "is prepared to use armed forces to assist any such nation or group of such nations requesting assistance against armed aggression from any country controlled by international communism."

In the meantime, containment came to be defined also as preventing extension of Soviet influence which might occur without armed aggression. From the outset, the Soviet Union had been seen as having capabilities for what early planning papers termed "ideological warfare." The Marshall Plan had been inspired in part by concern about Communist parties in Western Europe. Debate on aid to Greece and China had been complicated by awareness that their governments' enemies were largely indigenous. Acting case by case, the United States by 1950 had developed a policy of helping other governments resist domestic Communist enemies by every means other than direct commitment of American military force. This included covert operations. But the assumption prevailed among the public that there might be circumstances, even in Europe, in which the United States would acquiesce in local Communist success. When assisting in the formulation of the North Atlantic Treaty, John Foster Dulles, then a senator from New York, felt it necessary to seek assurance that American obligations would automically cease if a signatory government turned Communist; and in 1950, after reviewing the contingency of a Communist takeover in part or all of Italy, Truman and his NSC concluded that the United States would probably have to be limited to helping a non-Communist Italian government hold whatever remnant of power it retained.[23]

23. *FRUS, 1949,* 1: 361; *1950,* 3: 1486–91.

After 1950, however, it became increasingly the overt policy of the United States to contain the Soviet Union by preventing *any* extension of Communist influence. The change was reflected in the new attitude toward French operations against the Viet Minh. It found expression in declarations by the Eisenhower administration regarding Guatemala. Dulles, as Eisenhower's secretary of state, induced the Organization of American States to adopt a resolution declaring "the international communist movement . . . a special and immediate threat to the national institutions and the peace and security of the American States." By the beginning of the 1950s American energies were directed first toward preventing the success of a Communist-infiltrated faction in Laos and then toward helping South Vietnam cope with Communist-led guerrillas. The United States also led efforts to prevent supposed Communists from taking control of the newly independent Congo republic.

There were limits, to be sure. In Laos, Vietnam, and the Congo, the United States lent aid to indigenous governments; it did not act wholly on its own. And the United States did not use military force to overturn the revolutionary regime in Cuba when its leader, Fidel Castro, proclaimed Cuba a communist state and an ally of the Soviet Union. The refusal of President Kennedy to commit American armed forces in support of the Bay of Pigs invaders supplied strong evidence that the objective of containment continued to be subject to limits. Nonetheless, the definition current in American official rhetoric had broadened significantly after 1950.

Moreover, the increasingly more comprehensive definition of containment had behind it military power far beyond that of the earlier period. President Truman's change of position concerning Korea had been accompanied by a complete change of heart concerning defense spending. He ordered the services to request whatever they needed to effect NSC 68. Outlays for defense rocketed from the originally planned $13 billion for Fiscal 1951 to $22 billion for that year, $44 billion for Fiscal 1952, $50 billion for Fiscal 1953, and $47 billion for Fiscal 1954. Thereafter, Eisenhower scaled down defense outlays to an average of about $44 billion per fiscal year. Even so, defense spending was three to four times what had been projected before the Korean conflict.

Forces funded by this higher level of spending fanned out across the world. Truman assigned four (later six) divisions to NATO, with accompanying air and naval forces, and an American general became Supreme Commander. Following the truce in Korea and the American-Korean treaty of alliance, the United States pledged to keep a substantial army in the Korean peninsula. Other forces, chiefly air force units, became based more or less permanently at sites all around the rim of the Soviet Union, and, with fifteen- to sixteen-carrier task forces, the navy maintained large fleets on the oceans and in the Mediterranean and China seas. Previously, the policy of containment had appeared limited not only because of the cautious language used in Washington but also by the fact that, in most areas, the United States and its associates did not maintain ready forces adequate physically to block an extension of Soviet or Communist power. After 1951 the United States seemed to have the ability to employ military power almost immediately in almost any part of the world.

As this change occurred, the military aspect of containment became increasingly prominent. Previously, the general emphasis had been more that evident in the Marshall Plan and then in Truman's "Point Four"— economic and social reconstruction designed rather to immunize areas against the infection of communism than to fortify them militarily. The Korean War was accompanied by a shift, most apparent in trends in foreign aid. The proportion ascribed to military assistance went from 12 percent in Fiscal 1950 to 41 percent by Fiscal 1960. To be sure, the Eisenhower and Kennedy administrations sponsored significant programs aimed primarily at economic and social betterment in underdeveloped countries. Nevertheless, it is not much of an exaggeration to say that before mid-1950 containment seemed to involve primarily an effort to create economic, social, and political conditions assumed to be inhospitable to communism, whereas from mid-1950 onward, the policy seemed primarily one of preserving military frontiers behind which conditions unsuited to subversion could gradually evolve.

Greatly increased spending for military forces and military assistance did not, however, buy freedom from dependence on strategic nuclear weaponry. The Eisenhower administration's "New Look" defense policy involved cutbacks in manpower, particularly for the army, in favor of investment in advanced technology, particularly in the form of medium-range and long-range land-based bombers, high performance carrier-based fighter-bombers, and eventually missiles. Dulles's famous speech, employing the phrase "massive retaliation," signaled a conclusion that protection of all vulnerable frontiers cost too much for the United States alone, that America's allies and associates were unwilling or unable to pay the difference, and that the administration was therefore reverting to a posture of backing its commitments with the threat of nuclear attack on communist homelands. Publicly protesting this posture, army leaders such as Generals Matthew B. Ridgeway, Maxwell Taylor, and James Gavin advertised the incapacity of the United States even to honor the North Atlantic Treaty without resort to a strategic nuclear offensive. In fact, at the time, tactical air forces and forward-based army and navy units were all equipped with "tactical" nuclear weapons, many of which neared or matched in yield and/or prospective side-effects the bombs used on Hiroshima and Nagasaki. It was recognition of the extent of dependence on strategic forces and nuclear firepower that drove a shift in the early 1960s to "flexible response," with an accompanying increase of 10 percent or more a year in levels of defense spending.[24]

The post-1950 change in American policy—toward a more expansive definition of containment, an emphasis on protection of military frontiers, but without abandonment of a primary reliance on the threat of strategic nuclear war—was much more a matter of the external appearances created by the government than a change of opinion either among political leaders or within the bureaucracy. Indeed, paradoxically, what American leaders said to one another behind closed doors became increasingly circumspect as what they said to the world became increasingly less so. In the late summer of 1946, White House Special Counsel Clark Clifford, aided by George Elsey, prepared for the president a summary of views being expressed by the then secretaries of state, war, and the navy, the Joint Chiefs of Staff, and other high officials. They wrote:

> The language of military power is the only language which disciples of power politics understand. The United States must use that language in order that Soviet leaders will realize that our government is determined to uphold the interests of its citizens and the rights of small nations. Compromise and concessions are considered, by the Soviets, to be evidence of weakness and they are encouraged by our "retreats" to make new and greater demands.
>
> The main deterrent to Soviet attack on the United States, or to attack on areas of the world which are vital to our security, will be the military power of this country. . . . In order to maintain our strength at a level which will be effective in restraining the Soviet Union, the United States must be prepared to wage atomic and biological warfare. . . .
>
> In conclusion, as long as the Soviet government adheres to its present policy, the United States should maintain military forces powerful enough to restrain the Soviet Union and to confine Soviet influence to its present area.[25]

NSC 20/4, a statement of "U.S. Objectives with Respect to Russia," approved by President Truman and his advisers in August 1948, said:

> To counter the threats to our national security and well-being posed by the USSR, our general objectives with respect to Russia, in time of peace as well as in time of war, should be:
> *a.* To reduce the power and influence of the USSR to limits which no longer

---

24. See particularly William W. Kaufmann, *The McNamara Strategy* (New York: Harper & Row, 1964); Desmond Ball, *Politics and Force Levels: The Strategic Missile Programs of the Kennedy Administration* (Berkeley: University of California Press, 1980); and David Alan Rosenberg, "The Origins of Overkill: Nuclear Weapons and American Strategy, 1945–1960," *International Security* 7, no. 4 (Spring 1983): 3–71.

25. John L. Gaddis and Thomas H. Etzold, eds., *Containment: Documents on American Policy and Strategy, 1945–1950* (New York: Columbia University Press, 1978), pp. 64–71.

constitute a threat to the peace, national independence and stability of the world family of nations.

  b. To bring about a basic change in the conduct of international relations by the government in power in Russia. . . .[26]

The Manichean rhetoric of NSC 68, meeting the appeal for "a gospel which lends itself to preaching," merely echoed what had been current for the past several years.

After the onset of the Korean conflict, comparable documents embodied their conclusions in increasingly more measured language. As early as August 1950, NSC 73/4 phrased the nation's fundamental objective as merely "to maintain the integrity and vitality of its free society and the measure of world order necessary thereto."[27] Soon after the Eisenhower administration came into office, the president ordered general reviews of both foreign policy and military policy. The complement to the "New Look" in defense was NSC 162/1, a summary of "Basic National Security Policy" which remained a touchstone text for the remainder of Eisenhower's term.[28] It described as very limited the area definitely covered by the containment doctrine—that of NATO, including West Germany and Berlin, Japan, Korea, Australia, New Zealand, and the American republics. It added, "Certain other countries, such as Indochina or Formosa, are of such strategic importance to the United States that an attack on them probably would compel the United States to react with military force." With regard to actual military responses, the document first of all incorporated a point insistently argued by Secretary of the Treasury George Humphrey and Budget Director Joseph E. Dodge—namely, that the domestic economic health of the United States had to be a governing consideration. Second, however, it warned against excess of faith in forces tailored to "New Look" premises:

Although Soviet fear of atomic reaction should still inhibit local aggression, increasing Soviet atomic capability may tend to diminish the deterrent effect of U.S. atomic power against peripheral Soviet aggression. It may also sharpen the reaction of the USSR to what it considers provocative acts of the United States. If either side should miscalculate the strength of the other's reaction, such local

26. *FRUS, 1948,* 1 (pt. 2): 663–69.

27. *FRUS, 1950,* 1: 376.

28. NSC 162/1, in *Documents of the National Security Council,* part 1: 1947–77 (Frederick, Md.: University Publications of America, Inc., Microfilm, 1978). Later versions of the BNSP can be found as NSC 5440 (1955), NSC 5602 (1956), NSC 5705 (1957), and NSC 5810 (1958), in ibid., and Declassified Documents (1980), 286B and 379A in ibid., First Supplement (1981). No later versions are yet publicly available, but a memorandum by Dean Rusk of February 4, 1961 (Declassified Documents [1978] 400B in ibid.), suggests that phraseology from the 1953 text still carried over into a review of long-range postwar policy being prepared by the new Kennedy administration.

conflicts could grow into general war, even though neither seeks or desires it. To avoid this, it will in general be desirable for the United States to make clear to the USSR the kind of actions which will be almost certain to lead to this result, recognizing, however, that as general war becomes more devastating for both sides the threat to resort to it becomes less available as a sanction against local aggression.

As for America's basic objective, it had become the fostering of "willingness of the Soviet leadership to negotiate acceptable settlements, without necessarily abandoning hostility to the non-Soviet world."

Such glimpses as we have of actual decision processes in the Eisenhower, Kennedy, and Johnson administrations show similar cautiousness in responses to particular challenges. The Eisenhower administration made much noise about Indochina during the last phase of the French–Viet Minh struggle, but it did not intervene. Eisenhower and Dulles talked as if the inshore islands of Quemoy and Matsu represented a vital interest. Dulles said that, with their capture, the Chinese Communists would "begin their objective of driving us out of the western Pacific, right back to Hawaii, and even to the United States!"[29] In private they actually agreed that only clear aggression against the Nationalist Chinese ally could serve as a casus belli and that they wanted Chiang to abandon the islands as soon as circumstances permitted.[30] The preference for, and willingness to blink away excesses in, covert operations in the Congo and in Central America, the Caribbean, and Asia surely reflected an underlying desire to minimize risks of having to make good on the publicly announced policy of containment or admit to a bluff. And nowhere was such caution more evident than in the approach of successive administrations to Vietnam, for the longer our retrospect, the more apparent it becomes that the puzzle lies not in the military intervention which later became the object of domestic protest but rather, given the ostensible national policy, the government's hesitancy and restraint.

Thus, it appears that the onset of the Korean conflict brought with it three changes: (1) a marked increase in the *apparent* extent and vigor of the commitment to contain Soviet and Communist expansion; (2) an order-of-magnitude increase in annual defense spending without, however, a corresponding change in basic strategy; and (3) on the part of American policymakers, increased conservatism in defining general national objectives and in contemplating the actual use of force for purposes of containment. In regard to the general problem of management of American–Soviet relations, the interesting question is why such a gap

29. Quoted in Gaddis, *Strategies of Containment,* p. 144.

30. See Elmo Richardson, *The Presidency of Dwight D. Eisenhower* (Lawrence, Kan.: Regents Press of Kansas, 1979), pp. 98–99, 155–60; and Fred Greenstein, *The Hidden-Hand Presidency: Eisenhower as Leader* (New York: Basic Books, 1982).

usually existed between public rhetoric and private calculation. If opinion among Truman's advisers was faithfully captured by the Clifford-Elsey memorandum, why was the public being told contemporaneously that the administration felt hopeful about negotiations, continued to believe that nuclear weapons could be placed under international control, and regarded as adequate a defense budget targeted eventually to represent only a slightly larger fraction of GNP than in the 1930s? If the NSC documents on Basic National Security Policy (BNSP) reflected a true consensus, why did the rhetoric of Eisenhower and Dulles and Kennedy and Rusk, including that establishing the equivalent of legislative history for otherwise cautiously worded security treaties and military assistance pacts, suggest that, as Kennedy put it in his Inaugural Address, the United States would "pay any price, bear any burden, meet any hardship, support any friend, oppose any foe to assure the survival and the success of liberty"? Why did Eisenhower feel obliged in 1954 to create a pretense that he would have intervened in Indochina if he had not been restrained by weak-kneed European allies? Why did he and Dulles have to bluster as they did about Quemoy and Matsu? Why did Kennedy reportedly come into office regarding Laos as a country not "worthy of engaging the attention of great powers," yet feel obliged to appear on television, with maps in bright red as visual aids, to declare that on its fate could hinge the "freedom and security of the free world"?[31]

It may serve other current purposes besides general historical understanding to speculate on why, in American efforts to manage Soviet relations during the two decades after World War II, what the government said in public mirrored only very dimly what the majority of officials actually thought.

Part of the explanation lies in perceptions of relevant audiences, including the Russians, the allies, the Congress, and the public. As the Clifford-Elsey memorandum testifies, most of Truman's advisers believed that the "language of military power" was the only language to which the Soviets would respond. For the most part, the actual Russian experts in the government, such as Kennan, Charles Bohlen, and Llewellyn Thompson, argued slightly differently, Kennan, for example, contending that Stalin would probably retreat in the Near East rather than risk a diplomatic rupture with either Britain or the United States.[32] But most people in both the State Department and the military establishment took the simpler interpretation. After Korea, the Russian experts

31. See Arthur M. Schlesinger, Jr., *A Thousand Days: John F. Kennedy in the White House* (Boston: Houghton Mifflin, 1965), pp. 329–32.
32. See *FRUS, 1946,* 7: 362–64 (Kennan); *FRUS, 1949,* 1: 292 (Thompson); *FRUS, 1951,* 1: 106–09 (Bohlen).

ceased to have much moderating influence, for they had been confidently forecasting that Stalin would not make any such risky move. From mid-1950 onward, it was the effective consensus in Washington that, to have any effect in Moscow, the U.S. government should take no risk of understating its willingness to use force or implying any lack of faith in its capacity to do so.

Similarly, especially after Korea, American officials felt that they needed to sound resolute and confident in order to buck up the Europeans and others in what had now come to be characterized as "the free world." As the 1953 statement on Basic National Security Policy observed, "If our allies were uncertain about our ability or will to counter Soviet aggression, they would be strongly tempted to adopt a neutralist position, especially in face of the atomic threat."

Particularly, however, it was thought to be the domestic audience that had to be addressed with incomplete candor. In the immediate postwar period, champions of a harder line toward the USSR kept urging an administration effort to mobilize public opinion. President Truman occasionally yielded, as, for example, when proclaiming the Truman Doctrine. These efforts involved some conscious overstatement. Acheson recounts in his memoirs how the Truman Doctrine message was designed to answer congressional pleas for language to "scare hell" out of the country.[33] Generally, Truman resisted the tactic prior to 1950 partly out of fear for his defense budget ceilings. After mid-1950 he allowed it to become standard practice. As one State Department memorandum observed, it seemed "necessary for the administration to oversimplify Soviet intentions in appealing to Congress and the people for support of the defense program."[34]

Perceptions are always functions in part of reality, in part of the mindsets of those perceiving. Truman, Eisenhower, Kennedy, and their advisers possessed real-world evidence of the utility of stern bluffing. After all, the Russians didn't take Berlin, and the Chinese didn't seize Quemoy and Matsu. Similarly, the failure of the NATO allies to meet their original force-level pledges, the hesitancy of the French about German rearmament, the mid-1950s negotiation initiatives by the British, the Suez episode, and the growth of concern about "decoupling" all provided warrant for feeling that it might be safer at the margin for Europeans to see the United States as inflexible rather than flexible.

And history perhaps more than current indicators supplied ample basis for an impulse to oversimplify what was presented to Congress and

33. Dean Acheson, *Present at the Creation: My Years in the State Department* (New York: Norton, 1969), p. 219.
34. *FRUS, 1951,* 1: 166–67.

the people at home. Traditionally, American discourse about international relations, or at least about issues of war and peace, had involved absolutes. Shared belief in the total evil of the enemy had been essential to the mobilization of national energies in both world wars. Essential, too, had been the idea that war engaged all energies and led to some kind of attainable peace. It took a long time, and a lot of evidence, before American political leaders could begin to believe that Congress and the public might reconcile themselves to what another line in Kennedy's Inaugural described as "a long twilight struggle, year in and year out."

An even stronger American habit of mind, continually in evidence, involved a mixture of pragmatism and presentism. Forrestal argued in 1947 against any arms limitation negotiations "because of the American tendency always to take for granted that other nations have the same objectives as ourselves. . . . I am most apprehensive of our people's taking the *discussion* of disarmament for the fact."[35] Similar fears surfaced in connection with Eisenhower's "Open Skies" initiative and all test-ban negotiations, and polls and other indications of oscillation between deep pessimism and high hopefulness in the period from Sputnik to the Eisenhower–Khrushchev Camp David talks to the collapse of the Paris summit lent these fears objective support.[36]

But the men at the head of the American government in the postwar decades were prone to notice particularly the elements of objective reality that justified oversimplification. For the most part, their thinking had been shaped by the experience of the 1930s. Assuming the paradigmatic relationship between states committed to different ideologies to be that between Britain and Nazi Germany, they were perhaps excessively fearful of engaging in wishful appeasement or otherwise failing to recognize the full malevolence of the foe. Furthermore, memories from before 1941 also disposed them to be on the watch for British statesmen arriving with furled umbrellas or Frenchmen making toward Vichy. Above all, those memories caused them to be on the lookout for signs in Congress or among the public of a turn toward isolationism. Though gradually diminishing in strength, this particular apprehension remained powerful all the way into the period of the Vietnam War.

There were important individual differences. Hoping against hope to avoid a costly arms race, Truman was comparatively slow to make the equation between Stalin and Hitler. Only after the North Korean attack on South Korea did he become a complete believer. Marshall, molded by the interwar experience of attempting to wring meager defense appro-

35. Walter Millis, ed., *The Forrestal Diaries* (New York: Viking, 1951), pp. 290–91.

36. See Ralph B. Levering, *The Public and American Foreign Policy* (New York: Morrow, 1978), pp. 87–89.

priations from a pinchpenny Congress, was relatively more pessimistic than others about the long-term success of any policy requiring continual high levels of defense spending. For obvious reasons, he and Eisenhower were somewhat more skeptical than most others about ever actually attaining levels of military preparedness adequate for a comprehensive commitment to containment. In Acheson, experience in championing intervention before 1941 and handling congressional relations during the war had induced a special sensitivity to signs of isolationism, while in Dulles, painful memories from the aftermath of the Versailles conference and internal struggles of the Republican party had encouraged wariness both of Englishmen and Frenchmen and of Congress and the public. Thus history in the heads of American statesmen led them in varying ways to see reality as imposing restraints on the degree of forthrightness permissible in public statements about foreign and defense policy.

To leave it there is, however, to be unfair to a generation of leaders as remarkable as those who created the United States. For while it is now apparent that they were to some extent engaged in creating illusions, it is not clear that they had many alternatives, not only because it was hard *not* to read the lessons of recent history as they did, but even more because they worked within the constraints of a governmental system poorly constructed to cope with the conditions of the cold war.

While the United States had gradually acquired a powerful national government, few Americans ever habituated themselves to the concept of there being a state with interests larger than or not identical with the combined and often conflicting interests of individual citizens. To a greater extent than in any other nation (except ones in the midst of revolution) American public opinion exercises direct control over government. It is the only source of legitimacy for either people or policies. Owing to the intricate congressional-executive relationship, it affects directly the internal activities of almost every agency. This is not to deny that people holding office can have great influence on what the people pay attention to and what their attitudes are. But American officeholders are somewhat like manufacturers of painkillers or producers of motion pictures. Their capacity to foretell public response is limited; their dependence upon it is absolute.

In the cold war, the officeholders' control of public opinion may in some respects have been less than in previous periods or circumstances, for people within the government tended to believe that the large majority of the populace did not, perhaps could not, understand the issues. Kennan wrote almost despairingly that he doubted whether a policy would be consistently pursued unless it had been "drummed into the minds of a very large number of persons, including quite a few whose mental development has not advanced very far beyond the age which is said to be the criterion for the production of movies in Hollywood."[37] Even such a thoroughgoing democrat as Hubert Humphrey doubted whether the people could comprehend and support a policy of containment which might involve sometimes deliberately cutting losses.[38]

Once the policy came to be defined as essentially military containment, another complication arose, for defense policy necessarily involves calculations about uncertain and often distant futures. The conventions of defense planning and procurement and the associated budgeting and appropriations process require a pretense of present peril on the assumption that most people, and most members of Congress, think and act only in the short term. Thus, after mid-1950 the difficulty of explaining and defending governmental policy rose by a power of two because public statements dealt with both incomprehensible foreigners *and* invisible futures.

In fact, the difficulty increased almost by a power of three because of the related fact of secrecy. Though never with any real success, the wartime and postwar State Department borrowed the practice of nations where relations between state and populace were different and attempted to preserve confidentiality. The military services guarded their affairs as if the cold war were a real war. A supposition, only partly true, that there were protectable mysteries concerning nuclear weapons aided the process. So did an increasing amount of activity that in its nature did have to be cloaked from public view, such as, for example, varieties of secret intelligence collection. But the net effect on government communication with domestic publics was harmful. Relations between officialdom and the press acquired a hide-and-seek quality. (Anyone who believes that this only became true in the era of Vietnam and Watergate should leaf through the 1950s columns of the Alsop brothers and Drew Pearson.) Officials became able to discount opinion among laymen because they had not "seen the cables." Indeed, officials at varying levels in varying agencies could discount each other because not every insider had the same sets of clearances. And on the outside, secrecy encouraged unin structed trustfulness or indifference or suspicion. All in all, it became deceptively easier for people in the government to be less than candid with the domestic audience in order to seek desired effects in Moscow or other capitals abroad.

And one comes back to the frailty of the American state, because the government, for practical purposes, communicated with its own public through the president. Secretaries of state and defense spoke mostly for

37. Quoted in Gaddis, *Strategies of Containment*, p. 52.
38. Hubert H. Humphrey, *The Education of a Public Man* (Garden City, N.Y.: Doubleday, 1976), pp. 318–28.

specialized audiences. Concerning foreign or defense policy, Congress as a rule addressed the whole nation only as it or its committees or members reacted to statements or proposals from the White House. The enormous task of providing the public with a framework for judging those policies belonged thus successively between 1945 and 1965 to a Missouri politician in his sixties, a professional soldier of the same generation, and two young senators whose ripest years had been spent in presidential primary campaigns.

Little wonder, then, that prior to 1950 "the government" did not disclose to the American public the extent of the commitments and risks being assumed for the objective of containment, and that after 1950 it did not disclose its actual reservations and misgivings about the promises it seemed to be making and the dangers that they entailed. The power of public opinion, the frailty of the state, and the nature of the issues make this entirely understandable.

In the American system, the executive branch cannot manage foreign relations except with sustained sympathy and support from Congress and the public. In the early cold war, as earlier and later, presidents set headings and Congress and the public usually stayed on course. But not all the time. Truman and Eisenhower both wanted to define the Soviet problem primarily in political and economic terms. Neither succeeded. A combination of forces, some from within their own administrations, some from outside, compelled them to accept definitions couched much more in military terms.

Whatever the definition, presidents and other national leaders felt that the issues had to be oversimplified or exaggerated. Before 1950 they understated them. Afterward, they overstated them. Electoral processes, the budget process, and the sheer mechanics of catching the public's attention all seemed to require it. Abroad, however, to friend and adversary alike, the United States government gave the impression of lacking subtlety or discrimination and of being unpredictable. That impression was to be reinforced in later years.

10

Détente

STANLEY HOFFMANN

What is most striking about the period of Soviet–American détente under Nixon and Kissinger is not its length but its design and intensity—one could almost say, its mythology. It was just a bit longer than earlier moments of grace, but not by much: there were less than three good years—1971, 1972, and the first nine months of 1973. But these earlier "waves" of détente had never been so strong and so determined, or risen so high.

What was the design behind this particular "era of negotiations," and why did it recede? Many explanations have been offered for its ultimate failure. Some have argued that the essence of the Soviet system and the nature of Soviet policy make any search for even partial accommodation a dangerous delusion. Others have put the blame on something far more accidental: the combination of Watergate, which undermined the president's authority, and of a congressional counteroffensive made possible by this decline of the presidency. My view is different: détente was the major part of an ambitious world policy that tried to force the Soviet Union, through a network of linked rewards and punishments, to play the role assigned to it by America's leaders in a "stable structure of peace" that would have preserved America's primacy and ensured the triumph of its very conservative notion of stability. The design was impressive but beyond reach, and the tools it used were inadequate. These flaws more than the circumstances of Watergate, explain why domestic support remained elusive.

I will begin by looking at moments of détente before 1969 in order to see why they vanished or languished. Then I will discuss the Nixon-Kissinger approach and try to explain what went wrong.[1]

The author thanks Professor Michael Smith for his suggestions and Professor John Gaddis for his comments.
1. I have already tried to do so in *Primacy or World Order* (New York. McGraw-Hill, 1978), chap. 2, and in my two reviews of Kissinger's memoirs in *Dead Ends* (Cambridge, Mass.: Ballinger, 1983), chaps. 2 and 3.

INTIMATIONS OF DÉTENTE

In terms of scope and deliberation, only the Soviet–American wartime alliance can be compared with the détente of the early 1970s. The alliance lasted a bit longer: from Pearl Harbor to Roosevelt's death. Its underlying philosophy aimed at obtaining Soviet cooperation both during and after the war. American policy combined concessions to Soviet security interests in Eastern Europe and East Asia, positive inducements of military and economic aid, symbolic attempts at building confidence in the wartime conferences, and what John Lewis Gaddis[2] calls counterweights: keeping the atomic bomb and organizing a world in which the remaining great powers other than the Soviet Union could be counted on to ally themselves with the U.S., and the lesser powers, represented in the General Assembly of the UN, could be expected to follow Washington's lead. The policy failed for reasons that have often been analyzed—and that we shall encounter again. First, as George Kennan never tires of pointing out, it was based on very dubious assumptions about Stalin's probable behavior, the evolution of the Soviet regime, and Moscow's susceptibility to "the power of [Roosevelt's] charismatic personality."[3] Second, the policy instruments were inadequate. Despite Churchill's exhortations and Harriman's advice, the president had refrained from using threats during the war. Thus, by the time Yalta began to unravel and Truman came to power, the Soviet Union was in central Europe and the United States had too few carrots and the unusable atomic stick.

One had to wait eight more years before an offer of détente floated briefly into the cold air of the containment policy. Upon becoming president in 1953, Eisenhower, learning that Stalin was dying, had overcome Dulles's "reservations" and delivered an appeal for peace to the Russian people.[4] A few weeks later, on April 16, 1953, he denounced the arms race, asked the new Soviet leadership to "awaken" to the peril of war, and made a "specific offer"—universal disarmament.[5] A few months later, at the United Nations General Assembly, he proposed the creation of a World Atomic Energy Agency and launched the Atoms-for-Peace program. The Soviet response was disappointing; but the American offers set a pattern that would be repeated in the future attempts at détente: Washington's focus would be on the arms race rather than on the political points of confrontation. When Eisenhower hoped that his General As-

2. John Lewis Gaddis, *Strategies of Containment* (New York: Oxford University Press, 1982), p. 11.
3. George Kennan, *The Nuclear Delusion* (New York: Pantheon, 1982), p. 25.
4. Dwight D. Eisenhower, *Mandate for Change* (New York: Signet, 1965), p. 168.
5. Ibid., p. 191.

sembly offer could expand into something broader, he meant joint humanitarian efforts.

The scent of détente appeared only in the spring of 1955, in circumstances that can be compared with those of 1969–1970. The new Soviet leadership had now consolidated its power. The long battle over West Germany's rearmament was over, and Washington's allies were pressing the United States to show some flexibility. Moreover, the Soviets had announced their intention to sign a peace treaty with Austria. The Geneva summit conference, in July, produced a brief "spirit"—but little more: Eisenhower focused on surprise attack and made his own open-skies proposal, which Khrushchev rejected. Bulganin showed that the Soviet interest in a relaxation of tension was linked with permanent political objectives: he proposed a pan-European security system, which the Western leaders rejected. And the discussion on Germany's future, at first vaguely promising, rapidly led to a familiar impasse. Some cultural and scientific exchanges began. But 1956 was to be a troubled year.

The experience was repeated in 1959, when Khrushchev's visit produced the "Spirit of Camp David." The Berlin crisis engineered by the Soviet leader the previous year was temporarily defused. But the discussion on disarmament and on a test ban, in which Eisenhower was interested, had been going nowhere; and when, in early 1960, a compromise on the test ban seemed on the verge of agreement, the U-2 affair and the fiasco of the Paris summit set it back once more.[6] The lesson of the 1950s seems clear. Militarily, the Soviet Union was too far behind the United States for disarmament talks to be more than propaganda exercises, and the issue of inspection made even limited agreements difficult. On political issues, each side was eager above all to consolidate its own camp. Khrushchev, it is true, had announced a policy of peaceful coexistence. But he could be quite aggressive in tone and manner, and bullying Western leaders into cooperation got him into trouble instead. Eisenhower, who never believed either in a Soviet desire for war or in an American need to close a nonexistent missile gap, nevertheless thought that Soviet ideology and relentless expansionism made accommodation highly unlikely.[7]

Once again, it was the nuclear issue that brought forth what might be called the first real détente—after the Cuban missile crisis. Kennedy did not try to exploit his victory at the Soviets' expense either in Cuba or in Berlin: not only did he avoid humiliating his opponent, he also tried to

6. See George Kistiakowski, *A Scientist in the White House* (Cambridge, Mass.: Harvard University Press, 1976), and Glenn T. Seaborg, *Kennedy, Khrushchev and the Test Ban* (Berkeley: University of California Press, 1981).

7. Dwight D. Eisenhower, *Waging Peace* (New York: Doubleday, 1965), chap. 15.

move decisively away from confrontation. In his June 1963 speech delivered at American University, President Kennedy appealed, in effect, for a new American image of the Soviet Union. The implacable nature of Soviet ideology was not mentioned any more. Not only was the Limited Test-Ban Treaty signed, but a sale of grain to the Soviet Union was approved. This change was made possible not only by the terrifying experience of the "missiles of October," but also by the secret correspondence between Kennedy and Khrushchev (initiated by the latter in September 1961)[8] and by the lifting of Soviet pressure on West Berlin.

A few distinctive features of this détente stand out. First, like Eisenhower's, Kennedy's policy focus remained above all on the issue of war: most of the measures he outlined in his General Assembly speech of September 20, 1963 dealt with the dangers of nuclear war and proliferation;[9] and Kennedy did not follow Walt Rostow's advice of linking a test-ban treaty to Soviet cooperation in Cuba and Laos.[10] Second, Kennedy seems to have believed that agreements on the nuclear issues, by consolidating a range of common interests, could lead later to "a more constructive and less hostile Soviet policy";[11] in the meantime, controversial political issues were to be "decoupled" from the negotiable, discrete military ones.[12] But the long-range objective seemed to be an "unostentatious" Soviet–American rapprochement against China (see n. 11 above). Thus, both in method and objective, Kennedy's détente was very different from Kissinger's. Nevertheless, third, the problem of domestic resistance to a change of course had already arisen: the American University speech was prepared without the knowledge and participation of the bureaucracy, and the Test-Ban Treaty itself met strong opposition both from the Joint Chiefs of Staff (whose resistance was one of the obstacles preventing a comprehensive ban) and in the Senate. And fourth, the Soviets—as before—tried to use the limited rapprochement in order to reach old objectives: Khrushchev pressed hard for a nonaggression pact between NATO and the Warsaw Pact.

Kennedy's assassination brought this attempt to an end. In the period that followed, it is difficult to talk of a coherent or consistent policy toward the Soviet Union: Johnson's priorities were elsewhere—domestic reform and, alas, "containment" in Vietnam. In America's relations with the Soviet Union, the years 1964–68 were years of rather muted containment

   8. Theodore Sorensen, *Kennedy* (New York: Bantam, 1966), pp. 622 ff.
   9. Ibid., pp. 837–38.
   10. Gaddis, *Strategies*, p. 230.
   11. Seaborg, *Kennedy, Khrushchev*, p. 217.
   12. Gordon A. Craig and Alexander L. George, *Force and Statecraft* (New York: Oxford University Press, 1983), chap. 9.

of Moscow and limited accommodation. One could perhaps speak of a de facto détente, a détente more improvised than thought through. There was now a certain smugness toward the Soviet rival. His defeat in Cuba was interpreted as a major event that taught him a lesson in necessary modesty and made dangerous new crises unlikely; the prudent diplomacy of Khrushchev's successors in Europe and the Third World was treated as evidence instead of being understood as a deliberate choice for a massive, if sober, buildup of Soviet capabilities, an investment in the future after the years of bluff and failed shortcuts of Khrushchev. Now that Soviet conduct in the world was quieter, Washington paid more attention to the noise from Beijing—especially at the time of the cultural revolution—than to the realities of power and the less spectacular aspects of Soviet behavior, such as Moscow's considerable aid to North Vietnam: many officials believed Hanoi to be a stalking-horse for a truly revolutionary and expansionist China and listened to Moscow's suggestions of possible solutions in Vietnam. Johnson and his advisers did not share their predecessors' fears about Soviet ideology (this was, indeed, the period when China denounced the Soviets as "revisionists," afraid of nuclear war, and derided the erosion of Soviet ideology), whereas these same advisers were taking Chinese pronouncements at face value.

The de facto détente developed along three different tracks. One, traced by the nuclear predicament, had been initiated by Eisenhower and Kennedy; it led, in these years, first to the agreement on the nonproliferation treaty and, in the last months of the Johnson administration, to the preparations for strategic arms control negotiations. A second track was, Johnson claims, his own idea: "Rather than try to achieve a single, comprehensive agreement, I thought it more sensible to try to find common ground on lesser problems";[13] hence, a series of agreements on civil aviation, consulates, cultural and scientific exchanges, and so on. A third track concerned political conflicts. Washington and Moscow were in constant touch over Vietnam, and they succeeded in avoiding a confrontation during the Six-Day War (which was followed by the meeting of Johnson and Kosygin at Glassboro). Johnson's October 1966 speech about "peaceful engagement" in Eastern Europe implicitly recognized the territorial division of the continent—nine years before the Helsinki agreements—and was intended to open the way to a general European settlement.[14] In this third area, the results can best be described as damage limitation.

13. Lyndon B. Johnson, *The Vantage Point* (New York: Holt Rinehart & Winston, 1971), p. 463. For a list of agreements, see Walt W. Rostow, *The Diffusion of Power* (New York: Macmillan, 1972), p. 373.

14. William G. Hyland, *Soviet–American Relations: A New Cold War?* (Santa Monica, Calif.: The RAND Corporation, R-2763-FF/RC, 1981), pp. 19–20.

Distracted by Vietnam, Washington was in no position to pursue any ambitious grand design; but the relative retreat from confrontation with Moscow and the rise of violent confrontation at home (generated by the Vietnam War) probably contributed to the mildness of America's response to the invasion of Czechoslovakia.

Three features of this semiabsentminded détente deserve special mention. First, domestic suspicion of the Soviet Union manifested itself again: Johnson, in 1966, failed to get Congress to remove special tariff restrictions on East–West trade, and it took two years for the consular convention to get through the Senate. Second, France and West Germany, worried by the opening of a dialogue between the superpowers under Kennedy, took advantage of the quasi paralysis of America's diplomacy under Johnson to launch their own approaches to Moscow: sweepingly in the case of de Gaulle (who coined the slogan: détente, entente, and cooperation); prudently in the case of the Kiesinger-Brandt government. Third, the domestic troubles of the Johnson administration led it to seek compensation by "peace-mongering" abroad: LBJ sought in vain to salvage a summit meeting from the wrecks of the Chicago convention and the invasion of Czechoslovakia. Still, with the benefit of hindsight one can see the years 1964–68 as a vital incubation period for détente: without the Europeans' initiatives and the unspectacular but steady progress accomplished by an administration trapped in Vietnam and devoid of strategic concept concerning the Soviet Union, it would have been much more difficult for Nixon and Kissinger to launch their enterprise.

THE NIXON-KISSINGER DESIGN

In his recent book, John Lewis Gaddis has stressed the similarities between Kissinger's views and the "asymmetrical containment" policies recommended by George Kennan twenty-odd years earlier.[15] These resemblances strike me as superficial and misleading. Gaddis confuses asymmetry in the *scope* of containment and asymmetry in the *means*. Kennan is the best (indeed, the only) example of the former: in his view, we should prevent the Soviet Union from encroaching upon our vital interests, but the areas of vital interest—and therefore the threats—are limited. By contrast, asymmetry in means, characteristic of the Eisenhower policy, in theory allows the United States to choose how, where, and when to respond to Soviet adventures; but in the Eisenhower period, as in the one that had preceded it, the scope of what the U.S. government deemed to be America's vital concerns expanded almost indefinitely: any extension of Soviet influence was seen as a threat to American interests.

---

15. Gaddis, *Strategies*, pp. 283, 308.

Despite all his statements about the limits of American *means* and his pleas for a sharper definition of American *interests,* Kissinger unquestionably believed in the need to protect American influence and position throughout the world against the global and "ruthless opportunism" of the Soviet Union; and he believed in the importance of "meeting conclusively"—namely, prevailing in—the challenges we faced.[16] We may want to teach Moscow to abstain from incremental gains, but until this lesson is learned, all such gains must be prevented. Nixon, too, described the United States as "the main defender of the free world against the encroachment and aggression of the Communist world."[17] Kissinger could write, and Nixon muse, about multipolarity. In fact they looked at the world in stark bipolar terms: to both, the Soviet–American relationship was the most essential factor in world affairs. The landslide metaphor often used by Kissinger makes this perfectly clear: the Soviet Union is just as responsible for troubles it has merely encouraged as someone who starts an avalanche by throwing a few stones. Multipolarity only meant that others—America's main allies, China, Washington's lesser clients—should now be prodded to do more to prevent such a landslide; the United States could not do it alone, but would remain the brain and the main secular arm of the global operation.

Just as Eisenhower had tried after Korea to find more economical methods of containment than those of NSC 68, so Nixon and Kissinger, still saddled with Vietnam, attempted to buttress containment in less exhausting ways. Military expenditures went down, and the concept of sufficiency—invented, it seems, by Donald Quarles in 1956[18]—was brought back to fame. One could no longer try to deter regional conflicts by threats of massive retaliation, but one could still try to avoid local entanglements of American forces by the policies outlined in Guam—massive support to allies and proxies. And, as in the heyday of Dulles's strategy, one could hope to deter the adversary by relying on uncertainty (of means) and unpredictability.

To be sure, there were innovations. Unlike Eisenhower and Dulles, Nixon and Kissinger worried little about the ideological threat of the Soviet Union (something for which, in later years, the neoconservatives have not quite forgiven them). They tried as well to avoid the flaws of policies based exclusively on projections of Soviet capabilities or assumed intentions. As NSC 68 and the hysteria following Sputnik demonstrated,

16. Henry Kissinger, *White House Years* (Boston: Little, Brown, 1979), pp. 119 and 64.

17. Richard M. Nixon, *The Memoirs of Richard Nixon* (New York: Grosset & Dunlap, 1978), p. 343.

18. According to Gerard Smith, *Doubletalk: The Story of SALT I* (Garden City, N.Y.: Doubleday, 1980).

such projections could be dangerously exaggerated. Instead they concentrated on Soviet behavior. Above all, they were far more willing than any of their predecessors to exploit splits in the communist world—particularly the Sino–Soviet conflict. They were also far more eager to obtain what could be called containment by negotiation. Indeed, the failure to engage the Soviets in negotiations at a time when the United States was comparatively much stronger is one of Kissinger's chief criticisms of earlier cold-war policies.[19] Another criticism stated that the separation of power and diplomacy had somehow emptied American policy of content: "it aimed at an ultimate negotiation but supplied no guide to the content of those negotiations."[20] What Nixon and Kissinger appeared to want was really quite grandiose: a far more diversified use of means, a complex system of incentives and sanctions aimed at inducing Soviet self-containment, and a conception of international order to provide the previously missing "content." The design tried to synthesize adversary containment with the "friendly embrace"—or ensnaring—that Roosevelt had had in mind; but Kissinger and Nixon recognized his illusions, and they were far more determined to use all the levers of power.

Doing more with less (as in Vietnam), they would not be satisfied with the fragmentary approaches of Kennedy and Johnson. Linkage was to provide integration through the network of rewards and punishments. Linkage also aimed at combining a short-term objective—obtaining Soviet help for extrication from the Vietnam trap, an intermediate aim— entangling the adversary in a cobweb of interests, and an ultimate goal— redressing what, to Nixon, seemed a dangerously unbalanced situation. Militarily, the Soviets were outspending the U.S.; politically, "they had a major presence in the Arab states . . . while we had none; they had Castro in Cuba; since the mid-1960s they had supplanted China as the principal suppliers of North Vietnam and, except for Tito's Yugoslavia, they still controlled Eastern Europe and threatened the stability and security of Western Europe."[21]

What made Nixon and Kissinger believe that a more powerful Soviet Union could be piloted toward self-restraint (*and* induced to restrain Hanoi)? Contrary to what many writers have asserted, they seem to have been remarkably free of some familiar illusions. They did not see the Soviet Union as a status-quo power, even if they rejected the theory of a Soviet master plan: "The Soviet practice . . . is to promote the attrition of adversaries by gradual increments."[22] They did not believe in the virtues

19. Kissinger, *White House Years*, pp. 62 ff.
20. Ibid., p. 62.
21. Nixon, *Memoirs*, p. 344.
22. Kissinger, *White House Years*, p. 118.

of personal contacts or in the stories about factionalism in the Kremlin. Nor did they believe that the Soviet quest for economic development would gain priority over foreign adventures. Thus, a first answer to the question must be: a mixture of necessity and calculation. At times, the White House behaved as if under siege, and with good reason. American opinion was tired of both the Vietnam War and the cold war; congressional determination to cut the defense budget led Nixon, in February 1970, to propose a defense appropriation lower than that of the previous year (and Congress cut it further). Liberals in Congress pushed for a relaxation of trade restrictions with the USSR and Eastern Europe. Abroad, the Brandt government had undertaken an ambitious détente policy of its own—sufficiently innovative and daring to arouse the suspicions of Pompidou and serious misgivings in the White House (Kissinger feared both a resurgence of German nationalism and a Soviet success in exploiting Brandt's eagerness to achieve a merely "selective détente"). The United States could (and did) try to "give the inevitable a constructive direction";[23] but precisely because it was inevitable, the United States could keep control of the alliance only by following (indeed, by trying to step ahead of) its allies. Thus, necessity accounts for much of the administration's strategy.

Moreover, the intensely bipolar view of Nixon and Kissinger led them to believe that Moscow could influence North Vietnam. They tried to get Brezhnev to wring concessions from Hanoi by subordinating the development of Soviet–American cooperation, which the Soviets said they wished, to Soviet help in Southeast Asia. This brings one to the element of calculation: Nixon and Kissinger believed in Soviet eagerness for such cooperation because mutual restraints in a costly nuclear arms race now made sense, given the weaknesses of the Soviet economy *and* the closing of the gap between the two strategic forces. They believed that the Soviet interest in trade and credits provided an opportunity, if not for reversing Soviet policy or priorities, at least for inducing restraint. They were determined to use a rapprochement with China as a powerful goad. And they thought that a policy that stressed negotiation, "patient and continuing communication,"[24] had a good chance, not only of preventing erosion or division in America's alliance systems, but above all of repairing the cracked domestic consensus, leaving only extreme "appeasers" or hardliners at the fringes.

But a careful look at the record suggests a second answer as well. The French have an expression for it: *l'appétit vient en mangeant*. Indeed, in the

23. Ibid., p. 530.
24. "U.S. Foreign Policy for the 1970's," *Department of State Bulletin 1602*, February 18, 1970 (Washington, D.C.: U.S. Government Printing Office, 1970), p. 323.

beginning, both the expectations and the results were limited, despite the rhetoric about the "era of negotiation": Vietnam, on the one hand; a complex set of links between the Berlin negotiations, the Soviet–West German agreement, the European Security Conference, and a possible summit, on the other—this was the scope of the attempt at political bargaining (and despite all the talk about linkage, the slow SALT talks moved according to their own logic).[25] Soviet attempts to discuss the Middle East were rebuffed by the White House. And presidential discretion was retained, and used, after passage of the bill of December 1969 allowing a liberalization of trade with Moscow. Kissinger himself notes that "as far as the Soviets were concerned, 1969 was a flight from concreteness."[26] There was no progress on Vietnam; 1970 was marked by Soviet evasiveness over the holding of a summit meeting and, above all, by four more or less indirect confrontations: in Egypt (where the United States, much to Kissinger's chagrin, failed to react to the Soviet shipments of antiaircraft missiles and personnel), in Jordan, in Cuba, and over Chile. The second "State of the World" message, published in February 1971, still stresses the differences in the two countries' approaches to world affairs and "contention across a broad range of issues."[27]

The change in appetite or ambition appears to have followed the "breakthroughs" in SALT in the spring of 1971 and in Kissinger's trip to China in July 1971. Interestingly enough, the geographical scope of cooperation did not change much: there was still no meeting of minds over the Middle East, for instance. But in August 1971, the Soviets formally invited Nixon to Moscow; in 1972, the Soviet Union gave the appearance of helping Washington in Vietnam—by receiving Kissinger in the middle of the North Vietnamese offensive and by proceeding with the summit despite the bombing of Hanoi and the mining of Haiphong. Above all, the number of joint enterprises increased dramatically: in addition to the "Eastern treaties" and to SALT I, MBFR and a European Security Conference were launched; bilateral agreements multiplied; agreements on expanded trade, MFN treatment and credit arrangements were prepared; and the accord on twelve basic principles of U.S.–Soviet relations emerged from the Moscow summit. The 1972 State of the World message, issued in February, listed the Soviet Union first among the areas of major change; a year later, the 1973 message talked about a "decisive turn" away from past confrontations.

Thus, for a while the Nixon-Kissinger strategy seemed to work. Firm

25. See Kissinger, *White House Years*, p. 550, on the modesty of Kissinger's expectations at this point (July 1970), expressed in a memo to Nixon.

26. Ibid., p. 147. Cf. also, on p. 144: "Inconclusive exchanges in 1969 degenerated into a series of confrontations that lasted through 1970."

27. "U.S. Foreign Policy for the 1970's," *Department of State Bulletin 1656*, February 25, 1971 (Washington, D.C.: U.S. Government Printing Office, 1971), p. 403.

resistance to local shifts in the balance of power attempted by Soviet clients (as in the case of India during the Bangladesh conflict, according to the American leaders), a deaf ear to suggestions from Moscow that would have rewarded Moscow's friends (such as Sadat), a compromise settlement in Vietnam safeguarding the Thieu regime—all these showed the vigor of the determination to contain. The Berlin agreement; a SALT treaty which, in addition to banning ABMs (except for two sites on each side), froze "Soviet deployments of offensive weapons, in which they had an advantage that was likely to continue to grow in the absence of a freeze,"[28] but allowed for all the new American strategic programs; Moscow's restraint in providing arms to Sadat and the Soviets' cautious dissociation from the traditional Arab position for a settlement, resulting in a break between Sadat and Moscow (July 1972)—all these seemed to prove the success of the strategy of inducing self-containment. The gamble taken on worrying Moscow into compromises, not confrontations, through a carefully modulated China policy paid off. And yet, even in the period of greatest accomplishments—the year between the Moscow and the San Clemente summits—one could detect in the American strategy some ominous contradictions between statements or appearances and reality.

Thus the official line discounted the importance of ideology in international affairs: only the realities of power mattered. This seemed to suggest a more restricted definition both of threats to American interests and of those interests than in the days of John Foster Dulles. And yet, ideology slipped in through the back door: in the distinction between moderates and radicals and the definition of radicals as all those who rely on Moscow to promote their cause, or all those whose victory would ("objectively," as *Pravda* would say) further Moscow's interests. Such a definition allowed for, justified, or required American opposition to Allende in Chile, to Sadat before the expulsion of Soviet advisers in July 1972, and to the Italian Communist party; it explained the "tilt" toward Pakistan in 1971. As I have suggested elsewhere, this grand oversimplification made Kissinger's pronouncements about the balance of power sound more like Metternich than Castlereagh: "Communist ideology," wrote Kissinger, "transforms relations between states into conflicts between philosophies and poses challenges to the balance of power through domestic upheavals."[29]

The same conclusion emerges from a second contradiction: that between the formal declaration of indifference to domestic regimes—only external behavior matters and ought to be the object of foreign policy—and the sharp limits Kissinger tried in fact to put on domestic changes in

28. Kissinger, *White House Years,* p. 1244.
29. Ibid., p. 62.

the noncommunist parts of the world, even when those changes could not have been attributed to Soviet aggression or Cuban subversion. Again, the most glaring example is that of Chile; but Kissinger's initial policy for southern Africa, the continuing aid for the faltering FNLA in Angola, his reluctance to try to negotiate a return of Sihanouk in Cambodia, his failure to react to Yahya Khan's atrocities in East Bengal, and the un-limited support to the shah of Iran, also come to mind.

There was a third contradiction: between the attempt to define "a concept of our fundamental national interests" capable of avoiding "both overinvolvement and isolationism"[30] as well as of distinguishing between marginal assets and essential ones (no more Vietnams!), and the deter-mination to resist even—indeed, especially—challenges at the margin, so as to "overpower" them early, before they become unmanageable.[31] This was a clash between an effort to formulate a doctrine that would provide continuity and guidance, and—as Kissinger recognized in the second volume of his memoirs—a purely intuitive approach, which required asking the public to trust the leader's conviction that what might appear insignificant at first could, if left unchallenged, grow into a disaster. It was a clash between confidence in the existence of truly permanent interests, and the fear that perceptions of defeat or loss, even in objectively insig-nificant cases, could snowball and induce either dangerous risk-taking by the adversary, or a negative bandwagon effect among the neutrals or the allies, or a loss of self-confidence in one's public.[32] Thus, a demand for "a shared sense of proportion" and for a recognition of limits confronted a claim of our "responsibility to defend global security even against ambig-uous and marginal assaults."[33]

Finally, there was a contradiction between the appearance of a U.S.–Soviet condominium, which the two sets of principles adopted in the summits of 1972 and 1973 could not fail to suggest, and the far more profound reality of implacable containment, of intractable hostility to the expansion of Soviet influence. However much Nixon and Kissinger *sounded,* in each case, as though they wanted cooperation and accom-modation, they *acted* on the premises of unending, if more manageable,

30. Ibid., p. 65.

31. Ibid., p. 890. See also Henry Kissinger, *Years of Upheaval* (Boston: Little, Brown, 1982), p. 446.

32. Cf. Kissinger's speech on U.S.–Soviet relations in February 1976: "To claim that Angola is not an important country, or that the United States has no important interests there, begs the principal question. If the United States is seen to waver in the face of massive Soviet and Cuban intervention, what will be the perception of leaders around the world? . . . And what conclusions will an unopposed superpower draw when the next op-portunity for intervention beckons?" Henry Kissinger, *American Foreign Policy,* 3d ed. (New York: Norton, 1977), p. 321.

33. Kissinger, *Years of Upheaval,* pp. 982, 981.

rivalry. These premises, and the four contradictions, left very little room for compromise.[34]

FLAWS IN DESIGN

Why did disappointment come so soon, first in influential circles of the Congress and the interested public, later in the government as well? Kissinger's own answer puts the blame partly on Moscow's "fundamental assault" (see n. 34 above) on détente, partly on "our crisis of authority," and on the destruction by Congress of the indispensable "sticks" (a military buildup) and "carrots" (because of the Jackson-Vanik Amendment). This hardly explains everything, unless one accepts the idea that the combination of a stronger American defense posture and of the economic benefits which this amendment obliged Moscow to forego would have sufficed to deter Brezhnev from launching such an "assault."

Actually, the flaws of the strategy can be divided into three categories: flaws of design, execution, and domestic support. The most obvious difficulty in design is the deep difference in the two governments' conceptions of and expectations from détente. They might converge on the same agreements and compromises for a while, but these were just stepping-stones toward or means to quite incompatible ends. The Soviet Union had no intention of giving up ideological conflict or support to countries and groups capable of changing the international "correlation of forces" in ways favorable to Moscow: "The purpose of détente was to make the process of international change as painless as possible."[35] Moscow had not become converted to Western notions of international stability—that is, to the status quo or to merely peaceful change: it provided Sadat, throughout 1973, with the arms he needed for the war he planned. The Soviet leadership was interested in two strategies, both of which were opposed by its American counterparts. One was the promotion of "international social change" in ways that would not provoke an American counterchallenge, namely, entail high risks; a relaxation of tensions would be useful for this purpose, and the Soviets developed, to that effect, the highly artificial distinction between the level of interstate affairs—regulated by agreements—and that of "internal social and political life which forges ahead under any international conditions."[36] The other strategy

34. Cf. this excerpt from a letter of Kissinger to Golda Meir (spring 1974): "If I explained in detail what I am doing, I would gain Meany but lose the Russians." Kissinger, *Years of Upheaval,* p. 1030.

35. Aleksandr Bovin, quoted by Dimitri Simes in "The Death of Détente?" *International Security* 5, no. 1 (Summer 1980): 10.

36. From a paper on "Relaxation of International Tensions," prepared in 1978 by the Institute of the USA and Canada (Moscow).

was aimed at a form of condominium: not merely the formal recognition of equality, but a sharing of decisions about areas of mutual interest, if necessary at the expense of one's respective allies and certainly at the expense of China: hence the incessant Soviet pressure, documented by Kissinger, for a jointly imposed settlement in the Middle East, or for a nonaggression pact including a guarantee that nuclear weapons not be used on the soil of the two superpowers, or for "some common ground for a policy against China."[37]

Nothing could have been further from the Nixon-Kissinger strategy. The clash sharpened over the issue of "marginal gains." Again and again, they explained that in the nuclear age the pursuit of marginal interests was both unnecessary (for a limited advantage would not affect the overall balance of power) and dangerous (because of the risk of confrontations); and they made it clear that they would "resist marginal accretion of Soviet power even when the issues seem ambiguous,"[38] thus making it also clear that small or peripheral gains mattered. There could be no progress toward international order, Kissinger said after Angola, if the Soviet Union were permitted to exploit military opportunities resulting from local conflicts.[39] Obviously, each side expected the other to change its behavior, and believed—wrongly—that the other had good reasons to do so. Moscow appears to have interpreted the turmoil in America in the late 1960s, and also the Guam doctrine, as signs of an American retreat from the role of "world policeman." The reduction of the defense budget and the antidefense mood in Congress and in the country must have suggested to the Kremlin, as Dimitri Simes has argued,[40] a greater willingness to accommodate Moscow. The Soviet leaders could have thought that the new administration was moving away from containment, or at least toward "asymmetrical containment" à la Kennan.

Conversely, Nixon and Kissinger seem to have believed that, given the proper mix of incentives, the Soviet leadership could be escorted from its traditional relentless expansionism to a policy of restraint; the "breakthroughs" of 1971–72 were interpreted in this way. Nixon and Kissinger even expressed the hope that the spread of Soviet influence in the Middle East and in Southeast Asia might give the Soviets a new interest in regional stability.[41] The Soviets' economic failings and needs, fading ideological appeal, political stagnation, and fear of an American-Chinese alliance would, if containment was preserved, drive them to coexistence on our

37. Hyland, *Soviet-American Relations*, p. 27.
38. Kissinger, *Years of Upheaval*, p. 301.
39. Kissinger, *American Foreign Policy*, p. 317.
40. Simes, "The Death of Détente?" pp. 15 ff.
41. "U.S. Foreign Policy for the 1970's," A Report to the Congress by Richard Nixon, February 9, 1972 (Washington, D.C.: U.S. Government Printing Office, 1972), p. 19.

terms. It was true that the conflict on its Asian border incited the Soviet Union to seek stability on its European one, as de Gaulle had calculated. But de Gaulle may have been too optimistic about the degree of change Moscow would therefore tolerate in Eastern Europe, and the American leaders were too optimistic about Soviet changes of behavior in the rest of the world.

Both sides could agree that, without détente, the difficulties that developed between them during the October war might have been much worse.[42] But the Soviets wanted to use détente as a way of safeguarding their influence in a Middle Eastern settlement, whereas Kissinger was determined to use it as a cover for the elimination of Soviet influence.[43] Sooner or later, both sides were frustrated: the Soviets, once they found that détente meant no permanent slowing down of American military efforts, no resignation to Soviet regional gains, and no American retreat from reconciliation with China; the Americans, once they realized that the central strategic stalemate made the Soviets only more eager to seek limited, regional advances[44] and that the Soviets' arms buildup did not slow down. Both preached self-restraint, but each meant by it the other's restraint—the other side's refraining from doing what one did not want it to do.

A second flaw in design brings us back to the theme of American contradictions. What exactly did Nixon and Kissinger mean by détente? Their statements oscillate from very narrow to very loose definitions. The narrow ones suggest little more than containment without tears: what was there in it for the Soviets? The loose ones promise vague and broad cooperation: was this really what we wanted? Sometimes, Nixon and Kissinger, apostles of the "principle of concreteness,"[45] insist on the specificity of agreements to be reached. At other times, champions of linkage, they talk of a new structure of peace fundamentally different from "a classical balance of power" (both because one would no longer seek marginal advantages and because of "the element of consensus," everyone's stake in the status quo).[46] Sometimes détente is presented as supercon-

42. For Kissinger, see his *Years of Upheaval*, p. 246: "The USSR suffered a major setback in the Middle East and accepted it; the conflicts between us, while real, were managed." For Brezhnev, see his speech in India, in Simes, "The Death of Détente?" p. 14: "If the current conflict would explode in an environment of general international tension and the sharpening of relations between . . . the United States and the Soviet Union, the confrontation in the Middle East could become far more dangerous and be on a scale threatening general peace."

43. Kissinger, *Years of Upheaval*, p. 594.

44. Cf. Kissinger's speech to American ambassadors in Europe in December 1975, reported in the *International Herald Tribune*, April 12, 1976, p. 21.

45. Kissinger, *White House Years*, p. 128.

46. "U.S. Foreign Policy for the 1970's," A Report to the Congress by Richard Nixon, May 3, 1973 (Washington, D.C.: U.S. Government Printing Office, 1973), p. 232.

tainment, as in Kissinger's 1973 Pacem in Terris speech,[47] or when, in 1976, at the International Institute for Strategic Studies (IISS), he insisted that the very concept "had always been applicable only to an adversary relationship" and should not be measured "by criteria that should be reserved for traditional friendships."[48] At other moments, they stress the commitment to work together over a broad range of issues and the need for mutual benefits.[49] Sometimes détente is presented as no more than an exercise in damage limitation: preventing the use of inevitably growing Soviet power for unilateral advantages and political expansion.[50] At other times it is celebrated as the beginning of a new era.

The reasons for these vacillations are clear: the more prudent definitions prevail either in moments of crisis (such as October 1973) or during the period of decline (1976), the more exalted ones accompany the summit meetings or the efforts to blunt the Jackson counteroffensive. Much depends on the audience and on the specific message one wants to drive home at a given moment. But what left leeway to maneuver also signaled a fundamental dilemma. The narrow definitions—telling the Soviets, for instance, not to try to split America's alliances, not to practice selective restraint (in Europe but not in the Third World), not to use ideological competition as a cover for the expansion of their power[51]—demand of the Soviets far too high a price for cooperation; while the loose definitions risk exciting the Soviet appetite for a condominium one was determined not to grant (as the partial elimination of Soviet influence in the Middle East in 1973–74 showed), creating excessive expectations (or fears) at home, and worrying allies and friends periodically suspicious of superpower chumminess.

Thus, one always ends with the deepest flaw in the design: the basic unrealism of the Nixon-Kissinger brand of realpolitik. It dangled in front of Soviet eyes unspecified delights which it had no intention of really providing, since the last thing in the world the American leaders wanted to do was to acknowledge a Soviet right to intervene all over the world as an equal partner of Washington: it would have wrecked America's al-

47. Kissinger, American Foreign Policy, pp. 123–24.

48. Henry A. Kissinger, "The 1976 Alastair Buchan Memorial Lecture," presented at the International Institute for Strategic Studies (IISS), London, June 25, 1976, in Survival 18, no. 5 (September/October 1976): 198.

49. Kissinger, American Foreign Policy, pp. 167–69 (statement to the Senate Foreign Relations Committee, September 19, 1974).

50. See Kissinger's speeches: "America's Permanent Interests" (March 11, 1976), Department of State Bulletin 1919, April 5, 1976 (Washington, D.C.: U.S. Government Printing Office, 1976), p. 427; "The Future and U.S. Foreign Policy" (March 16, 1976), and "Foreign Policy and National Security" (March 22, 1976), Department of State Bulletin 1920, April 12, 1976, pp. 463 and 487.

51. Kissinger, IISS speech (see n. 48 above).

liances, the entente with China, the whole strategy of denying "the Soviets all opportunities for expansion,"[52] and it would never have received domestic support. Moreover, it demanded from the Soviets, in return, a price which they would not pay—the "end to the constant probing for openings and the testing of every equilibrium." "It is up to *us* to define the limits of Soviet aims";[53] but Kissinger overestimated the ability of the United States to put the limits where he wanted them to be, or the likelihood that the only "mutual benefits" with which the Soviets would content themselves were those of trade, arms control, and the "legitimacy" conferred by summitry. Pushed out of the Middle East, why wouldn't they try to do to the West in parts of Africa or around the edges of the Persian Gulf what had been done to them?

The focus on the Soviet aspect (however distant) of every crisis anywhere was both the heart of the conception and the reason for its utopian quality. Only if the Soviets were blocked everywhere would they become convinced of the need for "moderation." But given the meager compensations offered, why would they not keep trying to prove to the United States that it was the American conception that neither paid off nor was affordable? Indeed, as noted above, it required a willingness to be, always and everywhere, vigilant and active, which not only went against the national mood but also undermined the "cooperation" part of the policy. Moreover, it often invited failure: in the Middle East before October 1973, in Angola in 1975, it refused to foster negotiations, either between the parties in conflict (so as not to provide the Soviet Union's clients with a "reward") or, over these parties' heads, directly between Washington and Moscow (so as not to play "condominium"); this resulted in the October war in the Middle East, in the Soviet and Cuban victory in Angola. The policy seemed calculated to provoke that coalition of hawks and doves so bitterly denounced by Kissinger.

FLAWS IN EXECUTION

These flaws in design were aggravated by flaws in execution: the policy instruments turned out to be inadequate. The delicate mix of incentives and rewards required central control: all the threads had to be in the hands of the two men in the White House. This not only led to some picturesque incidents with a State Department that was being kept in the dark about such essential decisions as the opening to China and the summit with the Soviets. It also turned out to be triply counterproductive: by producing the kind of sloppiness in negotiation that Gerard Smith has so acidly documented in his account of SALT I (with a double process, in

52. Kissinger, *White House Years*, p. 1204.
53. Ibid., p. 119.

Helsinki and in Washington),[54] or the kind of internal conflict that marked American policy in the Middle East as long as Kissinger pursued a strategy drastically different from Rogers's; by preventing the two American leaders from concentrating sufficiently on certain issues for sheer lack of time (the SALT II negotiation, in 1973–74, was an example of this)[55]; and by provoking opposition in the Congress and in the country against such a formidable concentration of power and of back channels, in secrecy. All of this, say Kissinger and Nixon, was justified by the need to avoid bureaucratic paralysis. But a complex, long-range policy requires bureaucratic involvement and institutional memory; otherwise, support within the government itself will be weak, and resentment high.

Nixon and Kissinger counted heavily on the virtues of linkage. But there was a problem: linkage could work reasonably well in a first phase as an incentive toward agreements; "if you want trade, and arms control, and a recognition of the territorial division of Europe, you must be forthcoming on Berlin, on limiting offensive systems, on cooling Egypt's demands for arms." (However, even in that phase, the linkage with Vietnam did not work well.) But once détente is, so to speak, in orbit, the issue becomes one of preventing the Soviets from, or punishing them for, doing hostile things, and the tools first used as goads must now be used as possible sanctions, the carrots must become sticks—a much more difficult operation. Kissinger himself, in a very defensive speech after Angola, pointed out that neither the suspension of SALT nor that of grain sales would restore the local balance of forces: "cutting off grain would still lose Angola," and SALT and trade "benefit us as well as the Soviet Union and are part of the long-term strategy for dealing with the Soviet Union."[56] More recently, Nixon has pointed out that the "punitive use of economic sanctions" is "usually ineffective, and sometimes counterproductive."[57] In other words, linkage-as-sanction runs into these obstacles: domestic opposition, inability to affect the crisis at hand, a risk of overshooting the mark (by removing benefits, one also removes a factor of restraint), and self-inflicted wounds. To suspend arms control when the Soviets misbehave suggests that arms control is a favor we do them—a suggestion that is both wrong and likely to play into the hands of the hardliners. And commerce is not a faucet that can be turned on and off easily, in capitalist societies.

This suggests a second problem of execution: the "perverse effects" of one's moves or tools. These were of two kinds, both dangerous for the

54. Smith, *Doubletalk*.
55. Nixon, *Memoirs*, p. 1026; cf. also Kissinger, *Years of Upheaval*, p. 271.
56. Kissinger, *American Foreign Policy*, p. 329.
57. *The New York Times*, August 19, 1982, sec. A, p. 27.

very delicate balance of containment and cooperation entailed by détente. On the one hand, trade—which was supposed to induce Soviet restraint—created dependencies among powerful and often vocal American groups (farmers and businessmen) as well as in the West European countries and in Japan. This contributed to immobilizing the tool, so to speak, and made the Soviet Union—except for the brief period of the post-Afghanistan grain embargo—relatively more immune to manipulation than the West. The allies' attachment to their own, quite different, more limited and specific détente made them reluctant to support linkage-as-sanction, once Soviet–American relations deteriorated. However, especially with respect to trade (but also—increasingly—in the realm of arms control, given the saliency of the issue of intermediate nuclear forces), American policy toward the Soviet Union had to be coordinated with that of allies eager to preserve *their* islands of détente and to keep arms control alive.[58]

On the other hand, arms control agreements and the solemn declarations of principle signed at the 1972 and 1973 summits and, in 1975, in Helsinki, produced perverse effects of the opposite kind: they fueled tension rather than accommodation. SALT I produced what some have called a sausage effect: inciting both sides to produce whatever weapons had not been limited (and the result, between 1972 and 1980, was not only a vast increase in the number of warheads but also the buildup in both arsenals of new weapons for nuclear war-fighting; this undermined further the concept of mutual assured destruction that had been at the core of arms control theory at the outset). The United States worried increasingly about the vulnerability of its land-based missiles and of NATO's installations threatened by the SS-20; the Soviets worried about new American technological developments such as the Trident missiles and submarines and the cruise missiles. SALT II would have had no chance of surviving the Senate debate—or of obtaining the grudging approval of the Chiefs of Staff—without the accompanying increase in the defense budget, the decision to build the MX, and the agreement to deploy new medium-range nuclear weapons systems in Europe. The ambiguities and interstices of the SALT I treaty allowed the Soviets to resolve all uncertainties in their favor, and this in turn led its critics to denounce not only multiple "violations" by the Soviets, but also the administration's laxity in pursuing these. Similarly, the platitudes of the three declarations lent themselves to denunciations of Soviet infringements, brandished as evidence of Moscow's shameless exploitation of détente to its own advantage. At San Clemente, Brezhnev had warned Nixon of the risk of a war in

58. On the differences between the U.S.–Soviet and West European détente, see my essay, "The Western Alliance: Drift or Harmony?" *International Security* 6, no. 2 (Fall 1981): 105–25.

the Middle East if diplomatic immobility continued.[59] But when Sadat
went to war and the Soviets resupplied Syria and Egypt, many saw these
moves as a brazen violation by Moscow both of the commitment to eschew
unilateral advantages and of the commitment to make every effort to
avert the risk of nuclear war.

These "perverse effects" resulted in part from the specific weaknesses
of each of the instruments. General declarations violated the very rule of
concreteness which Kissinger had decreed. As Kennan put it, they led
inevitably into far more trouble than "specific agreements which left aside
all questions of motive and purported only to specify what each of us
would do, when we would do it, and under what conditions it would be
done."[60] To be sure, Kissinger presented the content of these statements
as "an aspiration and a yardstick by which we assess Soviet behavior,"[61]
but it was bound to be a boomerang. For there would necessarily be a gap
between aspiration and behavior (either because the promise was fatuous
or because its execution would have been disastrous for the Soviet empire). If these statements were meaningless, didn't they underline the
hollowness (and overselling) of détente? If they were real commitments,
didn't they illuminate the casual Soviet disregard of obligations? In either
case, didn't they show Soviet cynicism?

Arms control turned out to be an imperfect tool of policy as well. In
the first place, the obvious link between one's arms-control posture (and
opportunities for bargaining) and one's military posture is troublesome.
Uncertainties and weaknesses in one's military policy will make satisfactory arms-control deals much more difficult to obtain. And American defense policies exhibited both uncertainties and weaknesses. The administration was wedded to the notion of sufficiency *and* to the idea that
reliance on the threat of mutual destruction was no longer credible (nor
morally defensible). The former led to a policy of neither sharp cutbacks
nor sharp increases; the latter, to the development of war-fighting options that were bound to complicate arms control (even if, as Kissinger
later said, these options were a mere palliative for the increase of conventional forces).[62] The logic of "sufficiency" would have entailed resignation to Soviet numerical superiority in some respects, as long as Moscow
could not count on destroying most of America's retaliatory forces or on
eliminating all counterforce options available to the United States. But,
the clash between "hard" interests and perceptions reappearing, "the
appearance of inferiority—whatever its actual significance—can have se-

59. Cf. Kissinger, *Years of Upheaval*, pp. 297–98; Hyland, *Soviet–American Relations*, pp.
26–27.
60. Kennan, *Nuclear Delusion*, p. xxi.
61. Kissinger, *American Foreign Policy*, p. 154.
62. Kissinger, *Years of Upheaval*, p. 1176.

rious political consequences. With weapons that are unlikely to be used and for which there is no operational experience, the psychological impact can be crucial" (a strange non sequitur). "Thus each side has a high incentive to achieve not only the reality but the appearance of reality":[63] this suggested that the United States had to match, and to catch up with, Soviet efforts—a recipe for a race, not for arms control.

This would not happen, of course, if arms control became the way of constraining Soviet programs that seemed threatening. But the comparative weaknesses in the American defense posture had their effect precisely here. One could simply not obtain through negotiation what one did not want (or was not able) to achieve through competition. Nixon wrote in his diary that if we don't get " some constraints on the Soviets at this time" (June 1974) and if "we get into a runaway race, it may be that they will be uninhibited and we will be inhibited."[64] But what chance was there that they would stop their construction programs without any equivalent American concessions? Their refusal to do so in SALT I made it impossible to "reach meaningful controls over offensive forces"[65] and to curb the development of MIRVs. Once the combination of Soviet heavy missiles and MIRV began to threaten Minuteman, what chance was there that they would accept to slow down the MIRVing of their missiles and to allow the United States a larger number of MIRVed missiles, if the United States also insisted on exact equality in launchers? Clearly, "demands for equal aggregates for which we had no unilateral program"[66] either would be unacceptable, or else would have to include equal aggregates in MIRVed launchers, as SALT II ultimately did. But this left America's land-based missiles at risk. The "State of the World" message of 1973 is a perfect expression of official schizophrenia: it praises SALT I for confining "competition with the Soviets to the area of technology where, heretofore, we have had a significant advantage,"[67] but it also warns that "competition could inexorably intensify to the point that there could be a high premium on striking first," to the point where the Soviets could threaten the United States with their MIRVed heavy missiles.

Even if the United States had had a more ambitious defense program and a better negotiating position, a second problem of arms control would have plagued the use of this instrument: the extraordinary complexity of the issues, which ensured an inevitable lag between diplomacy and technology. The results of such negotiations "tended regularly to be outdated

63. Kissinger, *American Foreign Policy*, p. 160.

64. Nixon, *Memoirs*, p. 1025.

65. Smith, *Doubletalk*, p. 156.

66. Kissinger, *White House Years*, pp. 264–65 and 1027–29.

67. "U.S. Foreign Policy for the 1970's," A Report to the Congress by Richard Nixon, May 3, 1973 (Washington, D.C.: U.S. Government Printing Office, 1973), p. 201.

before they were even arrived at."[68] SALT I succeeded in banning
ABMs because of their technical troubles, but by 1972 the "genie" of
MIRV was out of the bottle; by 1979 there had been formidable new
advances in accuracy and mobility.

Trade and arms control also suffered from two additional difficulties—one, so to speak, outer-directed, and one inner-directed. The first
one could be called the acrobat's dilemma. If the acrobat, jumping from
one trapeze to the other, makes it, he'll be applauded. If not, he'll be dead;
and so, unless he must jump (or has a safety net), why do so? Arms control
and trade were supposed to turn a previously competitive relation into a
mixed one. But as long as there remained a strong element of competition
in this relationship, how far should one go in making concessions that
could prove dangerous (as did the combination of having conceded, or
rather acknowledged, unequal numbers of launchers in the interim
agreement of SALT I, and of having failed to ban MIRVs and to get the
Soviets to agree to the American definition of heavy missiles)? Or how far
should one go in providing the rival with advantages he could use to
strengthen either his economy or his armaments, *even* when, in exchange,
one retains the freedom to pursue one's own military programs or the
benefits from trade? For as Rousseau had explained, in a competitive
relation, it is not the common interests but the respective gains that matter, and each side remains obsessed with the imperative of limiting the
other's advantages. Thus, daring in the use of these tools was ruled out:
the more so, as in one case—arms control—the momentum of the race
seemed to favor the rival, so that one was even more unwilling to give up
chips, and in the other instance—trade—large imbalances in commerce
and payments made vast expansion difficult anyhow, unless one was
willing blatantly to subsidize one's competitor.

This conflict of concerns—the competitive ones leading to caution and
suspicion, and the concern for weaving a dense enough web of interests to
instill self-restraint in Moscow—explains the other difficulty: that of internal coordination. In the case of trade, Kissinger was afraid that the
enthusiasm of private businessmen and of departments catering to special interests would run away with the policy (and thereby both create the
perverse effect of American dependency described above and provoke a
backlash), as in the story of the grain "deal" of 1972, when the Soviets
"outmaneuvered" the United States merely by "skillfully using our free
market system."[69] In the case of arms control, Kissinger found himself
gradually paralyzed by the Pentagon's insistence on what he considered
nonnegotiable proposals. As a result, the 1973 summit merely produced a

68. Kennan, *Nuclear Delusion,* p. xxi.
69. Kissinger, *White House Years,* p. 1270.

statement of principles that "could mean anything,"[70] the 1974 summit failed to break the stalemate, the Vladivostok formula failed to deal with cruise missiles and Backfire bombers, the January 1976 compromise was shelved by President Ford.

There was a last instrument that proved hard to control. Blocking Soviet probes and pushes in the post-Vietnam era required relying on proxies, helped by the United States. This was a kind of roulette. In the Middle East, the United States had a winning number—Israel, although the need to limit Arab reprisals and the will to eliminate Soviet influence in the Arab world induced Kissinger to moderate Israel's victory. But in Vietnam, our proxy, despite much American aid, collapsed when Hanoi launched what appears to have been planned as a limited offensive in the spring of 1975; so did the Lon Nol regime in Cambodia. And in Angola, when covert support for the National Front for the Liberation of Angola (FNLA) no longer sufficed to prevent the victory of the Soviet-backed Popular Movement for the Liberation of Angola (MPLA), Kissinger made the mistake of endorsing, or tolerating, a South African intervention, which precipitated that of the Cubans. Of course, in each case the success of the proxies depended in no small part on the amount of support Kissinger could obtain for them from Congress: Israel has always fared well under such circumstances. This brings us to the vital problem of domestic support.

THE WANING OF DOMESTIC SUPPORT

There was a vicious circle. Centralization of policy at home was deemed necessary for success abroad. Success abroad would bring consensus at home. But discord at home could cripple the instruments and therefore ensure failure abroad. It is hard to disentangle cause and effect. Kissinger, of course, blames the fate of SALT (and of détente in general) on Watergate, and on the convergent opposition of "a liberal idealism unrelated to a concept of power and a conservative dogmatism unleavened by a sense of proportion or strategy."[71] My view is different: the deeper reasons for failure are those I have reviewed so far, and it is they which largely explain the domestic opposition.

It is true that any attempt at combining and balancing competition and cooperation risks meeting suspicion at home: liberals often like to avoid confrontation, and hardliners distrust cooperation because of their conviction that the Soviet system is essentially evil and that its behavior can be

70. Kissinger, *Years of Upheaval*, p. 272.
71. Ibid., p. 1021.

affected only by external resistance.[72] One group is bothered by punishments, the other by rewards. However, it is also true that the American public has shown, over the years, a desire for both strength and peace, containment and negotiations, arms and arms control. Theoretically, therefore, it should not be impossible to work out the right mix. Why did this one not succeed at home?

Part of the answer lies in the related issues of oversell and excessive expectations. Kissinger, in his memoirs, explains that he always shared the conservatives' fear that détente would lull the public into complacency about defense: "Our policy did involve the risk of lowering vigilance through the fact of constant negotiations—this surely was the Soviet strategy."[73] But he acknowledges Nixon's penchant for hyperbole and, on the other hand, asserts that détente "fostered the only possible psychological framework" for resistance to Moscow.[74] The fact is that the claims of "breakthroughs" made it possible for some to believe that, indeed, the Soviet Union was turning into a status-quo power and would become less repressive at home and in its empire—a view that rekindled the angry fires of the cold warriors. Above all, the heavy emphasis on giving up the quest for marginal advantages—a utopian goal which the United States itself had no intention of seeking—almost guaranteed that every Soviet attempt would raise, on the old or new Right, the cry that the policy was clearly failing and that "incentive payments" to the Soviets were nothing but appeasement.[75] And the leaders' self-congratulation about linkage incited those who feared appeasement to turn linkage into blackmail so as to squeeze more concessions from Moscow.

Indeed, the bipolar emphasis of Nixon and Kissinger could not fail to arouse both the liberals and the conservatives—the latter being the more dangerous in the long run. The liberals would object to a policy that judged every issue not on its merits but according to the state of play between Moscow and Washington: Chile, Bangladesh, Cyprus and—in 1975–76—Portugal and Angola come to mind. The conservatives, applying the same yardstick as Kissinger, would then brand as defeats of America and as casualties of détente not only the debacles of Vietnam, Cambodia, and Angola, which could be partly blamed on the persisting

72. On different views of the Soviet Union, see Robert E. Osgood, "Containment, Soviet Behavior and Grand Strategy," *Policy Papers in International Affairs*, no. 16 (Berkeley: Institute of International Studies, 1981), and Alexander Dallin and Gail W. Lapidus, "Ronald Reagan and the Russians," in Kenneth A. Oye et al., eds., *Eagle Defiant: United States Foreign Policy in the 1980s* (Boston: Little, Brown, 1983).

73. Kissinger, *Years of Upheaval*, p. 1031.

74. Kissinger, *White House Years*, p. 237.

75. Cf. Theodore Draper, "Appeasement and Detente," *Commentary* 61, no. 2 (February 1976): 27–38.

"Vietnam syndrome" in the Congress, but also, a little later, purely or essentially domestic developments abroad: in Afghanistan (1978), South Yemen, Iran, and Nicaragua. If one wants a partial relaxation of tensions with Moscow, it is dangerous to draw attention to the (spurious) fact that every event can be chalked up as either a gain or a loss in the bipolar contest. For if it is a zero-sum game, why fool oneself with prospects of cooperation?

One of the reasons why the hardliners' opposition was more dangerous than the liberals' was the administration's inclination to appease it rather than to fight it. Nixon and Kissinger had no desire to accommodate their critics to their left; these were treated with a combination of derision and exasperation. But Nixon and Kissinger shared to a large extent the "philosophical case" of the conservatives and the hardliners against the Soviet regime and policies; Kissinger, in his memoirs, often expresses the regret that Senator Jackson chose to oppose him rather than to be an ally: "it was a national tragedy that those who shared similar strategic analysis should conduct a civil war over tactics."[76] Perhaps because of this alleged similarity, Kissinger first tried to come to terms with him. The White House accepted his amendment to SALT I, which set the course for the quest for equal numbers in SALT II: a "fatal error,"[77] according to Hyland, since it meant, among other things—in Gerard Smith's words—that the administration was "vomiting on its own much-vaunted freeze agreement."[78] The SALT I team was dismantled to please the senator. Nor did Kissinger at first meet head-on the challenge of the second Jackson amendment.[79] This was—as he implicitly admits—a grave miscalculation. For the gap was really much deeper than a disagreement on tactics: both sides wanted, basically, to contain; but one thought that containment could lead to a thaw, that Soviet behavior was susceptible to inducements, whereas the other saw nothing but implacable hostility and an endless vista of confrontations: accommodation—détente's maximum goal—was unthinkable; damage limitation—the minimum—required no rewards.

The exploitation by Senator Jackson of the issue of Jewish emigration was a brilliant stroke. Not only was it a way to sabotage détente, by changing its objective (from affecting Soviet external behavior to affecting Soviet internal policy) and thereby weakening a crucial tool (trade and credits), but it also captured for the hard-line constituency two overlapping sets of people who could have been expected to support at least parts of Kissinger's strategy: liberals, suspicious about the Holy Alliance aspects of

76. Kissinger, *Years of Upheaval*, p. 1031.
77. Hyland, *Soviet–American Relations*, p. 55.
78. Smith, *Doubletalk*, p. 442.
79. Kissinger, *Years of Upheaval*, pp. 985 ff.

it in the Third World but favorable to trade, arms control, and political negotiations; and supporters of Israel, who had little to complain about a team that had, in fact, eviscerated Secretary of State Rogers's attempt at a comprehensive settlement in the Middle East, and obtained, quietly, an increase in Jewish emigration from the USSR. Jackson's coup consisted of redirecting the liberals' qualms about the neglect of human rights abroad from the Third World to the Soviet Union and empire, and of obliging pro-Israeli groups (especially Jewish liberals) to choose between overt support of a Jewish cause and loyalty to the administration's strategy: a choice which became much easier after the October war and Soviet support for Israel's enemies.

This was a turning point, insofar as it dramatically shifted public attention from the détente spectaculars with China and the Soviet Union to the shuttle diplomacy in the Middle East, in which Moscow played a very small and glum role. Détente with Moscow somehow shrank in the public eye. MBFR was never treated, even by the administration, as more than a charade, the European Coal and Steel Community (ECSC) was above all a European show for which the administration showed little enthusiasm, political negotiations with the Soviets faded away; there remained only the byzantine complexities of SALT, the debates over the virtues of trade, and the familiar routines of containment. The one area of success and prestige was that in which a major player, Sadat, had actually switched allegiance from Moscow to Washington, and a Soviet ally, Assad, was bargaining with Kissinger alone.

In this atmosphere, and with the fall of Nixon—widely interpreted in Moscow as the result of a plot against détente—domestic support shrank. The story is too familiar to be repeated here: the votes against further involvements in the Vietnam and Cambodia wars, in 1973, had made an American reengagement in the crisis of April 1975 impossible, and they were confirmed by the new Congress at that time. A few months later, that same Congress prevented an increase of American aid to the anti-Marxist forces in Angola. On the right, the Jackson-Vanik Amendment passed after a long contest. Jackson, with the help of supporters in the Pentagon, managed to set the limits of the SALT II proposals the administration could offer; and the theme of human rights, kept alive by post-Helsinki repression in the Soviet Union and in Eastern Europe, also kept the anti-détente coalition together.

Commentary and the forces gathered in the Committee on the Present Danger argued that détente equals appeasement. What made this view fashionable way beyond the conservative and neoconservative fringes was a combination of three factors. One was worry about the changes in the strategic balance, a worry fully shared by Kissinger—but he still seemed, to his critics (and to so significant a "defector" as James Schlesinger), more eager to achieve compromises in SALT than to give up the vain hope of constraining the Soviets through arms control, to recognize fully the perils of Soviet nuclear superiority, and to concentrate on increasing America's nuclear defenses. A second factor was growing indignation at Soviet human rights violations—what might be called the Solzhenitsyn effect, clumsily handled by Kissinger and Ford. A third one was the evidence of fiascoes abroad: in Southeast Asia, in southern Africa. The first factor was the hardliners' preserve, the second caused an unholy alliance of liberals and conservatives, the third one engendered a bizarre coalition of hardliners arguing that the cooperative elements of détente had to be given up since the liberals had destroyed the counterweights and "sticks," and of liberals arguing for a radically different, less contentious and bipolar approach to the Third World.

And so we come to the depressing year 1976, a year when *both* superpowers had excellent reasons to believe that they had lost their wagers. The Soviets could observe the end of the decline in America's defense budget, a presidential decision not to proceed with SALT—under attack from Ronald Reagan—nor to refer to détente, a failure of their Communist allies in Portugal, a challenge to their authority by the other West European Communist parties, and a shrinking of their influence in the Middle East; Angola was a meager compensation. However, what Congress had denied to Moscow—trade expansion and credits—had been amply obtained from America's allies. Ford and Kissinger were on the defensive, as the tone of all of the latter's major speeches clearly shows. He was obliged to hit at the national "rhetoric of weakness" and, in effect, to do battle on two fronts: warning the Soviets to stop pushing ahead in the Third World and attacking his critics for removing his leverage. He still defended détente—but less by praising its achievements than by denying that a return to a harder policy would improve America's overall position, and by keeping up the hope of ultimate Soviet restraint, of ultimate agreements on the settlement of conflicts, and of a better world.[80]

AGONY AND DEATH UNDER CARTER

I will not analyze in detail the long agony of détente under Jimmy Carter, in 1977–79. I have done it elsewhere,[81] Samuel Huntington does it admirably in the next chapter, and there never was a strategy comparable to that of Nixon and Kissinger.

The Carter administration, in foreign affairs, was an increasingly un-

80. See especially his IISS speech (cf. n. 48 above).

81. Stanley Hoffmann, "The Perils of Incoherence," *Foreign Affairs,* special edition: *America and the World, 1978,* vol. 57, no. 3 (1979); and "Requiem," *Foreign Policy,* no. 42 (Spring 1981).

comfortable coalition of two groups, neither of which made détente the cornerstone of its policy. One group—later denounced by the cold warriors and by the other group as the "McGovern wing of the Democratic Party"—believed that the bipolar focus of the preceding administrations had been a grave error. Attention had to be shifted to global issues (several of which, like nonproliferation and human rights, would require antagonizing friends) and to regional conflicts judged on their own merits. This entailed both a demotion of the Soviet–American relationship (unwelcome to Moscow) and, insofar as those relations were concerned, a quite different mix of conflict and cooperation: less overt conflict over Third World issues, no longer seen in East–West terms, but more conflict both over Soviet internal behavior because of the preoccupation with human rights, and—initially—over nuclear arms control because of Carter's impatience for deep reductions; more cooperation—if possible—in the hope of stopping the spread of nuclear weapons and of curtailing the flow of conventional arms abroad. As for the issue, so important to Moscow, of joint action in the Middle East, there was a significant reversal of the Carter administration in the fall of 1977, which must have sharpened the Soviets' misgivings.

Those misgivings were largely fed by the presence and weight of the other faction, which departed from Kissinger's approach in two ways. Like the first group, it wanted to pay greater attention to global issues and to the local roots of international and regional conflicts. Unlike the first group, it felt a deep worry about Soviet power and expansionism, which it proposed to confront by seeking what was euphemistically called a "more balanced détente," that is, a harder line than that attributed to Kissinger. This resulted in the alliance with Jackson over the March 1977 SALT II proposals, which required the Soviets to give up a sizable fraction of their heavy missiles in exchange for an American renunciation of weapons not yet built. It also entailed enthusiasm for improving relations with China beyond the point of delicate triangular balance reached by Kissinger. For reasons different from those of the first group (which was concerned above all with heeding Egypt's and Israel's own inclinations), this faction too, after Sadat's journey to Israel, showed itself eager to keep the Soviets out. It pushed for, and obtained, an increase in defense spending, particularly for NATO's conventional forces. And it used, for the first time, economic sanctions—over the issue of human rights in the Soviet Union.

The logic of this group was quite incompatible with that of the first one. It led, in fact, to a heightened concern about Soviet or Cuban encroachments in the Third World (for instance, in Zaire and East Africa), and to the temptation of resurrecting linkage-as-sanction. Since some of the forms of cooperation desired by the first group—over conventional arms control—predictably got nowhere, and since the reluctance of Car-

ter to intervene in the Horn of Africa, or in defense of the Shah, or against
the Sandinistas, allowed many hardliners to denounce his passivity, his
administration ended up with the worst of all worlds: a Soviet Union that
seemed to have, in the words of several commentators, little to fear *and*
little to expect from Washington; a demoralized liberal group under
attack both within the administration and outside; a strongly anti-Soviet
faction of officials whose actions (such as the normalization of relations
with China) contributed to Soviet hostility but which was still held back
from opposing Soviet moves in the Third World by Carter's own inhibi-
tions; and a rising "new orthodoxy" in Congress and in the country, which
denounced whatever was left of cooperation with Moscow and sang the
litany of American defeats.

What was left, in 1979, was mainly SALT; and the long story of
SALT II, under Carter, confirmed the points made above: the complexity of the issues made a quick agreement impossible, and when, several
years later, the final draft essentially filled out the outlines of Kissinger's
compromises of 1974 and 1976, the gap between Soviet programs and
American ones had only widened; the effort to slow down Moscow's race
by negotiation had failed. Once again, SALT "produced a conglomera-
tion of measures that virtually ensured an explosion in offensive weapons."[82] It also produced a coalition of adversaries: those who thought it
provided too little arms control, those who thought it ratified American
strategic weakness. Moreover, the negotiation itself had been slowed
down by the vicissitudes of the Soviet–American relationship, despite the
avoidance of formal linkage. The episode of the Soviet brigade in Cuba
showed the extent to which the SALT process had fallen hostage to the
general deterioration. Afghanistan gave a coup de grace to a policy that
had been comatose for years.

LESSONS

A few key lessons can be drawn from this experience:

1. The most important one is the necessity for modesty, in three different respects. First, there must be modesty in the definition of America's
interests. An extensive definition, in terms of threats, with the threats
themselves being defined so broadly as to include most challenges to the
status quo, cannot but lead to all the frustrations of either "symmetrical
containment" or "asymmetrical containment" in the Dulles or Kissinger
modes. Thirty-five years later, the wisdom of Kennan's conception seems
evident to me, even though there appears to be no way to convince everyone, in Congress or in the public, that certain "defeats" are merely apparent, that some setbacks are highly reversible, and that a rigorous hier-

---

82. Hyland, *Soviet–American Relations,* p. 60.

archy of threats can safely be established and can be followed without hysteria. But an extensive definition leads, sooner or later, to just as serious a loss of self-confidence and sense of insecurity.

Second, there must be modesty in our expectations about Soviet behavior. It is impossible to block all attempts to spread Soviet influence, nor are all such attempts equally threatening. Setting the limits of Soviet behavior simply cannot mean forcing Moscow to behave as a status-quo power, to give up all efforts at changing the "correlation of forces," and to play in the world concert the part we have assigned to it. We should aim at affecting the means and the intensity of the contest.[83] We cannot expect Moscow to stop supporting anti-Western forces in the Third World any more than Moscow can expect us to endorse its domination of Eastern Europe. But we can try to prevent Soviet power from injecting itself in the Third World through aggression and subversion, or from gaining military bases in areas of vital interest close to the United States, just as Moscow can be expected to resist Western attempts at disrupting openly its power in its East European glacis. Each one, in other words, will go on playing its own game; how it plays, and where, is what should be gradually regulated.

This suggests, in the third place, a modest place for cooperation, both within our overall relationship with Moscow and within our foreign policy as a whole. Condominium is clearly out of the question. It is not in our interest to make of the Soviet Union a partner in the settlement of conflicts far removed from its areas of vital interest. It is not in our interest to sign vague statements of principle. It is not likely that trade can ever become a major factor in Soviet–American relations, given strategic considerations, the problems of Soviet payment for American imports, and also Moscow's own unwillingness to become too dependent on outside sources of supply. It is not likely that explicit general agreements on "rules of the game" can be reached, except in the form of meaningless generalities. Once we recognize that neither side could really obtain what it may have hoped from the original détente, the place of cooperation appears more limited—although by no means insignificant, as we shall see.

This triple need for modesty does not entail a plea for timidity in proposals: there are issues of policy in which incremental progress may not be good enough, and where bold offers make sense (in several areas of the arms contest, for instance); and there are moments when new opportunities may arise for imaginative departures from the routine. But the kinds of modesty I suggest are justified not only by experience but also by the nature of the Soviet Union's system and world policy, and by that of

83. See my suggestions in *Dead Ends*, chaps. 6 and 7.

the American system of government, with its fragmentation and discontinuity.

2. I remain skeptical of linkage as an indispensable foreign policy technique in dealing with the Soviets, partly for the reasons given above (the difficulty of using linkage effectively for sanctions, "perverse effects"), partly because several of the areas of negotiation deal with issues of common or convergent interests: so to suspend bargaining or performing in these areas when the Soviet Union misbehaves in another, is like shooting oneself in the foot—something worth doing only if the effect on Moscow is more than symbolic. On balance, as Kissinger recognized when he discussed Angola, countermeasures, to be effective, have to be taken in the area in which the mischief occurred—which, of course, is also not possible in every instance. This does not mean that there cannot occasionally be obvious linkages within the same area, between an item that one side wishes resolved in its favor and an item that is in the interest of the other; this is what happened in SALT, and also in the negotiation of the treaties on Berlin and on Soviet–German relations. Linkage as incentive—if you do X, it will be possible for me to do Y—is certainly a useful technique. And there is undeniably a de facto link between a given negotiation and the general state of Soviet–American relations: when the latter deteriorates, active cooperation declines, if only because of rising opposition in the Congress and in the public. Thus the picture that Nixon and Kissinger sometimes conveyed, of a relationship that could entail simultaneously acute (if, preferably, low-level) confrontations at every point of pressure and active collaboration, is not very realistic: if the confrontations are many and sharp, their cumulative effect will dampen and perhaps drive out the collaboration.

3. Arms control bargains cannot be the centerpiece of Soviet–American cooperation. Either the superpowers, having learned from the SALT process, attempt to negotiate limited agreements quickly—a comprehensive test ban or a ban on antisatellite weapons; in this case, the measures will not be of sufficient scope to serve as a linchpin. Or else they resort to more informal methods, such as the "TAC talks" suggested by Joseph Nye;[84] these are likely to be useful but unspectacular. Or else they return—as is being done currently—to complex and comprehensive negotiations; but these are plagued by the flaws mentioned above, and they tend to become "an end in itself," if not "an orphan and a victim"[85] driven by the arcane logic of their own technical difficulties, dependent on the vicissitudes of the superpowers' military posture and defense plans as well

84. Joseph S. Nye, "The Future of Arms Control," in Barry M. Blechman, ed., *Rethinking the U.S. Strategic Posture* (Cambridge, Mass.: Ballinger, 1982), pp. 236 ff.

85. Kissinger, *Years of Upheaval*, p. 1029.

as isolated from other affairs, yet likely to suffer grievously if these affairs turn sour and if arms control remains as the only conspicuous edifice still standing in a field of ruins.

4. Soviet–American cooperation, aiming at the modest goals described here, ought to be presented, not as the cornerstone of a vague new structure of peace, but as a way of moderating the inevitable competition, of affecting Soviet calculations (rather than objectives), and of creating a climate in which, over time, desirable changes in the domestic practices of the Soviet Union and the satellite countries might occur. Cooperation must entail the use of several instruments simultaneously. Arms control—informal or formal—is a vital necessity in order to reduce the danger of nuclear war (both by curtailing first-strike weapons and by improving communication between the two sides), in order to restore crisis stability and to make possible the limitation of damage if war breaks out. Economic relations, within certain important limits (restrictions on military hardware and the avoidance of credits that amount to subsidies), can serve mutual economic interests, and the prospect of their further development can inject some prudence into Soviet behavior. Political agreements in areas where both sides have interests and clients, and where no settlement is possible without the ultimate participation of both—such as the Middle East—are also indispensable. Cultural and scientific exchanges represent one way of penetrating the insulation of the Soviet Union and of introducing fresh air into the cage. The recreation of such a network is indispensable, not because one can hope to "ensnare the bear" and persuade Moscow thereby that its interest lies in giving up political gains abroad, but because one can hope to affect the way in which it seeks those gains, because otherwise one would widen the gap between the United States and its allies—a gap Moscow has been eager to exploit—and because the combination of military balance, preventive diplomacy in the Third World, and cooperative relations with Moscow has a chance of limiting the cost, number, and scope of the confrontations which the unending contest breeds.

5. The most difficult and important task remains the marshaling of domestic support. Two lessons can be derived here from the story of the brief détente era. One is the need for educational leadership—for leaders who explain clearly and patiently the purposes and methods of their strategy (this requires, of course, that they have one). Nixon and, above all, Kissinger, tried to do so, but one of the two problems they ran into was the set of contradictions and the general unrealism I have tried to describe; what is needed (going against the national grain) is an education in complexity and modesty—in self-confidence through reliance on a balance of strength and skill, on a mix of overt American efforts and of timely exploitation of favorable currents in a world too elusive for control

by any one power. Another problem was their formidable insistence on their own control.

But, one might object, won't a more decentralized method of reaching decisions prevent any strategy from emerging? And doesn't the record show that domestic support has existed only when the Executive oversold the Soviet danger and stressed the imperative of worldwide vigilance and persistent containment? Can one mobilize Congress and the public for a modest and complex policy? Let us, however, remember that the apparent new hard consensus of the late 1970s has led to a growing disparity between the public's ambivalent mood and the original ideology of the Reagan administration, as well as to a gradual accommodation of this administration to external and domestic realities.[86] And let us draw this second lesson from the détente era: the need for a deliberate strategy of cooperation with Congress, of organizing support in the country, and of early and frontal opposition to and isolation of systematically hostile groups. This, in turn, as I. M. Destler notes in his chapter, requires consensus at least within the Executive itself. To conclude on a cheerless note, there has been no sign of any such strategy for several years.

86. See my *Dead Ends*, chaps. 1 and 8.

11

Renewed Hostility

SAMUEL P. HUNTINGTON

FROM 1972 TO 1982

Several notable events occurred in the course of a few weeks in the late spring and early summer of 1972. In mid-May West Germany ratified its treaties with the Soviet Union and Poland and signed the Treaty on Traffic Questions with East Germany. The Biological Weapons Convention agreed to by the United States, the United Kingdom, and the Soviet Union was opened for signature and the Seabed Arms Control Treaty was ratified by the same three powers. In late May, President Nixon visited Moscow and signed the SALT treaty strictly limiting antiballistic missile systems, an interim agreement limiting strategic offensive weapons, a statement of "Basic Principles of Relations" between the two superpowers, and several other agreements with the Soviet Union. In early June the three Western occupying powers and the Soviet Union signed the final protocol of the Four Power Agreement on Berlin. In early July the United States agreed to sell the Soviet Union 17 million tons of grain valued at $750 million, and a major U.S. oil company entered into a five-year agreement with the Soviets jointly to develop Soviet oil and gas reserves. Preparations were announced for initiating the Conference on Security and Cooperation in Europe (CSCE) and the talks on Mutual and Balanced Force Reductions (MBFR) in Europe. All in all, the skies were filled with planes bearing diplomats to negotiations, and the air was rich with the promise of détente.

Ten years later, in the spring of 1982, things were rather different. The American president journeyed not to Moscow to sign agreements but to the United Nations to denounce Soviet "tyranny," "repression," "aggression," "atrocities," and "the most massive Soviet build-up of military power in history."[1] The United States itself was embarked on its largest peacetime military build-up in history, and it was extending its sanctions against the Soviet Union over Poland in an effort to block construction of a natural-gas pipeline to Europe, at the cost of much irritation of its West

---

1. *The Washington Post,* June 18, 1982, p. 1.

European allies. Of the negotiations begun in 1972, the MBFR talks had produced nothing, the CSCE meeting had become an arena for ideological warfare, and the SALT II talks had led to an unratified and, in President Reagan's view, a "fatally flawed" treaty. A new round of START talks had begun with the Soviet delegate blaming the United States for the "sharp deterioration" in relations because it was "pressing forward with material preparations for war."[2] The United States was pressing for the removal of Soviet troops from Afghanistan and Cuban troops from Angola. Confrontation, not cooperation, between the superpowers was the order of the day.

How and why did this seemingly major change in U.S.–Soviet relations come about in less than a decade? The first question concerns whether the change was real or only apparent. Were the relations between the two superpowers in fact that different in 1982 from what they had been in 1972? Some might argue that the ultimate reality of those relations is necessarily competitive and that the apparent accord in 1972 was superficial, unreal, and largely a product of American misperceptions of the fundamental nature of the relationship. Others might argue contrariwise, but to the same effect, that despite all the combative rhetoric and gestures of 1982, the underlying realities were also not much different from what they had been ten years earlier. In the presence of their nuclear arsenals, both sides were proceeding cautiously; both agreed to abide by portions of the expired SALT I and the unratified SALT II agreements. New arms-control negotiations had been launched concerning intermediate-range and strategic weapons. Discussions were under way looking forward to a heads-of-state summit. Technology was embargoed but grain was traded. The Soviets had not invaded Poland; the United States had not sent marines to Central America.

Do these arguments in favor of continuity hold up? In one respect, they do. Clearly the changes in the rhetoric, polemics, and perceptions of U.S.–Soviet relations have been greater than the changes in the other elements of those relations. Outside of rhetoric, harmony was not imminent in 1972, and war was not imminent ten years later. Words and images, however, are not to be dismissed. They themselves are a key part of international reality, and they influence and shape other aspects of that reality. Without the increasingly hostile rhetoric of U.S.–Soviet relations in the late 1970s and early 1980s, it is very unlikely, for instance, that the United States would have gone ahead with the reconstruction of its military strength planned by the Ford administration, inaugurated by the Carter administration, and intensified by the Reagan administration. Without the rhetoric on both sides about the end of the cold war and a

2. *The New York Times,* June 30, 1982, sec. A, p. 6.

new era in superpower relations, Americans would not have reduced their arms as they did in the early 1970s, nor would American business-men and Soviet bureaucrats have rushed to trade with each other. By any standard, however, the material reality of and future prospects for Soviet–American relations in terms of economics, military affairs, arms control, politics, and diplomacy were very different in 1982 from what they had been ten years earlier.

How can this change be understood and explained? In some cases of historical analysis it is useful to think in terms of regular oscillations or cycles in policy and relationships. The pursuit of one set of policy goals through one set of means generates results, reactions, and frictions that then lead to the development of different policy goals and means; the pursuit of these then produces a return toward ones similar to those of the first phase. Conceivably, U.S.–Soviet relations could follow this course: containment, détente, and then "renewed hostility," the very title given this chapter, which suggests a return to something that had existed pre-viously. Politics and policy in America, moreover, are perhaps peculiarly prone to move in cyclical patterns.[3] Yet three phases suggest only the possibility, not the existence, of a cycle; détente could be conceived as only a brief interlude in an otherwise consistently competitive relationship. Alternatively, the third phase in the relationship could be thought of as significantly different from both of the earlier periods and building on what happened in those phases. In 1982, competition was pervasive, but it was carried out within and through a framework of agreements, under-standings, and ongoing negotiations. U.S.–Soviet relations in 1972 and 1982 had, in fact, far more in common with each other than either had with U.S.–Soviet relations in 1962 or 1952.

At times it may also be useful to speak of historical tides and turning points. Again, however, the metaphor is misplaced. It is hard to identify real turning points in history: history does not turn corners like a person walking; at best it moves in a broad, turning circle like a huge ocean liner. In similar fashion, the tidal analogy is inapposite: tides are either going in or out, and their turning points can be calculated precisely.

If any metaphor is helpful in understanding U.S.–Soviet relations it might be waves. A major change in these relations can be thought of as a wave that is generated by ocean winds and currents and moves toward the shore; gathers force and momentum; reaches a point where the shoaling causes it to break; after breaking continues inward up the beach, its penetration varying with the shape of the beach; and then recedes, its

3. For some cycles in American politics, see Samuel P. Huntington, *American Politics: The Promise of Disharmony* (Cambridge, Mass.: The Belknap Press of Harvard University Press, 1981), pp. 147–49.

recession overlapping and often becoming whipped up into the next incoming wave. Waves may vary in height, frequency, regularity, and on a calm day there may be none at all. They may overlap each other in confusing and mischievous ways, giving rise to undertows, rips, and cross-currents. In this sense, the détente wave slowly gathered force during the 1960s, became stronger, peaked in 1972, broke, reached its high point on the beach a year later, and then began to recede, as the renewed hostility wave began to move in and overlapped with the receding wave of détente.

What winds gave rise to the hostility wave of the 1970s? A variety of breezes undoubtedly contributed to it, including unrealistic and contradictory expectations on both sides. The three major ones at work, however, would appear to be:

1. The continuing across-the-board Soviet military buildup during the 1960s and 1970s, coinciding for seven years with a real decline in U.S. military spending;
2. The extension of Soviet–Cuban military influence in the Third World, most notably in Angola and the Horn of Africa;
3. A growing conservative domestic political trend that was the single most significant feature of American politics during the 1970s and that was fueled with respect to foreign policy by reaction to the U.S. defeat in Vietnam.

These currents interacted with and reinforced each other so as to wash away the foundations of détente that existed at the beginning of the 1970s. In all probability no one of these winds would by itself have generated the hostility wave. The Soviet military buildup went on for almost a decade after the Cuban missile crisis without arousing significant American fears or, for that matter, attracting significant American attention. Renewed hostility required in addition the stimulus of Soviet Third World expansion, suggested by the October War in the Middle East and made evident by Angola. It also required an intellectual and political environment in the United States that would encourage the sounding of tocsins, in Wells's phrase,[4] as the proper response. If the political climate in the United States had been different, quite conceivably the Soviet actions could have generated a move toward accommodation, delimitation of spheres of influence, and the structuring of a loose global superpower condominium. If the Soviets, on the other hand, had moderated their military buildup and had refrained from taking advantage of the opportunities to extend their influence in the Third World, the conservative political trend in the United States would probably have remained overwhelmingly focused on domestic social and economic issues.

4. See Samuel F. Wells, Jr., "Sounding the Tocsin: NSC 68 and the Soviet Threat," *International Security* 4, no. 2 (Fall 1979): 116–58.

If these three winds were responsible for the hostility wave, the next questions, of course, concern the causes of the winds. The conservative political trend in the United States clearly had deep roots in American society: in the development of the American welfare state in the 1960s, the slow disintegration of the New Deal political coalition, the evisceration of the "public philosophy" associated with that phenomenon, the persistent inflation generated by Vietnam and oil price increases, the economic and demographic rise of the South and West, the revival of religious fundamentalism, and a natural reaction to the crises, disorders, and confrontations of the 1960s. The Soviet military buildup represented a rationalization and generalization of earlier Soviet military efforts, a response to the humiliation of the Cuban missile crisis, a reaction against and away from Khrushchev's efforts to cut back military spending, and the feeling that the time had come for the Soviet Union to establish in practice its position as a global power equal to the United States. Soviet actions with respect to the Middle East and Africa undoubtedly reflected in part this estimate that the Soviet Union should now exert influence farther afield and also that it should take advantage of the opportunities offered by America's preoccupation with extricating itself from Vietnam and with avoiding involvement in anything comparable in the future. In short, the causes that gave rise to winds generating the hostility wave were historically discrete. Except for a loose link between Soviet expansion and Soviet military strength, they sprang from separate sources. That they happened to come together in the 1970s was a coincidence of history.

The brief period when détente was at its peak ended with the October War. The shift away from détente to hostility then went through three major phases. The period from the fall of 1973 to the advent of the Carter administration in the winter of 1977 was marked by the recession of détente and the gathering of the forces that would force President Ford in 1976 virtually to disavow his predecessor's achievements in 1972. A second period followed for the first two-and-a-half years of Carter's administration until the early fall of 1979. This was characterized by efforts to define a relationship that included more or less equal portions of both cooperation and competition. There then began a third period which continued into the Reagan administration at least through 1982, in which the emphasis in the relationship was on competition, confrontation, and hostility.

The Cresting of Détente: 1972–1973

Nixon's visit to Moscow in May 1972 marked the cresting of the détente wave. Its momentum continued through the first part of 1973. Congress overwhelmingly approved the SALT accords in the late summer of 1972. Agreements concerning trade, credits, and the still outstanding lend-lease debts were signed in the early fall. In November the SALT II talks got underway in Geneva, and a month later the Standing Consultative Committee authorized by the SALT I agreement was established. In January 1973 the Vietnam cease-fire agreement was signed, and the MBFR talks began in Vienna. In the late spring and early summer, Brezhnev first visited Bonn, where he signed an economic cooperation agreement, and then Washington, where he signed the Agreement on the Prevention of Nuclear War. The first round of the CSCE talks got under way in Helsinki during the summer. U.S.–Soviet trade shot up from $106.6 million in 1971 to $702.6 million two years later. All in all, the relaxation of tensions, the multiplication of contacts and exchanges, the signing of agreements, and the proliferation of negotiating arenas were the order of the day.

The core of détente was the perceived mutual interests of the two sides in trade and arms control. The Soviets needed trade with the West, particularly the United States, to promote economic development and to avoid economic reform. Elements of U.S. business saw substantial Soviet trade opportunities, and the U.S. administration saw increased trade as a means of enhancing the Soviet stake in international stability. Both sides would gain from arms-control agreements regularizing and limiting the competition, with an additional benefit to the Soviets from the formal U.S. recognition of their equality as a superpower. The overall military balance of the early 1970s was not markedly unfavorable to either side and thus seemed to provide a secure underpinning for arms-limitations agreements. In fact, however, the trends in the military balance during the years of détente overwhelmingly favored the Soviet Union. This was one major weakness in détente, for Americans seemed to assume that détente meant the continuation of the existing military balance, while the Soviets seemed to assume that it meant the continuation of the prevailing trends in that balance. Despite Soviet declarations of their intention of continuing ideological and political competition within the détente framework, Americans also assumed that they would not use détente "as a cover to exacerbate conflicts in international trouble spots," as Henry Kissinger put it during the October War.[5] In a similar vein, but in reverse, the Soviets undoubtedly assumed that détente was incompatible with Western "interference" in internal matters such as treatment of dissidents, Jewish emigration, and their relations with their satellites. Détente was thus strongest in the core areas of negotiated mutual benefits—trade and arms control. It was weakest where the interests were too sensitive, asymmetrical, and diffuse to be negotiated: Soviet involvement with the Third World and Western involvement with human rights.

5. See his speech at the Pacem in Terris Conference, Washington, D.C., October 8, 1973, quoted in Henry Kissinger, *Years of Upheaval* (Boston: Little, Brown, 1982), p. 239.

The Recession of Détente, Fall 1973–Winter 1977

Détente did not end in the fall of 1973. The October War was, however, the first major event to highlight its weaknesses and its fragility. During the following three years, American and Soviet statesmen committed to détente—Brezhnev, Nixon, Kissinger—tried to maintain its momentum, particularly in the central areas of trade and arms control. In both areas, however, the hoped-for achievements failed to materialize, in large part because of the antagonisms and concerns that blossomed forth in the other three major areas of Soviet–American relations. The Soviets became increasingly concerned with U.S. and, to a lesser extent, European pressure with respect to human rights, particularly Jewish emigration. Americans were aroused by apparent Soviet complicity in the launching of the October War, the extensive Soviet efforts to encourage and support the Arab states in that conflict, and the Soviet threat to introduce its troops into the Middle East. Two years later Soviet support for Cuban intervention in Angola refueled these concerns. In addition, American leaders, both within and outside the government, became increasingly alarmed by the Soviet military buildup and the virtually across-the-board relative decline in U.S. military capabilities vis-à-vis those of the Soviets. By 1976 roughly three-quarters of the American public still favored détente, but it had also become a concept that American politicians either rejected or avoided.

During the years 1973–76 the two administrations under the foreign policy guidance of Henry Kissinger made serious efforts to negotiate arms-control and trade agreements with the Soviet Union. Until 1975, however, they remained relatively indifferent to the changing military balance and to human rights issues. They also adamantly opposed Soviet efforts to extend their military presence and influence in the Third World. In Kissinger's view, such efforts were to be stopped by local counteraction—diplomatic, covert, or military if need be. It was useless and self-defeating to attempt to prevent Soviet Third World expansion by attempting to link it to either SALT or trade. "[E]xpansion can be checked only where there is a local balance of forces; indirect means can succeed only if rapid local victories are foreclosed."[6] The administration had acted along these lines during the imbroglio over Soviet expansion of their base facilities in Cuba in 1970. It acted along similar lines when it alerted U.S. military forces in response to possible Soviet deployments to

6. Henry A. Kissinger, "The Permanent Challenge of Peace: U.S. Policy toward the Soviet Union," address, Commonwealth Club and World Affairs Council of Northern California, San Francisco, Calif., February 3, 1976 (Washington, D.C.: Department of State, Bureau of Public Affairs, Office of Media Services, 1976).

the Middle East. It was prepared to take action to prevent the North Vietnamese conquest of South Vietnam in 1974 and 1975. It attempted to take what it considered to be appropriate counteraction against Soviet–Cuban intervention in Angola in 1975–76.

These latter two cases indicate the extent to which the administration's view of the forceful actions needed to sustain détente lacked a solid base in U.S. public opinion. The early and mid-1970s were the years when the proportion of the American public that identified itself as isolationist increased dramatically (from 8 percent in 1964 to 23 percent in 1974), when Americans were generally unwilling to use American troops to defend other countries, including close allies, and when elites in the media and Congress were even more suspicious of and opposed to anything that smacked of potential military involvement or covert action. Reflecting these sentiments, Congress in 1973 sealed the ultimate fate of Indochina by prohibiting future American military action there, and then, in 1975, prevented the administration from providing financial and material support to the anti-Soviet forces in Angola.

At the same time that public and congressional opinion obstructed the administration's efforts to counter Soviet military expansion, it also obstructed the administration's efforts to promote the expansion of Soviet trade. Senator Henry Jackson first raised the issue of Jewish emigration with respect to the trade reform bill in 1972. In 1973 provisions were added to the bill linking U.S. granting of most-favored-nation (MFN) status and Export-Import Bank credits to the Soviets' allowing free emigration from their country. President Nixon vetoed the bill. A year later, after complex negotiations in which the secretary of state mediated between Soviets and senators, a revised bill was passed. The Soviets, however, denounced the bill and rejected the earlier-negotiated trade agreement. The ceiling had been reached on U.S.–Soviet economic relations.

In the course of one year, Congress had thus twice defeated administration initiatives in Soviet–American relations: it had prevented both the extension of credits and most-favored-nation status, on the one hand, and anti-Cuban covert action in Angola, on the other. In terms of defining the limits of détente, the Congress wanted to promote human rights in the Soviet Union, while the administration wanted to stop Soviet expansion in the Third World. The result, from the viewpoint of the leading American détente-ist, was the worst of all possible worlds: "constant pinpricks of the Soviet bear (denial of MFN status, for example), but not coupled with a readiness on our part to run the risks that alone could produce Soviet caution (in Angola, for example)."[7]

Throughout 1973–76, U.S. public opinion was overwhelmingly un-

7. Henry A. Kissinger, *White House Years* (Boston: Little, Brown, 1979), p. 1143.

sympathetic to the strengthening of U.S. military forces. So were the dominant groups in Congress. During this period, however, officials in the executive branch gradually became more concerned with what appeared to be continuing unfavorable trends in the military—particularly the strategic—balance. This concern was fueled both by new Soviet programs and by the reevaluation of past and continuing Soviet programs. Soviet military spending was increasing at a rate of 3–4 percent a year; Soviet conventional forces were being strengthened and modernized; the Soviet navy had acquired the capabilities to maintain significant forces in the Indian Ocean, the Mediterranean, and elsewhere; the Soviets were beginning deployment of a new generation of intercontinental missiles. Most alarming from the American viewpoint was the Soviet progress in MIRVs. The Soviets flight-tested a new generation of ICBMs that could carry MIRVs in the winter of 1975.

In addition, the United States began to reexamine its earlier appraisals of the Soviet military effort and to focus on the extent to which that effort had been underestimated. In 1974 Albert Wohlstetter published his analysis of the failure of U.S. intelligence to predict the rate and size of the Soviet ICBM buildup in the 1960s.[8] In 1975–76 the CIA revised upward its estimates of the percentage of the Soviet GNP going for defense from 6–8 percent to 10–15 percent and also increased its estimate of the extent to which Soviet military spending (in dollars) exceeded U.S. military spending from 20 to 40 percent.[9] Coincidentally, various presumably well-informed people, such as former chief of naval operations Admiral Zumwalt, alleged that the Soviets had been engaged in "massive violations" of the SALT I agreements.[10] This combination of events led to a more general concern with the extent to which U.S. policymakers were getting a comprehensive and accurate picture of Soviet intentions and capabilities, leading, in turn, to CIA director George Bush's appointing the "B team" of outsiders to make an independent assessment of what the Soviet Union was up to.

The administration was generally sensitive to the need to halt and to reverse, if possible, what by 1975 was the seven-year decline in U.S. defense spending. The question was how ready it should be to sacrifice what was left of détente in order to achieve this goal. Secretary of State Kissinger grimly stuck with both the concept of détente and the desirability of working out compromises to remove the obstacles to a strategic weapons

8. Albert Wohlstetter, "Is There a Strategic Arms Race?" *Foreign Policy*, no. 15 (Summer 1974), pp. 3–20, and "Rivals But No 'Race,'" *Foreign Policy*, no. 16 (Fall 1974), pp. 48–81.

9. *The New York Times*, October 23, 1975, p. 29; February 28, 1976, p. 12.

10. International Institute of Strategic Studies (IISS), *Strategic Survey 1975* (London: IISS, 1976), p. 53.

agreement. Secretary of Defense Schlesinger, on the other hand, was much more willing to highlight the Soviet threat in order to strengthen American defenses. This difference was one factor, albeit perhaps not the principal one, leading to Schlesinger's departure from the administration in the fall of 1975 and his joining the growing circle of critics urging the administration to take a tougher stand regarding the Soviets.

As we have indicated, mass public opinion generally remained pro-détente, anti-defense spending, and anti-foreign involvement down through 1976. At the same time, however, the traditional liberal public philosophy was losing its intellectual vitality. This manifested itself first with respect to domestic issues and the reaction against Lyndon Johnson's Great Society programs and the expectations they had generated. The final defeat in Vietnam in April 1975, however, also cleared the way for a conservative, nationalistic reaction in foreign affairs. Conservatism was on the march intellectually and politically in the middle and late 1970s. Presidential politics in 1976 was distinguished by Jimmy Carter's defeat of the more traditional liberals in the contest for the Democratic nomination and by the extent to which Ronald Reagan came close to defeating President Ford in the Republican contest.

In its annual *Strategic Survey* for 1972, the International Institute for Strategic Studies announced that the cold war had been "buried." In its survey for 1973, however, it spoke of "Tensing the Détente." By 1975, it reported that a "general 'détente fatigue'" was pervading the West.[11] It seems likely that a parallel and perhaps comparable process had been under way on the Soviet side. The widening of economic détente, at least with the United States, ceased at the end of 1975. The rising concern in the U.S. with what might be negotiated in the SALT II talks certainly must have reinforced Soviet doubts as to whether a treaty could be arrived at that would be satisfactory from their point of view. The weakening of the American presidency during and after Watergate had caused Nixon to embrace détente as his unique contribution to world peace and then caused Ford to carry it forward in order to demonstrate just the opposite. By 1976, however, détente and its architect in both administrations, Henry Kissinger, were under serious fire from major elements in the Republican party, and Ford, who had embraced détente in order to demonstrate that he was president, now had to back away from it in order to remain president. In the end, the increasing suspicions among Republicans concerning détente, and particularly the SALT II negotiations, forced the administration to accept language in its foreign policy plank that virtually disassociated itself from the policies it had been following vis-à-vis the Soviets.

11. International Institute of Strategic Studies (IISS), *Strategic Survey 1972* (London: IISS, 1973), p. 1; *Strategic Survey 1973* (London: IISS, 1974), p. 2; *Strategic Survey 1975* (London: IISS, 1976), p. 5.

Competition and Cooperation, Winter 1977–Fall 1979

The political context of the Carter administration differed significantly from that of its predecessor. Carter was outside the liberal mainstream of the Democratic party; he more closely fell into the populist tradition in American politics, and populists may be liberal or radical on some points while being highly conservative on others. In the foreign policy side of his administration, Carter delegated to his top officials full control over second- and third-level appointments in their departments. These positions were filled overwhelmingly by people from the liberal wing of the Democratic party. The Coalition for a Democratic Majority (CDM), an organization of more moderate Democrats, indeed claimed with some justification that with one or two marginal exceptions none of the thirty people it recommended to the administration had been selected for a major foreign policy post. The administration was thus often perceived as tilting in a highly liberal, dovish direction on foreign policy issues. This situation was reinforced by a more general phenomenon. Republican administrations are normally more vulnerable to criticism from the left than from the right; with Democratic administrations it is just the reverse. The Ford administration had its critics on both the right and the left, but the weight increasingly was from the right. For the Carter administration, the criticism was from the start overwhelmingly from the right. This criticism often made the administration appear considerably more dovish and irresolute in its dealings with the Soviet Union than it actually was.

The administration's political vulnerability on this score was reinforced by its failure to counter Soviet-Cuban military intervention in the Horn of Africa, by the rhetoric often employed by many of its senior officials, and by several highly publicized weapons decisions (the B-1, the neutron bomb) that tended to obscure its broad increases in military spending. Perhaps even more serious, however, in creating an impression of weakness and irresolution were the major internal developments, in the form of two coups and two revolutions in four countries, all of which brought to power regimes considerably less friendly to the United States than their predecessors. These were the April 1978 coup in Afghanistan, the June 1978 coup in South Yemen, the toppling of the Shah and Khomeini's accession to power in Iran in February 1979, and the victory of the Sandinistas over Somoza in July 1979. All these developments could be considered, and by many were perceived as, American defeats. Yet all were almost entirely the product of domestic forces within the respective societies, with virtually no known Soviet involvement. With the possible exception of the downfall of Somoza, it is not clear that any U.S. administration could have done anything to prevent them from happening. Yet they did happen; and they all were in some sense American "losses," and hence they all contributed to the development of the widespread feeling that the Carter administration could not or would not adequately protect American interests in the Third World.

The political vulnerability of the administration combined with the perceived impact of events abroad provided the opportunity and the stimulus for a rising tide of hard-line criticism. A major source of this criticism was the Committee on the Present Danger (CPD), formed two months before Carter was inaugurated by a bipartisan group of senior figures, many of them former officials, that included Paul Nitze, Eugene Rostow, Lane Kirkland, David Packard, Richard Allen, Max Kampelman, and Dean Rusk. During the next several years this committee waged a vigorous campaign in favor of a greatly enhanced U.S. military effort and a SALT II treaty much more favorable to the United States than any of three administrations had found possible to negotiate. At the same time, another major source of criticism of the administration's military policy and Soviet policy emerged from those intellectuals and writers associated with the neoconservative movement. In the late 1960s and early 1970s this movement was generally associated with the journal *The Public Interest* and was primarily concerned with domestic policy. In the mid-1970s, however, a neoconservative foreign policy wing emerged, centered on *Commentary* magazine and including such people as its editor, Norman Podhoretz, his wife, Midge Decter, Robert Tucker, Richard Perle, Richard Pipes, Walter Laqueur, and Jeane Kirkpatrick. While the CPD group focused primarily on the Soviet military buildup, the neoconservative critics more sweepingly attacked Soviet repression and expansion, with a particular focus on the Middle East. In this they were also joined by *The New Republic*, which increasingly combined its traditional liberalism on domestic issues with a tough line in foreign affairs. Many Jewish intellectuals who had been ardent critics of U.S. involvement in Vietnam in the late 1960s had become by the late 1970s ardent supporters of military strength and strong anti-Soviet and pro-Israeli policies.[12]

The exercise of influence in American politics with respect to any particular set of policy issues is a function of: first and foremost, intensity of concern with those issues; second, expertise with respect to the issues; third, money and public-relations skills; and fourth, demonstrated capacity to organize and deliver voting blocs in response to actions on those issues. In a sense, almost everyone in American society has a diffuse interest in U.S.–Soviet relations. Only a very small number of groups, however, are intensely concerned with them. Outside of government agencies, these include right-wing anticommunist organizations; liberal

12. A position summed up in the not exactly immortal but most expressive words of *New Republic* publisher Martin Peretz when asked to reconcile his 1960s Indochina and 1970s Middle Eastern views: "Dovishness stops at the delicatessen door!"

and pacifist groups worried about war; academic, journalistic, and policy experts specialized in this area. It is a small public. A somewhat larger range of groups is intensely concerned with particular aspects of U.S.–Soviet relations, such as human rights or the military balance. Some of these groups will also have deep and highly specialized knowledge of these topics. When deep concern and deep knowledge are combined, they can be an important influence in the American policymaking process, as the history of the Committee on the Present Danger suggests. Some aspects of U.S.–Soviet relations also concern to some degree the larger and more prominent interest groups in American society: farm organizations, labor unions, business corporations and trade associations, veterans' organizations. By and large, however, U.S.–Soviet relations are not central to the interests of these groups. They might and they often have taken positions on particular issues of U.S.–Soviet relations, but they generally do not devote large amounts of effort, time, and resources to attempting to influence decision-making by legislative or executive officials in this area. They all have many other higher priority concerns. In the shift in U.S. opinion and policy toward the Soviet Union, these larger groups consequently did not play a prominent role. That shift instead reflected the interaction between the efforts of a small, intensely concerned, and deeply knowledgeable set of actors, on the one hand, and the broad trends of feeling and opinion among the mass public, on the other.

After 1976 the intellectual initiative clearly lay with the critics of détente, and the events of those years, combined with the seeming ambivalence and wishy-washiness of the Carter administration, produced major changes in U.S. public opinion in the course of a few years. Down through 1976, while there had been some manifestations of public concern over the rising strength of the Soviet Union, public opinion still remained basically in its post-Vietnam mode, hostile to foreign interventions and military buildups. Between 1976 and 1978, however, public perceptions of the decline in U.S. military strength vis-à-vis the Soviets increased significantly. By 1978 some 56 percent of the public thought that the United States was falling behind the Soviet Union in power and influence. General support for détente peaked at the end of 1976 and remained high into 1978. Yet by June 1978 some 53 percent of the public wanted the United States to get tougher with the Soviets, while only 30 percent favored a reduction in tensions. Less ambiguously, from 1969 through 1976, a substantial plurality of the public thought the United States was spending too much, as opposed to too little, on defense. In March 1977, for the first time since 1960, a public opinion poll showed more people (27 percent) believing the U.S. was spending too little on defense than believing the U.S. was spending too much on defense (23 percent). By late 1978, twice as many (32 percent) thought the U.S. was spending too little as thought it was spending too much (16 percent). Support for SALT II remained high, at over 70 percent, well into 1978. It then began to drop precipitously, with only 42 percent of the public backing a SALT treaty in November 1978 and only a minority of 30 percent supporting the treaty in September 1979, as against 39 percent opposing the treaty.[13] American public opinion turned against the SALT II treaty just as Brezhnev and Carter were affixing their signatures to it. Thus by late 1979, the post-Vietnam syndrome had faded from the scene, with significant pluralities of the American public feeling the United States was lagging behind the Soviet Union in military strength and overall influence in world affairs, supporting a tougher line against the Soviets and a U.S. military buildup, and opposing ratification of the SALT II treaty.

In its first three years in office, the Carter administration thus confronted: a continuing Soviet military buildup; Soviet-Cuban military intervention in the Horn of Africa; the "loss" of four countries to governments less friendly to the United States than their predecessors; an escalating attack on détente from informed, influential, and vocal elements of the American elite; and a public opinion that was increasingly anti-Soviet, anti-SALT, and pro-defense. How could and did it respond to these changed developments?

For two-and-a-half years the administration was divided in its response, between those like Zbigniew Brzezinski, the assistant to the president for national security affairs, who favored a stronger stand against the Soviets, and those, such as Secretary of State Cyrus Vance, who were more accommodating in their approach. All concerned, however, tried hard to moderate and downplay their differences. Both the differences and the efforts to reconcile them were manifest in the comprehensive study of the global balance of power and national strategy (Presidential Review Memorandum 10) which the administration undertook on first coming into office. This study was in a sense the Carter administration's equivalent of NSC 68. The differing viewpoints of State, ACDA, and OSD, on one side, versus NSC and JCS, on the other, produced a document which warned of the Soviet buildup and the need to combat it but did not portray as stark a threat as its predecessor had or recommend as large a U.S. military expansion. The final report concluded that: U.S.–Soviet relations are and probably will continue to be a mixture of cooperation and competition; a rough asymmetrical balance of military

    13. Survey results reported in "Opinion Roundup," *Public Opinion* 1, no. 3 (July–August 1978): 24; 2, no. 2 (March–May 1979): 25; 2, no. 5 (October–November 1979): 40; 3, no. 1 (December–January 1980): 22; and in John E. Rielly, ed., *American Public Opinion and U.S. Foreign Policy 1979* (Chicago: Chicago Council on Foreign Relations, 1979), p. 15.

power exists between the Soviet Union and the United States; the trends in the most important areas of the military balance are adverse to the United States; the United States has substantial advantages over the Soviet Union in almost all the nonmilitary elements of national power—economic strength, political appeal, diplomatic access, technology—except for covert-action capabilities.

The eventual product of the PRM 10 exercise, Presidential Directive (PD) 18, signed by President Carter on August 24, 1977, defined the goals of U.S. national strategy as: (a) to maintain an overall military balance vis-à-vis the Soviets no less favorable than the existing one, the achievement of this goal requiring an annual 3 percent increase in defense spending; (b) to use U.S. nonmilitary advantages to encourage more cooperative behavior by the Soviets; (c) to promote in competition with the Soviets fundamental U.S. values such as human rights and national independence; and (d) to use U.S. nonmilitary advantages and, if necessary, U.S. military forces to prevent the expansion of adverse Soviet influence in critical areas of the world. The more detailed provisions of the directive spelled out the need to maintain parity in strategic forces, to give high priority to the development of a stronger conventional defense of Europe, and to create a rapid deployment force for possible use in the Persian Gulf or other areas.[14]

The cautious phrasing of the PRM 10 final report and of PD 18 reflected the divisions of opinion within the administration. Over time, however, the actions of the Soviets tended to shift the balance toward those who wished a harder line. By the end of 1977, Brzezinski was more actively pushing the administration to take a firmer stand in dealing with the Soviets. After some hesitation, President Carter delivered in March 1978 a tough anti-Soviet talk emphasizing the need to build up U.S. defenses. The positive response to this speech encouraged White House political advisers to believe that a strong defense was good politics. At Annapolis in June, however, the president addressed U.S.–Soviet relations in another speech that was widely perceived as having two mutually incompatible halves, one written by Brzezinski and one written by Vance. The lines of division clarified and sharpened within the administration, but its leader steadfastly refused to become fully committed to one side or the other.

While many in the Carter administration remained highly dovish in their views of the Soviet Union, the administration did not have the same

14. For authoritative descriptions of PD-18, see *The New York Times*, August 26, 1977, p. 1; Harold Brown, address, National Security Industrial Association, Washington, D.C., September 15, 1977; and Zbigniew Brzezinski, *Power and Principle: Memoirs of the National Security Adviser, 1977–1981* (New York: Farrar, Straus, & Giroux, 1983), pp. 177–78.

commitment as its predecessor to either the concept or the process of détente. Top administration spokesmen routinely endorsed détente but in a context which made it clear either that détente described only one aspect of U.S.–Soviet relations or that détente encompassed a very mixed and complex relationship between the two superpowers. The standard administration formulation of U.S. relations with the Soviet Union, reflected in PRM 10, spoke of both cooperation and competition. U.S. policies were defined in similar terms. Our relationship with the Soviet Union, as Carter summed it up in February 1979, "is a mixture of cooperation and competition." The United States must "not let the pressures of inevitable competition overwhelm possibilities for cooperation," nor "let cooperation blind us to the realities of competition." As president, he said, he "had no more difficult and delicate task than to balance the two," and, as he said on another occasion, to avoid the swings "from an exaggerated sense of compatibility with the Soviet Union, to open expressions of hostility."[15] Statements by the president and other administration spokesmen adhered fairly consistently to the competition and cooperation theme. It was both a fairly accurate label of U.S.–Soviet relations during these years and an accurate reflection of the divergent tendencies within the administration.

Both the makeup of the administration and the nature of the pressures to which it was subjected from events abroad and politics at home made Carter administration Soviet policy significantly different in many respects from that of its predecessor. First, the Carter administration assigned human rights a central and highly visible position in its foreign policy. Its first actions vis-à-vis the Soviet Union after coming into office—the presidential letter to Soviet dissident Andrei Sakharov and the receiving of another dissident, Vladimir Bukovsky, at the White House—could not have been better designed to convey to the Soviets the message that the Executive was seizing from Congress the initiative on the troubling and irritating human rights issue. The administration maintained this emphasis throughout its first three years. The president repeatedly returned to the theme of Soviet "abuse of basic human rights" and their efforts "to export a totalitarian and repressive form of government."[16] In mid-1978, when the Soviets tried and convicted Shcharansky and Ginsburg, the administration responded with the first use of economic sanctions in the post-détente period, canceling a computer shipment and

15. Jimmy Carter, address, Georgia Institute of Technology, Atlanta, Georgia, February 20, 1979, in Publication no. 57 (March 1979) (Washington, D.C.: Department of State, Bureau of Public Affairs, Office of Public Communications, 1979).

16. Jimmy Carter, address, U.S. Naval Academy, Annapolis, Md., June 7, 1978, in Publication no. 8948, General Foreign Policy Series 307 (Washington, D.C.: Department of State, Bureau of Public Affairs, Office of Public Communications, June 1978).

imposing restrictions on the export of gas and oil technology. (Like its successor, it also undercut some of the effectiveness and meaning of these actions by then allowing Dresser Industries to go ahead with the construction of a $141 million drill-bit factory in the Soviet Union.) At the Belgrade conference Ambassador Goldberg vigorously and publicly pressed the Soviets on their nonimplementation of the Helsinki accords. The administration's active pursuit of the human rights issues reflected both the deep commitment of many of its top officials and the extent to which this issue enabled it to rally support from liberal Democrats, conservative Republicans, and Jewish groups in both parties.

The Carter administration also lacked the Nixon and Ford administrations' views on the central role which the development of economic relations could play in creating the basis for "strategic" linkage, in Sonnenfeldt's phrase.[17] Some economic interests close to the administration were anxious to exploit the possibilities for trade, but there was no pervasive addiction to the idea of trade as a peace-bringer, and the administration had fewer roots than its predecessor in both the business community and the farm bloc. PRM 10 had stressed the adverse trends in the military balance and also the substantial economic and technological advantages of the United States. PD 18 had directed that these advantages be capitalized on in dealing with the Soviets. With respect to human rights and then Afghanistan and Poland, the administration attempted to pursue this course. Inevitably, however, significant differences existed between State and Commerce, on the one hand, and Defense, Energy, and the NSC, on the other, and the use of economic leverage was fragmentary, halting, and inconsistent.

With respect to the military balance, U.S. defense spending bottomed out in 1975 and 1976. The Ford administration halted the decline in the U.S. military effort, and the Carter administration committed itself to a 3 percent annual increase in real defense spending in conjunction with the NATO allies. In fact, defense spending rose 1.9 percent in Fiscal 1977, 0.5 percent in Fiscal 1978, and 3.9 percent in Fiscal 1979. The administration gave top priority to improving what it viewed as the seriously dangerous situation in central Europe. It also approved the development of the MX and cruise missiles, while canceling the B-1 and postponing the neutron bomb. In PD 18 the president had ordered creation of a rapid deployment force oriented toward Persian Gulf contingencies, but it was not until late 1979 that serious efforts were made to bring this force into existence. Congress was generally favorably disposed toward what the administration proposed and probably would have been willing to ap-

17. Helmut Sonnenfeldt, "Linkage: A Strategy for Tempering Soviet Antagonism," *NATO Review* 27, no. 1 (February 1979): 3–5, 20–21.

prove more. In part this reflected the change in public opinion on defense; in part, also, it reflected the willingness of a Democratic Congress to approve what a democratic president wanted and the extent to which the administration's most vocal critics were those who were urging it to do more rather than less for defense.

The Carter administration attempted to expand the number and scope of the arms-control negotiations under way with the Soviets. Most of these efforts, such as the talks on the Indian Ocean and conventional arms transfers, came to naught as competition and antagonism increased in 1978 and 1979. With respect to SALT, the administration initially attempted to secure a significant cutback in strategic forces in order to reduce the vulnerability of U.S. silos to Soviet heavy missiles. This effort, of course, failed and probably would have failed even if it had been handled in a more discreet and diplomatic fashion. In due course, however, the SALT negotiations resumed and produced an agreement in the spring of 1979 that did not differ significantly from the overall outlines of the agreement the Ford administration was negotiating when it went out of office. The agreement was, however, criticized for not solving the vulnerability question and hence legitimizing a Soviet advantage in heavy missiles, for not incorporating adequate restrictions on the Soviet Backfire bombers, and for not being sufficiently verifiable. The signing of the treaty by Carter and Brezhnev in Vienna symbolically represented the final lingering legacy of the era of détente.

The Ford administration had tried to counter the spread of Soviet influence in the Third World, but had been prevented from doing so by Congress. For almost three years the Carter administration did not, with one minor exception, take any significant counteraction to Third World military actions by other states. In the winter of 1977–78, it did not respond militarily to the Soviet-Cuban military intervention in the Horn of Africa. The following spring it did provide logistical support for Belgian and French efforts to repel the Katangan invaders of Zaire. In the winter of 1978–79, however, it did not respond militarily to the Vietnamese invasion of Cambodia. President Carter was generally reluctant to turn to military force as an instrument of foreign policy. At some point in his administration he also became seized of the idea that he could be the first president since World War II during whose term no American servicemen were killed in action, and he clearly wanted desperately to make that aspiration a reality. (And if one classifies as accidental the deaths of the eight Americans at Desert One, he did.) Undoubtedly, if the administration had proposed any form of military intervention in either the Horn or Indochina, it would have faced great resistance from Democrats in Congress. The absence of response in these cases, coupled with the violent changes of government in four Third World countries, however, also intensified conservative criticism of the administration. By the fall of 1979 the political and diplomatic basis for the "cooperation and competition" posture that the administration had adopted two-and-a-half years before had virtually disappeared.

The Cresting of Hostility, Fall 1979–?

The failure of the Carter administration's effort to define a stable and continuing U.S.–Soviet relationship that was partly cooperative and partly competitive was due to the same winds that had generated the hostility wave in the first place. The divisions within the administration, its seeming indecisiveness and ineffectiveness in the face of the decline of American power, and the rhetoric of many of its officials, all provoked intensified criticism from hard-line advocates. The Soviets further contributed to this end, even in the form of such a minor nonaction as their refusal to make any gesture to help the administration solve the problem it had created for itself in the Soviet-brigade-in-Cuba fracas in the early fall of 1979. This controversy was, of course, closely followed by the Iranian hostage seizure, and then, most significantly, by the Soviet invasion of Afghanistan. In many respects, however, the basis of the Carter two-track relationship had disappeared even before Soviet divisions arrived in Kabul. The SALT II treaty was in trouble, having been approved by only a 9 to 6 vote in the Senate Foreign Relations Committee and facing probable disapproval in the Armed Services Committee. The Senate had also moved to increase defense spending considerably beyond what the administration had requested: "We have come to the end of an era," as Senator Sam Nunn summed it up.[18] The cooperative track of the Carter policy was rapidly disintegrating, and it only remained for the Soviet invasion of Afghanistan to eliminate it entirely.

Significant changes in public opinion also occurred in the fall of 1979. As we have noted, in early 1977, for the first time since the early 1960s, more Americans were in favor of increasing defense spending than were in favor of decreasing it. The largest plurality, however, favored the existing level of defense spending. In September 1979, for the first time since 1960, more Americans (38 percent) supported a defense increase as against maintaining the current level (36 percent) or a decrease (16 percent). By December 1979, before the invasion of Afghanistan, 51 percent of the public favored an increase, 31 percent the current level, and 9 percent a decrease. The following year percentage of support for more defense spending went up into the mid-sixties before dropping off in the fall of 1981. Also, just before Afghanistan, 75 percent of the American

18. Senator Sam Nunn, quoted in *The San Francisco Chronicle*, September 23, 1979, sec. B, p. 3.

public said they thought it very likely or somewhat likely that the United States would be involved in a war within three years, more than double the percentage who had thought so a year before. Initial public support for Carter's post-Afghanistan sanctions against the Soviet Union was overwhelming, and in general during 1980 and 1981 the public maintained what *Time* referred to as "a fiercely hawkish mood."[19]

The character of an administration is defined by those who leave it as well as those who enter it, and the breakdown of the Carter two-track approach was signaled by changes in its personnel. In late 1978 Paul Warnke resigned as Arms Control director, an action which, it was thought, would facilitate Senate approval of the SALT II treaty. In April 1980 Secretary Vance resigned. The occasion was the Iranian rescue mission, which he opposed; the reason was that his view of the world and of the Soviet–American relationship had been invalidated by events. Schlesinger's departure from the Ford administration had reflected that administration's continued efforts to salvage what it could from détente. Vance's departure marked the final end of the two-track effort in the Carter administration. Also in 1980 Max Kampelman became the first officer of the Committee on the Present Danger to enter government when he was appointed by Carter as U.S. representative to the CSCE talks. He was the advance guard of the other CPDers—Nitze, Rostow, Pipes, Allen—who occupied top foreign policy positions in the Reagan administration.

Officials of both the Carter and the Reagan administrations have emphasized the policy differences between them. In fact, however, a high degree of continuity exists in the American approach to the Soviet Union through 1980, 1981, and 1982. The Reagan administration intensified and brought to new heights the rhetorical exchange with the Soviets which Carter had originated in 1980 and also articulated a philosophy that gave promise of greater military strength, more aggressive diplomacy, and more active ideological and economic competition. The dynamics of politics, however, made the changes in the substance of policy not all that great.

For a political movement with strong policy preferences, getting into office is like a wave breaking on the beach. Momentum carries it forward for a while but the generating force has been spent. Inevitably it peaks and begins to recede. Just how far it goes up the beach and how quickly it recedes varies from one case to another. By 1982 signs existed that the hostility wave that had begun to form a decade earlier now might be

19. *Time* 115, no. 6 (February 11, 1980): 22; "Opinion Roundup," *Public Opinion* 3, no. 1A (February–March 1980): 22–23; Alvin Richman, "Public Attitudes on Military Power, 1981," *Public Opinion* 4, no. 6 (December–January 1982): 45.

starting to recede. As we have noted, Democratic administrations are likely to sustain stronger criticism from the right than from the left. If Carter had been reelected in 1980, his second administration would have been under continuing pressure to take a tougher line with the Soviets and to do still more for defense. He would also have faced secondary criticism from the left wing of the Democratic party, who would have attacked him along Kennedy lines for neglecting the traditional Democratic commitment to minorities and the poor. That criticism, however, would have been inherently limited because: (a) the Republican party and the most probable alternative administration to Carter were far more unsympathetic than he to these traditional liberal concerns; and (b) many Democratic liberals were in the Carter administration, and many of those who were not either wanted to be or at least wanted to maintain good relations with those who were.

With the Reagan administration, the political situation was just the reverse, with the principal opposition coming from the left and the secondary opposition from the right. The Carter administration was drawn rightward toward a more moderate position; the Reagan administration tended to be drawn leftward to a more moderate position. Quite apart from the pressure of events, pressure from Congress, the Democrats, the media, allies, political demonstrations, and at times the bureaucracy all pushed in this direction. After hardly a year in office, the Reagan administration was being denounced by its previous ideological enthusiasts, who spoke of "Carterism without Carter" and expressed "The Neo-Conservative Anguish over Reagan's Foreign Policy."[20] With respect to U.S.– Soviet relations, this moderating tendency toward continuity was visible on a number of fronts.

The Reagan administration increased and accelerated the defense buildup which the Carter administration inaugurated. The Carter administration proposed a 5 percent increase in the military budget; Reagan pushed for a 7 percent increase. Real military outlays went up 3.8 percent and 4.1 percent in FY 1980 and FY 1981 and an estimated 7.7 percent in FY 1982. For the Committee on the Present Danger, the Reagan defense program was clearly a major improvement over that which had been proposed by Carter. A year after the administration had come into office, however, the committee asked the question: "Is the Reagan Defense Program Adequate?" and, despite its members in the administration, felt compelled to come to an essentially negative answer: "The Administra-

20. Norman Podhoretz, "The Neo-Conservative Anguish over Reagan's Foreign Policy," *The New York Times Magazine*, May 2, 1982, pp. 30 ff.; Robert W. Tucker, "The Middle East: Carterism without Carter?" *Commentary* 72, no. 3 (September 1981): 27–36; Walter Laqueur, "Reagan and the Russians," *Commentary* 73, no. 1 (January 1982): 19–26.

tion's defense program is a minimal one. It will not halt the unfavorable trends in the U.S.–Soviet military balance, let alone reverse them."[21] Given the major cuts the administration had already made in domestic programs plus the unprecedented budget deficits it faced, it seemed unlikely that increases in defense spending would move much out of the 5–7 percent range in the coming years. Conceivably, more Democrats in Congress in 1983 and 1984 could produce increases below that range.

With respect to arms control, after Afghanistan the Carter administration asked the Senate to postpone consideration of the SALT II treaty; the Reagan administration interred it. The administration backed away, however, from what seemed to be its original position that it should postpone negotiations until after it had rectified the military balance. In what certainly appeared to be reactions to public pressure both in Europe and at home, the administration agreed to talks on both theater and strategic nuclear weapons and announced initial proposals which, among other things, seemed to be carefully crafted to weaken its critics.

In the area of economic relations, the Reagan administration explicitly rejected the idea, common to the approaches of both Kissinger and Carter, of economic linkage. It espoused what in effect was a theory not of economic diplomacy but of economic warfare designed to weaken Soviet strength rather than to change Soviet behavior. In practice, however, the administration's record did not seem all that different from its predecessor's. Both administrations were faced with Soviet or satellite use of military forces in parts of the world where an American military response was impossible. The Carter administration responded to Afghanistan with embargoes on grain and technology, restrictions on Soviet fishing off U.S. shores, an Olympic boycott, and draft registration. The Reagan administration responded to Poland with the suspension of remaining high technology exports, postponement of the talks on an extension of the grain agreement, and restriction of credits to Poland. These efforts were, however, jeopardized by its earlier cancellation of the grain embargo. It also failed in its attempt in the case of the pipeline to apply economic leverage against its allies in order to induce them to wage economic warfare against the Soviets. As it recognized, without cooperation from the allies in the application of economic measures against the Soviets, it would also be unable to resist for long the demands of American businesses that they be allowed to share in Soviet trade. Although failing to gain the allies' acquiescence in a policy of economic warfare, however, the administration did get them to agree to attempt to develop a common framework for Western economic policy toward the East.

21. Committee on the Present Danger, *Is the Reagan Defense Program Adequate?* (Washington, D.C.: Committee on the Present Danger, March 17, 1982), p. 34.

Significant differences did exist in the approaches of the two administrations to the Third World. During this period neither administration was confronted with the need to respond to Soviet military action in an area of the world where American military action might be appropriate. The two administrations tended to define the problems of conflict and insecurity in the Third World, however, in very different terms. The Carter administration tended to highlight the local roots of insecurity. The Reagan administration, on the other hand, particularly in its treatment of Central America in 1981, emphasized external Soviet and Cuban involvement. Such an emphasis, of course, could much more easily provide the justification for the introduction of American troops into a Third World conflict, and the administration certainly gave the impression that it would be much more willing to do so than its predecessor had been. How tough the Reagan administration would in fact be in a Third World crisis had not been put to the test by mid-1983. That was one of the more significant nonevents of the early 1980s.

MORE WAVES?

The sources of the hostility wave, we argued, are to be found in the Soviet military buildup, Soviet Third World expansion, and the conservative political trend in the United States. In appraising the future of Soviet–American relations, it is, consequently, necessary to evaluate the extent to which these factors will persist. The probability that the Soviet military buildup will continue is high. The momentum is there and with it a set of vested interests and fixed expectations. While American military budgets have gyrated widely, there has been a certain relentless consistency about the growth of the Soviet military budget. "When we build, they build," as Harold Brown put it; "when we cut, they build."[22] During a succession struggle and consolidation it seems particularly unlikely that any individual leader or clique would want to take the initiative in challenging what has been a staple of Soviet bureaucratic existence. On the other hand, aspiring leaders will have to have plans for dealing with Soviet economic problems. If they do not reduce the defense burden, they will almost inevitably be driven to propose meaningful economic reforms or to support further expansion of economic détente with the West, or at least with Western Europe and Japan.

From the beginning of the 1980s through 1982 the Soviets adopted a rather low profile in the Third World outside of Afghanistan and, to some degree, Iran. They sat relatively passively on the sidelines while Western powers attempted to negotiate, and did negotiate, some settle-

22. Harold Brown, unpublished testimony on the Fiscal 1980 budget before joint session Budget Committee, U.S. House of Representatives and U.S. Senate, 1979.

ments in southern Africa and the Middle East. It may be that the Soviets felt sufficiently preoccupied with Afghanistan and Poland. It may be that the tough positions assumed by the U.S. government during these years deterred them from risking adventures that might lead to superpower confrontations. It may also be that no suitable opportunities arose which they thought they could exploit. The future of renewed hostility depends in large part on whether a Third World crisis develops which becomes a test of strength between the superpowers. In the absence of such a crisis, the feelings of alarm and the fear of war that peaked in the United States in 1980 will undoubtedly continue to recede.

Finally, as far as U.S. domestic politics is concerned, the conservative winds continued strong. It would not appear, however, that they gained in velocity in the early 1980s, and some "neo-liberal" countercurrents appeared to be emerging. All in all, the political environment in the mid-1980s will not be as likely as it was in the late 1970s to generate alarms about Soviet actions or be as insensitive to foreign challenges as it was earlier in that decade.

At least two of the winds that gave rise to the renewed hostility wave thus seem to have moderated. In the absence of major new breezes, U.S.–Soviet relations are likely to remain in a state of stagnant hostility. Conceivably, however, Soviet restraint in the Third World, a liberal domestic trend in the United States, widespread concern about nuclear war and large defense budgets, plus pressures from American allies, could generate a neo-détente wave. Such a development would dramatically raise the issue as to whether U.S.–Soviet relations might swing as far in one direction between 1982 and 1992 as they did in the opposite direction between 1972 and 1982. What possibility, if any, is there of stabilizing American policy on a balanced, middle-of-the-road course?

In different ways, both Henry Kissinger and Jimmy Carter tried to do exactly that. They both failed. Kissinger's concept of détente and Carter's theory of mixed cooperation and competition were undermined by Soviet actions and by the rising wave of anti-Soviet feeling in the United States. Ronald Reagan rode that wave and expressed its sentiments in about as extreme a fashion as a political leader could who had serious intentions on high office. Once in high office, however, the ebbing of the hostility wave forced him to adjust his policies into the mixed, two-track direction which Kissinger and Carter had been forced to abandon.

If it is assumed that some middle ground—containment and coexistence, cooperation and competition—is a rational policy for the United States to follow vis-à-vis the Soviet Union, three possible conclusions can be drawn from these experiences.

One would be that the leaders of the Ford and the Carter administrations made insufficient efforts to persuade the American public of the wisdom of a balanced policy toward the Soviet Union or that they pursued the wrong tactics in attempting to do so. A larger, better-conceived educational effort is required to establish American policy on a stable course, and if such an effort were forthcoming it could succeed.

An alternative conclusion would be that nothing can change the pattern of American behavior, that American opinion inevitably oscillates between extremes, and that the dynamics of American politics force administrations toward either bellicosity or appeasement. The hostility wave undermined the efforts of two administrations to pursue a balanced course. A new détente wave would, in this view, not only erode the Reagan administration's efforts to pursue a tough line with the Soviet Union; it would also produce a swing back to the viewpoints, illusions, and inadequacies of the early 1970s. Allies, adversaries, and American statesmen have no alternative but to accept this inherent dynamic in the American body politic and to make the best of it.

A third conclusion is somewhat more hopeful. Perhaps one should conclude that administrations that consciously and explicitly attempt to follow a balanced course will inevitably be pushed off that course in one direction or another by public opinion and, possibly, by the Soviet actions which such a course may encourage. Administrations that adopt an unbalanced but more consistent posture vis-à-vis the Soviet Union, however, are likely to come under significant pressures to moderate their stance and may be led to a middle-of-the-road, balanced policy in practice. By talking like Ronald Reagan, in short, Ronald Reagan may end up acting the way Jimmy Carter wanted to act but could not. Moderation, especially in practice, may be the child of extremism, particularly in rhetoric. Statesmen, in this view, should not attempt, in the Kennan mode, to escape from or dam the tides of public opinion but rather to ride them and channel them to serve their country's purposes. To accomplish this, however, requires political leadership of unusual insight and skill.

12

Soviet Policy toward the United States

DIMITRI K. SIMES

Since World War II, the relationship with the United States has continuously been among the central considerations of Soviet foreign policy. Few Soviet moves in the world arena can be understood in total isolation from the superpower rivalry. America simultaneously became for the Soviet Union a source of constant fear, a constraint on further geopolitical advances, a yardstick by which to measure successes, and an example for imitation. Of course, the relative weight of these different images of the United States varied over time, but some mix of them was always on the mind of Soviet policymakers.

This is not to suggest that the Kremlin has been obsessed with America. The Politburo had neither the luxury, nor the predisposition to focus on only one actor in the international scene—even one as important as the United States—relegating all others to secondary status. The consolidation and later the maintenance of the Russian empire in Eastern Europe and the troubled Chinese connection were considered priorities in their own right. Nor would Moscow be prepared to sacrifice tempting opportunities in the Third World either out of respect for American power or the desire to win American recognition and cooperation. In short, the centrality of the United States in Soviet foreign policy thinking should not be exaggerated. Dealing with the United States undoubtedly occupied a top position on the Soviet foreign policy agenda, but there were other crucial items that the Kremlin was unwilling to neglect.

Moreover, the very multiplicity of Soviet images of the United States virtually assured a degree of ambiguity and inconsistency in Soviet–American policy. Moscow, for example, frequently yearned for reassuring signs that the United States accepted Soviet equality. At the same time, however, it adopted a hostile posture and attempted to undermine Washington's international positions—also in an effort to prove its own superpower status. The objective of the two types of behavior was the same—to put an end to the United States' exclusive predominance in global affairs—but the means chosen to achieve this aim were often profoundly different and sometimes mutually incompatible.

From the Soviet standpoint, the bloody victory which had been achieved over Germany at enormous cost established the USSR as a leading power on the European continent, destroying the so-called capitalist encirclement forever. Furthermore, the victory had been won not just over Germany; as far as the Kremlin was concerned, Germany, Japan, and Italy represented an imperialist "strike force." "Now this strike force was eliminated," as one official history of Soviet foreign policy claimed. [1]

The Soviets were aware, however, that the decline of imperialism could not be considered definite because the United States, like the Soviet Union, had managed to improve its position as a result of the war. It was the United States that opposed Moscow's efforts to consolidate its hold over Eastern Europe. It was the United States that had severely restricted the Kremlin's opportunities for further gains through the Marshall Plan and the Truman Doctrine. It was the United States that had first built an atomic bomb and, according to Soviet suspicions, intended to use its initial nuclear monopoly and then its superiority to blackmail the USSR. And finally, it was the United States that, because of its global power-projection capabilities, moved to replace Britain and France as the dominant presence in Africa and Asia.

The 20th Congress of the CPSU in 1956, while breaking on many foreign policy issues with the Stalinist legacy, gave the following uncomplimentary evaluation of America's postwar policy:

Imperialist powers headed by reactionary American circles began soon after the conclusion of the war to pursue a policy of dealing with the world "from a position of strength," which reflected the desire of the most aggressive elements of these powers to suppress workers and democratic and national liberation movements, to undermine the socialist camp and to establish their own control over the world. In practice, this theory means an unrestricted arms race, the creation of American military bases along the borders of the USSR and the people's democracies of the socialist camp, the unleashing of a so-called "cold war" against the socialist states and the preparation of bloody new wars.[2]

Needless to say, this interpretation, which was written under Nikita Khrushchev's guidance, is biased and self-serving. But it would be a mistake to dismiss it as simple propaganda. With their notorious self-righteous insensitivity to the perceptions, interests, and fates of other states, Soviet leaders probably indeed felt threatened and victimized.[3] A con-

---

1. A. A. Gromyko and B. N. Ponomarev, eds., *Istoriya Vneshnei Politiki SSSR, 1917–1975* [The history of the foreign policy of the USSR] (Moscow: Nauka, 1976), 2:20.

2. *XX Sezd Kommunisticheskoi Partii Sovetskogo Soyuza, Stenograficheskiy Otchet* [XXth Congress of the Communist Party of the Soviet Union, stenographic report] (Moscow: Politizdat, 1956), 2:411.

3. A. Arbatov, *Bezopasnost v Yadernyi Vek i Politika Vashingtona* [Security in the nuclear age and the policy of Washington] (Moscow: Politizdat, 1980). For a revealing account of covert U.S. actions against the USSR during the early postwar years, see Harry Rositzke, *The CIA's Secret Operations* (New York: Harper & Row, 1980).

vincing argument can be made that no American administration, excessive rhetoric aside, ever seriously intended to go beyond containment of Soviet power. But this was not necessarily how the Soviets viewed U.S. actions and statements, many of which left room for sinister interpretations, especially given the unusually suspicious cast of mind displayed by Soviet leaders who had matured politically during the Stalinist era. Moreover, containment was simply unaccepable to the Kremlin, which balked at a policy that would limit its freedom of geopolitical maneuver and challenge the legitimacy of the Marxist-Leninist promise of world revolution (and thus the legitimacy of the Soviet regime as its standard-bearer). Finally, by putting the Soviet empire in a straitjacket, and depriving it of geopolitical momentum, containment carried with it the danger of encouraging resistance among the disaffected peoples of Eastern Europe.

Since 1945, the United States has been considered a principal challenge to Soviet security and an obstacle to Soviet international ambitions by every leader in the Kremlin from Stalin to Andropov. Over time the emphasis gradually shifted from more defensive to more offensive perceptions of how to deal with the American problem. Great changes both inside and outside Russia's sphere of influence understandably affected Soviet notions of what exactly its rival could do to harm the Kremlin's interests. But a fundamentally adversarial attitude toward the United States was always among the leading themes of Soviet foreign policy.

Yet, especially after Stalin's death, this attitude was coupled with a thinly disguised respect and even admiration for the United States— admiration which occasionally seemed to have almost sentimental overtones. And acceptance from Washington became an extremely desirable status symbol for Moscow.

Khrushchev explains in his memoirs why he was extremely eager to visit the United States. According to him, "America occupied a special place in our thinking about the world. And why shouldn't it? It was our strongest opponent among the capitalist countries, the leader that called the tune of anti-Sovietism for the rest."[4] But despite this, or rather precisely because of this, Khrushchev was gratified to be asked to come to Washington. He felt that:

If the President of the United States himself invites the Chairman of the Council of Ministers of the USSR, then you know conditions have changed. We'd come a long way from the time when the United States wouldn't even grant us diplomatic recognition. We felt pride in our country, our Party, our people and the victories they had achieved. We had transformed Russia into a highly developed country. The main factors forcing the President to seek improved relations were our economic might, the might of our armed forces and that of the whole socialist camp.[5]

4. *Khrushchev Remembers: The Last Testament*, Strobe Talbott, ed. and trans. (Boston: Little, Brown, 1974), p. 369.
5. Ibid., p. 374.

Leonid Brezhnev was a cooler and less emotional leader than Khrushchev. And by the early 1970s, he presided over a nation much stronger
both economically and militarily. His first summit with President Richard
Nixon brought the reward of formal U.S. recognition of the USSR as
another superpower. Nevertheless, in his contacts with Henry Kissinger,
Brezhnev demonstrated a frequent need for reassurance that in fact he
and his country were not second best.[6] Here lies an important asymmetry
in American and Soviet images of each other. Fear and competitive impulse were present on both sides. But in the American case they were
mixed with contempt; in the Russian, with jealousy and respect.

THE FORMULATION OF SOVIET POLICY TOWARD AMERICA

An attitude of deferential assertiveness colored all Soviet postwar policies
toward the United States. But beyond this, there were sharp differences
in both the style and the substance of Soviet international behavior, including that vis-à-vis America, due, among other factors, to a significant
evolution of the policymaking processes, as well as to the circumstances
under which the Politburo reached its decisions.

Soviet foreign policy in general, and that toward the United States in
particular, was over the years formulated in different ways, under different conditions, and with different priorities in mind. The least is known
about the foreign-policymaking process during Stalin's last years. But
some basic data is on record. All important decisions were reached by
Stalin himself. The aging dictator increasingly came to distrust even his
closest associates. He suspected Vyacheslav Molotov, who after 1939
served first as Minister of Foreign Affairs, and then as the Politburo
member responsible for international activities, of being an American
spy.[7] Stalin's suspicions were not without consequences. A number of
officials and academics associated with Molotov were arrested and pressured to testify against their patron. The whole foreign policy establishment lived in constant fear.

Before the war, of course, purges were the norm. But those who had
access to Stalin differentiate between his prewar and postwar behavior.
According to knowledgeable sources, soon after the victory Stalin's mental health began to deteriorate. He became less and less confident and, on
occasion, plainly incoherent. The great terror of 1937–39 was monstrous,
but from Stalin's selfish standpoint, it served some practical purpose by
eliminating all those who could even potentially challenge his rule. On the
basis of observations made by close aides, in the late forties and early

6. Henry Kissinger, *Years of Upheaval* (Boston: Little, Brown, 1982). pp. 229–31.
7. *Khrushchev Remembers*, p. 309.

fifties the dictator was displaying signs of irrationality bordering on senility. He was no longer a formidable, if terrifying, leader who used to impress even his most antagonistic interlocutors.[8]

Outside the Party and government bureaucracy, no alternative sources of expertise on America were allowed to exist. The Institute of World Economics and International Relations was closed in 1947, and writings of Soviet America-watchers (those few who were not purged) were extremely simplistic and polemical. There was not much difference between their scholarship and the propagandistic anti-American products of the media.

Such a domestic situation did not favor the development of an enlightened and imaginative policy toward the United States. The international environment also made the conduct of anything but a unidimensionally hostile and essentially defensive strategy very unlikely. While the 1948 Berlin blockade was obviously an offensive action, generally speaking the Kremlin was more preoccupied with rebuilding the Soviet armed forces, trying to eliminate the American lead in the nuclear field, consolidating Soviet gains in Eastern Europe, and feuding with Tito's Yugoslavia.

Historians disagree about whether Stalin, fearing remilitarization of West Germany, was interested in finding some negotiated solution after the failure of the Berlin blockade.[9] But there is little doubt that any plausible deal would have included recognition of the legitimacy of Moscow's control over Eastern Europe—with the possible exception of East Germany. Such a deal would also have required a withdrawal of U.S. forces from Germany and probably from the European continent altogether. Washington—especially in the midst of the Korean War—was not willing to take chances. Was there a missed opportunity? The answer is uncertain. Potential gains were not sufficient to encourage American policymakers—as George Kennan observes—"to toy" with proposals which "could easily alarm and disorient Western opinion."[10] The risky pursuit of every marginal opportunity is not necessarily an act of political wisdom.

---

8. Ibid., as well as collaborating revelations by two of Stalin's top generals with whom the author talked in Moscow 1969–72.

9. For a fairly optimistic view of Soviet flexibility, see Marshall D. Shulman, *Stalin's Foreign Policy Reappraised* (New York: Atheneum, 1969), pp.1, 264; and Adam B. Ulam, *Expansion and Coexistence: The History of Soviet Foreign Policy, 1917–1967* (New York: Praeger, 1973), pp. 534–39. For an alternative perspective, see Robert C. Tucker, *The Soviet Political Mind: Stalinism and Post-Stalin Change* (New York: Norton, 1971), p. 98; and William Taubman, *Stalin's American Policy: From Entente to Détente to Cold War* (New York: Norton, 1982), pp. 196–97.

10. George F. Kennan, *Memoirs, 1925–1950* (Boston: Little, Brown, 1967), p. 446.

As far as the Korean War is concerned, Khrushchev was probably not being disingenuous in suggesting that the Soviets sanctioned Pyongyang's invasion of the South. But they did not initiate this action and they did not really encourage it.[11] And in the course of the war, Moscow took considerable care, while helping its client, to remain on the sidelines and to avoid any possibility of a premature military conflict with the United States.[12]

Stalin's American policy was dominated by efforts to isolate the recently formed Soviet empire from U.S. influence by pursuing economic autarky and strengthening the Soviet military machine in order to protect the security of the state and achieve superiority over its immediate neighbors. Little effort was made to expand the USSR's international reach, to develop global-force projection capabilities or to establish ties with newly independent Third World nations whose leaders were denounced as "imperialist lackeys."

After Stalin's death things began to change quickly. Even before Khrushchev succeeded in prevailing over his rivals in the leadership, important shifts took place in both the rules of formulation and the net product of Soviet foreign policy. First, in Stalin's absence the element of irrational defensiveness quickly disappeared. Molotov and his close associates, Dimitri Shepilov and Andrei Gromyko, were all pragmatic and fairly experienced in world affairs. Khrushchev himself was relatively ignorant about the international scene but remarkably open-minded and willing to experiment. Georgy Malenkov, appointed chairman of the Council of Ministers after Stalin's death, felt a need to give more emphasis to consumer industries and questioned for the first time in Soviet history the winability of war if it were fought with nuclear weapons.

The willingness to depart from Stalin's legacy made Soviet foreign policy considerably more dynamic and sensitive to the intricacies of evolving international realities. A partial reconciliation with Yugoslavia took place. A peace treaty with Austria was signed. Soviet troops were withdrawn from Finland. Diplomatic relations with Japan were established. And a summit meeting with the United States, Great Britain, and France occurred in Geneva. The meeting did not result in breakthroughs on any major issues, and the spirit of Geneva was short-lived. However, it fit into a pattern of lesser paranoia toward the West, a pattern that provided the background for the important policy conclusions announced at the 20th Party Congress.

In relations with the Third World there was also considerable reassessment. Bridges to India, Indonesia, and Egypt were rapidly built. Their

11. *Khrushchev Remembers,* pp. 367–68.
12. For a different account, see M. S. Kapitsa, *KNR: Tri desyatiletiya—tri politiki* [PRC: Three decades—three policies] (Moscow: Politizdat, 1979), p. 53.

leaders were embraced by Khrushchev, and almost overnight the Soviet media discovered that they were not capitalist puppets but, rather, heroic personalities representing national liberation movements. Simultaneously, Soviet military strategy underwent modification. The role of the navy was upgraded and, under the new command of Admiral Sergei Gorshkov, the first initial steps were undertaken to transform the Soviet fleet into an ocean-going force.[13] Decisions were also reached to create an intercontinental nuclear capability.

The 20th Party Congress codified the new trends in Soviet foreign policy. The leadership publicly stated that a new world war was not inevitable and could be avoided. An alliance with the Third World was declared to be one of the cornerstones of Soviet foreign policy. And there was an implicit recognition that the process of de-Stalinization had implications not only for the Soviet Union itself, but for the Soviet empire as a whole. From now on, the suppression of Hungarian revolt notwithstanding, some tolerance of diversity was accepted in Soviet bloc states so long as Moscow's domination was not challenged.

The period of 1953–56 became an important turning point in Soviet foreign policy. And the change seemed to be supported by leadership consensus, as its fundamental directions outlived Khrushchev's dismissal in October 1964. Starting in 1956, however, and especially after the defeat of the so-called anti-Party coup in June 1957, Khrushchev more and more began to act not just as a first among equals, but as a dictator free to ignore the views of his colleagues and subordinates. It was during this era of Khrushchev's supremacy—later described as voluntarism by his successful rivals—that the Soviet Union engaged in risky ventures both in terms of befriending the United States and confronting it. The Party leader's eccentricity during the trip to America and his daring invitation to Dwight D. Eisenhower to visit Russia, the U-2 incident, the Berlin crisis, and the Cuban missile adventure were all the results of personal rule by a new, easily excitable, and intellectually undisciplined Soviet leader. Khrushchev had a tendency both in domestic and foreign policy to take crucial steps without giving much thought to their consequences.

At home he was not satisfied with the release of millions of concentration camp inmates and the rejection of police tactics as a means of settling debates among the elite. He launched a noisy campaign against Stalin's "cult of personality" that discredited the Communist regime, encouraged all kinds of liberal and reformist tendencies, and made his own emerging "cult of personality" look particularly conspicuous. In the foreign arena, Khrushchev regularly threatened his associates with either excessive rapprochement with the West or with excessive confrontation with it. There

13. S. G. Gorshkov, *Morskaya Moshch Gosudarstva* [The naval power of the state] (Moscow: Voenizdat, 1976), pp. 290–96.

was also a feeling that he was too quick to make commitments to Third World nations such as Egypt and to give up on alliance with China. Fascinated with foreign policy, Khrushchev increasingly preferred to bypass regular institutional channels and to rely primarily on his own instincts and a few close personal aides. The practice of using his son-in-law, Aleksei Adzhubei, whom he appointed as an editor of *Izvestiya* and as an unofficial ambassador-at-large, generated particular resentment among the foreign policy establishment and the elite as a whole. Together with periodic reorganizations of the Party apparatus, reforms in the state economic management, and shake-ups in the armed forces, risky and sometimes embarrassing games in the world arena were among the reasons the Soviet ruling strata finally had enough of Khrushchev.

His dismissal greatly affected the operational rules of the Soviet foreign policy formulation process. After roughly six years of collective leadership, Leonid Brezhnev by 1970 succeeded in becoming the principal Soviet foreign-policymaker. But despite his great authority, the General Secretary consistently acted with care, trying to shape a leadership consensus rather than imposing his own views on the Politburo. Under his stewardship, Soviet foreign policy became considerably more consistent, predictable, and informed. It also tended to avoid defining priorities, making hard choices and shifting gears in response to new circumstances. As Brezhnev and those around him were aging, a growing conservatism in the Kremlin transformed what initially appeared as the steady, confident, and assertive international course of an emerging superpower into the immobilism of old ideas and patterns of behavior. Afghanistan, despite the aggressive nature of Soviet intervention, was an illustration of this trend. Moscow's involvement was not carefully considered but, rather, represented a reactive pattern of escalation and miscalculation.

The Politburo possessed the ultimate authority under Brezhnev. From a primarily pro forma group of Stalin's handpicked loyal lieutenants, the Politburo had turned, under Khrushchev, into an advisory body filled with personal allies and protégés of the leader. Brezhnev's Politburo resembled more a supreme legislative-executive committee of the Soviet elite, with the General Secretary occupying the position of a chairman of the board who had great personal authority but who could not, and did not want to, monopolize the formation of policy. In several instances, when confronted with issues of profound importance, Brezhnev at the very least tried to involve his colleagues in determining responses. In the course of discussing ICBM limitations with Kissinger during the secretary of state's visit to Moscow, Brezhnev went so far as to claim that, "If I agree to this, this will be my last meeting with Dr. Kissinger because I will be destroyed." The General Secretary was probably exaggerating, and the next morning the Soviets made some important concessions. But interestingly enough, the shift in Moscow's position occurred only after a six-hour Politburo session which delayed a scheduled meeting between Kissinger and Brezhnev.[14]

This tendency to shape a consensus rather than taking decisions unilaterally was coupled with a change in the Politburo's structure. Under both Stalin and Khrushchev, senior officials were regularly shifted between agencies, having little reason, as a result, to develop strong institutional loyalties. This was not so in the case of Brezhnev's Politburo. Most of its members have been identified, if not with specific agencies, then with issue areas, for the better part of their careers. This is particularly evident in the national security establishment. Minister of Foreign Affairs Andrei Gromyko was appointed to his post in 1956 after having joined the ministry as a department chief back in 1939. Minister of Defense Dimitri Ustinov spent more than forty years in a variety of positions on both the Party and government sides of the military-industrial complex. He was made People's Commissar of Armaments in 1941 at the age of thirty-three. During his 1965–76 tenure as a Central Committee Secretary, Ustinov was in charge of coordinating the defense industry.

The same is true for new General Secretary Yuri Andropov. Like Ustinov, he served on both the Party and the government sides of the bureaucracy but inevitably was preoccupied with matters of national security. He joined the Foreign Ministry and was soon made ambassador to Hungary in 1953. In 1957, he was brought back to head the Central Committee's Department of Liaison with Ruling Communist Parties. In 1962, still in charge of the same department, he was promoted to the rank of Central Committee Secretary. From 1967 to 1982, he served as chairman of the KGB, at first as a candidate and, since 1973, as a full member of the Politburo. And in May 1982, he was returned to the Central Committee Secretariat to take over Mikhail Suslov's international portfolio.

As a result, key Politburo members responsible for national security formulation have a lot of experience, have worked with each other over long periods of time, and have strong ties (particularly in Gromyko's case) to the institutions they represent in the leadership. During the Stalin and Khrushchev eras, principal aides were sent to Central Committee departments and government ministries in order to run them on behalf of the central authority. Brezhnev's setup came close to allowing Politburo members to wear two hats—one as the overseer of their agency on behalf of the entire leadership, and the other as articulator of their agency's preferences to the Politburo. A situation of dual responsibility if not of dual loyalty has been permitted to develop.

14. Kissinger, *Years of Upheaval*, pp. 1023–24. See also Richard Nixon, *The Memoirs of Richard Nixon*, (New York: Grosset & Dunlap, 1978), p. 616.

The combination of a consensus-oriented decision-making style and greater bureaucratic participation in the Brezhnev regime has created an unprecedented premium on information and competence. New research institutes under the auspices of the Academy of Sciences have been organized and already existing ones have won both funds for additional staffing and, more importantly, new access to policymakers. The precise role of the institutes remains in doubt. Some informed sources claim that, with the exception of academician Georgy Arbatov, its director, the Institute of the U.S.A. and Canada does not have good connections with senior officials and serves primarily internal and external propaganda purposes.[15] Such accounts should be treated with care. Abundant evidence indicates that a number of the institute's senior officials and functionaries have close informal connections with their counterparts in the bureaucracy.

Also, it would be surprising in a highly centralized Soviet think tank—and all Soviet think tanks are heavily centralized—to find that many people in addition to the director would have official dealings with the higher-ups. This is not the way Soviet institutions operate in general. But Arbatov acts as a transmission belt introducing those in power to data, conclusions, and, more rarely, policy recommendations developed by his research subordinates.

The importance of the institutes should not be overstated. Naturally American students of Soviet affairs for whom scholars from Moscow are a principal, if not the only, window into the black box of the Kremlin's policy formulation have a tendency to ascribe to these think tanks a greater role than they probably deserve. And Soviet researchers are not above telling stories designed—for political or more often for selfish reasons—to present themselves as much more informed and influential than they actually are. Nevertheless, it would be quite unfortunate if, after years of undue fascination with the *institutchiki,* the Americans began to dismiss them out of hand. The strength of the institutes and even of their directors, such as Arbatov (who is also a member of the Central Committee and Supreme Soviet) is, in all likelihood, not in their ability to affect operational decisions on concrete technical issues. For this they have neither adequate data nor an adequate place in the bureaucratic structure. Their true accomplishment has been to sensitize the Soviet elite to general international, political, economic, and social trends; to educate it about new threats to, and conversely, new opportunities for the USSR; and to help it to see the world as it is rather than the way it is supposed to be according to Marxist-Leninist dogma.

15. For more on this, see Dimitri K. Simes, *Détente and Conflict: Soviet Foreign Policy 1972–1977* (Berkeley, Calif.: Sage, 1977).

Westerners' preoccupation with the research institutes and their staffs has tended to make us miss the fact that a new breed of foreign policy specialists has risen through the Soviet bureaucracy to positions of importance just below the Politburo. Many of these individuals have graduated from the Foreign Ministry's Institute of International Relations, which upon its establishment in 1944 became the launching pad for many careers in the international field. While political reliability has been considered a prerequisite for entrance into this privileged college, its graduates have nevertheless also received impressive language and substantive training. Later, the Higher Diplomatic School, now renamed the Diplomatic Academy, has given well-taught refresher courses to middle-level professionals. Quite a few of the early graduates of both these institutions, men currently in their fifties and early sixties, presently staff the top echelons of the Foreign Ministry, the KGB, the Central Committee International Department, some even belonging to Brezhnev's, and now Andropov's, groups of personal aides.

The Soviet leadership has thus had an opportunity to be reasonably well informed about international developments. This has been especially true in the case of the United States, which has been the particular focus of research and information-gathering. Never before has the Kremlin been so knowledgeable about events.

Soviet understanding of the United States is a different matter. While Soviet analyses of America have become considerably less ideological and more sophisticated, even Moscow's best analysts frequently make serious errors—especially in their forecasting. In the 1970s, not only did they assume that détente enjoyed increasingly broad popular and elite support in the United States, but, with few exceptions, they hoped that Ronald Reagan could become another Nixon and reestablish superpower cooperation. But before judging Soviet commentators too harshly, one should remember that many of the same misperceptions existed in the United States among the most informed commentators.

Whether or not the leadership has been frequently exposed to conflicting advice is not entirely clear. Simplistic clichés such as "hawks" and "doves" notwithstanding, there are grounds for believing that serious debates have taken place on a variety of important issues involving relations with the United States. To what extent the visibly sharp disagreements among academics and media commentators have mirrored differences among members of the Politburo is impossible to assess. But the presence of these disagreements indicates at the least that there is an element of uncertainty in the leadership's thinking which individuals at lower levels have either tried to influence or to use as a shield for expressing their own views.

In the final analysis, it seems unlikely that Brezhnev's Politburo would have adopted major policies if one or more institutional actors had had strong objections to them. The late Soviet leader was able to make a gesture to the United States during the Vienna summit by agreeing to disclose the production levels of the Backfire bomber, something Gromyko had previously argued that the Soviet Union was not obliged to do.[16] Similarly, Brezhnev proved to be in a position to display flexibility on the more meaningful point of negotiating fundamental changes in the nature of the U.S.–Soviet Agreement on the Prevention of Nuclear War.[17]

Consistently, the Party leader avoided taking steps in the USSR's relations with the United States that could have put him at odds with any powerful elite faction.

The Kremlin was unresponsive to constant requests from the Nixon-Kissinger team to restrain a variety of Soviet allies, ranging from North Vietnam to Egypt. The standard Soviet reply was that Hanoi and Cairo did not take guidance from Moscow.[18] There was a considerable element of truth in this assertion. Also, there was little reason for the Politburo, détente notwithstanding, to help its principal rival solve its foreign policy problems. Most importantly, however, the Politburo had to be very careful not to appear either to Third World nations or, more crucially, to the Soviet elite as placing a higher priority on cooperation with its imperialist adversary than on alliance with national liberation movements. A break with the Soviet commitment in this area would have been costly for the leadership's image among the Soviet elite.

The Party apparatus, the military, and the security services have been the big beneficiaries of the Brezhnev era. Under Brezhnev, the Party apparatus's representation on the Politburo grew considerably in comparison with what it enjoyed during Khrushchev's rule. Not only did the military find Brezhnev a sympathetic supporter, but the relative pluralization of the decision-making process, combined with the military's virtual monopoly on information regarding military operations and technology, allowed the generals and admirals to acquire an unprecedented degree of institutional autonomy.[19]

Under Brezhnev, the KGB, after years of limited respectability during Khrushchev's de-Stalinization campaign, again moved back into the first ranks. Between 1967 and its chief's transfer to the Secretariat, the KGB had representation in the Politburo, and even with Andropov's departure

16. Strobe Talbott, *Endgame: The Inside Story of SALT* (New York: Harper & Row, 1970), pp. 14–15.

17. Kissinger, *Years of Upheaval*, pp. 274–86.

18. Nixon, *Memoirs*, p. 391.

19. For more on this, see Dimitri K. Simes, "The Military and Militarism in Soviet Society," *International Security*, vol. 6, no. 3 (Winter 1981–82).

and the death of his former first deputy, Semyon Tsvigun, the security service still puts more members on the Central Committee than it did in the late 1950s. It has received strictly positive media coverage; has, for all intents and purposes, been politically rehabilitated; and, like the military, has escaped being operationally controlled by any Central Committee department.

Any new policy toward the United States would have to win, if not the support, then at least the tacit acceptance of these crucial bureaucratic actors. As a result, Brezhnev was confronted with fairly narrow margins within which he could operate without considerably changing the Politburo's policy-formulating style.

THE ROOTS OF SOVIET POLICY TOWARD THE UNITED STATES

There is a tendency to overintellectualize in hindsight the reasons why Soviet and American leaders embarked on the path of détente. In the behavior of both countries there is less evidence of grand design than there is the appearance of nations reacting to circumstances, but reacting in such a way that certain patterns evolved eventually, but not necessarily intentionally. On U.S. policy, William Hyland is correct when he observes:

It is ironic that Nixon and Kissinger became identified with the policy of détente. Initially at least, neither saw a prospect for more than a narrow, limited accommodation with the Soviet Union. Rather than a broad relaxation of tensions, they offered Moscow a number of specific issues (e.g., Berlin) for negotiation within a general framework, in a process that came to be designated as linkage.[20]

A fundamentally new relationship with the United States was probably not among the Soviet leadership's priorities. The Politburo perceived American involvement in Vietnam as both an obstacle to any rapprochement with the United States and an opportunity to undermine Washington's international positions. On several occasions, Soviet officials underlined that any improvement in the U.S.–Soviet relationship would require an end to American involvement in Vietnam. Even after the first summit had taken place in Moscow, Brezhnev found it wise to sound a cautionary note in a major foreign policy address he made at a joint Central Committee–Supreme Soviet meeting to commemorate the fiftieth anniversary of the USSR. After declaring that, "in the course of further contacts, new significant steps to develop Soviet–American relations may become possible," he felt compelled to add, "but, and this should be clearly stressed, a lot will depend on how future events evolve,

20. William Hyland, *Soviet–American Relations: A New Cold War?* (Santa Monica, Calif.: The Rand Corporation, 1981), p. 22.

and in particular, on how the problem of ending the war in Vietnam is resolved."[21]

Several developments pushed the Politburo in the direction of some normalization with the United States. First, during the late 1960s the Kremlin had aggressively pursued a policy of détente with Western Europe. The Soviets sought recognition of the postwar division of Europe; they wanted to secure their western frontiers in a time when antagonisms with China were growing; and they were interested in enhanced economic cooperation, particularly when it became clear that economic reform had been blocked by the Party apparatus and the central industrial ministries. The Soviets perceived an influx of Western credits and technology as one possible escape route from the need to modify their system of planning and management. In addition, there was a definite hope in Moscow that better relations with the West European nations would lead to a weakening, and possibly even to the eventual collapse, of the NATO alliance. Soviet analysts interpreted the French departure from NATO's military organization as the beginning of a major new trend, and they were looking for new candidates to join France in the process of dissolving the transatlantic ties.[22]

This building of bridges to Europe (and to a lesser extent the attempt to establish an economic interrelationship with Japan) in order to isolate the United States and China was the closest thing to a grand design with respect to foreign policy that the Soviet leadership possessed in the late 1960s. But the logic of events finally forced the Kremlin to reassess its reluctance to include the United States in the process of rapprochement. The consolidation of Soviet relations with the Federal Republic of Germany required clarification of West Berlin's status. But agreement on this subject was impossible without America. The simultaneous admission of the GDR and the FRG to the United Nations also could not take place without U.S. acceptance. And America's European allies absolutely refused to take part in a conference on European security and cooperation—Moscow's favorite pet project at the time—unless the United States and Canada were also invited to participate.

Finally, both the West European and the Japanese governments and business communities demonstrated considerable hesitation about rushing into major long-term investments in the USSR without some form of American involvement. In the absence of such an involvement, the risk of Soviet breach of trust—for instance, because of a sudden outbreak of

21. *Pravda*, December 22, 1972.

22. In late 1968, the Institute of World Economy and International Relations produced for its official customers a special issue of its *Information Bulletin* which was devoted to NATO and which forecasted an extremely bleak outlook for the alliance.

international tension—was viewed as too great. So, paradoxically, the Politburo found itself in need of an improvement in relations with the United States in order to carry out a policy (a meaningful and stable rapprochement with Western Europe) that at least initially, had been intended to move against the United States.

Of course, there was also the Chinese factor. A little more than a month after the inauguration of Richard Nixon, bloody clashes broke out along the Ussuri River. Summer produced further confrontations on the border with Sinkiang. On his way back from Hanoi, where he had been attending Ho Chi Minh's funeral, the chairman of the Council of Ministers, Aleksei Kosygin, made a brief stop in Beijing. But his talks at the airport with Zhou Enlai were inconclusive at best. A few days later, on September 16, Viktor Louis, a Soviet citizen who writes for English newspapers and is reputed to have KGB connections, published an article in London's *Evening Press* warning that: "The Soviet Union is adhering to the doctrine that socialist countries have the right to interfere in each other's affairs in their own interests or those of others who are threatened. The fact that China is many times larger than Czechoslovakia and might offer active resistance is, according to Marxist theoreticians, no reason for not applying this doctrine."[23] Simultaneously, a number of Soviet diplomats stationed abroad hinted that the Kremlin was seriously entertaining the possibility of military action against China.[24]

More importantly, the USSR continued its buildup of troops in the military districts bordering on the PRC. Rumors of war were not limited to Western capitals. Classified war games (called situational analyses) were conducted in Moscow, and the possible American reaction to a Soviet military move against Beijing was among the principal considerations.[25]

Meanwhile, the United States was making initial approaches to China—approaches that most definitely were carefully watched in the USSR. On January 20, 1970, Ambassador Anatoly Dobrynin asked Kissinger for a briefing about a meeting between American and Chinese ambassadors in Warsaw, reminding the secretary of state that anything connected with U.S.–PRC contacts was a "neuralgic" point for Moscow.[26] Concern about a possible accommodation between its principal adversaries encouraged the Soviet leadership to be more forthcoming in its relations with the United States. And there is little doubt that one crucial

23. Quoted from Robin Edmonds, *Soviet Foreign Policy 1962–1973: The Paradox of Super Power* (Oxford. Oxford University Press, 1975), p. 50.

24. Henry Kissinger, *White House Years*, (Boston: Little, Brown, 1979), p. 184.

25. The author had the opportunity to talk to three participants and organizers of these "war games" in Moscow in 1970.

26. Kissinger, *White House Years*, p. 524.

reason Nixon's visit to Moscow was not canceled, as the Ukrainian party boss Pyotr Shelest had apparently recommended, was because the American president had just returned from a trip to China. The Politburo was plainly fearful of allowing a situation in which Washington would have better relations with Beijing than with Moscow. In later meetings, Brezhnev and other Soviet leaders rarely missed an opportunity to remind Nixon and Kissinger about the great dangers of Chinese policy and the inherent advantages of isolating its adventurist leadership. But, at a minimum, Soviet policy was designed to avert the worst possible outcome—a strategic arrangement between the United States and the PRC directed against the USSR.

Finally, with Nixon and Kissinger in the White House, the United States itself began to look to the Soviets as both a more acceptable and more needed partner. In Moscow, the phased U.S. withdrawal from Vietnam, Nixon's Guam doctrine, and his promise to move from confrontation to negotiation encouraged the belief that the "lessons of Vietnam" and a more basic appreciation of the new "correlation of forces in the world arena" had led some "realistic elements among American ruling circles" to begin to accept new, more narrow limits on the United States' power and geopolitical presence.[27] Of course, at first the Politburo treated Washington's new rhetoric with some suspicion. As Brezhnev put it: "The Soviet government viewed positively the statement of the US desire to move 'from an era of confrontations to an era of negotiations.' However, we know that in politics the only way not to err is to believe in practical deeds, not verbal declarations. And we cannot fail to see that the peaceful statements of the American Administration are at odds with its aggressive actions, aggravating the international situation."[28]

But gradually, the combination of signals from Washington, evidence of U.S. disengagement in Vietnam, and American flexibility in SALT persuaded the Politburo that there were indeed new and encouraging elements in American thinking, as well as a new willingness to accept a more modest role in the world and to allow new leeway for the Soviet Union.

On the other hand, the Nixon administration's toughness in Vietnam, its firm position during the 1970 India-Pakistan war, its success in pushing appropriations for an ABM through Congress, and its decision to MIRV Minuteman missiles communicated to the Kremlin that it was dealing with a flexible but formidable opponent that could not be pushed around. In this context, Nixon is probably correct when he observes that,

27. *Pravda*, August 14, 1970.
28. *Pravda*, June 13, 1970.

had his administration "lost the ABM battle in the Senate [it] would not have been able to negotiate the first nuclear arms control agreement in Moscow in 1972."[29]

At roughly this time, the Soviet military began to turn around on SALT. After initial suspicions (some of which were openly aired in military publications), the General Staff began to feel that SALT did not threaten Soviet weapons programs, and that furthermore it was an effective way to enhance confidence in the other side's intentions and consequently to rationalize military planning.[30] The ABM treaty, initially rejected out of hand by Kosygin in Glassboro, also began to look more appealing to the Soviet military-industrial complex. For one thing, the United States was better equipped technically to win on ABM. For another, the Soviets were at that time preparing to proceed with an accelerated research and development program for new generations of MIRVed ICBMs and SLBMs. Budgetary constraints therefore encouraged the defense establishment to make hard choices, and under the circumstances it seemed logical to sacrifice the less promising ABM.

The requirements of its European policy, the split with China, and its new image of the United States were fundamental reasons for the Soviet Union to become interested in rapprochement with America. From the very beginning, however, the Politburo went almost out of its way to stress that détente with America did not mean recognition of the international status quo, abandonment of the Soviet commitment to national liberation movements, or acquiescence in U.S. efforts to contain Moscow's emerging global reach.

BUILDING A NEW RELATIONSHIP WITH THE UNITED STATES

But whatever the original Soviet reasons for seeking accommodation with the United States, the Politburo, and Brezhnev personally soon began offering conceptual rationalizations of the new relationship—rationalizations that gave the impression, not of geopolitical maneuvering, but of accommodation to fundamental change in international politics. To what extent Soviet leaders believed their own optimistic pronouncements remains unclear.

There were major flaws in Soviet analysis of U.S. foreign policy. While Moscow was keenly aware of its pragmatic reasons for normalization with America, it tended to assume that on the U.S. side a very important

29. Nixon, *Memoirs,* p. 418.
30. For more on this, see Kenneth A. Myers and Dimitri Simes, *Soviet Decision Making, Strategic Policy, and SALT,* final report prepared for the U.S. Arms Control and Disarmament Agency by Georgetown Center for Strategic and International Studies, Washington, D.C., December 1974.

reassessment was taking place. This reassessment was thought to go beyond tactical shifts in policy, such as a temporary response to American Vietnam sentiment, a desire to enlist Moscow's help in arranging an honorable peace with Hanoi, and a fear that Western Europe would engage in détente without the United States if necessary. Soviet officials and analysts were increasingly coming to the conclusion that U.S. political realignments were more far-reaching. The new conventional wisdom in Moscow assumed that there was a new "correlation of forces" in the world arena which was more favorable to the Soviet Union, on one hand, and which restricted American freedom of maneuver, on the other. Moreover, a dominant school of thought in Moscow held that the "ruling circles" in the United States were gaining an appreciation of the significance of the "correlation of forces" and might therefore be prepared to reconcile themselves to living with the Soviet superpower.

Vietnam was perceived not just as a trauma affecting U.S. willingness and ability to conduct an assertive global diplomacy, but as a yardstick in American thinking about itself and the world. From now on the United States was expected to accept that there were not one, but two genuine superpowers. Accordingly, the Soviet Union would not need to make a painful choice between seeking American friendship and attempting to modify the international status quo to its advantage.

Needless to say, this was a convenient interpretation for the Soviet leadership to adopt. It did not mean, however, that the Kremlin had developed such contempt for the United States that it saw no reason to modify its behavior in order to promote a better relationship with it. Receiving Richard Nixon in Moscow a few days after the bombing of Hanoi and the mining of Haiphong Harbor was not a routine matter.[31] It created problems for the Soviets' image as the champion of the "anti-imperialist struggle" and staunch supporter of national liberation movements. Anwar Sadat, for one, was suspicious that the Soviet Union was reaching an accommodation with the United States at Egypt's expense.[32] And Sadat's concern was far from unique among Third World leaders.

The record indicates that between 1972 and 1975 the USSR was relatively restrained in the Third World. It did support and resupply Egypt and Syria during the October 1973 war in the Middle East, but the decision to open hostilities against Israel was made in Cairo and Damascus, not in Moscow. And the Soviet Union could not do less and still have retained its prestige in the Arab world. Moscow's threat to intervene unilaterally to save the encircled Egyptian Third Army was in response to a desperate Sadat's pleas in a situation where Moscow, together with

31. *Istoriya Vneshnei Politiki SSSR, 1917–1975*, p. 521.
32. Mohamed Heikal, *The Road to Ramadan* (New York: Ballantine Books, 1975), p. 172.

Washington, had helped to arrange a cease-fire. With its credibility at stake, the Politburo issued a threat but simultaneously indicated its strong preference for a joint action with the United States to restrain Israel.[33] From the Soviet standpoint, abandoning allies was definitely not a part of détente.

Elsewhere there were no major instances of Soviet troublemaking. Vietnam was an obvious exception. But there was a tacit understanding of sorts between the Brezhnev leadership and the Nixon-Kissinger team that both powers would live up to their commitments in Vietnam without allowing the conflict to have a negative spillover effect on the U.S.–Soviet relationship. Naturally, the lack of particularly tempting opportunities was a major factor in Soviet caution. It is impossible to know how the USSR would have reacted if the civil war in Angola had occurred during the superpowers' honeymoon. The fact remains, however, that the Soviets were at least careful in dealing with the inevitable connection between their behavior in the Third World and the status of their relations with the United States.

The Soviets were equally made aware that their relations could not be entirely divorced from the way they treated their own citizens. Under considerable U.S. pressure, Moscow allowed somewhat greater freedom for emigration, particularly for the Jews and (under separate arrangement with Bonn) for the Volga Germans. There was also greater tolerance of contacts with foreigners, including those between American reporters and Soviet citizens. Soviet concessions in the sensitive area of domestic political controls were both reluctant and marginal; and yet they cannot be dismissed entirely out of hand. The regime did not consider any benefits the United States could have feasibly offered sufficiently important to justify an internal relaxation. But it was willing to make some adjustments which, despite their token nature, complicated the business of running a totalitarian state.

Whether such minor modifications in Soviet foreign and domestic policies were meaningful requires a judgment regarding their potential to lead to other, more profound changes. And this judgment is impossible to make, because at the very time when détente was taking its first steps, Vietnam and Watergate considerably reduced the U.S. ability both to cooperate and to compete with the Soviet Union. The Brezhnev leadership was probably, in any event, disinclined to make major sacrifices in the name of rapprochement with the United States. But a combination of the Jackson-Vanik and the Stevenson Amendments—made possible by a dramatic decline of the executive branch's authority—restricting Soviet access to American credits and trade, signaled Moscow that the economic

33. Kissinger, *Years of Upheaval*, p. 241.

rewards it had anticipated receiving from the United States would be more difficult to obtain. At the same time the United States, contrary to Soviet expectations, allowed itself to be defeated in Vietnam. Soviet propaganda had, of course, been predicting this outcome for years, but private Soviet analyses had consistently argued that Hanoi would have to be satisfied with a compromise political solution. Nixon was seen as being fully committed to avoiding American humiliation. And the improved performance of the South Vietnamese army backed by U.S. air power was seen as evidence that the United States might actually succeed in sustaining Saigon's rule at an acceptable cost.[34]

Total U.S. disengagement from Vietnam thus came as a surprise to the Soviet Union. And the Clark Amendment, banning even indirect U.S. military involvement in Angola, was bound to encourage the Kremlin to believe that America was losing its appetite for geopolitical wrestling in less than crucial Third World regions. In short, by 1975, while still remaining optimistic about the long-term prospects of the U.S.–Soviet relationship, the Politburo in all likelihood felt neither so enthusiastic about the advantages of cooperation nor so concerned about the dangers of confrontation that it was willing to forego intervention in Angola.

The temptation to act as the arbiter of the Angolan civil war might have been enhanced by the fact that Soviet hopes vis-à-vis Portugal, Angola's colonial master, had just been frustrated. And after bad news from Chile, Egypt, and Portugal, the Soviets could have been looking for some "easy" foreign policy success to prove their geopolitical momentum. This could have been particularly important to the Soviet leadership on the eve of the forthcoming 25th Party Congress. In addition, Chinese assistance to other factions in Angola had, at least initially, probably challenged the Soviets' competitive instincts. Finally, South African involvement on the side of the MPLA's opponents made Soviet-Cuban intervention less controversial among the African states, and hence more attractive to the Kremlin.

Of course, without its newly developed air- and sea-lift capabilities, Moscow would have been hard put to support the Cuban intervention. And, while the effort to upgrade Soviet abilities in this area predates détente, it did not slow Soviet programs down. Nor did it change the basic commitment to strengthen Soviet armed forces across the board. There were several reasons why U.S.–Soviet rapprochement in general, and arms control negotiations in particular, did not have a noticeable effect on military planning in Moscow. To start with, if it had been a shift in the correlation of forces, including military forces, which had initially per-

34. This was the dominant view among scholars at the Institute for World Economy and International Relations in Moscow in 1969–72.

suaded Washington to accept détente with the USSR, would it not be logical to conclude that a further shift would only contribute to accommodation on Soviet terms? Since the prevailing view among the Soviet elite was that détente was a manifestation of the Soviets' new power and the Americans' new weakness, there was no reason to be too concerned about complaints in the United States regarding growing Soviet military capabilities. Such complaints were dismissed as an inevitable, but not terribly threatening, outcry on the part of those Americans who could not reconcile themselves to the "new international realities," a sort of rearguard action by cold warriors.[35]

Furthermore, Soviet perceptions of the military balance were naturally different from those in the United States. Each side in a competition has a natural tendency to focus on its own vulnerabilities. Worst-case scenarios discussed in Moscow would probably look like ridiculous fantasies to most American observers. But chances are that the Americans' worst-case predictions would look similarly outlandish when evaluated in Moscow. It is incredibly difficult for geopolitical rivals to take one another's nightmares seriously. The U.S. lead in technology was traditionally respected by the Soviet Union. Also, Soviet calculations of the military balance were not based, as they were in the United States, primarily on an assessment of U.S. and Soviet capabilities vis-à-vis each other, but rather on the assumption that in the case of war Russia might be confronted by a coalition of hostile states and would need forces to deal with all of them simultaneously. China was one consideration; NATO's European allies were another. And the unreliability of Warsaw Pact nations only added to the concern. Nobody could be sure whether their forces were more of an asset or a liability in a war. But even in peacetime, the Soviet Union's perception of its defense requirements had to be influenced by a need constantly to keep the East Europeans in line.

In short, while on the one hand the Politburo probably felt the self-confidence and assertiveness associated with emerging superpowers, on the other hand it was not sufficiently secure in the existing military balance to accept American definitions of parity. These were definitions which, in the Soviet view, failed to take account of Russia's basic loneliness in the world arena.

No Western leader could have been expected to accept the legitimacy of the argument that the Soviet Union was entitled to have superior forces on the ground in view of the fact that they had many adversaries and no genuine friends. Nevertheless, even if the Politburo was a principal

35. L. I. Brezhnev, *O Vneshnei Politike KPSS i Sovetskogo Gosudarstva: Rechi i Stati* [On the foreign policy of the CPSU and the Soviet state: speeches and articles], 2d ed. (Moscow: Politizdat, 1975), p. 660.

source of its own predicament, Brezhnev and his colleagues had to take a surrounding hostile environment into account. They could, of course, have asked themselves a number of soul-searching questions about the reasons for their loneliness and reshaped Soviet foreign policy. But soul-searching the Brezhnev regime was not.

Domestic imperatives also discouraged a benign view of military requirements. In the long run, the Soviet economy would have benefited from a reduction in the defense burden, and a military slowdown would have improved Moscow's chances for gaining access to massive Western credits and sophisticated technology. But the Politburo was faced with an immediate challenge to build and sustain the elite consensus in favor of détente.

More importantly, there was an essential national security consensus among the Soviet establishment on the need for an adequate military posture. And the Soviet decision-making process, with its notorious secrecy and compartmentalization, put the military in a strong position to determine what this adequacy specifically meant. There had to be budget and technological constraints.[36] However, it was hard to challenge the marshals and the admirals who had a near monopoly on expertise and information regarding military-operational matters and forces' capabilities and deployments.

Conceivably, policymakers might have been under greater pressure to cut defense spending if the Soviet economy had then been experiencing slowdowns of the magnitude of the 1980s. But although the rate of annual economic growth was continuously declining, it still totaled approximately 4-5 percent (roughly the level of the rate of annual defense-spending increases), and this allowed the Politburo to postpone major decisions about resource allocation. Conversely, the Soviets were not at all convinced that the United States was exercising genuine military restraint. Soviet commentators were critical of the Nixon administration's decision in the wake of the Moscow summit to ask Congress for such new strategic systems as the B-1 bomber and the Trident nuclear submarine. MIRVing of American ICBMs and SLBMs was actually enlarging the U.S. lead in strategic nuclear warheads. And the selected nuclear targeting concept enunciated by Secretary of Defense James Schlesinger was treated in Moscow as another signal that the United States was interested, not only in modernizing its strategic forces, but also in making them more usable.

Ample evidence now indicates that Soviet programs actually had the

36. Thomas W. Wolfe, "Military Power and Soviet Policy: Critical Choices for Americans," in *The Soviet Empire: Expansion and Détente*, William E. Griffith, ed. (Lexington, Mass.: Lexington Books, 1976), p. 157.

greater momentum and shifted the strategic balance in Moscow's favor. But the point is that whatever restraint the United States exercised after SALT I, it was neither sufficiently unambiguous nor sufficiently permanent to have much impact on Soviet weapons acquisition decisions.[37] And the U.S. systems were also not close enough to deployment to provide the Soviet military with real incentive to make negotiating concessions. And finally, with a development life span of five to ten years, most Soviet strategic systems would have had to have been approved in the pre-détente period in order to be ready for deployment by the mid-1970s.

Under these circumstances, it was hardly surprising that the Soviet Union, while for the most part observing the letter of SALT I (with the exception of some marginal, not necessarily intentional violations), was not ready to comply with the spirit of the agreements—at least, not as the spirit was understood in the United States. The Soviet leadership viewed SALT as a "pivotal salient" in the U.S.–USSR relationship. SALT was a symbol of Soviet strategic equality. It was expected to have a beneficial spillover effect on other areas of U.S.–Soviet contacts. It had the potential to retard, and possibly to block, some American weapons programs that exploited the U.S. technical edge. And it added an element of predictability and certainty to the Soviets' own strategic planning. Finally, the Soviet Union was not above trying to lull the United States into a false sense of security. Even if there were early signs that SALT actually might have helped the Nixon and Ford administrations to introduce the bargaining-chips concept as a justification for obtaining new types of strategic armaments, it took time for the Soviet leaders to realize their misconception.

Protection of Soviet systems remained a critical ingredient of Soviet SALT strategy. ABM, of course, was limited by the 1972 treaty. But this reflected a rather unique combination of circumstances, including uncertainty regarding the expected performance of the Soviet system, the fear that the American ABM would prove to be far superior, and the need to make a judgment as to whether the ABM or ICBM-SLBM modernization was the better way to invest limited resources. To proceed simultaneously with two programs on this scale would have required either a substantial increase in the share of the defense budget devoted to strategic forces or a significant boost in defense spending altogether. No similar choices had to be made in the middle and late seventies, and the Politburo failed to agree on major alterations in its deployment plans.

There were several instances, however, when the USSR indicated some interest in negotiated solutions which, while primarily designed to stop Trident and MX, implied that the Soviets might have been prepared

---

37. Soviet uncertainty regarding the impact of détente and SALT on U.S. military programs is well reflected in Arbatov, *Bezopasnost,* pp. 149–212.

to stop some of their new programs. In 1974 at Vladivostok, Moscow offered to ban all types of new strategic systems, meaning that the Kremlin was willing to give up its Typhoon submarine. But the Typhoon was at that point just on the drawing board and appeared a poor trade-off for Trident and other U.S. systems the USSR wanted to prohibit. Washington was not interested. Several years later, in May 1978, Gromyko suggested to Jimmy Carter that a total ban be declared on all new types of ICBMs. But as Strobe Talbott reports, the proposal was treated as a poor joke.[38] The American MX was much more important to U.S. strategic planners than a new Soviet ICBM—presumably solid-fuel follow-on to the SS-11—could be to Kremlin strategists. The Soviet offer was viewed as a crude attempt to derail the MX. Furthermore, there was some skepticism regarding the seriousness of the trade Gromyko had offered. U.S. officials still remembered how the Soviets, contrary to American hopes, had utilized ambiguous language in the 1972 Interim Agreement to deploy new ICBMs, embarrassing Kissinger in the process.

In short, in the military as in the geopolitical competition, the Soviet Union tended to rely primarily on unilateral efforts rather than cooperative arrangements with the United States, détente notwithstanding. There was an element of flexibility in the Soviet response to both Third World opportunities and military procurement. But the flexibility existed essentially on the margins. To go beyond the margins, if this was at all possible, would have required time, use of major positive and negative incentives encouraging Soviet moderation, and the pursuit of a patient, purposeful, and skillful American diplomacy. By 1974–75, Leonid Brezhnev was at the peak of his power, and he invested his personal prestige in making détente a success story. He was talking about the "materialization of détente,"[39] about making détente irreversible,[40] and even about establishing not just normal, but friendly, relations with the United States.[41] The Soviet leadership is not at the mercy of a nonexistent Soviet public opinion. And the existence of a pro-détente constituency among some foreign policy officials, analysts, and economic managers would not have caused the Kremlin political trouble if it had decided to change course. But once Brezhnev associated himself publicly and proudly with the new relationship with the United States, he developed a vested interest in giving it a chance. And as long as this relationship did not require alienating major elite constituencies and sacrificing important interests in other areas, the general secretary was likely to have some room for maneuver.

38. Talbott, *Endgame*, pp. 159–60.
39. Brezhnev, *O Vneshnei Politike KPSS*, p. 853.
40. Ibid., p. 687.
41. Ibid., p. 750.

The paralysis of American foreign policy did not allow the Nixon and Ford administrations to explore the ultimate limits of Soviet flexibility. The passage of the Jackson-Vanik Amendment greatly soured the relationship. The Kremlin's involvement in Angola drove the first nail in its coffin. At the same time, neither side was entirely sure of the profound nature of their disagreement. Both were hopeful that the damage could be repaired. But both also shared the expectation that the other side was the one that should do most of the repairing.

DÉTENTE WITHOUT STRINGS ATTACHED

Long after President Gerald Ford was compelled to drop the very word *détente* from his election campaign vocabulary, the Soviets continued to claim that the "positive accomplishments" of the early seventies could and should be preserved. Many of the same reasons which pushed the Kremlin to enter détente were still valid. And the relative success of Soviet relations with Western Europe may have suggested that a rapprochement between the two social systems was not entirely out of sight. But the Soviet interest in a lasting accommodation with the United States was not matched by a willingness to modify Soviet behavior in accordance with American requests. Not only did the Kremlin find many of these requests unacceptable, but it also had difficulty grasping what Washington was up to.

The Politburo was not solely at fault in this confusion. Under President Jimmy Carter, the United States' Soviet policy was not well defined. It suffered from many serious contradictions and failed to speak with one voice. On one hand, the new administration appeared to take a more tolerant attitude to the Soviets' Third World exploits. Carter promised to reduce U.S. defense spending and canceled the B-1 bomber without trying to use SALT to win concessions from the Soviets. News accounts revealed that consideration was being given to modifying the Jackson-Vanik and Stevenson Amendments, yet at the same time that the president launched a campaign to improve human rights in the Soviet Union. Few things the U.S. president could have done would have been equally alarming, not only to the Politburo, but to the Soviet elite as a whole. After all, if dissidents were immune to prosecution, if unofficial Russians were allowed to communicate with foreigners, if Jews and representatives of other ethnic and religious minorities had won the right, rather than the privilege, of emigration, then it would be a significantly different Soviet Union.

The Helsinki Final Act did not make Carter's criticism of Soviet repression more legitimate in Soviet eyes. Whatever was stated in this document was not legally binding and could not be used as a mandate to meddle in Soviet internal affairs. Carter, the Soviets complained, had grossly violated the previous norms of the relationship. And toward what end did he choose to support Soviet dissidents? Could he be so sentimental and naive that he was willing to jeopardize contacts with the other superpower simply out of some abstract conviction or because of a misplaced sympathy with the underdog? Or did the U.S. president have something more sinister in mind—for example, creating domestic trouble in the USSR? The answers to these questions were not readily apparent; and there seemed to be some disagreement among Soviet analysts about Carter's motives. But the controversy over human rights, while it did not eliminate Soviet interest in détente, made the Politburo increasingly suspicious about many other aspects of the United States' Soviet policy.

Carter's ill-fated March 1977 SALT proposal is a case in point. The Soviet leadership rejected it out of hand. Chances are that a number of components of this initiative would have been resisted by the USSR. But in a more cordial, less emotionally charged climate, it is also likely that Moscow would have reacted with greater calm and would have treated the package as something deserving serious study. Later, some Soviet spokesmen privately voiced regret that the Soviet Union was too hasty in denouncing the proposal. Apparently Carter's letter to Andrei Sakharov and his meeting in the White House with another Soviet dissident, Vladimir Bukovsky, coupled with the unorthodox and polemical manner in which the March 1977 initiative was disclosed, colored Soviet perceptions and contributed to the unqualified *nyet* from the Kremlin.

Geopolitically, despite Carter's declarations that his Third World policy would not be guided by "an inordinate fear of communism," the Soviet Union discovered itself increasingly at odds with the Democratic administration. In the Middle East, after signing an October 1, 1977, joint statement on the need for a comprehensive settlement (in which the Kremlin would play a major role), the United States quickly discovered that both Egypt and Israel distrusted the USSR and wanted America alone to act as an intermediary. Pressure from the Jewish community worked in the same direction. Washington could hardly be expected to insist on its rival's participation, but the USSR was understandably disappointed and bitter. To convey the depth of Soviet displeasure, Brezhnev granted a special interview to *Pravda* accusing the United States of blocking "genuine settlement."[42]

Soviet intervention on Ethiopia's side in the Ogaden war became an additional source of superpower disagreement. The strong U.S. protests against another Kremlin operation in Africa were dismissed by the Polit-

42. *Pravda*, December 24, 1977.

buro with considerable annoyance. The USSR argued that it acted at the request of a legitimate government, aiding it to rebuff foreign—in this case Somali—aggression. The fact that the Somali attack would have been difficult to mount without years of Soviet military training and arms assistance did not moderate the Kremlin's self-righteous indignation. Referring to American opposition to Soviet Third World advances, Leonid Zamyatin, chief of the Central Committee's International Information Department and a frequent spokesman for the Politburo, dryly commented during the June 1979 Vienna summit that his superiors were "quite surprised at the ease with which in the United States some sphere of the earth far from the United States is proclaimed a sphere of vital interest to the United States."

On top of everything else, Moscow was becoming increasingly concerned with the American tilt toward China. Again there was no certainty regarding how far the United States was prepared to go in building a semialliance against the USSR. Nor was there a consensus among Soviet analysts about Washington and Beijing's ability to overcome disagreements over Taiwan. But the Carter administration's gradual shift away from even-handed treatment of the two Communist adversaries was beyond doubt and could not but cause deep resentment in the Kremlin.

Why, if the Brezhnev leadership still cared about preserving what remained of détente, would it not see the wisdom of avoiding the heavy-handed behavior that contributed to U.S. disenchantment with the USSR? Did the Soviet Union have some master plan to reshape the world order that it was pursuing despite all obstacles and against all odds?

Obviously, no outsider can know for sure. But one should always be aware of the analytical danger of ascribing to opponents much greater foresight, consistency, and determination than is possessed by oneself. The issue is not whether the Soviet leadership under some ideally favorable conditions would like to achieve world domination. A more relevant question is how far the Politburo is prepared to push in a complex international environment that does not allow a significant shift in the global equilibrium without certain costs and exposure to certain risks.

Soviet spokesmen offer little assistance toward interpreting their country's motives. Soviet exploits in the Third World are verbally justified by a solemn and selfless commitment to national liberation movements. On occasion, when a state or faction in which Moscow takes an interest is located in near proximity to the USSR, the Kremlin may issue a warning that it cannot remain indifferent to what transpires in countries close to the Soviet Union's borders. No wonder, with explanations like these, that many in the West look for some far-reaching scheme behind Soviet actions.

But the aging Politburo of the late 1970s and early 1980s hardly projected the images of Caesars, Napoleons, and Hitlers. Soviet foreign policy suffered from incoherence, a reluctance to make choices, and an inability to act boldly both as an adversary and as a partner.[43] Thus, a more plausible explanation of the Soviets' aggressive pursuit of geopolitical gains in the Third World suggests that, lacking real U.S. leverage and in a climate of deteriorating relations, the Politburo was simply unprepared to accommodate American concerns. On the contrary, there could even have been a strong urge to prove to the United States and the world in general that the Soviet Union is a major global actor that cannot be pushed around. Similarly, disintegration of the much celebrated détente was enhancing the attractiveness of visible successes which would demonstrate that history was on the Soviet side.

The attempt to build the domestic and international legitimacy of the Soviet regime through a diplomacy of force has to be seen in this context. Of course, the Politburo did not decide to invade Afghanistan because of failures in the Soviet economy and the détente policy. But a general feeling that things were not going as they ought would probably have encouraged the Soviet leadership to view defeat in Afghanistan as particularly unacceptable and victory there as particularly tempting.

In Afghanistan, the Soviet Union found itself in a situation where it was supporting the failing, disobedient regime of Hafizullah Amin. The Kremlin could, of course, have abandoned Amin and let his regime die a natural death. But, bitter at Washington over the Cuban brigade controversy and aware of the turmoil in Iran that removed the shah and his formidable army as factors to cope with, the Soviets were predisposed to take their chances and to use their own forces to put an end to the rebellion.

In Kampuchea, the Soviets went along with the Vietnamese invasion, providing Hanoi with equipment and logistical support. Still, as in the case of Korea, the initiative came primarily from the ally rather than from the USSR itself. Those who, like Kissinger, have negotiated with the Vietnamese have been uniformly impressed by their dogged determination. Again, Moscow naturally could have declined to help Hanoi. But Vietnam was viewed as an important ally with great appeal in the Third World, as of immense help in encircling China, and finally as not to be relied upon to resist advances from China and even Washington if Moscow refused to cooperate. Pol Pot's regime had shortly before been described by Carter as the greatest violator of human rights in the world. Was there much reason to believe, some Soviet analysts argued, that the

43. For more, see Dimitri K. Simes, "Assessing Soviet National Security Strategy," a paper presented at the National Security Affairs Conference, National Defense University, October 8, 1982.

United States would make too much of an outcry over the Vietnamese invasion as long as the Soviet Union were not directly involved? And if the Carter administration did object—well, it seemed always to find something to object to. But what would it really do to penalize the USSR? Probably nothing that could outweigh the Soviet desire to stay on the good side of the Vietnamese and to help them eliminate Chinese influence in Kampuchea.

Yuri Andropov's accession to power did not bring radical departures in the Soviet attitude toward the United States. There was an initial improvement in the conduct of Moscow's foreign policy. But even here, perhaps because of the new General Secretary's failing health, the change did not go very far. Andropov and his colleagues seem to see little opportunity to improve relations with the United States. Reagan's seriousness about arms control is questioned in Moscow, some recent overtures by Secretary of State George Shultz and other senior U.S. officials notwithstanding.[44] And tough-minded Reagan's policy produces a resentful defiance rather than flexibility among the Soviet elite.

The Kremlin's handling of the Korean airliner tragedy is a perfect example of how marginal considerations for improving the U.S.–Soviet relationship are to the current Soviet mindset. Explaining an embarrassing situation to the domestic audience and avoiding appearing weak to the outside world clearly took precedence over the need to appear responsible and civilized to Americans and to the West in general.

Not that the Politburo is categorically rejecting any rapprochement with the United States. On the contrary, Andropov and other Soviet leaders rarely miss a chance to underline their commitment to peace and disarmament. But they appear to be skeptical about the Reagan administration's willingness to accept rapprochement on terms acceptable to the Soviet Union. As Andropov declared in his first major speech at the November 22, 1982, Central Committee Plenum:

All are equally interested in preserving peace and détente. Therefore, statements in which the readiness for normalizing relations is linked with the demand that the Soviet Union pay for this with preliminary concessions in different fields do not sound serious, to say the least. We shall not agree to this and, properly speaking, we have nothing to cancel: We did not introduce sanctions against anyone, we did not denounce treaties and agreements that were signed and we did not interrupt talks that were started. I should like to stress once more that the Soviet Union stands for accord but this should be sought on the basis of reciprocity and equality.[45]

44. *Pravda,* June 17, 1983.
45. *Pravda,* November 23, 1982.

To sum up, since 1975–76, while maintaining an interest in détente, the Soviet leadership increasingly refused to accept U.S. efforts to tie any strings to the bilateral relationship. The United States was perceived as neither so powerful an adversary nor so promising and reliable a partner that the Kremlin could be persuaded to subordinate its other interests and to forego other opportunities for the sake of its American connection. Inevitably, since the United States was the predominant global player, the Soviet Union had to view its own superpower status through the prism of competing with Washington.

LESSONS

This competitive urge is unlikely to change with Yuri Andropov's accession to power. There is little the United States can do to persuade the Soviet Union to change the Kremlin's fundamental interests in maintaining the Soviet system of government, perserving its domination in Eastern Europe, deploying multipurpose armed forces second to none, and being perceived as a truly global player. But maintenance of the Soviet system means that democratic liberties taken for granted in the West will have to be suppressed. Preservation of the Soviets' hold over Eastern Europe requires force and coercion. Multipurpose armed forces designed to respond to a variety of worst-case scenarios will undoubtedly appear threatening to many nations. And finally, acting as a global player presupposes that the Kremlin will continue to behave competitively in the Third World, challenging the American self-image and, on occasion, its truly important interests.

U.S. policy can affect Soviet choices only on the margins. But the margins are not totally irrelevant. The fact that several hundred thousand Jews were allowed to emigrate did not make the Soviet Union a democracy but was an encouraging sign in both human and political terms. Greater freedom of communication between Soviet citizens and foreigners, which, like Jewish emigration, increased and then virtually disappeared during the 1970s, was in retrospect a minor, but positive change. In Eastern Europe, no plausible Soviet leadership would tolerate an outright threat to its control. But how tight this control is going to be, to what extent it will interfere with economic and social reforms and even with some modicum of foreign policy autonomy is not set in concrete. The Soviet military buildup probably cannot be stopped or even considerably slowed down through arms control, but it may be channeled on occasion in less dangerous directions, and some particularly destabilizing systems may be blocked altogether. And in the Third World, it makes a difference whether Moscow limits itself to security assistance, relies on proxies, or uses its own troops.

Unfortunately, the record of both the U.S. ability to send clear messages to the Kremlin and the Soviet ability to interpret them correctly is anything but encouraging. Washington has been most successful when it has restricted the opportunities for Soviet imperial expansion by building an impressive military deterrent and by organizing a fairly reliable—if frequently troubling—alliance system. Moscow, accordingly, has been compelled to recognize that there are limits to how far and how fast it can proceed in the global arena without provoking a direct confrontation with the United States and its allies.

Yet, in too many instances the Politburo has underestimated U.S. determination and has initiated, or at least sanctioned, adventures, some of which, in all likelihood, it later came to regret. The Berlin blockade, the North Korean attack, the placing of Soviet missiles in Cuba, the spring 1972 North Vietnamese offensive, and the unleashing of Cuban troops in Angola were all actions undertaken or approved by the USSR without adequately anticipating the U.S. response. An impression of greater American permissiveness than in fact existed on several occasions brought both nations to the brink of disaster and probably contributed to the collapse of détente.

Conversely, in the early 1950s, the Soviets seem to have been unduly alarmed by American talk of "liberation," and in the 1970s and 1980s, U.S. preoccupation with human rights issues raised suspicions in Moscow that the United States was attempting to undermine the Soviet regime. Of course, this failure to distinguish between policy and rhetoric, between a concerted strategy and the incoherent product of the U.S. political process, could not provoke an outright conflict. Cynical practitioners of geopolitics and champions of ideological crusades themselves, the Soviet leaders are not easily impressed and are quite capable of seeing the difference between empty, even if provocative, gestures and serious threats to their own rule.

Nevertheless, the domestic security of their regime is a paramount concern of the Soviet elite. It is also one area where the national security establishment is particularly obliged to be sensitive to the views of other sectors of the bureaucracy. Accordingly, it would be an error to underestimate the considerable impact that U.S. challenges to Soviet internal legitimacy have on the Kremlin's willingness to deal with America in an open-minded, constructive fashion.

Other contributions to this volume elaborate on why the U.S. has failed to perform better in its policy toward Russia. But there is another side to the story. The Soviet Union has often not been sufficiently sensitive to American signals. To suggest that Moscow's policies are simply responses to American actions would be ethnocentric exaggeration. Russia's rulers—as preoccupied with the United States as they appear to be—

have also to be guided by their nation's domestic determinants, by their perceived security requirements, and by long-reaching international ambitions inherent in their historical tradition, ideology, and search for legitimacy. Many of these overriding hopes and fears have only an incidental connection to America. Furthermore, it is not only what America does but also what it *is*—namely, a global power representing opposite values and capable of destroying the USSR—that forces the Kremlin to see the United States as its principal foreign policy problem.

Yuri Andropov's accession to power has the potential of making the conduct of Soviet foreign policy more professional. The lack of direction and immobilism of the late Brezhnev era may be at an end. Andropov's Soviet Union may prove to be simultaneously a more formidable opponent and a less difficult partner. Here lie some new challenges to, and opportunities for, the United States. Yet neither history nor the current state of Soviet political and economic affairs offers much hope that whatever America does—in terms of competition, cooperation, and a mixture of the two—will halt the rivalry. That is a hard notion to adjust to, but there seems to be no alternative except self-delusion.

PART IV

Policy Conclusions

13

Can America Manage Its Soviet Policy?

JOSEPH S. NYE, JR.

Democracy can only with great difficulty regulate the details of an important undertaking, persevere in a fixed design, and work out its execution in spite of serious obstacles. It cannot combine its measures with secrecy or await their consequences with patience.
—Alexis de Tocqueville, *Democracy in America*

The essays in this volume are replete with examples of incoherence and inconsistency in American policy toward the Soviet Union. But does it matter? Though the record of American policy since 1945 is far from perfect, it has not been disastrous. Moreover, coherence in the process may not be the key consideration. Effectiveness is more important than efficiency, and some periods of relatively efficient management may not have been the most effective. Could one not argue that, despite its messiness, U.S. policy has been relatively successful in the postwar period? Is there a problem?

HOW WELL HAVE WE DONE?

At a high level of abstraction, the United States has sought three broad goals in its relationship with the Soviet Union: avoiding nuclear war; containing the spread of Soviet power and ideology; and gradually encouraging change in the nature and behavior of the Soviet Union. It is evident that the United States has been wholly successful in the first of these objectives and successful to a lesser extent in the second and third.

Nuclear war has been avoided, as has all direct armed conflict (though not limited wars with Soviet allies in Korea and Vietnam). Nuclear arsenals on both sides have grown greatly, but there have also been some substantial, if imperfect, efforts at arms control. Most important, the nuclear arms race has not led to nuclear conflict, and both sides have learned some prudent practices of crisis management since the Berlin and Cuba crises of the cold war period. Attributing credit may be difficult. Adam Ulam, for example, argues that what kept the Berlin and Cuba crises from erupting into wars was not only U.S. policies but also Soviet prudence.[1] The fact remains that war has been avoided.

Assessing our success in relation to the second general objective—the containment of Soviet power and ideology—is more debatable. First, there is the undeniable fact of increased Soviet military capability. During the cold war period, the United States enjoyed a distinct nuclear military advantage which it saw as balancing superior Soviet conventional capabilities. This strategic advantage was at its peak after the Kennedy buildup of the early 1960s. Faced with steady Soviet military growth, American policymakers in the mid-1960s concluded that trying to maintain strategic superiority would be both infeasible and too costly to attempt. Subsequently, Vietnam and domestic turmoil diverted resources away from the strategic budget to the point where Soviet gains in some areas, particularly land-based missiles, led some Americans to fear that even rough parity had been lost. While the significance of ICBM vulnerability is highly contested, and few American officials have expressed willingness to trade forces with the Soviet Union, most Americans agreed that Soviet military power had greatly increased since the early 1960s. Where they tended to disagree was over how inevitable that change was and how significant it was for our foreign policy objectives.

American success at political containment is also debated, in part because of ambiguities over whether the goal was the containment of Soviet power or of communist ideology. Some, like Norman Podhoretz, argue that communism is a curse, whether dominated by Moscow or not, and that the cost of our political relationship with China is "the loss of political clarity that it inevitably entails."[2] From this point of view, the existence of Marxist regimes in Angola, Laos, Vietnam, Cambodia, Mozambique, South Yemen, Ethiopia, Afghanistan, and Nicaragua is a serious setback for American foreign policy. Moreover, even those who do not worry about the ideological coloration of poor countries would admit that some of these governments are more susceptible to Soviet than to American influence. This represents an extension of Soviet influence to areas far beyond its borders.

On the other hand, it can be argued that there has been a diffusion of power away from both superpowers since the 1950s. In key areas such as Europe and Japan, the political appeal of Soviet ideology has greatly diminished since the 1940s and 1950s. Yugoslavia began the fracturing of Soviet ideological power, and the Soviets as well as the United States "lost" China. The Soviets as well as the Americans have seen Third World

---

1. Adam Ulam, *The Rivals* (New York: Viking, 1971), p. 389.
2. Norman Podhoretz, *The Present Danger* (New York: Simon and Schuster, 1980), p. 67.

clients collapse and governments turn hostile.[3] Moreover, marginal Third World gains are not nearly as significant to the balance of power in the world as the fact that the key areas of Western Europe, Japan, and the Middle East—though geographically closer to the Soviet Union—have remained politically closer to the United States. In addition, the Soviet empire in Eastern Europe is far from the politically secure bastion that the Soviets might hope it to be. In short, while the United States has not prevented the Soviets from gaining some influence in the Third World, from a geopolitical point of view the Soviets have tended to win the small ones rather than the big ones.

In terms of economic power, while the Soviet economy grew impressively in the postwar period until recently, so also did the American economy. In fact, in recent years the Soviet Union has not closed the economic gap with the United States and the Soviet gross national product still remains at little better than half the size of the American. Khrushchev's 1959 threat to overtake and bury the United States has turned out to be a hollow boast. Although American economic preponderance has declined, with the U.S. share of gross world product dropping from 33 to 22 percent of the total over the past thirty years, this relative decline has not been matched by a commensurate Soviet gain. On the contrary, the Soviet share of gross world product also declined in the past decade from 12.5 to 11.5 percent of the total.[4] Moreover, most of the American loss of relative share in world product went not to the Soviet Union but to our allies in Europe and Japan. The recovery of Europe and Japan was our deliberate foreign policy objective, in part as a means of combatting communist influence, and our success in maintaining those alliances means that our loss has not represented a Soviet gain.

A third general objective of American policy in the postwar period, albeit one that has not been pursued at all times, has been to encourage change in the nature and behavior of the Soviet Union. This has varied, from George Kennan's conception in the 1940s of waiting for Soviet power to mellow, to the Reagan administration's efforts to use economic pressures to accelerate particular types of change inside the Soviet Union. As both Dimitri Simes and Strobe Talbott have described, there have been significant changes in the Soviet Union. Although Lenin's authoritarian party structure remains, Stalin's excesses have been alleviated. Some of these changes have been influenced in part by contacts with Western society. Awareness of Western affluence and ideas stimulates popular expectations and makes it more difficult for Soviet leaders to portray

3. Richard Feinberg, *The Intemperate Zone* (New York: Norton, 1981), p. 129.
4. Herbert Block, *The Planetary Product in 1980: A Creative Pause?* (Washington, D.C.: U.S. Department of State, 1980).

America in terms of simple "demonology." It is far less certain, however, that deliberate American governmental efforts have had significant results in bringing about social change inside the Soviet Union, and in some instances they have had contrary effects. In some cases, efforts to foster emigration, internal liberalization, and human rights through quiet diplomacy or increased contacts have had marginal beneficial effects. But this third objective is a difficult one to manage when dealing with a society like the Soviet Union, and it may be just as well that, with a few exceptions, this objective has tended to rank a distant third in our priorities.

Finally, one could argue that, although oscillations have occurred in U.S. policy toward the Soviet Union, the behavior is not purely cyclical. Things never return to exactly where they were. And oscillations are typical of some aspects of the relationship more than others. For example, if one looks at defense spending or public attitudes of trust in the Soviet Union (see charts 1 and 2), oscillation is quite striking. When one looks at trade and social exchanges (charts 3 and 4), one sees a continuing upward trend rather than a reversion to the levels of earlier periods. This confirms Samuel Huntington's argument in chapter 11 that the return to hostility was not exactly the return to cold war that some observers had predicted. On the contrary, a residue of trade and contacts, as well as arms control and crisis management, make the current period of renewed

Chart 1   Public Spending and National Defense Budget Outlays
           (Billions of Constant 1980 Dollars)

Source: United States Budget, FY 1948–83

Chart 2   U.S. Public Opinion of the Soviet Union*

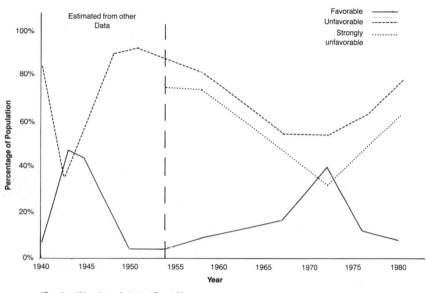

*Question: "How do you feel about Russia?"
Source: Gallup polls for period ending after 1955; pre-1955 data from Ralph B. Levering,
The Public and American Foreign Policy.

hostility quite different from the 1950s trough in the cycle of attitudes.
Thus an optimist could argue that the United States has not done badly in
pursuing its major objectives over the past four decades and that there has
even been some progress, albeit glacial, in improving the quality of the
relationship. The optimist might argue that American policy has been like
a drunk coming home from a bar: he may wander from the path from
time to time and follow a circuitous and inefficient route, but the important point is that he eventually reaches home.

The Costs of the American Policy Process

A pessimist would be less complacent. Maybe we have just been lucky thus
far. Some of the wanderings were prolonged and painful detours; and in
a nuclear age there is always the danger of a disastrous fall into an open
manhole. Moreover, the metaphor can be misleading by implying that
there can be an end to the continuing need to be attentive in managing the
relationship. Even if one agrees that the postwar record has not been bad,

Chart 3   U.S.A./U.S.S.R. Trade in Billions of U.S. Dollars
(Figures Quoted in Constant 1981 Dollars)

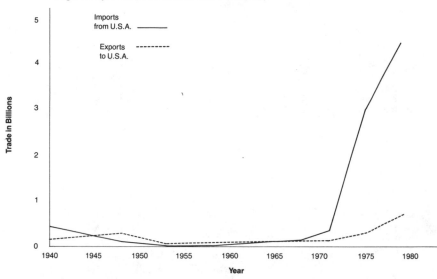

Imports
from U.S.A. ————

Exports - - - - - - -
to U.S.A.

Source: United Nations Statistical Yearbook, 1949–80/81.

Chart 4   International Tourism
(Numbers in Thousands)

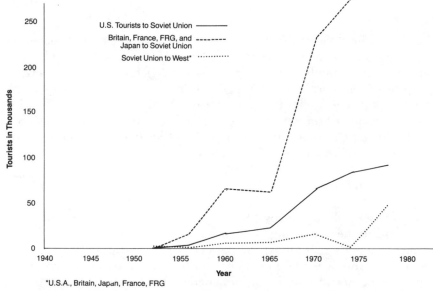

U.S. Tourists to Soviet Union ————

Britain, France, FRG, and - - - - - - -
Japan to Soviet Union

Soviet Union to West* · · · · · · · · · · ·

*U.S.A., Britain, Japan, France, FRG

Source: United Nations Statistical Yearbook, 1949–80/81.

there are significant past and potential costs to a policy marked by incoherence and inconsistency. Certainly the recent experience of negotiating major agreements in trade and arms control and then failing to ratify them, and of applying sanctions inconsistently, make it difficult to build a long-term framework for managing the relationship. There are several reasons why an inefficient process is likely to have a cost, if only the cost of opportunities foregone. It may be that equivalent or better outcomes could be achieved at lower levels of cost to our society if we followed a more coherent and consistent policy process.

First, oscillation and incoherence can be costly in terms of encouraging intransigence in our opponent and wariness about cooperative U.S. positions when we get around to them. Desired Soviet responses to our tactical moves will be delayed if Soviet leaders learn that by simply waiting they can cause the United States to drop the tactic and turn to something else. It is characteristic of U.S.–Soviet negotiations that, after the Soviets reject an American proposal, elements in the American polity proceed to bargain publicly with each other rather than with the Soviet Union.[5]

Indeed, the Soviet Union has had a long time to study American inconsistency and incoherence. During the period of nonrecognition in the 1920s, our policy "came close to being the very opposite from what Washington had intended," and in the 1930s the high expectations held out by both sides at the time of recognition soon eroded in a triumph of domestic over external considerations.[6]

Second and more dangerous, incoherence and inconsistency can lead to Soviet misperceptions of American intentions and concerns. Stalin must certainly have been surprised by Truman's reaction in Korea so soon after the U.S. secretary of state had declared it to be outside our defense perimeter. Khrushchev seems to have been surprised by Kennedy's reaction to the installation of Soviet missiles in Cuba so soon after accepting defeat in the Bay of Pigs episode. In the 1970s, Soviets who argued that the fall of Saigon and the failure of the United States to respond in Angola indicated that the United States was compelled to follow a policy of détente in accordance with the vague Marxist notion of a historical change in the "correlation of forces" between capitalism and socialism may have been surprised by renewed demands in the United States for defense spending and a return to hostility at the end of the decade.

Soviet intentions are opaque to us because of Soviet secrecy. Our

5. Congressional Research Service, *Soviet Diplomacy and Negotiating Behavior* (Washington, D.C.: U.S. Government Printing Office, 1979).
6. John L. Gaddis, *Russia, The Soviet Union and The United States* (New York: Wiley, 1978), p. 285.

intentions may be opaque to them because of incoherence and cacophony. They may be a "black box" to us, but we may confuse them with our "white noise." Efforts to sort out intended from unintended signals and to understand the intentions of our policy must be difficult for the Soviets. For example, even practiced observers of the American scene disagreed on how to interpret American reaction to an alleged Soviet combat brigade in Cuba in 1979—a clumsily handled incident that set back the ratification of SALT II. Some saw it as an accidental product of the impending electoral process; others believed it was "no accident," but a signal that Carter had turned his back on détente and arms control.[7] Sometimes creating uncertainty in the mind of an adversary can enhance deterrence. But misperceptions may lead to unintended confrontations that can lead to a failure of deterrence and the onset of war. In dealing with a stronger Soviet Union in an age of nuclear parity, the United States may not have as much leeway for incoherence, inconsistency, and inefficiency as we had in earlier periods. In an age when two such disparate societies aim 50,000 nuclear weapons at each other, the costs of miscalculation could be catastrophic.

A third cost of incoherence and inconsistency lies in weakening support from our allies and other countries. This might be called the "third audience problem." Most foreign policy issues involve at least two audiences. Political leaders try to mobilize domestic support for their policies as well as to send signals to foreign governments. But an effective policy toward the Soviet Union involves more than just the U.S. public and the Soviet government. As argued above, success in balancing Soviet power is dependent on allying major countries to the United States rather than to the Soviet Union. And as charts 5 and 6 make clear, the economic role of other countries is becoming increasingly important. An effective strategy for dealing with the Soviet Union cannot be considered in bilateral terms alone. With reduced American preponderance, more attention must be given to the concerns of allied and other countries. Oscillation and inconsistency confuse, not only the Soviets, but also our allies, and make it more difficult to maintain a common position. It was not only impossible to obtain allied agreement to cancel the natural-gas pipeline from the Soviet Union while the United States lifted its embargo against Soviet grain exports, but the effort to do so managed to turn an East–West issue into a West–West dispute and presented the Soviets with a political windfall. As several of the chapters in this book point out, dividing Western alliances has been a long-standing Soviet foreign policy ob-

---

7. Based on conversations at the Institute of the United States and Canada, Moscow, May 1981. See also Gloria Duffy, "Crisis Prevention in Cuba," in Alexander L. George, ed., *Managing U.S.–Soviet Rivalry* (Boulder, Colo.: Westview Press, 1983), pp. 285–318.

Chart 5   U.S.A., Soviet, and World GNP
          (1980 Constant Dollars)

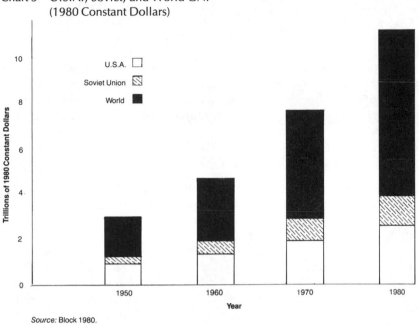

Source: Block 1980.

Chart 6   U.S.S.R. Trade in Billions of U.S. Dollars
          (Figures Quoted in Constant 1981 Dollars)

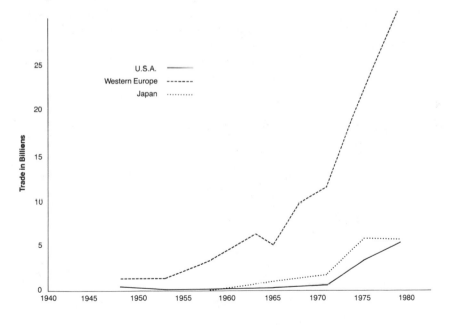

Source: United Nations Statistical Yearbook, 1949–80/81.

jective, and maintaining such alliances is a key to an effective policy toward the Soviet Union.

Thus one can agree with the optimist that the overall management of the U.S.–Soviet relationship in the postwar period has not proven disastrous but also agree with the pessimist that the past and potential costs of incoherence and inconsistency are too high to allow one to feel sanguine about the future.

THE CAUSES OF INCOHERENCE AND INCONSISTENCY

No foreign policy can be fully consistent. By its nature, foreign policy involves balancing competing objectives in a frustrating and changeable world. Every country faces a problem of relating ends and means—of defining its goals and interests so that they can be met within available levels of resources. The Soviets have not always been consistent or coherent in their policies: Khrushchev was certainly far from clear in his foreign policy signals and eventually was fired for his "harebrained schemes."[8] But as I wrote in chapter 1, the inconsistency and incoherence in American foreign policy are rooted in our political culture and institutions. The eighteenth-century founders of the republic deliberately chose to deal with the danger of tyrannical power by fragmenting and balancing power rather than centralizing and civilizing it. In a sense, a potential degree of incoherence and inconsistency in foreign policy is part of the price we pay for the way we chose to defend our freedoms. In the words of Congressman Barber Conable, "The American people are sufficiently skeptical so that, given the choice between efficiency and impotence, they will usually choose impotence."[9] For better *and* worse, we are a government of "separated institutions and sharing powers."[10]

The executive branch has certain natural advantages over the Congress in the constitutional "invitation to struggle" for control of foreign policy. Even so, the Congress has a broad set of legitimate means to block, divert, or alter foreign policy initiatives if it so chooses. The system tends to work best when two conditions are fulfilled: (1) the president has a relatively coherent strategy and smooth executive branch process; and (2) there is a general executive-legislative compact, sometimes symbolized as "bipartisanship" in foreign policy.

By and large, this was the situation during the cold war period. I. M.

---

8. Ulam argues that Khrushchev's pressure on Berlin was an invitation to a thoroughgoing accommodation, "but he certainly chose a strange way to pursue these objectives." *The Rivals,* p. 285.

9. Quoted in "What the Next 50 Years Will Bring," *U.S. News and World Report,* May 9, 1983, p. 33.

10. Richard Neustadt, *Presidential Power* (New York: Wiley, 1980), p. 26.

Destler lists three conditions that contributed to the relative harmony between the branches of government in that era: (1) deference to the president on the big questions; (2) sufficient centralization in the Congress to allow congressional leadership; (3) a general consensus on the Soviet threat and how to meet it. By the late 1960s, all three of these conditions had greatly eroded.

It is important, however, not to idealize the cold war policy process. First, the period of the "imperial presidency" was more the exception than the norm in the politics of foreign policy. Second, even when conditions were favorable, there were problems with the process of managing our relations with the Soviet Union. As Ernest May argues, even under favorable conditions the Executive's need to develop sustained support from Congress and the public often requires oversimplification. Exaggeration is part of the process of collecting power in a polity characterized by fragmented institutions and dispersed political elites. It is difficult to maintain nuances, fine-tuning, or small adjustments in course. In the early postwar period, as the inherited Roosevelt strategy eroded, the Truman administration understated the Soviet threat; but in searching for a new consensus it later overstated and overly militarized both the threat and the response. In May's view, the shift from management of the relationship as one involving primarily political and economic competition to one primarily military in character is largely to be explained in terms of how men in the executive branch perceived changing requirements and opportunities for mustering domestic support. This does not imply cynicism. The drafters of a planning document like NSC 68 in 1950 took the Soviet military threat seriously, but they saw exaggeration as necessary to motivate a democratic polity into a prompt and adequate response.

The cold war era was also marked by difficulty in framing and maintaining support for a strategy that established a consistent and effective relationship between ends and means in American policy. This difficulty was exacerbated by our liberal political cultural reaction to the harsh reality of Soviet expansion and the resulting excoriation of the Soviets in our domestic electoral competition. As I argued in chapter 1, when liberal moralism faced the reality of amoral Soviet policy, there was a sense of shock and indignation. Analogies were drawn to the 1930s, and Stalin was portrayed as similar to Hitler. As Alan Wolfe argues, there was a bipartisan consensus during the cold war, but the rhetoric of foreign policy was consistently tugged to the right in the competition between the political parties.[11] In these circumstances, it was difficult to maintain support for

11. Alan Wolfe, *The Rise and Fall of the Soviet Threat* (Washington, D.C.: Institute for Policy Studies, 1979), p. 36.

Kennan's conception of selective containment by limited means, since it depended on "the ability of national leaders to make and maintain national distinctions between vital and peripheral interests, adversary capabilities and intentions, negotiations and appeasement, flexibility and direction."[12]

The exaggerated threat described in NSC 68 called for means that were far in excess of what was domestically feasible—which in turn was part of the reason for the exaggeration. A gap developed between election rhetoric and policy implementation. The Republicans spoke of "rolling back" communism in 1952, but within six months Eisenhower adopted more modest goals and his fiscal conservatism led him to reduce the demand for military means. Similarly, Kennedy came into office sounding like an echo of NSC 68, but later in 1963 he tried to adjust goals and means to a more modest direction in some aspects of policy (though not in Vietnam). In short, even in the cold war era, when the parts of the political system worked relatively harmoniously with each other, that harmony had to be purchased at a considerable price. As James A. Nathan and James K. Oliver state: "Policy consistency built on the smothering of the inherently conflictual institutional relationships of the American system contributed by the late 1960s and early 1970s to the collapse of the policy consensus in the 1970s. The coherence of bipartisanship led ultimately to a complacency in Congress and an atrophying of its role in policy formulation."[13]

Nixon and Kissinger developed a strategy that placed fewer demands on American resources in the effort to relate ends and means. An opening to China was used as a means to encourage better Soviet behavior. Arms control agreements codified Soviet parity but were also intended to constrain further Soviet growth at a time when our defense budget was under domestic attack. Trade and a web of cooperation agreements were tacitly linked to imroved Soviet behavior in relation to Third World crises. The Nixon approach to détente was dictated, not by goodwill toward the Soviet Union, but by the need to adjust to changes in Soviet military power and in American domestic conditions.

An effective foreign policy strategy must set forth a general long-run vision that combines a reasonable and persuasive account of Soviet intentions and capabilities with an account of our long-term goals and the feasibility of our means for achieving these goals. In that regard, the Nixon concept of a two-track approach combining selective containment

---

12. John L. Gaddis, *Strategies of Containment* (New York: Oxford University Press, 1982), p. 88.

13. James A. Nathan and James K. Oliver, *Foreign Policy Making and the American Political System* (Boston: Little, Brown, 1983), p. 254.

with economic incentives made sense, although Stanley Hoffmann points out that the design was still too ambitious in its view of our ability to control Soviet behavior. Equally important, a strategy must include a third dimension, which is domestic political acceptance of the strategy as desirable and feasible. And in that area the Nixon-Kissinger strategy was not successful.

The usual explanation is that the "accident" of Watergate derailed the Nixon strategy. Watergate certainly had an effect in contributing to public mistrust and sapping executive strength. It may also have emboldened the Soviets to take greater risks. But the trouble with Watergate as a full explanation is that it pays insufficient heed to some of the deeper causes in the American political structure. Not only was the Nixon-Kissinger strategy overly ambitious in its broad definition of American interests, but it was difficult to implement in our political system. It relied on fine-tuning where fine-tuning is difficult to manage. It relied on secrecy in a system in which the media are a virtual fourth branch of government. It depended upon personal control that worked when things went well but that left few congressional and bureaucratic allies to share the burden when things went badly. Moreover, it provided insufficient points of access for allied countries to learn what was happening. Only when there is such access can allied leaders gradually adjust their policies without suffering public shocks that are jolting to democratic politicians.

Perhaps the most damning of Hoffmann's criticisms is that eventually the Nixon strategy succumbed to the typical American tendency to exaggerate as a means of building and maintaining consensus. In this case, it was not the exaggeration of the threat but the exaggeration of Soviet change. Pressed by Vietnam and domestic turmoil, Nixon compensated by exaggerating the new structure of peace that was being created. Moreover, as Hoffmann says, the appetite for détente grew with the eating; détente was oversold to the American public. The net effect was a sense of deception and disillusionment in response to Soviet actions that accentuated the ensuing turn of the cycle of attitudes in the direction of renewed hostility.

At the same time, the domestic problems of the Nixon-Kissinger strategy were also related to the period. It might have been more successful in an earlier period, but by the late 1960s the American political constellation was undergoing some profound changes that would have made any strategy difficult. A basic trend was the ideological realignment of the two major political parties that started with the Goldwater candidacy in 1964 and culminated in the Reagan election of 1980. The long-standing coalition of southern conservatives and northern urban groups in the Democratic party, stemming back to Civil War days and reconfirmed in the Roosevelt coalition of the Depression, began to fall apart under the social stresses of the 1960s.[14] While some southern conservatives remain in the Democratic party and some liberals remain Republican, their numbers are much lower in the 1980s than before the gradual party realignment began.

During the two decades of realignment, party activists tended to pull the two parties away from the center. At times, the activists became more concerned about winning the ideological struggles to control each party than winning elections by centrist appeals. Among the results were the growth of ideological challenges to presidents in their own party primaries; shortening of presidencies; and increased controversy over foreign policy (which in turn contributed to further party disarray). Not surprisingly, among the casualties were the bipartisan tradition in foreign policy and deference to the president—two of the conditions that had helped to smooth relations between the separate branches of government in the cold war era.

Gradual party realignment was not the only problem in this period. Huntington cites the reaction against the welfare state and cultural changes of the 1960s, the revival of religious fundamentalism, the economic and demographic rise of the South and West, and the neoconservative challenge to liberalism. And reactions to the Vietnam War had a deeply divisive effect. William Schneider describes the role that television played in forcing international news upon the noninternationalist majority of the public and the increased volatility this created in public attitudes. Robert Bowie notes the corrosive effects on public trust of deceptive practices by presidents Johnson and Nixon and the way this contributed to the development of anti-Establishment attitudes.

Another political trend that accompanied the rise of anti-Establishment attitudes was the "democratization" of institutions. This took several forms. In the Congress, the weakening of seniority and the committee system opened opportunities for younger congressmen but also weakened congressional leadership. The net effect, says Destler, was to make executive-legislative bargaining more difficult and to open the way for more entrepreneurial congressmen (and ambitious staffs) to create surges in attention and neglect of various issues affecting U.S.–Soviet relations. In the society as a whole, the emphasis on participation and reduction in authority tended to erode deference to the president. Schneider finds this particularly true of the media in the post-Vietnam and post-Watergate 1970s. He sees them as increasingly perceiving their role in adversarial terms, as a loyal opposition to all governments. Whatever the

14. See the essays in Joel Fleischman, ed., *The Future of American Political Parties* (New York: Prentice-Hall, 1982), particularly Gary Orren, "The Changing Style of American Party Politics."

benefits of such a role, there tend to be costs in terms of the president's ability to communicate a long-term strategy and sustain a consensus around it.

Thus the 1970s would have been a difficult period to implement any strategy of relations toward the Soviet Union, much less one that depended upon fine-tuning, linkage, secrecy, and personal control. As the decade wore on and the conservative trend in the cycle of American politics gathered strength, the domestic climate for détente worsened. As Huntington notes, the period of renewed hostility at the end of the decade was a product of the coincidence of a conservative trend in American politics interacting with a Soviet military buildup and extension of Soviet-Cuban military influence in several Third World countries. Given the earlier American exaggeration of the benign shift in Soviet behavior at the height of détente, some increase in defense expenditures and toughening of attitudes was appropriate in the 1970s, but the subsequent degree of renewed hostility was the result of the combination that Huntington describes.

Huntington's argument about the breakdown of détente reminds us of the important effect of Russian behavior on American politics. The American political process may exaggerate and amplify Soviet actions, but the Soviets have contributed to the process by their seeming failure to take into account the effects which their actions have on American politics. When Stalin permitted the invasion of Korea, he confirmed the views propounded in NSC 68 and contributed to the massive increase in defense spending it called for. Some détente, albeit a weakened one, might have survived Watergate if it had not been for the Soviet airlift of Cuban troops to Angola. SALT might have been ratified had the Soviet involvement in Ethiopia and the invasion of Afghanistan not taken place.

Georgy Arbatov, a leading Soviet expert on the United States, declares that if détente had been pursued more vigorously many events in the Third World "might have taken a different shape" and "been managed by political means." He rejects Soviet responsibility for the breakdown of détente, placing the blame on American hawks and arguing that Soviet restraint in the Third World would only have whetted their appetites.[15] Huntington does indeed show that there are few groups with intense interest in U.S.–Soviet relations and that a group such as the Committee on the Present Danger had the key requisites of intensity, expertise, and money. But their capacity to affect public opinion and votes was greatly enhanced by their ability to point to Soviet actions that appeared to corroborate their arguments. Dimitri Simes may be correct in his description

15. Georgy Arbatov, "Commentary," in Arthur Macy Cox, *Russian Roulette: The Super-power Game* (New York: Times Books, 1982), p. 180.

of the improvements the Soviets have made in moving from crude demonology to a better understanding of American politics, but their actions show that there is still a long way to go. Their actions raise doubts
about both their intentions and their ability to predict the way Americans
will react. One wonders how much they will improve before the next turns
in the American political cycle.[16]

WHAT IS TO BE DONE?

Looking ahead, there are grounds to hope for improvement in our management of relations with the Soviet Union. Public opinion at the mass
level is still centrist in its demands for a policy that balances "peace and
strength," though, as Schneider points out, mass public opinion does not
weigh international issues very intensely and events can pull noninternationalist opinion back and forth between its dual concerns. More important is the fact that the process of party realignment may be nearing its
completion, with the attendant effect that party activist opinion may move
back toward the center as the activists focus on winning the mass vote
rather than struggling for the soul of the party. If so, the result may be a
return to stronger and longer presidencies. This would alleviate the discontinuities caused by the turnover of the top of the executive branch in
our system that inevitably follows each change of presidency. In addition,
it could improve the prospects for bipartisanship in foreign policy and
thus ease the struggles between the executive and legislative branches. An
optimist might add the hope that economic constraints and the lessons of
the 1970s may deter the new Soviet leadership from Third World adventures of the sort that proved such irritants in American politics in the last
decade.

But even if the optimists are correct, there are still problems to be
faced, as we saw from our inspection of the cold war period. The problems of exaggeration will remain; though ironically, if the optimists are
correct, the next exaggeration may be of benign change in Soviet policy
rather than the current one of the Soviet threat. Developing a clear strategy for the long run is not easy in American politics. Indeed, for reasons I
discussed in chapter 1, it is difficult for Americans to think of relations
with the Soviet Union as a long-term process to be managed indefinitely
rather than as a near-term problem to be "solved."

16. On how far the Soviets have come and have to go, see William Zimmerman, *Soviet
Perspectives on International Relations, 1956–1967* (Princeton: Princeton University Press,
1969), and Morton Schwartz, *Soviet Perceptions of the United States* (Berkeley: University of
California Press, 1978).

The Choice of Strategy

The first requirement for successful long-term management is a flexible strategy that combines a sensible vision of the future and a definition of our interests with appropriate means in a manner that can sustain domestic support. As John Lewis Gaddis points out, since 1947 there have been variants of one basic strategy—containment.[17] The broadest choice in strategy is between containment and totally new approaches. If one assumes that options such as isolation or a joint U.S.–Soviet condominium are not feasible in domestic or international politics, then there are two basic alternatives to containment: one in the direction of a more active confrontation with the Soviet Union and the other in the direction of a less active American role.

Those who are deeply pessimistic about our ability ever to manage Soviet relations successfully might be tempted to urge a less active American role. From this point of view, the only sensible strategy is to encourage the development of a multipolar world in which Soviet power will be balanced and contained by others as much as by the United States. So long as nuclear bipolarity is combined with ideological rivalry, the American public will remain obsessed with the Soviet Union, and the electoral process will press politicians toward exaggerations in the formulation of policy. In a true multipolar world, one would have to consider the Soviet Union as a potential partner in shifting coalitions balancing Chinese, Japanese, and European power. In these circumstances, our domestic politics would show less of a fixation on the Soviet Union, and policy might be easier to manage.

There are a number of problems with such a strategic vision, however. Our experience of multipolar balances comes from the prenuclear age. There may be greater dangers of miscalculation in the management of deterrence if coalitions shift quickly in the nuclear age. Moreover, even if the end result were desirable it might be destabilizing to try to get from here to there, since the process would involve the massive nuclear arming of Germany and Japan, with uncertain effects on Soviet perceptions. In fostering such proliferation, we might be throwing wide open the lid of Pandora's nuclear box, as others rush to emulate. Moreover, the benefits in terms of American politics and policies toward the Soviet Union might prove to be ephemeral. After all, there were ideological hostility and wide oscillations in our policies toward the Soviet Union in the period of multipolar balance before World War II.

There is a kernel of wisdom in the vision of the multipolar strategy. A

17. Gaddis, *Strategies of Containment*.

degree of multipolarity already exists at the political, if not the military, level. Containment of Soviet power is not a task for the United States alone, as Nixon's opening to China made clear. And the increased economic strength of Europe and Japan must be factored into any strategy. It is even conceivable that over the very long term such a world may evolve. But to set as our goal the creation of such a world would not only be difficult; it would have the high cost of threatening the basis of the postwar alliance strategy that has worked so far, in return for uncertain domestic and international benefits in the future.

The other major alternative to containment is an active policy of confrontation designed to force change in the Soviet Union. At times the Reagan administration has shown inclinations in this direction, though by and large the main lines of its policy have hewed to the existing path of containment. Some who urge a confrontation strategy offer a long-run vision of a Soviet empire in decline. Economic growth has slumped from 6 percent to roughly 2 percent a year. Corruption and inefficiency are rampant. Demographic trends will exacerbate the nationalities problem inside the Soviet Union, and there is restiveness in the empire in Eastern Europe. In these circumstances, it is argued, curtailment of trade and scientific exchanges and the threat of a new arms race could force the Soviets to change, or at least force them to turn from expensive external adventures to domestic economic reforms.

This strategy also raises fundamental questions. Is it prudent in a world of nuclear-armed powers to try to press an opponent to the wall? The reckless performance of Austria-Hungary on the eve of World War I would indicate that declining empires can be very dangerous actors in the balance of power. Moreover, do we really know how to bring about reform in the Soviet Union? Is there good reason to believe that, faced with a choice, the Soviets would choose butter rather than guns? Or that they can be prevented from producing adequate guns? Strobe Talbott argues that hard times are more likely to breed hard lines.[18] In addition, Marshall Goldman and Raymond Vernon raise questions about the economic assumptions that underlie a confrontation strategy, and recent CIA reports indicate that "the ability of the Soviet economy to remain viable in the absence of imports is much greater than that of most, possibly

18. David Satter, "Soviets Limit Personal Liberties at Home as Relations with the West Deteriorate," *The Wall Street Journal*, September 29, 1982. "Russian-language radio broadcasts from abroad, which were heard by millions of people in the Soviet Union during the 1970s, are now being jammed consistently. Emigration from the Soviet Union, which reached a peak of 5,000 persons a month in late 1979, has all but ceased. And the number of telephone lines connecting the Soviet Union with the West has been reduced by two-thirds" (p. 36).

all, other industrialized countries. . . . Consequently the susceptibility of the Soviet Union to economic leverage tends to be limited."[19]

Nor is it clear that in a period of low economic growth we have the means to implement such a strategy, either in terms of budgetary resources or in the curtailment of trade that is profitable to significant electoral groups like farmers or to our allies. The effort to enforce such a strategy would certainly prove costly, yet the historical record shows that Soviet resistance is likely to be far more coherent and sustained than American persistence or consistency in the strategy. Once again, we are faced with a strategic option that presents formidable problems of feasibility combined with high present costs in return for very uncertain future benefits.

Thus the difficulties of the alternatives, both in terms of the uncertainty of their goals and the feasibility of their means, drives us back to the historically proven center ground of containment. But there are many paths to choose among in the center, and the slogan of containment can be misleading. If containment is thought of as balancing Soviet power by a variety of political and diplomatic means, then it is merely the traditional common sense of balance-of-power politics. But if containment implies a broad definition of American interests that leads to efforts to counter every Soviet action or ally in the Third World, it would soon surpass our means, including the critical resource of domestic political support. The lesson of Vietnam is that an overly ambitious definition of interests that creates a gap between ends and means can lead to severe oscillations in foreign policy attitudes. One might label a centrist strategy as "containment with communication and negotiation" or a "managed balance of power" approach.

The important point is that conflict with the Soviet Union is endemic in the structure of the bipolar relationship. Hopes to terminate the conflict quickly by accommodation or victory are unlikely to be realized. The problem is one of long-term management. At the same time, successful management of a balance of power requires communication and negotiation between the opponents.[20] And a successful foreign policy for managing such a balance requires reliance upon multiple sources of strength—economic, political, military—and a selectivity in goals that maintains a balance between ends and means. The essays in this book offer three important lessons to guide such a strategy.

First is the importance of a moderate design to insure that policy can

19. Henry Rowen, chairman of the CIA National Intelligence Council, *The New York Times*, January 9, 1983.

20. See Paul G. Lauren, "Crisis Prevention in Nineteenth-Century Diplomacy," in George, *U.S.–Soviet Rivalry*.

be durable and robust. Some aspects of our policy process can be improved (as we shall see below), but others are deeply rooted in our political culture and institutions. Our problems are more constitutional than organizational. There are no quick fixes. A basic principle for a durable strategy is to cut the coat of foreign policy to fit the rather rare eighteenth-century domestic cloth that we have inherited. The importance of this principle cannot be overstated: we have ignored it at our cost. In chapter after chapter, we read that fine-tuning is impossible, secrecy difficult, oversimplification likely, and pluralism of views of the Soviet Union unavoidable. Thus a successful strategy must be moderate in three ways: in its definition of American interests; in its cautious rather than optimistic expectations of Soviet behavior; and in its assessment of American politics—meaning a hardheaded appraisal of what resources the electorate will devote to what interests and for how long. This does not mean a low profile in countering Soviet power. On the contrary, it means recognizing that only a moderate strategy will be robust enough to survive our domestic climate and be durable in the face of any tendency toward pendular swings in attitudes. Only a moderate strategy will allow leaders to close the gap between ends and means. The point seems obvious until one reflects on how often we have failed to achieve it.

A second lesson from this volume, stressed particularly by Talbott and Simes, is that the Soviet Union is also unlikely to change quickly but does evolve slowly and unevenly. Thus we will continue to be faced with a closed and secretive society that is difficult to understand. On the other hand, the Soviet Union has opened up somewhat over the past thirty years. There are more contacts. There is more sophistication in the perception of outside reality. There are more pinholes letting light into the black box.

Specifying a broadly shared, long-range goal is an important precondition for creating the policy legitimacy needed to undergird a durable strategy. Avoiding nuclear war by counterbalancing Soviet power and gradually reducing the risks associated with nuclear deterrence is such a goal.

If misperception and miscalculation are the conditions that are most likely to cause a breakdown of nuclear deterrence, then one of the long-term security objectives in our strategy should be to encourage a process of evolving openness and communication. The Soviet Union remains very opaque to us, as a number of legislators noted when trying to decide how to vote on the MX missile. "When you play cards against someone," noted Congressman Dan Glickman of Kansas, "you ought to know something about them. Unfortunately, our judgments turn out to be highly subjective for the most part." Or, in the words of Senator Richard Lugar of Indiana, "We try to figure out where they're coming from, but it could well be the blind leading the blind."[21] Increased contact and communication can help to poke holes in the black box of Soviet society and gradually increase its transparency.

Change inside the Soviet Union will be gradual and hard to gauge, and we can at best encourage rather than hope to guide it. Nonetheless, this possibility suggests that a managed balance-of-power strategy should involve routine and regular communication. From this point of view, our tactics should include engaging the Soviets in prolonged strategic discussions; holding talks at high level on force structure and stabilization measures; and considering crisis-prevention techniques, not necessarily in the expectation of signing formal agreements, but as a means of enhancing transparency and communication.[22] It also follows that trade, scientific and cultural exchanges, and tourism should be evaluated by the same standard and not solely by the current criteria of economic benefits and short-term security interests. A managed balance-of-power strategy does not rest on expectations that increasing engagement will win Soviet trust or greatly constrain Soviet actions. Nor does it rest on any immediate liberalizing effects of "goulash communism." In the first instance, it rests on the importance of enhancing transparency and communication.

A third major lesson that can be drawn from this book is that indirect means of containing or balancing Soviet power are as important as direct dealing with the Soviets. Both because the Soviets will resist efforts to change them quickly and because our politics tend to undermine our own persistence in pursuing such efforts, our direct efforts will often face frustration. An indirect approach is more likely to succeed both at home and abroad. We may be most successful in containing Soviet power by constraining their opportunities in the rest of the world. Maintaining the Western alliance system has been the key to the success of containment thus far, and this is an area where the pluralism of American institutions can be a help rather than a hindrance by providing multiple points of access and reassurance. As Destler points out, in the recent period Europeans nervous about Reagan's nuclear rhetoric were able to get access to and reassurance from key congressional chairmen. Similar points are made by Bowie and Hoffmann in regard to the importance of transgovernmental contacts among bureaucracies.

The growing complexity of world politics, with its increasing actors and issues and the inevitability of turmoil in the Third World as fragile polities come under the stress of social modernization, means that we can

21. "Gambling on the Russian Response to the MX Missile," *The New York Times*, June 4, 1983.

22. For elaboration, see J. S. Nye, "The Future of Strategic Arms Control," in Barry Blechman, ed., *Rethinking the U.S. Strategic Posture* (Cambridge, Mass.: Ballinger, 1982).

never hope to control completely the milieu of world politics as part of a strategy of containment. But a realization of these problems and of the diffusion of economic power to our allies should reinforce our attention to the indirect dimensions of our policy in managing relations with the Soviet Union. As Alexander George points out, crisis prevention is not merely a bilateral issue. Or, as Goldman and Vernon argue, a strong world economy with effective linking among the noncommunist market economies may be a more robust economic strategy than one that tries to fine-tune East–West trade or breaks Western unity over an abortive attempt at embargo. An effective strategy rests on the comparative advantage of America's economic power and presence in the world economy as well as on the traditional political and military aspects of balancing Soviet power.

At a level of specific issues, the book provides a number of more detailed suggestions about a managed balance-of-power strategy. Managing the defense and nuclear issues is basic, not only because a strong defense and clear signals are essential for an effective policy of deterrence toward the Soviet Union, but because, as Destler, Betts, and Schneider point out, domestic and allied confidence in the strength of our deterrent is a necessary condition for the rest of our policy toward the Soviets. Betts argues that uncertainty about security exacerbates the domestic debate and hinders effective steps toward arms control. Both May and Betts point out the dangers in the practice of exaggerating the Soviet threat as a means of generating support for the defense budget. The net effect is inconsistency, as the public eventually reacts to the exaggeration. To counter this tendency, Betts recommends steps for improving our estimates; integrating arms control with defense planning; negotiating in smaller (but related) packages; and avoiding the rhetorical excesses that prove disruptive to the alliance and to domestic support for a consistent defense program over the long term.

Looking at crisis management and prevention, Alexander George urges that we eschew large dramatic gestures and formal agreements such as those of 1972 and 1973, but that we engage the Soviets in quiet discussions of classic techniques (neutralization, buffer states, spheres of concern) for avoiding crisis escalation. Such talks could extend or be related to discussions of nonproliferation of nuclear weapons or of particularly dangerous conventional weaponry. Equally important will be efforts at home to redefine our interests in the less expansive terms of selective containment. As originally outlined by George Kennan, the most cost-effective way of containing Soviet power is through reliance on the swelling nationalistic currents in other states. This entails learning to live with disagreeable regimes and distinguishing those Third World situations where our interests would be deeply involved (for example, Saudi

Arabia) from those where they are less centrally involved (for example, Southeast Asia).

A critical problem, of course, is maintaining domestic support for carefully graded degrees of interest in Third World conflicts, particularly since adventuresome Soviet policies, like those pursued in the 1970s, may create a degree of American interest where none existed before. And such questions can become clubs in domestic political debates. Two devices can be used to prevent such debates from driving a managed balance-of-power strategy seriously off course. The first is presidential education of the public about the problem of limited ends and means. The second is a continuing quiet dialogue with the Soviet Union about the interests they have in the process of crisis prevention if they do not want to see a repetition of the 1970s escalation in public hostility toward the Soviet Union, with its concomitant effects on defense issues and trade. This is not a tactic of linkage; rather, it is an education of the Soviets in the inevitability of inherent linkage through a better understanding of public opinion in the United States.

As for the economic component of a managed balance-of-power strategy, Goldman and Vernon warn against too ambitious an approach. While they admit the importance of controlling a narrow set of technologies where we are sure of the direct military relevance, they caution that we know too little about the net effects on the Soviet economy and have too poor a grasp of our own or of allied political processes to engage in a policy of detailed linkage or finely-tuned leverage. The signals we would try to send would inevitably come across as too confusing to justify the costs we would incur in trying to send them. Because interest groups will always be hard to control—witness Reagan's capitulation to the farmers—and the effects on the Soviet Union are debatable, it is better to focus controls on those situations, such as trade in technology, that shorten military lead times, where a clear and present danger is demonstrable.

While it is silly to approach Soviet trade with a laissez-faire attitude, a total embargo is also unrealistic. An effective policy of broad economic denial is simply not available at acceptable levels of cost in terms of the Western alliance, which is a central feature in balancing Soviet power. Whatever Americans may think of the wisdom of their position, the Europeans and the Japanese can be expected to weigh quite heavily the economic dimensions of any policy toward the Soviet Union. At the same time, any effective efforts at denial will increasingly require the cooperation of the Europeans and the Japanese. Goldman and Vernon argue that, since a strong denial policy is ruled out as infeasible and costly to alliance relations, the U.S. should pursue increased economic ties with the Soviet Union, in the hope of exploiting the advantages from such a policy. Within limits, that makes sense. Those limits include restrictions on militarily significant technology and on the development of trade patterns that increase the vulnerability of democratic governments to Soviet pressure because of an excessive level of dependence in particular sectors. Goldman and Vernon caution that the economic consequences of a broad denial policy could disrupt Western trade, unless the West concurrently could find common rules of the game on the basis of which to expand those economic contacts. As a supplement to efforts to develop common rules, they urge the strengthening and invigorating of the alternative economic opportunities that Western Europe and Japan might enjoy—namely, a more effective intra-Western trading system. In short, the American comparative advantage lies in strengthening the open international economy in which we presently loom large and the Soviets small, rather than squandering Western unity over futile efforts to prevent the Soviets from gaining any benefits from that economy.

Finally, as already indicated, Talbott urges caution and realism in our expectations of bringing about social change in the Soviet Union. An idealistic concern for human rights is a domestic American reality that a managed balance-of-power strategy must accept. Americans cannot live by balance of power alone. Nevertheless, a confrontational human rights policy is likely to be counterproductive in terms of the interests of Soviet citizens. Sometimes, however, minor improvements can be made through quiet diplomacy. In general, Talbott argues, the fate of human rights in the Soviet Union is adversely affected by the worsening of the overall climate of U.S.–Soviet relations. Both Simes and Talbott believe that government actions that promote social contact and quiet diplomacy rather than public government efforts targeted at individuals or Soviet policies are more likely to serve both human rights and our long-term objective of enhancing the degree of openness and communication in the relationship.

Improving the Policy Process

Even if the coat of strategy must be cut to fit the cloth of American political reality, there are still some specific steps that might be taken to improve the quality of the tailoring. A variety of suggestions have been made both in the chapters in this volume, and by others, to improve the quality of U.S. management of relations with the Soviet Union. These would entail changes at the constitutional, organizational, and attitudinal levels.

At the constitutional level, there have been suggestions for constitutional amendments that would make congressional terms coterminous with that of the president or would lengthen the presidential term to six years.[23] The first might strengthen presidential influence over Congress; the second would allow more time between the disruptive electoral cycles to carry out the negotiations of difficult detailed agreements with the Soviet Union.

It can be argued that these approaches visualize the president as a manager who needs to be freed to concentrate on substance, whereas his proper role is to concentrate on politics. In the logic of democratic theory, politics disciplines substance to the will of the people. If the implicit role is the role of prime minister in a parliamentary system, one finds that prime ministers are constantly concerned with politics, while substance is left to subordinates. Moreover, if a country is going through the kind of weakening and shifting of party loyalties that characterized the past American decade, there is no guarantee that a lengthened term would shield negotiations from politics. Nonetheless, one amendment or the other, or both, might make the job of political management easier. The problem is that the amendment process is lengthy and cumbersome. Reforms could well take more than a decade, if they are achievable at all. And who knows where America will be in its political cycles by that time?[24] Moreover, constitutional conservatives properly warn against the unforeseen and unintended effects of major changes in our basic framework that could come back to haunt us in the future. Constitutional remedies often sound good, but by their very nature they are not easy.

At the organizational level, improvements have been suggested for the legislature, for the executive, and for the relations between them. Of the latter, Destler cites Warren Christopher's proposal of a "compact" between the branches that would reaffirm presidential authority over foreign policy in return for promises of more effective consultation and agreement to abide by broad constraints that the Congress imposes.[25] Such a compact would be helpful, but as Destler indicates, its negotiation and enforcement would not be easy if it were detailed. And if it were not detailed, it would remain primarily hortatory, like the symbol of bipartisanship in foreign policy. Certainly efforts should be made in that direction.

Destler suggests other organizational changes to improve congressional processes: Some form of joint committees or subcommittees on arms control, establishing guidelines and procedures for ratification analogous to the 1974 trade legislation, might help arms-control agree-

23. Lloyd Cutler, "To Form a Government," *Foreign Affairs*, vol. 59, no. 1 (Fall 1980).
24. For further criticisms, see Arthur Schlesinger, Jr., in *The Wall Street Journal*, December 24, 1982.
25. Warren Christopher, "Ceasefire between the Branches," *Foreign Affairs*, vol. 60, no. 5 (Summer 1982).

ments. In addition, a managed balance-of-power strategy would involve constant negotiations of one sort or another with the Soviets. Creating a regular ongoing process of meetings and negotiations might help to overcome the fact that Congress's cooperative involvement in the management of Soviet affairs is now rare, in contrast to the continual nature of its conflictual involvement through defense programs.

All such organizational efforts pale, however, in comparison to the importance of the question whether underlying political conditions will allow legislative and executive leadership that can redevelop the practice of bipartisanship in foreign policy. While there is a certain artificiality in the argument that politics should stop at the water's edge, such artifices can help to restrain some of the excesses that otherwise grow out of the structure of separated institutions sharing powers.

Informal devices can be used to alleviate the institutional split between the executive and legislative branches. Stanley Heginbotham has described how the norms and rules of the diplomatic and congressional games differ with regard to publicity, attention to detail and nuance, consistency of approach, intercultural sensitivity, and constituency orientation. The differences cannot be wished away, and to deplore them does little good. Heginbotham suggests that the cleavage is worst among those who focus singlemindedly on one game—whether congressional or diplomatic. Various steps can be taken to increase the number of players who understand both games. Exchange programs that create a core of State Department officials who understand congressional approaches; patterns of interbranch hiring of staffers; and involvement of legislators in foreign visits (in this case involving the Soviet Union) are informal means to reduce the cleavage and make the policy process work more effectively.[26] And above all, constant presidential consultation with key legislators, including practical respect for the views received, is an essential informal means to develop bipartisan foreign policy support.

One could also devise more formal ways to bridge the executive-legislative gap and at the same time try to provide a central focus for the national debate on policy toward the Soviet Union. One device would be to establish a joint legislative-executive "Soviet assessment commission" to produce an annual assessment of the military, economic, and political aspects of the Soviet Union and its policies. Four members might be appointed by the president and four by the opposition leadership in the Congress. They might jointly select a ninth member to chair them. Their task would be to assess intelligence information and produce an annual report that would be the subject of annual hearings before the foreign

---

26. Stanley J. Heginbotham, "Congressional-Executive Consultation in Foreign Policy: What Works?" Library of Congress Congressional Research Service, mimeo (1982).

affairs committees (or possibly, a joint select committee). Such a report need not, indeed probably would not, be unanimous; but it could provide a focal point for debates that might well play a more central role than is provided by the current procedure, where entrepreneurial congressional staffers (usually from the wings of the two parties) work with executive branch leaders to produce a national debate over estimates that stress extreme positions. For example, a commission could lead to a careful discussion of the intelligence estimates on Soviet military spending that are currently often misused to support particular objectives.[27] While a Soviet assessment commission would not be a panacea, presidential commissions have frequently worked partly to depoliticize issues in American politics, and this pattern might be adapted to an interbranch mechanism.

A variety of suggestions have also been made for organizational improvements of the executive branch. For example, Marshall Brement, a State Department official with Soviet experience, has suggested the appointment of one official to oversee all aspects of the relationship; creation of a special bureau in the State Department; and improved development and use of expertise, including our embassy in Moscow.[28] Others have suggested that centralization of control over special subjects such as technology transfer be located in the White House.[29]

Such organizational changes have their pros and cons, depending on the circumstances of particular administrations and the presidential style in foreign policy that Bowie describes. But they are minor when compared with the question of a clear executive process and the importance of having a single authoritative spokesman on foreign affairs. The Carter administration developed a useful interagency coordinating procedure to inform the diverse arms of the executive branch of the various activities in U.S.–Soviet relations, but the procedure was dwarfed by the president's lack of clear strategy and failure to insure that only one person spoke for him on each issue. In the end, the American system allows only one czar of U.S.–Soviet relations—the president—and he should either use his secretary of state as his sole spokesman or replace him. Bowie describes several steps that could improve the decision-making process by

27. "CIA specialists responsible for Soviet military spending now say that their previous estimates of increases of 3 to 4 percent each year, after inflation, may be wrong and the rate of growth may have been no more than 2 percent." *The New York Times*, March 3, 1982, p. 1. The problems lie not in CIA methodology but in political misuse of inherently uncertain estimates.

28. Marshall Brement, *Organizing Ourselves to Deal with the Soviets* (Santa Monica, Calif.: The Rand Corporation, Study P-6123, 1978).

29. A 1982 Senate Subcommittee on Governmental Affairs declared the Department of Commerce "institutionally incapable" of enforcing export controls and advocated restructuring American efforts. *The New York Times*, November 15, 1982. See also Samuel P. Huntington, "Trade, Technology and Leverage," *Foreign Policy*, no. 32 (Fall 1978).

making the secretary of state the principal adviser and executor of foreign policy. The National Security Council must play a role in coordinating the efforts of many agencies, and the role of the NSC assistant will inevitably include advice and planning as well as facilitation of the policy process. But the secretary of state should be the sole spokesman and negotiator. Not only would this reduce inconsistency in public messages, but using the State Department provides more regular access for allies and a better use of our own expertise.[30]

The issue of expertise in the executive branch is important. The controversy over the U.S.–Soviet issue in domestic politics has always tended to tar the experts, but the tendency seems to have grown worse in the past decade. Moreover, bureaucratic conflict in Washington increases the temptation to deal with the Soviet embassy in Washington rather than go through the difficult process of clearing instructions to be sent to our embassy in Moscow. The result is to deprive ourselves of the benefit of our expertise. And the use of our embassy provides occasions for our ambassador to make contact with top Soviet officials, as well as to insure that the messages are delivered in the terms intended.

Expertise is particularly important in dealing with a country like the Soviet Union. As Bowie points out, the usual tendency of American politicians is to assume that their Soviet counterparts are like them and to project American ways of thinking onto the Soviet system. Such "mirror-imaging" can be disastrous when one is dealing with societies organized as differently as the United States and the Soviet Union are. Soviet leaders are recruited by very different routes, and their frame of reference is unique to their own society. The temptation of mirror-image thinking even infects some intelligence analysts. The intelligence services have tended to share rather than counteract the assumptions common to Washington at any given time. The remedy must be a greater investment in and broader institutional use and protection of people specially trained to understand the Russian language and Soviet political culture.

Greater public sophistication about the Soviet Union is also an important component of improvements that have been suggested at the attitudinal level. Educational efforts in schools and for the media can help. But most important is the president's use of what Teddy Roosevelt called the "bully pulpit." No other figure in the society commands the same attention. Presidents can help to shape public attitudes to expect less drama, fewer "solutions," and more consistent long-term management involving both conflict and cooperation in U.S.–Soviet relations. They

30. See I. M. Destler, "A Job That Doesn't Work," and Peter Szanton, "Two Jobs, Not One," *Foreign Policy,* no. 38 (Spring 1980). On Eisenhower's use of the NSC, see Fred Greenstein, *The Hidden-Hand Presidency* (New York: Basic Books, 1982), chapter 4. See also Zbigniew Brzezinski, *Power and Principle* (New York: Farrar, Straus & Giroux, 1983), chap. 15.

can also stress the importance of a strategy that is more modest in defining interests and combines balancing Soviet power (by various means) with communication and continuous engagement.

The way in which a president presents his programs can have a strong effect on the public attitudes that are necessary to sustain his efforts. Given that public opinion polls show continual support for a policy of "peace and strength," a two-track policy would seem a natural one in terms of domestic as well as international politics. But as Schneider writes, the noninternationalist majority can be pulled back and forth between its two concerns by random events and electoral campaigns. Depending on which value seems more threatened at the moment, the noninternationalist majority is drawn into a coalition with those who stress peace or those who stress strength. In practice, presidential leadership and communication are essential ingredients in explaining to the public how the balance is being maintained between firmness and cooperation in the actual implementation of a two-track policy.

Huntington suggests that this volatility of attitudes creates a natural politics of opposites that makes it easier for a moderate politician to urge increased defense spending and safer for a right-wing politician to urge arms control or moderation in attitudes. The best hope to reduce this volatility in attitudes is for a president to elaborate a two-track approach, such as the suggested managed balance-of-power strategy. Such an approach would lay out long-term goals for military strength as well as peaceful engagement. Without such a strategy, it will be difficult to curb the inevitable pressures of particular groups. Small groups with intense interests can have a disproportionate effect on perceptions. Only the president is well placed to reach the broad public. If he avoids his educational role, Huntington's description may become a self-fulfilling prophecy, and we shall continue in what May described as an exaggerated variance between rhetoric and policy.

In sum, while a number of specific measures can be taken to improve the process by which we manage our relations with our principal adversary, there are strict limits to what such changes can achieve. We can alleviate the tendency to oversimplify and exaggerate, which tends to amplify the oscillations in our policy. We can improve executive and legislative procedures and hope to reduce the incoherence of different parts of our polity speaking with different voices or taking contradictory actions. And we can hope that the tides in our storms of political realignment will eventually ebb sufficiently to allow the centrist orientation, bipartisan policy, and cooperation between the branches that reduces the excesses that otherwise grow out of our constitutional structure.

But our political culture and institutions do not change quickly or easily. The implications of this simple-sounding proposition are very significant. It means that there will always be limits to the types of strategies that we can successfully follow. As stated earlier, our ability to manage the Soviet relationship is less a matter of organization than of choosing an appropriate strategy. The basic principle for a durable strategy is to cut the foreign policy coat to fit our domestic political cloth. This does not mean appeasing the Soviet Union or failing to counterbalance Soviet power. Quite the contrary. What it means is that, if we pick an inappropriately ambitious strategy, we will fail in the long run because the American political process will produce oscillations and inconsistency. In a nuclear age we ignore such reality at our peril. The three major lessons of the book are that an appropriate strategy (1) must be modest enough to fit our domestic capabilities; (2) must focus on indirect effects through maintaining our alliances as much as on the direct bilateral relationship with the Soviet Union; and (3) should combine balancing Soviet power with economic engagement and continual and open communication. Over time, such a strategy may gradually increase the transparency in the relationship, reducing the dangers of miscalculation and increasing somewhat our understanding of what goes on within the opaque Soviet society. In short, our strategy should be not only to manage the current threat of Soviet power but also to seek to improve gradually the conditions that make it so difficult for a society organized like ours to manage its relationship with the Soviet Union.

Contributors

Richard K. Betts is a senior fellow at the Brookings Institution in Washington, D.C., and lecturer at Columbia and Johns Hopkins universities. He has been a lecturer in Government at Harvard, a staff member of the Senate Select Committee on Intelligence, and consultant to the National Security Council. Betts is author of *Soldiers, Statesmen, and Cold War Crises* (1977) and *Surprise Attack* (1982), as well as coauthor of *The Irony of Vietnam* (1979) and *Nonproliferation and U.S. Foreign Policy* (1981). He has also published numerous articles on strategic intelligence, conventional military strategy, government organization, arms control, and other subjects.

Robert R. Bowie is currently a Guest Scholar at the Brookings Institution in Washington, D.C. He was a member of the Harvard faculty from 1946 to 1980, first at the Law School, and then, from 1957 to 1973, as director of the Harvard Center for International Affairs. In government, he served in the Pentagon (1942–45); as special assistant to the Deputy Military Governor for Germany (1945–46); as General Counsel to the U.S. High Commissioner for Germany (1950–51), as director of Policy Planning, Department of State (1953–57); as counselor, Department of State (1966–68); and as deputy director for Intelligence (1977–79).

I. M. Destler, currently a senior fellow at the Institute for International Economics in Washington, D.C., is the author of *Presidents, Bureaucrats, and Foreign Policy* (1972) and *Making Foreign Economic Policy* (1980), and coauthor of *The Textile Wrangle* (1979) and *Coping with U.S.–Japanese Economic Conflicts* (1982). He did the research and writing for his chapter while a Senior Associate at the Carnegie Endowment for International Peace, where he directed the project on Executive-Congressional relations in foreign policy.

Alexander L. George is Graham H. Stuart Professor of International Relations, Stanford University. His first book, *Woodrow Wilson and Colonel House* (1956), written with his wife, Juliette L. George, is widely regarded as a classic study of the role of personality in politics. He is also

355

author of *Deterrence in Foreign Policy* (with Richard Smoke, 1974), which won the 1975 Bancroft Prize; *The Limits of Coercive Diplomacy* (with David K. Hall and William E. Simons, 1971); *Propaganda Analysis* (1959); *The Chinese Communist Army in Action* (1967); *Presidential Decisionmaking in Foreign Policy* (1980); *Force and Statecraft* (with Gordon A. Craig, 1983); and *Managing U.S.–Soviet Rivalry* (1983).

Marshall Goldman is the Class of 1919 Professor of Economics at Wellesley College and Associate Director of the Russian Research Center, Harvard University. He was the Fulbright Hays Visiting Professor at Moscow State University during the fall semester of 1977. His most recent book is *The USSR in Crisis: The Failure of an Economic System* (1983). Other monographs include *Détente and Dollars: Doing Business with the Soviets* (1975) and *The Enigma of Soviet Petroleum: Half Empty or Half Full?* (1980).

Stanley Hoffmann is Douglas Dillon Professor of the Civilization of France and chairman of the Center for European Studies at Harvard University. His most recent books are *Dead Ends: American Foreign Policy in the New Cold War* (1983) and *Duties beyond Borders* (1981). He was also a member of the Harvard Nuclear Study Group, which has just published *Living with Nuclear Weapons* (1983).

Samuel P. Huntington is Eaton Professor of the Science of Government and director of the Center for International Affairs at Harvard University. His many books on politics and international affairs include most recently *American Politics: The Promise of Disharmony* (1983) and, as editor and contributor, *The Strategic Imperative* (1982). During 1977 and 1978, he was Coordinator of Security Planning at the National Security Council. In 1970, he was a founder of the magazine *Foreign Policy,* and served as its coeditor until his entry into government.

Ernest R. May is Charles Warren Professor of History at Harvard University, where he teaches American history, the history of international relations, and, in the John F. Kennedy School of Government, a course on using history for policy analysis and public management. He has written, edited, or contributed to a number of books, most recently *Knowing One's Enemies: Intelligence Assessment before the Two World Wars* (1984). He has also served from time to time as a consultant for the National Security Council, the Office of the Secretary of Defense, other executive agencies, and committees of the Congress.

Joseph Samuel Nye, Jr. is a professor of government at Harvard University. From January 1977 to January 1979, Dr. Nye was Deputy to the Under Secretary of State for Security Assistance, Science and Technology, and chaired the National Security Council Group on Nonproliferation of Nuclear Weapons. He is a member of the Trilateral Commission, the International Institute for Strategic Studies, and the Council on Foreign Relations, and of the editorial boards of *Foreign Policy, International Security,* and *International Organization* magazines. His most recent book (coauthored) is *Living with Nuclear Weapons* (1983).

William Schneider is a resident fellow at the American Enterprise Institute in Washington, D.C. He is also a political consultant to Craver, Mathews, Smith & Company of Falls Church, Virginia, and to *National Journal* and *The Los Angeles Times,* where his articles appear regularly. He is coauthor of *The Confidence Gap: Business, Labor, and Government in the Public Mind* (1983) and *The Radical Center: New Directions in American Politics,* to be published by Simon & Schuster in 1985.

Dimitri K. Simes is a senior associate at the Carnegie Endowment for International Peace and a professorial lecturer in International Relations at the Johns Hopkins School of Advanced International Studies. Dr. Simes has formerly served as executive director of the Soviet and East European Research Program at the Johns Hopkins Foreign Policy Institute and as the director of Soviet Studies at the Georgetown University Center for Strategic and International Studies. He attended Moscow State University's School of History and the Graduate School of the Institute of World Economy and International Relations of the USSR Academy of Sciences, where he was also a research associate from 1967 to 1972.

Strobe Talbott is Diplomatic Correspondent for *Time Magazine,* based in Washington. He is the editor and translator of two volumes of Nikita Khrushchev's memoirs and the author of *Endgame: The Inside Story of SALT II* (1979).

Raymond Vernon is Dillon Professor of International Affairs in the Department of Government of Harvard University. He is the author of various articles on economic relations between the United States and the USSR.

Index